Acknowledgments

NO MATTER HOW TOUGH THINGS GOT, our support crew stood by us for this project. Calvin and Edna Howard (alias "Dad and Mom") put up with withering heat, bone-chilling cold, sandblasting winds, iffy river crossings, and my encounters with poison ivy.

My brother Leland and I traveled and hiked together. Special thanks have to go out to a photographer such as Leland, who can concentrate on his difficult job while his persnickety sister trails along in his wake, lugging books and maps instead of a good supply of cookies.

The remarkable patience of land administrators ought to have earned them points in heaven by this time. "I'll have to look in the boxes in the basement," they'd say, and then they were off to rummage in records from 1974 to dig out a needed fact. Mike Salamacha from the Kanab BLM field office epitomizes the army of back-country rangers who know all the stuff that's often missing from the pretty brochures —like how many feet of rope you really need to get past a dry waterfall in Bull Valley Gorge. We'll let Mike stand in for everyone, but know that there are a lot more people like him who protect and serve the land—and who would prefer that I put enough information into this book so that they don't have to rescue so many unfortunate hikers.

Local outfitters, conservation groups, and ranchers were also a valuable source of information. These people were generous with their time and gave us the benefit of their years of experience exploring areas that we only had time to visit once.

Last but never least, Westcliffe Publishers put up with all my struggles while I tried to organize this mix of information and inspiration. They never gave up on me, and their enthusiasm for the glories of wilderness adventure never diminished.

—*Lynna Howard*

The following companies generously supplied gear or discounts for our expedition:

CASCADE DESIGNS: Map cases, water filters, and SealLine® dry bags for river travel and wet canyon hiking. *(800) 531-9531, CascadeDesigns.com.*

CLIF BAR: Clif® and Luna® Bars, and Clif Shot®. *(800) CLIFBAR, clifbar.com.*

DVORAK'S KAYAK & RAFTING EXPEDITIONS: Kayaking and rafting outfitters and guides. *(800) 824-3795, dvorakexpeditions.com.*

LOWEPRO: Lowepro® Pro Trekker and Nature Trekker specialty backpacks for professional camera gear. *(800) 800-5693, lowepro.com.*

NIKWAX USA: Waterproofing systems for boots and gear. *(800) 335-0260, nikwax-usa.com.*

RIVERS WEST: H2P® (Hydro2Power Lock) System fleece, high-performance waterproof outerwear. *(800) 683-0887, riverswest.com.*

TRAILS ILLUSTRATED: Trails Illustrated® waterproof maps for most designated and proposed wilderness areas. *(800) 962-1643, trailsillustrated.com.*

Jerry Howard and his son Jesse take in the view at the 11,600-foot saddle above Priord Lake in the High Uintas Wilderness.

Table of Contents

8

NOTE: For definitions of abbreviations, see pp. 48–49

Fall color frames a backcountry road in the Wasatch Range.

Utah's
Wilderness
Areas

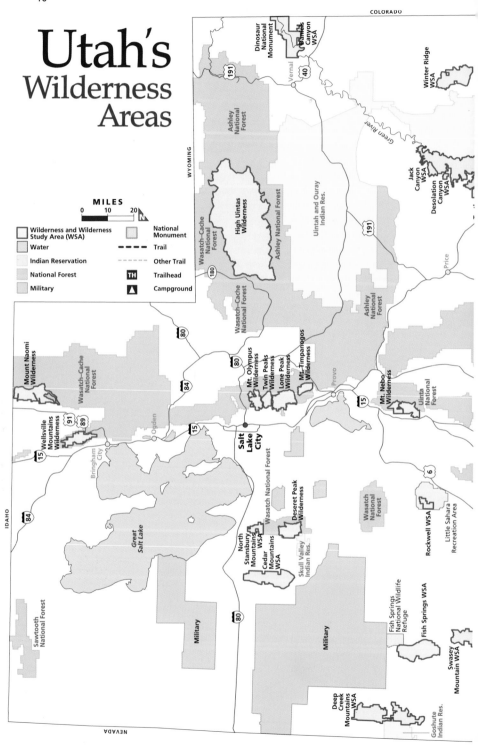

MILES

0   10   20

Wilderness and Wilderness Study Area (WSA)

Water

Indian Reservation

National Forest

Military

National Monument

--- **Trail**

---- **Other Trail**

TH **Trailhead**

▲ **Campground**

COLORADO

WYOMING

IDAHO

NEVADA

Dinosaur National Monument

Diamond Canyon WSA

Vernal

Winter Ridge WSA

Ashley National Forest

Green River

High Uintas Wilderness

Ashley National Forest

Uintah and Ouray Indian Res.

Jack Canyon WSA

Desolation Canyon WSA

Price

Wasatch-Cache National Forest

Wasatch-Cache National Forest

Ashley National Forest

Mount Naomi Wilderness

Wasatch-Cache National Forest

Mt. Olympus Wilderness

Twin Peaks Wilderness

Lone Peak Wilderness

Mt. Timpanogos Wilderness

Provo

Mt. Nebo Wilderness

Uinta National Forest

Ogden

Wellsville Mountains Wilderness

Salt Lake City

Bringham City

Great Salt Lake

Deseret Peak Wilderness

Wasatch National Forest

Wasatch National Forest

Rockwell WSA

Little Sahara Recreation Area

Sawtooth National Forest

North Stansbury Mountains WSA

Cedar Mountains WSA

Skull Valley Indian Res.

Military

Military

Fish Springs National Wildlife Refuge

Fish Springs WSA

Swasey Mountain WSA

Deep Creek Mountains WSA

Goshute Indian Res.

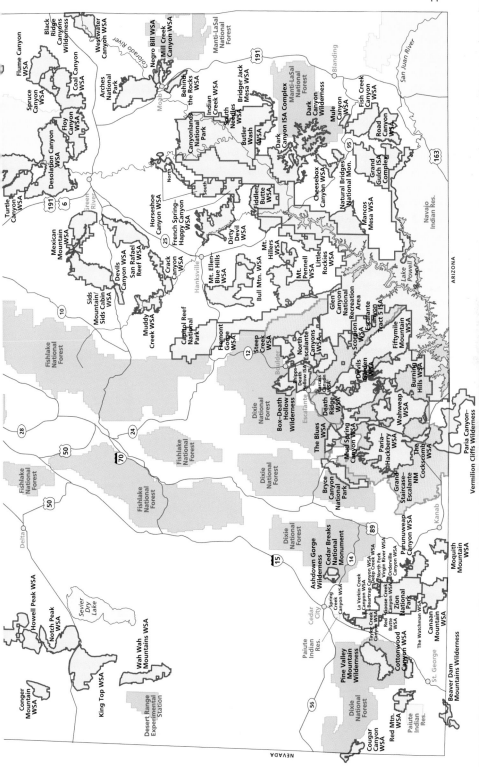

Utah Wilderness

Mountain, mesa, canyon, butte.
Reefs of rock, flaring desert skirts—
all reflect the beating heart of light.

Soaked in twice-bounced light,
horizon swells of cloud
bloom and give back the gloss.

Navajo sandstone drenched in gold
hands out a mute invitation;
cold-blooded slot canyons shoulder wide,
rinse in brief cousins of the sun.

We hike and note facts for a book
as light stirs the land
into this wayward beauty.

Even well-aimed facts miss the heart.

—Lynna Prue Howard, *"PrueHeart the Wanderer"*

Reflected light in a slot canyon paints this wall pure gold.

Preface

IT'S ONE THING TO SAY that Utah's wilderness areas are remarkably diverse, but it's another to experience that diversity. Here are a few excerpts from the diary I kept while my brother and I climbed over mesas, down into canyons, and up mountains as we conducted research for this book.

Grand Staircase–Escalante National Monument, June 2

We're hiking on a nameless mesa in southwestern Utah. It's midday and all this great, barren, empty space is crowded not with people, but with sensations. The wind pushes against us like a rude hand. An indifferent sun pours white heat down on our heads. The pressures of time and thirst push us forward. The landscape is drained of color and we are the only motion in it.

Near the close of day, a delicate blush appears like soft powder on the dun curves of sandstone. The transformation begins slowly, then quickens, until, with heart-stopping beauty, the whole mesa lies ripe with color under a thin swirl of cirrus clouds. In those cold, high clouds, the moisture is ice. Down here, we are hot, but cooling fast. Shadows create definition where everything looked flat before. Colors and shadows reach for their maximum saturation, peaking when our enemy, the sun, is below the horizon, its presence still reflected by the hazy sky. A mule deer peers at us cautiously and skeptically, as if to say, "I see you have been walking during the heat of the day. Don't you know how thin the margins are for survival?"

Brimstone Slot Canyon, May 15

An impressive slot canyon has to have walls close enough together to catch the brim of my brother's Indiana Jones hat. As he sidles sideways down the canyon, the walls snag his hat and it stays behind, hanging in the air like a still from a cartoon.

Narrowness is only one element of the jaw-dropping charm of slot canyons. It's the intricate, water-carved forms of the walls that I never tire of. The sensuousness of the walls comes briefly to life when shafts of sunlight turn the cold, dark underworld into a shimmering play of mauve, cobalt, and peach waves of stone.

High Uintas Wilderness, September 28

How long has it been since I walked in a trackless forest in a snowstorm? With every breath, there's some cause for joy.

We got up before dawn to climb one of many 12,000-foot-plus peaks while the first snow of the season still graced the landscape. Everything was blue when we started out. Blue snow, dark blue shadows, trees tinted blue. The sky was still overcast, but the day lightened on a fantasy of ice and snow. We saw four elk, shy and quick to slip away, as we made our way up the mountain.

Now we stop about halfway up, pausing in an open spot to photograph an amphitheater carved by glaciers about 25,000 years ago. The surrounding peaks are softly lit by sun coming through the thinning clouds, but the deep bowl itself is densely blue, a jewel of air.

In the rocks above treeline, we stop again to catch our breath. A topsy-turvy jumble of red slabs and boulders sports ice teeth, ice-lace mantillas, and other forms of wind-driven decoration. Last night, the snow-bearing wind came over the ridge from the west, so the glittering, elongated ice crystals face us as we climb. From the top we can see all the way to Flaming Gorge.

Diversity! To gather the information and photos for this book, my brother and I hiked, rafted, waded, climbed, and crawled through both designated and proposed wilderness areas of Utah. No matter what fuels the dreams of your adventurous soul, somewhere in Utah there's a wilderness waiting for you. The purpose of this book is to get you there.

—Lynna Howard

High mountain lake and autumn color,
Wasatch Range

What Is Wilderness?

"DESIGNATED WILDERNESS" IS DEFINED by Congress; "proposed" or "recommended wilderness" is defined by land managers, or by citizen groups—and then there's that elusive feeling we get when we think of wild, pristine landscapes and of breathing their undomesticated air. If you think that all of these ideas of "wilderness" are one and the same, you are in for some surprises.

Designated Wilderness

In 1997, Dr. Greg Thayn, a wilderness coordinator for the Bureau of Land Management (BLM), said, "Wilderness is whatever Congress says it is." Congress passed a law called the Wilderness Act of 1964, which defined what wilderness should be. In part, the act reads:

> A wilderness, in contrast with those areas where man and his own works dominate the landscape, is hereby recognized as an area where the earth and its community of life are untrammeled by man, where man himself is a visitor who does not remain…an area of undeveloped Federal land retaining its primeval character and influence, without permanent improvements or human habitation, which is protected and managed so as to preserve its natural conditions and which (1) generally appears to have been affected primarily by the forces of nature, with the imprint of man's work substantially unnoticeable; (2) has outstanding opportunities for solitude or a primitive and unconfined type of recreation; (3) has at least five thousand acres of land or is of sufficient size as to make practicable its preservation and use in an unimpaired condition; and (4) may also contain ecological, geological, or other features of scientific, educational, scenic, or historical value.

This all sounds great until you take the romantic ideal and process it through an evolving legal system and the subjective, often dissenting minds of many people. For instance, you can end up with a mini-mall of jewel-like wilderness areas such as the ones lined up along the Wasatch Front: Where the suburbs of Salt Lake City and Provo end, designated "wilderness" begins.

Along the approach routes near Mount Olympus and Twin Peaks Wilderness Areas, bright neon signs arch over the highways, flashing "No Horses," "No Dogs," "Watershed Protection Enforced," "No Campfires," and so forth. I think they should add a line of high-kicking neon Vegas showgirls at the end of the announcements.

Each of these five small islands of protected land is federally designated wilderness, therefore roadless and not recently logged or mined. However, on their western edges, finding a view that doesn't include freeways and noise poses quite a challenge. The eastern edges often abut ski resorts. The Wasatch Mountains resemble the Alps in their sculptural beauty, but hikers have to work hard to find a place in them with that untamed feeling.

These are legal/political wilderness areas, not wilderness in the broader sense of the word. Of course, that's a subjective judgment, too. If you're fresh off the streets of Manhattan, the Wasatch Front might satisfy all your wilderness expectations. To best enjoy these areas, hike them in the off-season when crowds subside; don't go on weekends or holidays when the traffic gets dangerous on the narrow, winding roads; backpack far enough in to escape the joggers; and seek out terrain that screens you from cities and ski resorts.

Utah has 16 *designated* wilderness areas totaling about 800,000 acres (see Appendix A). The Forest Service manages 13 designated wilderness areas, and the BLM manages the others. Of the 16 designated wilderness areas, the High Uintas Wilderness in the northeastern corner of the state comes closest to the romantic ideal, mostly thanks to sheer size. Congress designated the High Uintas and most of Utah's other wilderness areas in 1984, but one area, Lone Peak—the largest of five areas along the Wasatch Front—was designated in 1978. One new wilderness area was designated in 2000, Black Ridge Canyons Wilderness on the Utah/Colorado border; most of this wilderness area is in Colorado.

Proposed or Recommended Wilderness
The Wilderness Act of 1964 left the BLM out of the picture. The U.S. Forest Service, National Park Service, and U.S. Fish and Wildlife Service were included, but the BLM managed 22,932,588 million acres in Utah that were not considered—that's 42% of the state's total land area. The BLM manages the most arid regions in the state, and this might have been part of the reason for overlooking their wilderness value.

In 1976, the Federal Lands Policy and Management Act (FLPMA) passed, initiating an inventory of BLM lands. Most of the current wilderness study areas (WSAs) were identified in 1978–1980. The Utah Statewide Final Environmental Impact Statement (EIS) of 1991 finalized the inventory. FLPMA gave the Department of the Interior 15 years to complete the study. By October 1993, in compliance with the law, the BLM submitted a wilderness proposal to Congress. Instant study areas (ISAs) previously identified as natural or primitive got top priority when it came to inclusion in wilderness proposals. Wilderness study areas also met wilderness criteria.

Several citizen groups launched a vigorous debate over the BLM's recommendations and came up with their own proposals. When this book went to press, the BLM had put no new recommendations for wilderness designation before Congress; however, approximately 2.6 million acres (in addition to previous proposals for 3.2 million acres) were found to have wilderness characteristics. The BLM may manage some of these additional lands using its ACEC (area of critical environmental concern) and SRMA (special recreation management area) options, but it cannot declare them as wilderness study areas because its mandate from Congress expired at the end of the 15-year period. Only Congress can designate wilderness.

We based this book on the 1991 inventory, as far as proposed wilderness is concerned. But wherever possible, we have noted lands the BLM has identified as having at least some of the values associated with wilderness, as well as additional lands that citizen groups have recommended. In 1998, a citizen group coalition of many organizations increased their recommended wilderness acreage in Utah to 8.5 million acres and recruited members of Congress to submit the proposal. The Utah Wilderness Coalition's "America's Redrock Wilderness Bill" asks that more than 9 million acres in Utah be designated as wilderness.

What Are Wilderness Characteristics?

According to Congress, public land that is designated or proposed as wilderness should meet most of the following criteria, in addition to having scenic qualities:

• **Size:** The unit of land must be roadless and larger than 5,000 acres. Areas of less than 5,000 acres can be included if contiguous to other lands that have wilderness values.

• **Naturalness:** The area must be primarily affected by the forces of nature, and man's imprint must be substantially unnoticeable. Allowed impacts include trails, trail signs, bridges, fire towers, snow gauges, and pit toilets. Most BLM wilderness study areas are grazed by livestock and have associated human traces. Vestiges of past mining activities are also common. If these human imprints are minor, then they do not exclude the land from consideration as wilderness.

• **Solitude:** The size of the unit affects opportunities for solitude, but so does natural screening (such as the steep walls of a canyon). Avoiding the sights, sounds, and evidence of other people becomes increasingly difficult on well-used trails or in popular areas. The idea that a wilderness should be "soundproof" becomes a problem when flight paths cross overhead, and when cities or highways sit nearby. During its inventory,

Sunset pinks the Navajo sandstone cliffs along the Dirty Devil River.

the BLM sought "outstanding opportunities" for solitude, but this subjective judgment varies from person to person.

• **Primitive or unconfined recreation:** Opportunities for nonmotorized recreation such as horseback riding, hiking, fishing, kayaking, and sightseeing should exist.

• **Supplemental values:** Archaeological sites in many southern Utah wilderness study areas serve as good examples of supplemental values. They're not required for wilderness consideration, but are noted as adding to the value of an area. Ecological, geological, scientific, educational, and historical worth also fall into this category.

State land use also affects wilderness proposals and designation. In Utah, school trust lands—parcels that by law must be managed for maximum revenue—are scattered in a checkerboard pattern in each township. Roads and activity on school trust lands directly conflict with wilderness characteristics. In some cases, the problem is solved by trading out the school trust lands in a wilderness area for a block of land elsewhere. But in many cases, school trust lands still exist in proposed wilderness areas.

What Is Roadless?

"Searching for a definition of 'road' is currently no different from uncovering a definition of beauty; both exist only in the eye of the beholder."

—Rep. James Hansen (R-Utah), 1997

"Existing roads in inventoried roadless areas could be maintained under the proposed rule."

—USDA Forest Service,
"Roadless Area Conservation" bulletin, 2000

"The word roadless refers to the absence of roads that they have improved and maintained by mechanical means to ensure regular and continuous use. A trail maintained solely by the passage of vehicles does not constitute a road."

—Utah State BLM office,
"Utah BLM Statewide Wilderness Final
Environmental Impact Statement," 1990

"We maintain them by driving them."

—BLM archaeologist

"[Utah counties want to] torpedo wilderness designation…by asserting approximately 5,000 dubious [road] claims involving dirt trails, two-tracks, cow paths, sand wash bottoms and even rivers. Most of these byways they assert are largely impassable by car."

—Southern Utah Wilderness Alliance,
"The 1866 Mining Act: Imminent Threat to
Protection of America's National Lands," 1997

To be or not to be a road? Of all the characteristics of a wilderness, roadlessness has become the paramount, make-or-break factor. But no one can decide what is a road and what is not. In practical terms, there are several conclusions you can draw from the debate about roads: (1) roadless areas are not roadless; (2) road closures and road maintenance are always in a state of flux; and (3) a four-wheel-drive byway impassable by car is exactly what the locals call a road.

Most people who read this book are adventurers, day hikers, backpackers, photographers—people who are after that elusive "wilderness experience." This book makes a serious attempt to steer readers to hiking routes via existing and designated roads that everyone agrees are roads. However, it is possible that roads and unmaintained "vehicular ways" open to motorized traffic when I wrote this book might be closed in the future. (A "way" is a trail maintained solely by the passage of vehicles. This book notes ways where they are useful for access. Visitors can travel these ways in a four-wheel-drive vehicle or use them as hiking paths.) If you use the USGS 1:24,000 topographical maps, you'll see many four-wheel-drive roads and possible approaches to hiking routes. Use these roads with caution, respect closure signs, and check with local land administrators whenever possible.

Backcountry roads are often unsigned, and this is typical of Utah's public lands. Sometimes it's easier to get lost driving the roads than it is to get lost hiking. I usually carry three kinds of maps for serious backcountry travel: Forest Service or BLM large-scale maps to see an overview and the land uses allowed; Trails Illustrated maps for maintained hiking trails; and USGS 1:24,000 maps for terrain and "road" details.

This issue of roadlessness has created some other oddities that might baffle hikers new to the Western states. Why, for example, are there multitudes of named wilderness study areas on Cedar Mesa? Why not just give it all one name? A road corridor separates each WSA from its neighbors. Legally speaking, the proposed wilderness has to be "roadless," so the boundaries between areas are often four-wheel-drive roads or highways that are not officially included within the designated or proposed wilderness area.

"Cherry-stemmed" roads are access routes that protrude into a wilderness area like a finger stuck into bread dough. The wilderness boundaries are tightly drawn around the finger of road, and the road itself is excluded from the wilderness so that the area can be defined as "roadless." On a map, the road looks like a cherry stem laid on the landscape.

Common Wilderness Restrictions and Regulations

- Motorized and mechanized vehicles and tools are not permitted, including aircraft, ATVs, hang gliders, bicycles, and chain saws.
- Wheelchairs may be permitted by special order.
- Mountain bikes are not permitted in designated wilderness areas, but may be permitted in wilderness study areas. Check the regulations for the area you are visiting. When in doubt, stay on the roads.
- Group sizes are usually limited, varying from 5 to 20.
- Fees and permits may be required.
- Reservations may be required for heavily used areas.
- Leave No Trace guidelines must be followed.
- Pets and pack stock may be restricted to certain areas.
- Archaeological sites are protected by law, and defacing or removing artifacts is punishable by fines and/or jail time.
- Campfires are often prohibited.

Flash floods have uncovered layered mudstone at the bottom of this canyon in the Colorado Plateau.

Along the Trail

"Leave No Trace" Principles

Land managers have developed outdoor ethics guidelines that should govern the behavior of every backcountry visitor. In order to address issues specific to Utah's backcountry, the following information builds on the seven principles put forth by the nonprofit organization Leave No Trace. For more information, call the Leave No Trace Center for Outdoor Ethics at (800) 332-4100 or visit the website at lnt.org.

• **Plan ahead:** Proper planning makes it easier for you to stick to Leave No Trace guidelines. Choose gear, clothing, and food that will lessen your impact.

• **Hike single file:** Hike single file and stay on the trail to help minimize the trampling of fragile plants and soft ground. Never cut switchbacks. In places where there is no trail, or where it is necessary to leave the trail, choose the most durable surfaces to walk on.

• **Cryptobiotic soil:** In desert environments, take care to avoid stepping on cryptobiotic soil crust. Fungi, algae, moss, and lichen make up this bumpy-looking soil. Also known as cryptogamic or microbiotic soil, these conglomerations trap moisture, hold the soil in place, and prevent erosion.

• **Be courteous:** According to the current standard, bikers and hikers yield to horses, and bikers yield to hikers, but the prudent hiker will make room for a mountain biker. When passing a horse party, move off the trail on the lower side until everyone has passed. Don't leave your pack or other items next to the trail. Horses may shy when they spot an unfamiliar object. Mountain bikes are prohibited in designated wilderness areas, but may be allowed in proposed wilderness areas. Know the rules before you go, and stay on approved trails and roads.

• **Lessen the impact from horses, mules, and other pack animals:** Where pack animals are allowed, weed-free feed is usually required. Horse packers can get more information on responsible practices by requesting the "Backcountry Horse Use" booklet from the Leave No Trace office.

• **Concentrate impact in high-use areas:** In oft-traveled areas, select a well-established campsite at least 200 feet from streams and lakes. This principle reflects the philosophy that certain spots are sacrificed for repeated use without the intention of restoring them to a natural state.

• **Disperse impact in low-use areas:** If you visit an area that has seen less human impact, situate your cooking area on a durable surface, such as a large, flat rock. If you have them, wear light shoes instead of heavy, hard-soled hiking boots once you arrive at camp.

• **Campfires:** Once the traditional source of warmth, comfort, and safety in the backcountry, campfires leave signs of human impact that have become more of a problem as the number of visitors to the wilderness has increased. A small backpacking stove provides a quicker and more efficient way to cook.

Campfires are prohibited in many wilderness areas, so check the rules for the area you will be visiting. If you must have a fire, never create a new fire ring or build a fire in or near an archaeological site. Use an existing fire ring or build a "mound fire." To build a mound fire, find a source of mineral soil, such as a streambed during low water or the hole left by a tree that has blown over. Use a stuff sack to carry a large amount of this soil to the fire site, lay down a ground cloth, and use the soil to build a flat-topped mound 6 to 8 inches thick on top of the cloth. Gather wood from the ground—small bits no bigger around than your wrist work best—and build the fire on the mound. When it is time to break camp, scatter the few ashes, and then use the ground cloth to return the soil to its source.

I'm soured on the "scatter your ashes" rule, however. This advice has been given out for years, and as a result, many camping spots are black all over. In such campsites, you can't walk or set up a tent without acquiring a layer of greasy, hard-to-remove carbon. The idea behind scattering ashes is that the fire will definitely be out and that the scattered ashes will blow away or absorb into the terrain. Unfortunately, it doesn't work that way in real life. To help minimize this problem, you can empty the old ashes from an established ring with a shovel and bury them in a nearby hole or put them in a waste bag to carry out. Build a small fire, not a big one, and put it out thoroughly before you leave.

• **Campfires along desert rivers:** If campfires are allowed, rafters and kayakers might be required to have and use a fire pan. When the ashes cool, they are bagged and carried out like any other waste.

• **Pack it in, pack it out:** With the exception of human waste, leave nothing in the woods that wasn't there before. Pack out toilet paper, personal hygiene items, and uneaten food. Leaving food for animals or giving it to them directly habituates them to humans, alters their diet, makes them less self-sufficient, and can result in more aggressive animals (everything from squirrels to bears). Never feed a wild animal. You can cache water for longer hikes, but do not cache food.

• **Properly dispose of what you can't pack out:** Dispose of solid human waste via the "cathole" method. Dig a hole 6 to 8 inches deep and fill it in after use. An alternative to packing out toilet paper is forgoing its use and trying natural alternatives. Snow works well, and you can experiment with such items as smooth stones or closed, immature pinecones to find out what works best for you. Feminine hygiene products should be packed out. Tea bags or baking soda in a baggie or container will lessen odors. Some land administration offices provide plastic bags and sanitation instructions for backcountry travelers to use.

• **Waste disposal along desert rivers:** The river is the only biologically and chemically active cleansing agent in a desert. Land managers advise wilderness visitors to urinate in the river. Leftover beer (as if that would happen) also goes into the river, as do toothpaste and all soap residues. To dispose of coffee grounds, press them into a bandanna or other straining device, throw the liquid into the river, and add the grounds to the waste you are packing out.

When rafting or kayaking on a desert river, outfitters and private parties alike must bring the means to carry out all human waste. If everyone obeys the rules, the river corridor stays clean.

• **Archaeological and historical sites:** State and federal laws prohibit destruction or vandalism of archaeological sites. If you do much hiking on the mesas and in the canyons of the Colorado Plateau, you will find rock art that is not on any map, and the wonder of finding such compelling evidence of human creativity will stay with you forever. A different and unwelcome kind of wonder accompanies the discovery of sites that have fallen victim to vandalism.

Historical buildings, old mines, and cowboy rock art, or "cowboy glyphs," also dot the landscape. These sites should be left alone, as well. Old mines can be extremely hazardous, with aging explosives, cave-ins, and cyanide and other chemicals among just a few of their life-threatening features. On particularly hot days, snakes will seek the shade of abandoned mine shafts.

Weather and Safety

Beginning in April, my brother and I chased spring around Utah. We moved from south to north, from low elevations to high, entering each area at the end of the snowmelt, before the bug season, and well ahead of the days when a fiery sun would arrive to wither everything under its merciless gaze. We still found springlike conditions in the High Uintas in August. With this approach, it's possible to hike in Utah from March to November. However, many caveats surround this plan. Spring runoff from snowmelt, iffy road conditions, and freezing temperatures at night are just some of the potential problems. Please read the following weather and safety concerns as part of your pretrip planning.

• **Weather:** Carry the proper clothing for snow, rain, high winds, extreme heat, or a combination of these conditions, depending on where and when you hike. Sunscreen, lip protection, and a hat are essential gear.

In the desert, plan to hike in the early morning and late evening, and rest in the shade during the hottest part of the day. Limiting desert hiking to early spring and late fall is also a good way to prevent heatstroke.

Rugged mountain areas intensify the effects of weather systems. Combined with the colder temperatures of high elevations, a fast-moving weather system can put highcountry hikers in danger within a few minutes. Hail and snow flurries are common well into July at the higher elevations. Just a few feet of snow can result in avalanche danger. You'll see the "No Stopping, Avalanche Danger" signs on some of the access roads.

• **Lightning:** A serious concern for travelers on high, exposed ridges, mesas, and canyon rims, this hazard kills several hikers each year. Lightning tends to take the shortest path between sky and earth, so you should avoid high points of land or lone trees when a storm comes in. If possible, return to your vehicle. If not, experts recommend seeking out a low, treeless point in the terrain and squatting there until the storm passes, with your backpack or sleeping pad under you to insulate you from the ground. The National Outdoor Leadership School recently amended this advice to "seek gently rolling terrain." Strikes are infrequent in low, rolling terrain where there are few trees. Hiding in caves is not recommended.

• **Flash floods:** Flash floods can originate in a rainstorm 50 miles or more from your location. Never camp in a dry wash or slot canyon. Look around to determine the height of the floodplain, and camp well above it. July, August, and the first week of September are usually the worst months for flash floods, but they can occur at any time. Most ranger stations and visitor centers post a current weather forecast, so check there before you begin.

• **Fording rivers and streams:** A pair of river sandals or water shoes, combined with trekking poles, can help you keep your balance while fording mountain streams. Desert rivers tend to be full of silt, with muddy bottoms, and slot canyons can harbor the kind of mud that will suck the shoes right off your feet; for these situations, a pair of old, tightly laced hiking boots might prove preferable. Going barefoot to ford rocky-bottomed rivers is the ultimate no-no, as you need to protect your feet and ankles. Old hiking boots are not recommended for rafting or kayaking trips because they can act as a wedge to trap your feet in rocks if you take an accidental swim in the rapids.

• **River rafting and kayaking:** This book does not provide enough information for beginners to safely travel on wilderness rivers. When you apply for a river travel permit, you will receive safety information from the land administrators. Supplement that information with guidebooks written specifically for river runners, consider hiring one of the many excellent outfitters, and/or travel with more experienced friends. See Appendix B for outfitters and Appendix E for suggested reading.

• **Two-wheel or four-wheel driving:** Access roads to most desert wilderness areas and some forested areas are not paved. A road that two-wheel-drive cars can travel in good weather might become impassable when wet. We encountered supersuction mud in

A flash flood in Valley of the Gods

most of the arid areas, where a little rain seems to go a long way toward making the roads impassable (we changed that to "implausible"). On the other hand, long dry spells and high winds spell trouble in the form of drifting sand that closes roads to all but high-clearance, four-wheel-drive vehicles.

• **Private property:** With no buildings or people in sight, private land might look just like public land, but it is usually posted with identifying signs or with red or orange paint. Access roads to public land often cross private property, and vice versa. Respect private property and don't camp or hike there without permission from the owner.

• **Water:** The low moisture content of the air in desert locations and at higher altitudes in the mountains, combined with the greater respiration rate required for hiking, could result in dehydration, a potentially dangerous condition. Hikers should drink water or a combination of water and sport drinks frequently. The recommended amount is 1 gallon per day, per person.

The greatest peril concerning backcountry sources of drinking water is a small parasite called *Giardia lamblia*. Transmitted via the fecal matter of animals, it survives even in very cold water at high altitudes and causes severe intestinal discomfort in humans. Three methods of water treatment are recommended: boiling for three to five minutes, treating with iodine tablets, or using a filter.

In desert locations, water from natural sources might cause intestinal distress even after treatment. For example, water sources in the San Rafael Swell are so heavily laden with minerals that, depending on the source, they'll cause diarrhea or constipation. In such areas, particularly in southern Utah, the only option is to carry in your own fresh water.

An alpine garden in the High Uintas Wilderness

• **Injury and rescue:** If I could give only one bit of advice, it would be this: Turn around and go back if the going gets too rough for your skill level. Ditto if you are running out of daylight, water, food, or energy. It's better to miss something when you turn around than to risk not getting another chance to experience the stunning beauty of Utah's wilderness.

In many wilderness areas, cellular phones don't work. Even in places where a cellular phone will work, rescue teams might find it difficult to get to you. Whenever possible, don't hike alone, and be prepared to get yourself out of whatever you get into.

One of the most common injuries hikers suffer is a lower limb fracture incurred while canyoneering. When hikers elect to jump from boulders or the tops of dry waterfalls, a broken leg or ankle can result because the sand at the bottom is harder than it looks. The same injuries can happen when backcountry travelers drop into pools without knowing the depth of the water or the presence of underwater hazards. Whenever possible, use a rope to lower yourself and/or your pack, and to provide an extra measure of protection during all climbing activities. Canyoneering that requires a high degree of technical climbing skill is beyond the purview of this book.

It's easier to climb up slickrock than it is to climb down it. Despite its name, slickrock does not feel slick to the touch; in fact, it feels like very rough sandpaper. But tiny grains of sand on its surface can act as ball bearings and send you sliding. It is particularly treacherous when covered with snow or wet with rain. In some places you will find both ancient and modern-day "Moqui steps" carved into the sandstone. These toehold-size indentations are a time-honored aid to climbing slickrock. Plan to descend on a gentler slope.

Poison ivy grows in the moist pockets of canyons and near springs that issue from rocky cliffs. More virulent in the spring, these plants can wreak enough havoc to necessitate medical intervention. Read a good plant identification book and memorize the dastardly plant before you go into the backcountry.

Rattlesnake, scorpion, and tarantula bites account for fewer injuries than one might think, considering the widespread population of these biters and stingers. If you are going to hike far from help, carry a snakebite venom extraction kit. Never try to suck the venom from a wound with your mouth, as getting venom on your tongue will hasten its effect. If you are bitten, seek medical assistance immediately. As preventative measures, inspect and shake out your clothes and boots before you dress, keep your tent zipped, and don't put your hands and feet where your eyes can't see.

• **Hypothermia:** Rain accompanied by wind can cause hypothermia, the lowering of the body's core temperature to dangerous levels. It most commonly occurs when wet skin and clothing are exposed to heat-depleting winds. Symptoms include loss of coordination, shivering, and exhaustion. Prevention is the best medicine, but if hypothermia sets in, immediately warm the victim and protect him or her from the elements. Shelter the victim in a tent and give him or her many layers of dry clothing, as well as hot liquids—*but no alcohol.*

• **Acute mountain sickness:** This most common of high-altitude maladies can strike anyone, anytime, but visitors from lower elevations are more susceptible. Prevention, in the form of a few days of rest on arrival at altitude, is recommended. Symptoms of acute mountain sickness include headache, nausea, dizziness, shortness of breath, loss of appetite, and insomnia. The best treatment is to descend to a lower elevation,

A waterfall on the Provo River near the western border of the High Uintas Wilderness

drink plenty of water, and rest. The trails in Utah's mountainous wilderness areas seldom climb above 10,000 feet, so it is unlikely that more serious conditions such as pulmonary edema, the buildup of fluid in the lungs, will occur.

• **Tips for avoiding bears:** Your chances of encountering a bear are slim. We saw bear sign in Dark Canyon, the Uinta Mountains, the Wasatch Range, Death Ridge, and several other areas. We saw black bears in Desolation Canyon. If the bear population is a factor, it is mentioned in the individual chapters.

When camping in bear country, hang your food at least 10 feet up and 4 feet out from a tree trunk or rock. We use waterproof food bags and hang our food to keep rodents out, as well. Use only fragrance-free soap; this means no perfumed deodorant, lotion, shampoo, or laundry soap.

If you run from a bear, you are acting like prey. Black bears can sprint up to 35 miles per hour, twice as fast as an adrenaline-pumped backpacker. Don't run.

You may opt to carry oleoresin capsicum spray (pepper spray) meant to deter bears. Sprays designed to deter humans are not good enough. Bear spray will only work if it is sprayed in the animal's eyes, nose, or mouth. If you use the spray incorrectly, it will act as a strong attractant, sort of like catnip for bears.

If you come upon a bear on the trail, drop something (like your hat, but never food) and slowly back away, talking softly. The bear might stand on its hind legs to get a better view or smell of you. Standing is not an aggressive display. Bears show agitation and aggression by swaying their heads, huffing, clacking their teeth, lowering their heads, and laying back their ears. If a bear charges you, remain standing at first. The charge could be a bluff charge. Don't run. If the bear doesn't stop, use your pepper spray. If the bear does not retreat, assume a cannonball position on the ground, or lie on your stomach, with your arms and hands covering your head and neck. Leave your backpack on to protect your back.

Some recent research on bear attacks suggests that black bears can be fought off if you seize and maintain the high ground. Unlike grizzly bears, black bears apparently do not become more aggressive if you defend yourself. There is some disagreement on the best technique—should you play dead or fight back? In part, it depends on the bear, so there is no one-size-fits-all recommendation.

If you are close enough to photograph a bear, you are too close.

• **Avoiding other wild animals:** Many of the bear avoidance techniques will work for other large animals. Be particularly wary of females with young. Put up a fight if a mountain lion, elk, or moose attacks you. Experts suggest standing tall, waving your arms, making noise, and slowly backing up. Throwing rocks at or using a trekking pole against attackers might also prove effective. Children and small adults are more vulnerable to attack than are larger adults.

• **Rodents:** The droppings of deer mice and other rodents might carry the deadly disease hantavirus. Disturbing rodent nests or entering old buildings or mines increases your chances of breathing the airborne particles that carry the virus.

• **Cattle:** A system of fences and gates keeps cattle on their grazing allotments, which ranchers lease from the BLM or Forest Service. When visitors fail to close the primitive gates across roads and trails, the whole system breaks down. Gates, often made of barbed wire and cedar poles, can take quite a bit of muscle to hoist back into place and fasten upright. If you're planning on driving the backroads alone, attach a loop of chain to the end of a long bar and bring it with you on your trip. Loop the chain over the latch pole and lever the gate pole close enough to fasten the latch (usually the latch is just a circle of wire). Some ranchers leave a wooden or metal lever system attached to the gate pole.

If you come across a dead cow, make a note of the number on its ear tag and report that to the nearest land administration office. Using the ear tag identification, they'll know which rancher to call for removal of the carcass.

Equipment and Clothing

The Ten Essentials

1. Matches and lighter
2. Knife
3. Emergency shelter (tarp, ground cloth, and/or space blanket)
4. Food and water
5. Trowel for digging catholes
6. Extra clothes or jacket, as determined by season and location
7. Headlamp or flashlight
8. Maps and compass
9. First-aid kit
10. Sunglasses, sunscreen, hat

Additional Items for Day Hikes

Daypack
Moleskin and foot-care products
Insect repellent
Parachute cord or rope
Gloves
Extra socks
Insulating layer, both top and bottom
Raingear
Camera and film

Additional Items for Longer Hikes or Overnight Backpacking Trips
Sleeping bag
Insulating ground pad
Tent or shelter
Stove, fuel, and eating and cooking utensils
Bag for garbage
Food bag
Jacket/raingear
Long underwear appropriate for the season and elevation
Light shoes to wear around camp (water sandals or tennis shoes)
Water filter, iodine tablets, or other device for water treatment
Toiletries and personal hygiene kit
Repair kits for tent, stove, water filter, etc.
Pack cover

Optional Items

Handheld global positioning system (GPS)
Cellular phone
Bear spray
Water bag
Fire pan
Waterproofing for boots
Insulated cup
Baby wipes or hand wipes
Chair
Pillow
Journal
Reading material
Watch
Fishing gear
Ground cloth for tent
Binoculars
Candle lantern
Walking stick or trekking poles
Radio
Small basin or folding bucket
Kitchen sink

Clothing Tips
• **Protective clothing:** It's tempting to wear shorts and sleeveless shirts for warm-weather hiking, but unless you're on a paved trail and impervious to sunburn, think twice. There's often no other way to avoid poison ivy and rosebushes than to cover your skin. The temperature in slot canyons is like a refrigerator even in summer. Undeterred by insect repellent, deer flies and gnats feast on exposed flesh. Skin cancer cases are increasing exponentially. You can even get a sunburn through your clothing. Wet T-shirts, for example, may provide only 5 to 9 SPF (sun protection factor). Choose expedition-worthy clothes made from fabrics with 30-plus SPF. Look for features such as mesh vents, lightweight cloth, and light colors for warm-weather hiking. Choose several thinner layers for cool weather.

• **Gloves:** Gloves need to fit snugly so that they don't hamper you when you reach for handholds. Granite boulders, canyon walls, and slickrock pitches require you to use your hands frequently.

Gear Tips
• **Tents:** High winds and rocky or sandy surfaces can make it hard to set up a tent in desert environments. Bring a bit of extra cord to use for tie-downs. If you set up where tent stakes won't work, you can use the cord to tie rocks or logs to each stake-out point.

Waxing or lubricating your tent zipper will create a sticky trap for sand. Wash or shake sand out of tent zippers. Choose a light-colored, well-ventilated tent for desert hiking. Select a tent that can stand up to a load of snow for high-altitude hiking.

• **Raingear:** Your raingear should be a jacket and pants set, not a poncho.

• **Packs:** Internal-frame packs work better for tight places such as narrow canyons, and for routes that require climbing. External-frame packs hold the load away from your body and are cooler—good for well-maintained trails like those in the High Uintas. Your pack should not weigh more than one-third of your body weight. For example, if you weigh 120 pounds, your pack should weigh no more than 40 pounds (30 pounds would be better). You can lessen the weight you carry by using the smallest pack that will hold the gear and food necessary for your trip.

• **Insulated cups:** You can use an insulated cup as a mini-refrigerator if you precool it and add a napkin as insulation under the cap.

Geology and Ecosystems
Most of Utah falls within either the Basin and Range Ecoregion or the Colorado Plateau Ecoregion. The Wasatch Range divides the Middle Rocky Mountain and the Basin and Range Ecoregions. About 40% of Utah is Basin and Range, but there are far fewer proposed wilderness areas in the western desert. The Colorado Plateau accounts for more than 50% of Utah and contains the highest concentration of proposed wilderness. Recommended wilderness lands in national parks and national recreation areas are also concentrated on the Colorado Plateau.

Middle Rocky Mountain Ecoregion
At 13,528 feet, Kings Peak in the High Uintas Wilderness ranks as Utah's highest point. More than a dozen peaks over 13,000 feet (almost 4,000 meters) are also in the neighborhood. The Uinta Mountains, the longest east-west range in the lower 48 states, measure more than 150 miles long. The range is shaped like a huge arch

Jorge Canaca and Laura Lutz watch for raptors in the Wellsville Mountain Wilderness.

30 to 45 miles wide, with the arch flattened a little on top—a feature that puts all the 13,000-foot-plus peaks fairly close together in a single line. But the range is so immense and thickly forested below 10,000 feet that access is difficult. Precambrian rocks more than 600 million years old make up part of the Uinta Mountains. The rocks have been elevated by tremendous pressures from below to form part of the upswelling that makes up the Uintas.

Going back even farther in time, the oldest rocks in Utah can be seen in the Wasatch Range. The canyons along the Wasatch Front are a slide show of different layers of rock, the oldest from even earlier in the Precambrian era. The Wasatch Range rises along the Wasatch fault, an unstable geological zone that threatens the densely populated area nearby with potential earthquakes and landslides. The large, triangular facets on the lower slopes are evidence of movement along the fault. Parts of the Wasatch Range have moved about 10 miles eastward from where the sediments were first deposited. Water originating as rain and snowfall in the high country blesses the population that nestles next to the mountains. Protecting the watershed is serious business and some of the resultant regulations affect visitors to the wilderness areas.

Utah's justly famous ski runs follow the steep slopes of the Wasatch Range. Granitic intrusions that shoved upward during the Tertiary period (about 60 million years ago) have since eroded into the impressive, Switzerland-like shapes we see today. Glacier-carved cirques pockmark the crest of the range, and they often hold small lakes that lure hikers.

Basin and Range, Great Basin Desert, Mojave, and Sonoran Ecoregions

As you follow the old Pony Express Trail west of the Wasatch Range, you are still in the Rocky Mountains—sort of. Movements of the earth's crust formed the Rockies about 70 million years ago. More recently, a new (and still ongoing) episode of mountain building began. Chunks of the earth's crust broke, with the faults trending north to northwest. The chunks tilted and rotated above the fault, with one edge raised and the remainder of the block sloping down toward a future basin. The mountain ranges we see in the Basin and Range province are the edges of a succession of these chunks. The basins are filled with sediment so we see them as flat, but that's a disguise. Just imagine the visible part of the mountains extending farther downward, like a playground slide.

Every fault block forms a part of the Basin and Range and each is a slice of the Rocky Mountains that has been pulled away, pulled west from its original position by tectonic plate movement. The mountain blocks are still slowly moving away from each other, thinning the crust of the valleys as they go, spreading out, and leaving isolated ranges such as the Deep Creek Range sitting alone to lord over an attending desert.

In geological terms, 12,000 to 10,000 years ago qualifies as recent. Carrying boulders the size of houses, ancient Lake Bonneville burst through a natural dam on its northern edge and scoured out what is now the Snake River Plain in Idaho. Lake Bonneville used to cover about 20,000 square miles of northwestern Utah. In places it was a thousand feet deep. You can still see the old shoreline as plain as day along the Wasatch Front. Utah Lake (near Provo) and Sevier Lake (now a playa not far from the Wah Wah Mountains Wilderness Study Area) are both remnants of the giant water body of the past. Mountain ranges that used to be islands are now surrounded by desert. Plants and fish were also isolated and became island remnants of once-large populations. Lake Bonneville cutthroat trout in the Deep Creek Range are a famous example. The Pleistocene fish got trapped there when their habitat shrank. Another lake, the Great Salt Lake at the foot of the Wasatch Range, is a ready-made source of salt that has been harvested for thousands of years, first by American Indians and then by settlers. The freshwater Utah Lake to the south drains into the Great Salt Lake via the Jordan River.

When you drive westward from the Wasatch Range, you'll have the unmistakable experience of first encountering a basin, then a range, then another basin, and so on: Oquirrh Mountains, Cedar Valley, Onaqui Mountains, Rush Valley, Simpson Mountains, Dugway Range, Dugway Valley, Fish Springs Range, Fish Springs Flat, and, finally, the Deep Creek Range on the Nevada border. The Basin and Range province continues across most of Nevada.

While geology defines the Basin and Range province, precipitation, temperature, and plant types distinguish the Great Basin Desert. Still, the two cover much of the same area. The northern edge of the Great Basin Desert is Idaho's Snake River Valley. In Idaho, and in northern and western Utah, a lot of grass grows between the sagebrush and there are very few cacti. The land is classified as a cold desert because more than half of the annual precipitation comes in the form of snow. Deseret Peak Wilderness falls into this category. Farther south, cacti and drought-resistant shrubs replace some of the grass, but the desert is still classified as "cold," thanks to winter snowfall. The Great Basin is called a "basin" because precipitation that falls there doesn't drain to the Pacific or Atlantic Oceans. What little rain and snow falls there, stays there.

Exactly where Great Basin Desert ends and Mojave and Sonoran Deserts begin is a matter of debate. Farther south, where the hot deserts begin, the Beaver Dam Wilderness occupies a transition zone where Mojave and Sonoran meet Great Basin.

Dour lands lacking thick forest cover and having few lakes and streams are an acquired taste. Many acres bear the pockmarks of cow hooves or are so dry as to be unfit even for a scattering of bovines. These lands lack the kind of aesthetic beauty that pops up as backdrops for selling sport-utility vehicles. This kind of wilderness protects itself. Coyotes lope across it, pronghorn antelope cover its distances with springy legs, hawks oversee it with binocular vision, chukar partridges tempt fate on its precipices, and the sun seeks the edge of spring clouds to highlight the neon green of lichen on the black edges of broken cliffs.

At night, if you turn a slow 360 degrees to look into the darkness of west-central Utah, the only light is often from stars and moon. No city lights reflect off distant clouds; no fellow camper tells you about his new boots. Real solitude is the glory of the Basin and Range. In the vast desert spaces, the horizon is so endless that you swear you can feel the earth turning.

Colorado Plateau Ecoregion
The Colorado Plateau is 8.5 million acres of various kinds of sandstone, shale, and limestone deposited in horizontal layers from about 570 to 180 million years ago.

The layers were not uplifted to form the plateau until about 65 million years ago. Water and wind have intricately cut and carved much of the present-day Colorado Plateau, with deeply incised canyons providing some of the most unique hiking routes in the world. Equally impressive are the mesa tops that rise above the canyons, hiding in their relatively flat domain thousands of defiles, some of them "slots" as narrow as a zipper in the landscape.

Canyons that narrow to arm's length or to shoulder width can be found the world over, but the Colorado Plateau boasts more slot canyons than any other place. Many canyons only meet the "slot" definition for short distances. Slot canyons exist in Capitol Reef and Zion National Parks, in the San Rafael Reef, and along the tributaries of the Dirty Devil River. Water engulfed many canyons when the Colorado River was dammed to form Lake Powell. You can see slots right from the highway when you drive UT 276 and UT 95 north from Lake Powell. Measuring 16 miles, the longest

Geological Strata in Utah

Era	Period	Epoch	Age	Rock Examples
Cenozoic	Quaternary	Holocene	10,000 to present	Products of weathering and erosion
		Pleistocene	2–.01 million	Zion volcanics, Lake Bonneville develops
	Tertiary	Pliocene	5–2 million	Capitol Reef volcanics, Basin & Range faults
		Miocene	24–5 million	Wasatch fault, Colorado Plateau uplift
		Oligocene	37–24 million	Scattered volcanics, intrusions push upward
		Eocene	58–37 million	Mountain erosion, lake sedimentation
		Paleocene	66–58 million	Uinta and Wasatch Mountains rise
Mesozoic	Cretaceous		144–66 million	Kaiparowits Plateau & Wahweap WSA Straight Cliffs Mancos and Tropic Shale Dakota Sandstone Sevier Mountains rise Invading sea brings sandstone and coal
	Jurassic		208–144 million	Morrison Formation Summerville Formation Curtis Formation Entrada Sandstone Carmel Formation Temple Cap (Zion NP only) Navajo Sandstone Desert conditions over most of Utah Dinosaurs, footprints in San Rafael Swell
	Triassic		245–208 million	Kayenta Formation Wingate Sandstone (Moenave in Zion) Chinle Formation Moenkopi Formation Sea retreats westward, volcanoes spew ash that aids in petrified wood formation

slot canyon in the world is Buckskin Gulch in the Paria Canyon–Vermilion Cliffs Wilderness on the Utah-Arizona border. What all these slots are saying very loudly is "EROSION."

Canyons and clefts result when water rushes from high places to low places, seeking a way out through the maze of sandstone. During the Triassic period, rivers wound their way across low basins. There were no steep gradients, and

Sedimentary layers of the Moenkopi ribbon cliffs in the Muddy Creek WSA

Era	Period	Age	Rock Examples
Paleozoic	Permian	286–245 million	Kaibab Limestone White Rim Sandstone Cedar Mesa, Four Corners Uncompahgre Highland rises in E Utah and Colorado
	Pennsylvanian	330–286 million	Honaker Trail Formation, Canyonlands NP Salt, gypsum, potash deposit in SE Utah Oquirrh Basin marine and shale deposits in NW Utah
	Mississippian	360–330 million	Marine limestone deposited with fossil corals, snails, brachiopods in shallow sea
	Devonian	408–360 million	Most of Utah covered by sea, uplift of north-central Utah
	Silurian	438–408 million	Dolomite deposited over much of Utah Warm, tropical sea
	Ordovician	505–438 million	Marine limestone, sandstone, dolomite deposits, thickest in W Utah Trilobites preserved as fossils
	Cambrian	570–505 million	Sandstone, shale, then limestone deposited as sea deepens
Precambrian		over 570 million	Thick deposits of sedimentary rocks, later altered to marble, slate, quartzite Glaciation in Uinta and Wasatch Mountains In earlier Precambrian episodes of mountain building, rocks altered to gneiss and schist

rivers moved slowly enough to deposit about 500 feet of silt and sand. Logs falling into the rivers were buried in silt. Geologists have found clay minerals in the Chinle Formation that show evidence of distant volcanoes adding ash to the mix. Unstable silica glass in volcanic ash helped to petrify fallen trees.

You can see isolated examples of petrified wood on many of the trails and in the washes of the Colorado Plateau. Most have been significantly abraded and broken as they were carried downhill by flash floods or mudslides. Better specimens, including whole petrified logs, exist in the Wolverine Petrified Wood Natural Area, west and south of Burr Trail Road in the Grand Staircase–Escalante National Monument.

Capitol Reef National Park is dominated by one of the most visually arresting folds in the Colorado Plateau. Members of the 1869 Powell Expedition lent Waterpocket Fold its name for the many pockets in the cap of Navajo Sandstone that hold water after brief rains. To imagine what a fold is, take a telephone book, hold it horizontally, and push on it from both sides. It might crumple upward (an anticline), or downward (a syncline), or stay high on its spine side and drop down on its unbound side (a monocline). The Waterpocket Fold is a monocline, high on the west and lower on the east. It is aligned roughly north-south and stretches about 90 miles long. The Cockscomb Wilderness Study Area southwest of Capitol Reef is part of the even longer East Kaibab monocline.

Erosion has peeled all of the monoclines and other formations of the Colorado Plateau. Sheets of softer stuff, such as shale, have been carried away. Wherever the stone is weaker or softer, water swiftly cuts canyons, sometimes right through the

Petrified wood is exposed by erosion on a mesa near Fremont Gorge WSA.

skeletal lines of a monocline. Today, the Colorado Plateau makes for a hiker's paradise in the cooler spring and autumn months. Numerous trails through tortuous canyons provide a walk back through the strata of geological time, extending from the White Rim Sandstone of the Paleozoic era to the Mancos Shale of the Cretaceous period, from about 286 million to about 66 million years ago.

As you walk through time, you'll see a broad palette of colors. Red, pink, and yellow are derived mostly from minute amounts of iron oxides; bright yellow is the uranium-containing ore carnotite; green and blue are usually unoxidized iron minerals; lavender is manganese. Rock colors also differ depending on the direction the wind was blowing when ancient sand dunes were formed. Wind from the west brought pale colors and almost-white quartz particles. Wind from the northeast brought red sand. The sandstone we now enjoy on our hikes used to be a vast desert of dunes.

"Desert varnish" is a thin, shiny coat of iron and manganese oxides that forms on exposed surfaces. Scientists have recently discovered that desert varnish is "alive." Airborne dust, clay particles, and iron and manganese minerals all form a partnership with bacteria and microfungi to paint the streaks that can stretch more than a thousand feet long on canyon walls.

The layer cake of geological strata that gives its name to the "Grand Staircase" of tilted terraces in the western Grand Staircase–Escalante National Monument marches from high to low, from young to old, across 200 million years of geological history. At the top of the cake, the youngest layer is the pink icing of silt deposited by a freshwater lake that later became the eroded spires of Cedar Breaks National Monument and Bryce Canyon National Park. At the bottom are the deep red sandstones and badlands of the Vermilion Cliffs in the Paria Canyon–Vermilion Cliffs Wilderness.

Plants and Animals

Flora and fauna populations change between low and high elevations, and from dry to moist regions. A sampling of the different ecozones follows.

Along Streams and Rivers

• **Desert rivers and streams:** Today's hiker finds desert riverbanks choked with tamarisk, or salt cedar (*Tamarix pentandra*), a tree introduced from the Near East. Some sources say the shrub-sized tree was introduced to control erosion on Arizona's Gila River; others say it was imported as an ornamental shrub or to establish wind-breaks. Whatever the reason, the import has proven a grave error.

On first sight, the tamarisk has a certain lacy charm. In spring and summer, it sports a baroque filigree of pink flowers, multiple thin trunks, and frothy foliage. The foliage turns orange in late fall. In winter, tamarisk is evil decor—ugly, dark, and monotonous. Throughout the seasons, this phreatophyte extracts all the available moisture, sending down deep taproots and shutting out native species such as willows and cottonwood trees. On shallower watercourses, it can suck all the water out of a stream, leaving nothing but a damp strip of sand where life-giving water once ran. Impenetrable barricades limit access to stream banks and fords. Some researchers have begun testing imported Chinese beetles to eat the imported tamarisk.

• **Mountain streams:** Willows, alders, water birches, maples, and serviceberry are just some of the shrubs and small trees that line the banks of mountain streams and rivers, anchoring riparian ecosystems. Hikers will know they've reached lower elevations when cottonwoods (*Populus fremontii*) also line the riverbanks. Their extensive root systems play a large part in erosion control. The tree's name derives from the cloud of cottony seeds that it releases in spring and summer. Hopi Indians carve cottonwood roots into kachina dolls, representatives of supernatural beings.

Sagebrush Communities

• **Meadows:** Meadows that plainly outline drainage patterns dot sagebrush ecoregions at higher elevations. Sedges, grasses, flowering plants, and willows fill the meadows. Tall sagebrush and grasses prevail from the edges of the meadows to forest treelines. Monkey flowers and shooting stars join the sagebrush community where seeps keep the ground more moist.

• **Mormon tea:** In drier sections of sagebrush communities, we find plants such as Mormon tea (*Ephedra nevadensis*). The bushy ephedra shrubs stand about 3 or 4 feet tall and look like a bunch of short-handled brooms stuck in the ground. Ephedrine is a stimulant present in the plant. Head-high stands of this plant grow in the Deep Creek Mountains WSA and in most of the central and southern proposed and designated wildernesses, with exceptionally thick stands in the Black Box along the San Rafael River.

• **Sagebrush:** Sagebrush (*Artemisia tridentata* and *Artemisia rigida*) was named in honor of the Greek goddess Artemis, the virgin huntress or goddess of wild nature. Sagebrush is a god of sorts in its own right, a ruler of wild nature. It has the broadest ecological tolerance and can survive under the greatest range of environmental conditions.

• **Tumbleweed:** Actually Russian thistle, tumbleweed (*Salsola kali*) evokes the desolate, desert West. The nonnative plant arrived mixed in with the wheat seed that Russian and other farmers brought from their homelands in the late 1800s. Tumbleweed owes its distribution efficiency to its annual habits and its circular growth form. When the plants die in the autumn, they break away from their roots and tumble freely with the wind, scattering seeds as they go. Fortunately, Russian thistle is not an aggressive competitor, so it doesn't replace as many native species as does the pesky tamarisk.

• **Joshua trees:** Slow-growing and long-lived, Joshua trees (*Yucca brevifolia*) can survive for a thousand years. They are characteristic of the Mojave Desert, and forests of them flourish in the extreme southwestern corner of Utah. The "tree," actually a yucca of the agave family, has a thick, shaggy trunk that offers to the sun many clusters of daggerlike leaves. Indigenous peoples used the leaf fiber to make rope, sandals, mats, and baskets. The flowers and buds are edible, and the roots and stems can be used to make soap.

Badlands

The Blue Hills near the Henry Mountains are composed of Mancos Shale Formation, an example of soil chemistry that is not plant-friendly. When a lack of vegetation combines with convoluted terrain such as the Blue Hills, the area earns the title of "badlands."

You might spy vegetation-rich areas adjacent to "wastelands." On the Kaiparowits Plateau, for example, gray barrens fail to support the juniper woodlands and desert shrubs that grow elsewhere on the plateau. The barrens began as deposits in oxygen-poor pools or lakes that were stagnant. When time and erosion exposed them, shales from the Cretaceous period (140 to 60 million years ago) reacted chemically with oxygen, creating sulfuric acids, selenium, and salts—a toxic cocktail for most plants.

• **Prince's plume:** Prince's plume (*Stanleya pinnata*), with its multiple spikes of yellow blooms, is a sure sign of selenium-rich soil. Prospectors used to look for this plant in the otherwise barren landscape because it signaled the likelihood of uranium-bearing ore. The plant takes up selenium and substitutes it for sulfur in some of its amino acids. The altered amino acids in the plant are extremely toxic to livestock and wildlife. Don't add this plant to your diet.

• **Greasewood:** A low, spiny shrub with bright green foliage, greasewood (*Sarcobatus vermiculatus*) is another plant that has adapted to inhospitable soils. It grows in alkaline flats and playas where salty soil would kill other plants. Sodium salts accumulate in the leaves and roots. If you taste a leaf, you can easily note the salt content.

Piñon-Juniper Woodlands

• **Junipers:** Woodlands of juniper (*Juniperus osteosperma*) and piñon are common in Colorado, Wyoming, and Utah. Sids Mountain in the San Rafael Swell is an excellent example of an intermediate mesa topped with piñon-juniper woodlands. Often used to make fenceposts, the drought-resistant junipers sometimes form a transition zone between sagebrush communities and montane forests, mingling with both.

Gold aspen trees and red understory plants in the Twin Peaks Wilderness

• **Piñons:** Piñons (*Pinus edulis*) serve as an important food source for the Navajo and other local residents. The edible seeds, known as piñon nuts or pine nuts, are nutritious and tasty.

Forests

• **Ponderosa pines:** Stands of ponderosa pine (*Pinus ponderosa*) flourish in the warmest, driest forest sites. Parklike stands of ponderosa pine beautify many of Utah's wilderness areas, including the mesas above Dark Canyon Wilderness, the higher elevations in Zion National Park, and the Pine Valley Mountain Wilderness. Their thick, red trunks are fire-resistant, and, because the trees monopolize the soil resources, the understory around them is sparse.

• **Quaking aspens:** Because of their remarkable ability to adapt to different ecological conditions, quaking aspens (*Populus tremuloides*) are the most widely distributed of any tree in North America. The aspen's fine, saw-toothed leaves "quake" in the slightest breeze, and leaf movement is emphasized by the disparity between the bright green on top and the dull gray-green on the bottom of the leaf. Aspen trees of unusually large girth grow in the Mount Timpanogos Wilderness. The combination of scene-stealing, candy-red maples and antique-gold aspens makes the Wasatch Range famous for its show of colors in autumn.

• **Lodgepole pines:** This opportunistic tree often takes over after a fire, as it relies on the heat from the flames to melt the resin seal on its cones, releasing its seeds in an open, noncompetitive environment. Lodgepole pines (*Pinus contorta*) look like the weeds of the pine family, growing so closely together that they create a gloomy, impenetrable fence of skinny trunks. They grow so tightly together that they sometimes form what are called "dog hair" forests. Lodgepole pines are common in the High Uintas Wilderness.

• **Douglas firs:** Douglas firs (*Pseudotsuga menziesii*) frequently mix with lodgepole pines and other conifers. These tall, large trees are important to the lumber industry. In sharp contrast to the more open ponderosa pine forests, Douglas fir forests are cooler, darker, and blue-green in color.

• **Subalpine forests:** Engelmann spruce (*Picea engelmannii*), subalpine fir (*Abies lasiocarpa*), and limber pine (*Pinus flexilis*) dominate the subalpine areas of Utah's mountains. Dwarf, twisted versions, known as "krummholz," cling to life at the higher elevations. *Krummholz* is a German word meaning "crooked wood."

• **Bristlecone pines:** In Ashdown Gorge Wilderness and a few other dry mountain regions, bristlecone pines (*Pinus aristata*) grow in pure, beautifully sculpted stands. The pyramids in Egypt were under construction when some of the bristlecone pines in Utah's mountain ranges began as saplings, as long ago as 2700 B.C. The trees stop growing during harsh conditions and can survive fire, drought, wind, heat, and cold. A 6-foot-tall tree can be 900 years old. Bristlecone pines don't die of old age; they die when the soil is eroded from around their root systems.

Alpine Zone

Above the treeline, the thin soil is festooned with hardy grasses and thousands of miniature flowers and cushion plants. Most of the terrain above 10,000 feet is alpine.

Buttercups, moss campion, cushion phlox, forget-me-nots, and yellow stonecrop are common flowering plants, some of their blooms measuring only a quarter-inch across. In places they seem to spring from rock itself, with no apparent requirement for soil. High-elevation plant communities are very sensitive. To avoid damaging plants that might have taken as long as two decades to mature and blossom, stay on the trail, or on rocky surfaces, as much as possible.

Animals, Birds, and Bugs

Unlike plants, animals can move about to escape bad weather. Mountain goats, bighorn sheep, elk, and deer might all browse in alpine areas, but will seek shelter at treeline during the worst weather or migrate to lower elevations for the winter months. Alpine grouse, coyotes, hawks, and other smaller birds and animals will hunker down in the krummholz to evade the weather. If you look closely, you can see that they have worn paths in and out of the low cover.

Coyotes, mountain lions, black bears, and mule deer have a remarkably wide comfort zone, ranging from canyon floors to mountainsides. Desert bighorn sheep, black bears, and midget rattlesnakes share the shores of the Green River in Desolation Canyon. Wild turkeys live on the mesas above Dark Canyon; rare desert tortoises survive in a protected area next to the Beaver Dam Mountains Wilderness; rattlesnakes, scorpions, tarantulas, and hosts of lizards and rodents populate all the deserts.

Human History

When we travel, we move not only in space, but often into an awareness of earlier times. The variety of human history, the eroded face of geological time, even our own inner sense of time, all come to us as fresh revelations. Navajos with no electricity surf the Internet with solar-powered laptops and satellite connections. Hikers work their way down into rock formations more than 10,000 centuries old, and once there, finger-draw an e-mail address in the sand. Japanese and German tourists examine the monument where Mormon leader Brigham Young looked across the Salt Lake Valley in 1847 and said, "This is the place."

Ranching has been a way of life in Utah since the mid-1800s, and it got a big boost from industrious Latter-Day Saints (Mormons) who fanned out from Salt Lake City on orders

The Three Kings petroglyph in Dry Fork Canyon

from Brigham Young. Here's an excerpt from *Oh Ye Mountains High: History of Pine Valley, Utah*, a local history by Bessie Snow and Elizabeth Beckstrom:

> Snow fell deep in the 1880s, so grass grew lush and tall in the mountains….As soon as the forty day rain ceased [men] were chosen to find grazing for all the cattle….The men came upon large herds of wild cattle running loose in Bull Valley and on the Beaver Dam Wash….Some said they were the offspring of cows lost by travelers on the Spanish Trail….In the period from about 1880 to the turn of the century many men not realizing the results of over-grazing, allowed their herds to increase as fast as nature would permit.

Long before the pioneers were learning about the sins of overgrazing, other humans roamed over what is now Utah. When my brother and I were hiking in the Paria-Hackberry proposed wilderness we saw an artifact, a stone "shovel" as big as a man's hand, that was notched in the top for a wooden handle. In the same area, worked flakes of agate told a tale of someone patiently crafting arrowheads. A desiccated and delaminating horn from a bighorn sheep was probably left by an Indian hunting party. This was not a major archaeological site, just one of thousands across southern Utah.

Nearby, at the old Pahreah townsite, a graveyard marked the deaths of Mormon pioneers. They had farmed the area from 1860 to 1870, but had built on a floodplain. Flash floods inevitably came and washed all their crops and hopes away.

The next day we found rusted tin cans, old shell casings, and a datable monkey wrench minus its wooden handle, all from military training prior to or during World War II. On the top of a hill closer to the Paria River, we found a mining claim that consisted of a rotting piece of paper no longer entirely readable. It was buried under a cairn of rocks, the spot marked with an upright juniper post. The probable

An old cabin near the Kolab Canyons section of Zion National Park

reason for the claim was uranium, so this was relatively modern, from the 1950s. A yellow, cakelike, uranium-bearing mineral was embedded in layers of black rock near the claim, looking fascinatingly evil.

With a fake saloon, blacksmith shop, and hotel lined up along a single dusty street, a set for Western movies stood there aging in the sun and wind. Behind the set stood a spectacular backdrop of Jurassic mudstone. The ancient mud—now layered neatly into a multicolored cake below a cap of red sandstone—featured strata of saffron yellow, claret, violet, vermilion, warm gray, salmon, ochre, terra-cotta, lavender, magenta, and ash white.

The desert preserves its history of interactions with human populations. In a few days of hiking, we had seen evidence of most of Utah's human history and its relationship to the inhospitable terrain. All we needed was a piece of Spanish silver and a page from John Wesley Powell's diary and the story would have been complete. Powell was an explorer, bureaucrat, and amateur scientist and geologist of the late 19th century. Civil War wounds left him with only one arm, but that did not deter him from leading an expedition down the Green and Colorado Rivers in 1869. The Grand Canyon became "Grand" after his expedition, and the Colorado Plateau moved to the forefront of American dreams of the Wild West.

It is estimated that humans first arrived in Utah about 12,000 to 8,000 years ago. These Archaic peoples or Paleo-Indians were the first people to walk the mesas and canyon floors that are our hiking routes today. Spear points, along with bison and mammoth bones, are some of the clues archaeologists use to reconstruct the lifestyle of this hunter-gatherer culture. Clovis and Folsom points have been found in the San Rafael Swell area, near Dinosaur National Park, and along the Green River.

The rock art and ruins of southern Utah's earliest human occupants fascinate most modern-day visitors. Barrier Canyon–style rock art panels provide the clearest evidence of the Archaic peoples. Barrier Canyon pictographs (designs painted on rocks) in the San Rafael Swell date to about 5000 B.C. Such pictographs were once thought to be part of the Fremont culture, but have since been traced back to a much earlier time. At Horseshoe Canyon, occupants painted enormous panels on the canyon walls about 6,500 years ago. They produced red paint from hematite, yellow from limonite, and black from coal deposits.

The rock art, granaries, and dwellings of the Fremont and Anasazi cultures date from about A.D. 200 to about A.D. 1300. Evidence of a 30-year drought, and a preponderance of fortresslike cliff dwellings, has led some researchers to conclude that dwindling resources and conflict over land might have hastened the demise or migration of the Fremont and Anasazi peoples. Archaeologists call the earliest emergence of these groups that used horticulture, irrigation, and domesticated animals the "Basketmakers." The name derives from the elaborate woven baskets and clothing that the dry desert air kept preserved for archaeologists to find.

Anasazi and Fremont cultures are so similar that it's hard for a nonexpert to tell them apart. Differences in styles of basketweaving, pottery, and housing distinguish the two. Some experts think both cultures evolved from the Basketmakers, and others think that the Fremont culture migrated to the Colorado Plateau from the Great Basin.

Generally speaking, Fremont Indian sites are more plentiful north of the Escalante River. Fremont Indians lived in groups of up to a hundred people and built clusters of pit houses. They used caves, with crude improvements, for storage of grain. Petroglyphs, designs that were pecked onto rock walls, define Fremont rock art. The name "Fremont" derives from an ambitious white man, John Charles Frémont, who managed to have more than a hundred places and one group of historic peoples named after him. Frémont's haphazard career as the "Pathfinder" of the 1840s and 1850s was fraught with controversy. He covered more ground than any other explorers, including Lewis and Clark, but his judgment ranged from good to appalling. He later sullied his own reputation further with questionable dealings in the California goldfields.

Walled cities and distinctive cliff dwellings are hallmarks of the Anasazi culture. Names for these early peoples vary, depending on what authority is doing the naming. *Anasazi*, a Navajo word meaning "ancestral enemies," has been in use since 1936. Some present-day tribes, particularly the Hopi and other Pueblo Indians, find the term offensive. "Paleo-Indians," "Ancestral Puebloans," or "Pueblo Culture" have been suggested, but so far "Anasazi" has remained the predominant term.

Southern Paiute, Ute, Hopi, and Navajo tribes were the next wave of settlers and travelers. These tribes, which once roamed over much larger domains without a thought for the foreign concept of land ownership, are now the administrators of small, independent nations within the United States. They have their own regulations, fees, and permit systems for hiking, hunting, fishing, and camping. The Uintah and Ouray Indian Reservation next to Desolation Canyon and the High Uintas Wilderness, as well as the Navajo Reservation in southeastern Utah, are lands that present-day hikers encounter as they explore Utah's designated and proposed wilderness areas. When visiting tribal lands, please respect reservation regulations.

Spaniards and Mexicans fought with and traded with Indian cultures. In 1776 a Franciscan friar named Francisco Silvestre Velez de Escalante and his companion Francisco Atanasio Dominguez searched for a new route from present-day Santa Fe, N.M., to Monterey, Calif. Their trek took them all over Utah, including up to the Great Salt Lake. The Escalante River and Grand Staircase–Escalante National Monument bear the friar's name. Mount Timpanogos Wilderness in the Wasatch Range owes its name to the indigenous peoples living around Utah Lake, the Timpanogotzis, mentioned in the diary kept by the Dominguez-Escalante expedition.

Miners and trappers have traditionally pioneered routes into less populated areas, and Utah was no exception. For example, fur trappers worked the upper Green River as early as 1825, and Bear Lake was famous as a wild and woolly fur trader rendezvous circa 1812–1830. The trappers spread news of the land to miners. Most of the agriculture- and ranching-oriented pioneers who settled in Utah followed closely on the heels of miners.

Mormon pioneers like "Gunlock" Hamblin were charismatic men. Hamblin shot the bowl out of another man's pipe at 50 paces, thus securing the respect of the local Indian tribes and setting the scene for a waterhole to be known as "Pipe Springs" ever after. Mormons who practiced polygamy hid out in Pipe Springs from the law.

The influence of Mormon pioneers still marks Utah today. When you see an address such as "2370 South 2300 West," it's not a typographical error. The address relates to the local Mormon religious center, 23 blocks south and 23 blocks west of the temple.

Utah's population now includes a mix of many religions and skin colors. High-tech industries flock to the Salt Lake City–Provo area to take advantage of the motivated workforce. Construction for the 2002 Winter Olympics added to the boom. The beauty of nearby wilderness areas serves as an additional draw, but the state's growth has put added pressure on designated and proposed wilderness areas.

Land Hierarchy

National parks are some of the most scenic and most frequently visited public lands in the western United States. For example, Zion National Park may receive more than two million visitors per year while nearby wilderness study areas on BLM land average about 500 visitors annually. Administered by the National Park Service, national parks provide a significant number of amenities, usually including paved roads, visitor centers, improved campgrounds, tour bus facilities, and more. Fees and reservations are required for some uses. Backcountry portions of all five of Utah's national parks have been recommended for wilderness designation. The National Park Service also manages national recreation areas and national monuments.

Wilderness areas are, for the most part, defined by Grade A scenery, but might not have the knock-'em-to-their-knees impact of national parks. Designated wilderness is managed to maintain a roadless and primitive character (see What Is Wilderness?, p. 16). It is more difficult to access and has fewer amenities than national parks.

National forest lands cover mostly higher terrain, where forests of trees define the landscape. National forest lands that are not designated wilderness areas provide access for hunting, camping, hiking, boating, and other recreational uses via a system of forest roads, usually improved dirt or gravel. Both improved and unimproved camping sites exist on these public lands, which might also encompass ski resorts and reservoirs. The Forest Service also leases limited logging and grazing rights on these lands.

Bureau of Land Management lands are generally more arid than Forest Service lands. Cattle and sheep grazing, along with mining and gas/oil development, used to play major parts in the BLM's focus. In recent decades, recreational use has greatly increased on BLM lands, and an appreciation for the unique character of desert and near-desert environments has emerged. Most of the proposed wilderness areas in Utah are on BLM land. Visiting BLM land, with its lack of amenities, signs, trails, and water, makes for a different kind of wilderness experience. BLM land often offers unimproved camping and hiking at no or minimal cost. On BLM land, you have to take care of yourself and find your own way.

Indian reservation lands are extremely arid, for the most part. In Utah, the section of the Uintah and Ouray Indian Reservation in the foothills of the Uinta Mountains is a forested exception. Contacts for permits to camp or hike on reservation lands appear in Appendix B.

How to Use This Guide

UTAH'S WILDERNESS AREAS are grouped by geographic region with the exception of recommended wilderness on National Park Service lands, which is summarized at the end of the book. If you know the name of an area but have no idea where to look for it, check Appendix A for an alphabetical listing that shows the chapter in which the area appears. Helpful information in the Along the Trail introductory material on pp. 22–45 is not repeated in the individual chapters, so please read that section as part of your expedition planning.

An overview of each region introduces the chapters, which describe every wilderness or proposed wilderness in Utah. Regions are color-coded for easy reference as you flip through the book. At the beginning of each chapter, a short table of pertinent information about each area includes the following points:

Location: This lists the region in which the wilderness area is located. See the organizational map on p. 10 for a regional outline.

Size: Wilderness in Utah is a moving target. In preparing this book, I rarely found sources (including official sources) that agreed exactly on the acreage of wilderness or proposed wilderness. Boundaries are adjusted, school trust lands are traded out, things change. This book presents the most accurate and the most current information available at the time of printing.

Elevation Range: Two thousand feet can be the difference between winter and spring. If you are planning your trip with weather and snowmelt in mind, read the details in the overview and route descriptions to determine when roads will be open and trailheads accessible.

Ecoregion: The major ecoregions of Middle Rocky Mountain, Colorado Plateau, and Basin and Range are mentioned here and described fully in Along the Trail.

Miles of Trail: Miles are given for maintained trails, with notes as to additional primitive routes.

Administration: Land administrators are listed here, and their contact information appears in Appendix B.

Maps: Topographical maps in scales of 1:48,000 and 1:90,000 from Trails Illustrated cover many of the designated and proposed wilderness areas in Utah (see Appendix D). These waterproof maps show official hiking trails and routes. In addition to the Trails Illustrated maps, the USGS 1:24,000-scale maps are also listed. Add these to your map resources when you anticipate cross-country travel, or when you need extremely detailed topographical or backcountry road information. The Forest Service map High Uintas Wilderness is recommended for northeastern Utah. The BLM's Arizona Strip District map is recommended for southern Utah. The BLM also prints 1:100,000-scale topographical maps that you'll find useful for overviews.

Camping near the entrance to the Upper Black Box along the San Rafael River

The simplified maps that appear in this guidebook are not intended for orientation in the field. Please refer to this legend for all maps in this book:

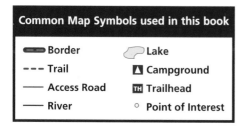

Common Map Symbols used in this book

▬ Border	⬭ Lake
--- Trail	▲ Campground
── Access Road	⊞ Trailhead
── River	○ Point of Interest

Recommended day hikes and backpacking trips follow the general information about the area. The description of and directions to each hike are preceded by these summary details:

One-Way Length: This gives the one-way mileage to the destination or recommended turnaround point. If you are walking to a specific endpoint and then back along the same route, double the given distance for total mileage. For loop trips, the one-way length is the total distance.

Low and High Elevations: This identifies the lowest and highest points on a particular hike, not the total elevation gain or loss. On many hikes, you might ascend and descend many times over. On some hikes into canyons, be aware that the highest elevation is often the starting point.

Difficulty: A difficulty rating of easy, moderate, strenuous, or extremely strenuous accompanies each hike. Hikes with low mileage, an easy-to-find route, and little elevation change earn an "easy" rating. "Moderate" hikes involve longer distances and/or greater elevation changes. Rough terrain, bushwhacking, stream wading, scrambling over boulders, substantial elevation gain, long distances, or a difficult-to-find trail lend a hike a "strenuous" designation. Routes that require top-notch physical endurance and skills are rated "extremely strenuous."

Abbreviations:
2WD = Two-wheel-drive
4WD = Four-wheel-drive
ATV = All-terrain vehicle (see "ORV"); motorized,
       includes four-wheelers and dirt bikes
BLM = Bureau of Land Management
CR = County Road
EIS = Environmental Impact Statement
FR = Forest Road
FS = U.S. Forest Service
GSENM = Grand Staircase–Escalante National Monument
ISA = Instant Study Area
NM = National Monument
NF = National Forest
NP = National Park
NPS = National Park Service

NRA = National Recreation Area

NWR = National Wildlife Refuge

ORV = Off-road vehicle (see "ATV")

Topo = Topographical map; refers to USGS 7.5-minute maps, 1:24,000 scale

Two-track = Route where two tracks cut by motorized vehicles are visible, but it is not graded and has grass or small shrubs growing in its center; if you are feeling generous, you can call it a "road."

USDA = U.S. Department of Agriculture

USGS = U.S. Geological Survey

WSA = Wilderness Study Area

Eroded sandstone in the White Cliffs area of Paria-Hackberry WSA

North-Central Utah

Although they are practically next door to each other, sharing the Cache Valley on their borders, Wellsville Mountains and Mount Naomi Wildernesses make quite a contrast. Wellsville is dry, while Mount Naomi is blessed with streams and lakes. Wellsville has one trail along its crest, and Mount Naomi has 60 miles of varied trails. Wellsville seldom sees visitors until the fall raptor count begins, but visitors besiege Mount Naomi from June to October. Wellsville is an isolated island of wilderness completely surrounded by private land, and Mount Naomi is the jewel in a much larger setting of Forest Service and state recreational lands, including more than 30,000 additional acres of roadless terrain.

Near the Mount Naomi Wilderness is Logan Canyon, famous in the rock-climbing community. Climbers come from all over the world to sample the cliffs, and a contingent of local climbers supports climbing clubs and classes. Climbing is restricted to routes that don't damage threatened plants such as the Maguire primrose.

The town of Logan has also spawned a dedicated group of cyclists that helps the Forest Service maintain hundreds of miles of mountain-biking trails. Utah's Wasatch Range is known for its "we-have-it-all" recreational opportunities, and the northernmost Wasatch peaks are no exception. In and around the Mount Naomi Wilderness, visitors can bike, hike, ski, and climb. Oh, yes, and nearby Bear Lake covers all the water sports.

In the Wellsville Mountains, an annual raptor count begins in August. HawkWatch International posts two experienced birdwatchers on the crest, and there they stay for two months, with a team of packhorses bringing up water and supplies. The raptor count draws day hikers as well, and the narrow spine of the Wellsvilles enjoys a brief busy season. In a typical year, 4,000 raptors take advantage of the updrafts along the western front as part of a migration route. Deer and elk hunting seasons begin in October, when the mountains play host to a migration of hunters from surrounding cities.

Mountain maples, box elders, and aspen trees flare into beautiful tapestries of color in late September and early October near the Mount Naomi Wilderness.

The high country doesn't melt free of snow until June, and even then you might find yourself crossing snowfields in shaded areas. In late July and August, temperatures can top 90 degrees Fahrenheit on the highest peaks and then fall to 40 degrees at night, so be prepared for wide-ranging weather conditions. Thanks to the spectacular show of fall colors, September and October are popular months to visit the mountains. Ticks are a problem in the spring, so check yourself daily to remove the little nasties. No matter how sparkling and clear the water looks, filter or treat all water from natural sources before drinking. Giardia parasites reside in all water sources within the Wellsville Mountains and Mount Naomi Wildernesses, as well as all of the Wasatch-Cache National Forest. When hiking in the Wellsville Mountains, take plenty of water with you.

Here's an excerpt from my travel diary:

Logan Canyon, September 27

Midstream in a tumbling waterfall, five rounded boulders wear coats of deep green moss and professorial beards of grass. Magenta and barn-red maple leaves, along with gold-fall from box elders, willows, and aspen trees, are caught in the moss and grass. The stream is so cold that it delivers an instant headache from my feet up. A shifting wind moves upstream and careless showers of leaves fall into the current, some shooting through the tongues of green water like tiny kayakers, some getting caught in the hole where a reverse current holds them in thrall and eventually sends them to the bottom. Evening softens the light until everything glows: lemony box elders, froth from the waterfalls, candied maples. The allure is in the brevity of the moment, in the river's pact with change. Just as you look, it is gone.

Mount Naomi Wilderness

Author Lynna Howard sits by High Creek Lake.

MOUNT NAOMI WILDERNESS IS KNOWN as the best wildflower viewing area in Utah. When we were there, it lived up to its fame, with Indian paintbrush, lupine, columbine, balsamroot, and dozens more all washing the mountainsides with color.

Moose, black bear, elk, and mule deer are abundant in the Bear River Range of north-central Utah. The crest of the range is an alpine paradise of flowers, lakes, and forest—all above 9,000 feet for 13 miles of its length before tapering off toward the Idaho border to the north and toward Logan Canyon to the south. The crest of the range is the boundary line of the designated wilderness, with lots of recreational opportunities in public land east of the boundary, but an abrupt switch to private land at the base of the range on the west.

LOCATION: North-Central Utah
SIZE: 44,523 acres
ELEVATION RANGE: 4,800 to 9,979 feet
ECOREGION: Middle Rocky Mountain
MILES OF TRAIL: 60
ADMINISTRATION: Wasatch-Cache NF, Logan Ranger District
MAPS: Wasatch-Cache NF: Ogden and Logan Ranger Districts. USGS 1:100,000: Logan. USGS 1:24,000: Mt. Naomi, Mt. Elmer, Tony Grove, Temple Peak, Richmond, Smithfield.

Although there are trailheads on the west flank, it's nicer to cruise through all the forested areas to the east and south in order to approach wilderness trails.

The busiest of these eastern trailheads is Tony Grove. From the town of Logan, drive east on 400 North (US 89) to enter Logan Canyon. In the canyon, drive carefully. The narrow, winding highway is used by mountain bikers, rock climbers, and scenery gawkers. There are also numerous pullouts and short spur roads to picnic areas and hiking destinations. Drive 19.5 miles of canyon road, then turn left at the Tony Grove sign. Drive west 7 miles on a paved road to the trailhead (older maps show this road as improved gravel). The trailhead and campground are usually a hive of activity; many day hikers opt to bag Naomi Peak from this base, but backpackers will find opportunities for solitude by hiking over the crest to High Creek Lake or Cherry Peak.

> **BACKPACK:** MOUNT NAOMI PEAK AND HIGH CREEK LAKE
> One-Way Length: 10 miles
> Low and High Elevations: 8,029 and 9,979 feet
> Difficulty: Moderate

Park in the overnight parking lot for backcountry travelers at Tony Grove. A fee is required if you opt to camp at Tony Grove. No fee is required for backcountry hiking. All trails are well marked and easy to find. The trail to Naomi Peak and the continuation to High Creek Lake is steep in sections, and most hikers will require a few rest stops along the way. Elevation gain from the trailhead to the peak is 1,950 feet.

At a sign where the trail forks, keep left for Mount Naomi (the right fork leads to White Pine Lake, a popular destination for those traveling by both horse and foot). Keep left again where another trail leading to White Pine Lake intersects. Quartzite ridges, stairlike steps, and pillars are remnants of retreating glaciers. The rock formations add to the scenic value of the trail.

Great views open up one after the other all along the trail. When you stop to catch your breath, you can pretend that you're admiring the view. In the spring, trickles of water come down the trail and alongside it, but by late July or August, it is usually dry. Carry enough water to see you through the first 5 miles. Hummingbirds flit around the flowers and over rock formations eroded from limestone. There are enough spruce and fir trees to provide occasional shade, so the hike is pleasant even on a hot day.

At the crest of the ridge, the trail forks, with the left fork leading to Naomi Peak. The straight-ahead fork says only "Cherry Peak" but it is also the trail to High Creek Lake. At the fork, you may want to stash your backpack before hiking to Naomi Peak. A few spots along the way to the peak require human four-wheeling, with hands and feet engaged to get around and over boulders. None of the route to the peak is difficult, but some care is required on the boulders. The view from the peak is one of Utah's best, with the entire range of the Uinta Mountains laid out to the southeast, and Basin and Range country stretching to the Nevada border on the west. You can see the Bear River, after which this mountain range is named, as it snakes through Cache Valley.

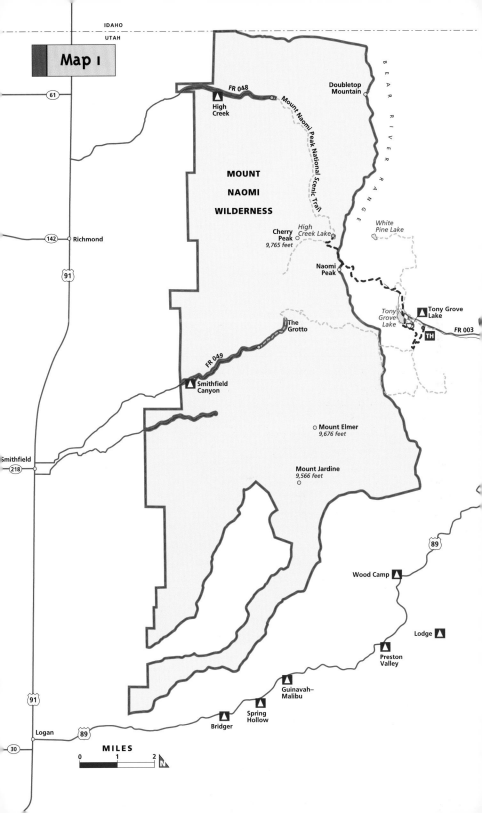

Return to the fork in the trail, cross the crest, and continue west to High Creek Lake. You'll descend from 9,800 feet on the ridge to 8,762 feet at the lake. The lake is completely hidden from view until you are right on top of it. A steep descent with several small switchbacks and one very long switchback leads hikers toward Smithfield Canyon before turning back toward High Creek Lake. The long switchback goes so far in the opposite direction that you might doubt you're on the right trail. Persevere. Water is plentiful in streams and waterfalls, especially in the last 2 miles of the hike; remember to treat all water before consuming.

High Creek Lake sits in a glacial cirque, with rocky cliffs around three sides. When we were there in August, pockets of old snow lay in the cliff shadows. It was springtime at 9,000 feet and the flowers were in their prime. Near High Creek Lake, we set up base camp and the next day we day-hiked to various points of interest.

Beautiful autumn color frames the right fork of the Logan River.

Wellsville Mountains Wilderness 2

A field of sunflowers colors the landscape.

THE WELLSVILLE MOUNTAINS are said to be the steepest range in the United States, with a very narrow base only 3–4 miles wide and an absolute elevation of 5,000 feet above the Cache Valley and Great Salt Lake Valley. The tallest peak in the range is Box Elder, at 9,372 feet, and the main ridge seldom dips below 8,000 feet in its 20-mile length. The Wellsville Mountains are on the border where the Middle Rocky Mountain Ecoregion ends and the Basin and Range begins. From the crest, hikers can see the distinctive basin-range configuration of western Utah.

Wellsville Mountains Wilderness sits in splendid isolation above several visible centers of civilization, but few

LOCATION: North-Central Utah

SIZE: 23,850 acres

ELEVATION RANGE: 4,680 to 9,372 feet

ECOREGION: Middle Rocky Mountain, Basin and Range

MILES OF TRAIL: 15

ADMINISTRATION: Wasatch-Cache NF, Logan Ranger District

MAPS: Wasatch-Cache NF: Ogden and Logan Ranger Districts. USGS 1:100,000: Logan, Tremonton. USGS 1:24,000: Honeyville, Wellsville, Brigham City, Mount Pisgah

Laura Lutz perches on the highest point in the Wellsville Mountain Wilderness to count migrating raptors for the annual raptor count.

hikers explore its rugged terrain. Even in a dry range like the Wellsvilles, shrubs and alpine groundcover manage a show of spring and fall color. For those willing to take the path less trodden, there are beauties and solitude to enjoy.

Overgrazing and burning caused massive erosion problems in the early 1900s. By the 1940s, people living below the mountains were fed up with being flooded out of their homes. They bought the mountain range and donated it to the Forest Service. A program of rehabilitation has been ongoing ever since. When you hike up to the ridge from Deep Canyon Trailhead, you can still see some of the gashes that spring flooding created. Most of the erosion problem is now solved and the gullies are overgrown with vegetation, but the mountains still do not support the number of trees you would expect. By late fall, what would be low undergrowth on a forested hillside has grown to a 6-foot-tall jungle that obscures the trail. Even the traffic of pack animals to support the raptor count makes little difference.

HawkWatch International, a nonprofit organization, sponsors an annual raptor count (see Appendix C). The group has been counting raptors along the Wellsville migration route from 1987 to the present. On the day we were there, the following bird sightings were recorded:

1 sharp-shinned hawk	1 merlin	5 American kestrels
2 Cooper's hawks	1 prairie falcon	3 golden eagles
2 turkey vultures	2 peregrine falcons	28 red-tailed hawks
4 northern harriers	2 ferruginous hawks	4 Swainson's hawks

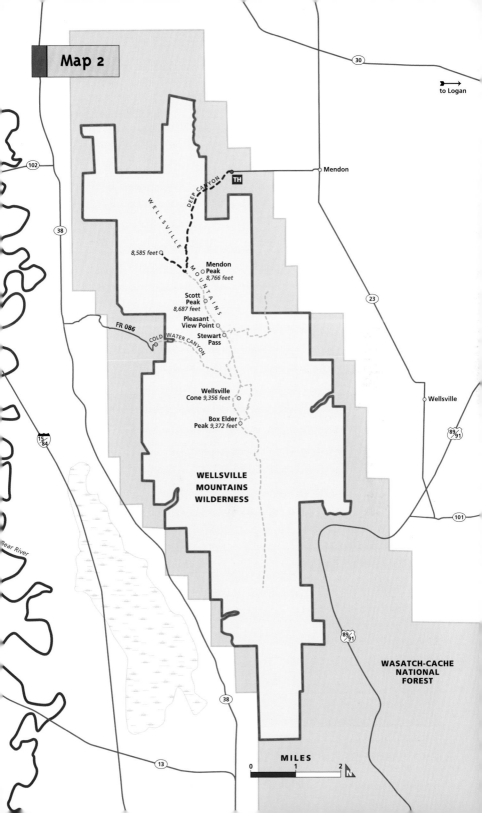

Late August and September are excellent times to visit. You can enjoy the stream of raptors cruising by just below the ridge, the fall colors are at their peak, and hunting season has not yet started (hunting begins October 9).

A lack of water and of campsites on the spine of the Wellsvilles discourages backpacking and encourages day hiking. You can devise loop hikes if you have a shuttle vehicle. Unimproved camping is available on the road to Coldwater Canyon (FR 086).

> **DAY HIKE:** DEEP CANYON TRAILHEAD TO RAPTOR WATCH AREA
> One-Way Length: 3.75 miles (8–12 miles with options)
> Low and High Elevations: 5,400 and 8,585 feet
> Difficulty: Moderate

From Deep Canyon Trailhead, this hike climbs 2,700 feet in only 3 miles. The trail is a solid footpath, but head-high plants bend over it, obscuring the way until you enter the alpine zone just below the crest. If you're sensitive to nettles and other plants, wear long sleeves and pants.

Three miles of steady uphill slogging brings you to a saddle on the ridgeline at 8,100 feet in elevation. At the saddle turn right (northwest) and hike north about 0.75 mile to the primary raptor watch location, an unnamed knob at 8,585 feet.

The Wellsville Mountains are said to be the steepest range in the United States, with a very narrow base and an absolute elevation of 5,000 feet above the surroundings.

Option: From the saddle you can also turn left (south) and hike along the ridgeline as far as time and energy allow. At Stewart Pass, Coldwater Lake Trail (038) comes up from the Cache Valley—a hike that meets a shuttle vehicle at Coldwater Trailhead makes for an 8-mile hike. To climb Box Elder Peak, continue south down the ridgeline 2 miles beyond Stewart Pass.

From the Cache Valley side of the Wellsville Mountains, the small town of Mendon is the closest supply point. To approach from the south on I-15, take exit 364 and drive east on US 91 through a gap in the Wasatch Range. US 91 turns sharply north once it rounds the southern end of the Wellsville Mountains. Turn left at an intersection with UT 23 and drive through the small town of Wellsville. Continue north to Mendon. In Mendon, turn left (west) on Third North at a "Raptor Count" sign with a binocular icon. Drive 2 miles to the trailhead and parking area.

To approach from the city of Logan, drive west on 600 South (Mendon Rd.). To approach from the north on I-15, take exit 394 and drive east on 20800 North (Short Divide Rd.) to an intersection with UT 142. Turn south on UT 142 to Newton. In Newton continue south on UT 23 to Mendon. In Mendon turn right (west) on Third North at the "Raptor Count" sign and continue 2 miles to the trailhead and parking area.

For the 8-mile hike option with a shuttle vehicle, access Coldwater Lake Trailhead from Mendon. Drive south on Main Street, crossing UT 23. Watch carefully for a small, faded brown-and-white "National Forest" sign and turn west on a gravel road. The road jogs west, then south into the foothills. The trailhead is about 3.5 miles from Mendon. The dirt sections of the road within the national forest might require a 4WD in bad weather. Higher-clearance 2WD vehicles can negotiate the road in good weather. The drive to the trailhead is a good fall color route.

Northeast Utah

The High Uintas Wilderness in northeastern Utah is far and away the largest of the designated wilderness areas in the state. The wilderness feels even larger to visitors because it is surrounded by a buffer zone of 199,000 acres of National Forest land.

A good deal of the Uinta Mountains is in the Wasatch-Cache National Forest. Conversely, much of the Wasatch Range is in the Uinta National Forest. Part of the Uinta Mountains falls within the boundaries of the Ashley National Forest. Does the Forest Service do this on purpose?

On-trail hiking abounds in the Uinta Mountains, with an extensive system of foot and horse paths. Most of the trails are destination-oriented and serve as access routes to many lakes. Famous as Utah's premier fishing destination, the Uintas offer the highest concentration of alpine lakes in the state. Utah's Division of Wildlife Resources manages 650 lakes in the Uintas—and those are just the lakes they bother with. There are more than 1,000 lakes and 400 miles of streams.

When it comes to exploration, the 56-mile-long Highline Trail is the crown jewel in the trail system. It's an understatement to say that the Highline Trail is arduous. Many people ride horses for the trip, with a string of pack animals coming along behind. If sharing the trail with horses ruins your day, choose some of the steeper trails that get less traffic, or check with the Forest Service for areas that are closed to horse use (these closures change periodically).

No matter which trails you decide to hike, you'll spend a lot of time in the trees. At lower elevations, the aspen groves are glorious, especially in the fall. At higher elevations, the forest floors are an incredible green in the summer months, nearly fluorescent with low shrubs. The sun filters through a thick conifer forest—a mixture of blue spruce, balsam fir, Engelmann spruce, Douglas fir, and lodgepole pine. In autumn, the understory flashes brilliant red under the blue-green and yellow-green conifers.

The Bear River flows through Christmas Meadows on the northwestern edge of the High Uintas Wilderness.

All this foliage and water makes an ideal habitat for mosquitoes, flies, and gnats. Deer wandered into our camp at dawn and moose grazed in the meadows. The only black bear we saw was crossing one of the access roads as if he owned the place, and I guess he did.

Access roads from the south cross sections of the Uintah and Ouray Indian Reservation. The wilderness and the mountain range are named after the "Uintats," the Ute Indians. Approaches to the wilderness from the north and west are across grasslands, where you see less of the desert environment that laps at the southwestern foothills. Here are the major approach routes:

> **South:** US 40 to UT 35, 87, 121; large town of Duchesne
>
> **East:** US 191 to several Forest Service roads; large town of Vernal
>
> **Northeast:** UT 44, 43, and FR 221; small town of Manila
>
> **North:** I-80 to WY 414, 410, and 150; city of Evanston, Wyoming
>
> **West:** UT 150; small town of Kamas, large town of Heber City

Note that heavy winter snowfalls close portions of UT 150, usually in late October. This route, also called the Mirror Lake Scenic Byway, truly is the most scenic drive through the Uinta Mountains. Dirt and gravel roads that lead from the major highways to access trailheads are listed in the text of the description for each suggested hike. The wilderness area is about four to five hours east of Salt Lake City (about 150 to 200 miles, depending on which section of the mountain range you plan to visit). Other areas of interest in northeastern Utah include the 104,709-acre Lakes Roadless Area west of the wilderness; Flaming Gorge National Recreation Area on the northeast; and the recommended wilderness in Dinosaur National Monument (see Chapter 42 for national monument information).

The best time to hike in the High Uintas Wilderness is July to early September. Some lower-elevation areas in the surrounding national forests can be enjoyed from late May into October. Hunters are numerous in the fall (late September to early November), so hikers should wear blaze orange (at least a vest or hat) for safety during those times. The highest elevations of the Uintas often hold remnants of snow well into July. The lowest elevation within the designated wilderness is 8,000 feet. When you hike above 10,000 feet, nights are always cold, and even on the hottest days of summer the temperature rarely rises above 80 degrees Fahrenheit. Review the Weather and Safety information in the Along the Trail section at the beginning of this book.

Land managers ask that all visitors register at trailheads, and that group sizes be limited to 14 people and 15 horses. Weed-free feed is required. Additional restrictions and fees may apply in some areas, such as the Mirror Lake Recreation Area.

An alpine meadow dotted with the blooms of Indian paintbrush and western bistort adds to the beauty of Helen Lake in the High Uintas Wilderness.

3 High Uintas Wilderness

Smiths Fork Canyon

LOCATION: Northeast Utah

SIZE: 456,704 acres

ELEVATION RANGE: 8,000 to 13,528 feet

ECOREGION: Middle Rocky Mountain

MILES OF TRAIL: 1,000-plus in wilderness and surrounding NF lands

ADMINISTRATION: Wasatch-Cache NF, Kamas, Evanston, and Mountain View Ranger Districts; Ashley NF, Duchesne, Roosevelt, and Vernal Ranger Districts

MAPS: Trails Illustrated: Maps #704 and #711. Forest Service: High Uintas Wilderness map. USGS 1:24,000: Christmas Meadows, Red Knob, Mt. Lovenia, Bridger Lake, Mount Powell, Gilbert Peak NE, Kings Peak, Hole-in-the-Rock, Fox Lake, Hoop Lake, Chepeta Lake, Mirror Lake, Hayden Peak, Explorer Peak, Oweep Creek, Garfield Basin, Mount Emmons, Bollie Lake, Rasmussen Lakes, Iron Mine Mountain, Granddaddy Lake, Tworoose Pass, Kidney Lake, Lake Fork Mountain, Burnt Mill Spring.

As you can see from the list of USGS topographical maps given in this chapter, there's a lifetime of hiking in the Uinta Mountains. The Forest Service map High Uintas Wilderness is adequate unless you plan to do off-trail hiking. If you need the detail of USGS 1:24,000 topos, get the free Index to Utah Topographical Map Coverage from the USGS in order to purchase only the maps you need for your trek. You might want to get topos for surrounding national forest lands that are outside of the designated wilderness. See Appendix D for map sources.

SHUTTLE BACKPACK HIKE: HIGHLINE TO EAST FORK BEAR RIVER
One-Way Length: About 24 miles, with about 3 miles cross-country
Low and High Elevations: 10,000 and about 11,600 feet
Difficulty: Strenuous

This hike perfectly melds traveling a well-established trail with just enough cross-country work to satisfy an adventurous spirit. This trek also has the added charms of enabling you to gawk at the scenery and hike on both sides of the spine of the Uintas. Allow three days for an expedition that includes time off for fishing.

The Highline Trailhead is on UT 150 (Mirror Lake Scenic Byway), 34 miles from Kamas, Utah, and 44 miles from Evanston, Wyo. Butterfly Lake Campground is near the trailhead. With a huge parking lot and amenities for equestrians, the Highline Trailhead looks like civilization run amok right on the boundary of the designated wilderness. However, once you get on the trail, most of the foot and horse traffic thins. So many destinations and varying routes split off from the Highline Trail that, apart from dodging road apples (horse manure), it's not bad.

The trail loses a few hundred feet in elevation as it leaves the highway to drop into the upper basin of the Duchesne River. The topography soon screens the noise of trucks and cars. Naturalist Basin (mile 6) is one of the most popular, and very much overused, destinations. With a few gradual ups and downs, the trail makes its way through the forest toward Rocky Sea Pass.

On this state-of-the-art trail, every intersection is signed, boggy places have causeways, and streams are bridged with logs. Wherever the trees let in a little sunlight, showy purple daisies, corn lilies, and Indian paintbrush bloom. When we were there, we got a taste of typical High Uintas summer weather as we crossed Rocky Sea Pass in a hailstorm. We donned jackets, hats, and gloves. Thousands of flowers in a natural rock garden on the south side of the pass bloomed fuchsia, red, yellow, and white. The dark clouds receded to the horizon and the westering sun highlighted both the Wagnerian pile of cumulus and the delicate flowers. This was exactly what we had come for. Total elevation gained from the trailhead to the top of Rocky Sea Pass is about 1,200 feet, over 7.5 miles.

In the first week of August, the remains of the previous winter's snowdrifts lay in the shadows on the north side of the pass. We paused on the 11,500-foot pass to take a 360-degree look at the humps of the Uinta Mountains fading into the distance.

We camped near a smattering of nameless ponds below Rocky Sea Pass, then hiked to Lightning Lake and Helen Lake the next morning (about 12.2 miles from the Highline Trailhead). Quite a few fishermen, and even more Boy Scouts, were trying their luck at Lightning Lake, but we found quiet campsites and beautiful views around Helen Lake. The alpine setting—with a few big trees at lakeside and Ostler Peak pushing a rocky shoulder into the sky—was the epitome of what the Uintas have to offer. Helen Lake is at 10,869 feet, at treeline.

The USGS topographical map Explorer Peak shows a trail going over the saddle northeast of Helen Lake (about 2 miles east of Ostler Peak); there used to be a trail in 1966, but there's no trail now. We followed visible tread to a watercourse and waterfall east of Helen Lake, where an old pack trail veers southeast. To stay on our course for the saddle, we followed a few rock cairns (no tread, no cut trail) for about another 0.5 mile east, then turned north to climb to the saddle via the least-steep route.

We thought we had good views from Rocky Sea Pass, but this beat them all. Views from the alpine meadows were tremendous, and once we reached the saddle, Priord and Amethyst Lakes shone below us to the north. A ptarmigan not used to human traffic ventured over as if for a conversation. Looking back the way we had come, we saw nothing but endless ranks of trees and mountains. Here was visual proof that the Uintas boast the largest continuous forest in the Intermountain West. Once you're on the saddle, at 11,600 feet, you can see a steep trail, eroded and covered with rockfall in places, that leads down to Priord Lake.

Brian Horton fishes for trout in Helen Lake in the High Uintas Wilderness. The Uintas are Utah's premier fishing destination. State Wildlife Resources manages 650 lakes—and that's just the lakes they bother to count!

At Priord Lake, we saw no signs of humans, but a lot of black bear, elk, and deer sign. The setting, and the hike down the Right Hand Fork of the Bear River, shows classic beauty. The "trail" periodically disappears until you are a bit below Norice Lake. Eventually, the trail becomes the usual wilderness foot/horse highway one expects in the Uintas.

It's 8.3 miles from Priord Lake to the East Fork Bear River Trailhead. We enjoyed the downhill trek, losing about 1,500 feet in elevation from the lake, plus another 750 from the saddle above it. The only fly in the ointment, or fly in the cowpie, came at the wilderness border, where a herd of cows had thoroughly trampled the trail and deposited the largest cowpies I'd ever seen—a tribute, I guess, to the quality of Uinta Mountain grass.

Our shuttle crew met us at East Fork Bear River. To reach this trailhead on the northeast corner of the wilderness, drive southeast on FR 058, which leaves UT 150 near the East Fork Campground. At the first intersection, turn south on FR 059. Continue on FR 059 past the Boy Scout camp to the trailhead, where the road ends. This is also the trailhead for Allsop Lake within the wilderness (8.5 miles), and Deadman Pass outside the wilderness boundary.

DAY HIKE: CHRISTMAS MEADOWS TO AMETHYST LAKE
One-Way Length: 6.5 miles
Low and High Elevations: 8,750 and 10,750 feet
Difficulty: Strenuous

Christmas Meadows Trailhead is accessed from UT 150 (Mirror Lake Scenic Byway), about 33 miles south of Evanston, Wyo. Drive south on FR 057 (the turnoff is about a mile north of the Stillwater Campground). The road ends at Christmas Meadows Trailhead and Campground. A stock ramp, toilets, and other amenities mark this as a busy trailhead.

Christmas Meadows is a beautiful spot, worth visiting even for those not hiking the trail. The trail is well marked and easy to find as it parallels the Stillwater Fork of the Bear River. At the intersection with the Ostler Fork Trail (Trail 149), bear left (east) as this trail follows the Ostler Fork, the outlet stream from Amethyst Basin. Ostler Lake is a good place to camp if you want to turn this into an overnight back-packing expedition, but do press on to view Amethyst Lake, which lives up to its colorful name and, at 42.5 acres, is impressive in size. Return by the same route.

Map 3

China Meadows

Trailhead

Henrys Fork

Hoop Lake

FR 221

Beaver Meadow Reservoir

FR 001

BIG PARK

Tamarack Lake

McCOY PARK

Spirit Lake

TH

Fish Lake

Jessen Lake

Spirit Lake

Gilbert Peak
13,442 feet

Island Lake

Wigwam Lake

Papoose Lake

Divide Lake

North Pole Pass

Chepeta Lake

Moccasin Lake

Highline Trail

Dime Lake

Brook Lake

Fox Lake

Taylor Lake

TH

Crescent Lake

Kings Peak
13,528 feet
(highest point
in Utah)

Cleveland Lake

Queant Lake

Yellowstone Creek

Lake Atwood

Allred Lake

Roberts Lake

Allen Lake

Carrot Lake

TH

FR 110

Pole Creek Lake

FR 117

Pole Lake

Pole Mountain Rd. / FR 117

Wandin

ASHLEY
NATIONAL
FOREST

Uinta Canyon

Swift Creek

Riverview

Reservoir

Yellowstone

Bridge

Central Utah

There are five designated wilderness areas in the central and southern Wasatch Range: Mount Olympus, Twin Peaks, Lone Peak, Mount Timpanogos, and Mount Nebo. The hiking season is generally from May to late September, with elevations ranging from 5,000 feet at the foot of Mount Olympus to 11,928 feet on the Mona Summit of Mount Nebo. Extreme avalanche danger in early summer prevents access to higher-elevation trails until late June or early July. The steep granite faces are popular with rock climbers, especially the southern side of Twin Peaks Wilderness along Little Cottonwood Canyon. It's so forbiddingly steep that there are no hiking trails into Twin Peaks from that side.

The Wasatch Range stretches about 160 miles from the southern border of Idaho to Nephi (south of Provo), ending in the last hurrah of Mount Nebo at the southern tip before fading into the Wasatch Plateau. Day-trippers from Provo and Salt Lake drive the winding, paved roads that make their way up and down the canyons between each wilderness area. Because of the wilderness areas' proximity to big cities and their water requirements, domestic animals are forbidden on most trails and camping is limited to three days in some areas. Campfires are also prohibited.

The names in the Wasatch Range have a mixed legacy. *Wasatch* is an American Indian word meaning "high mountain pass," and *Timpanogos* is derived from various spellings of the name that local Indians called their tribe. Spanish explorers recorded it as *Timpanogotzis* in 1776. In the Ute language it is sometimes translated as "rocky stream." Mormon pioneers named Mount Nebo after a mountain with the same name in Palestine. "Pfeifferhorn" in the Lone Peak Wilderness comes from the Swiss Alps and is a nod to the similar shapes found there. Mining and lumbering activities that flourished here from 1863 to 1910 left us with names like Mill A Gulch and Alexander Basin. The mines increased the need for cutting big timber, so the two went hand in hand to strip parts of the Wasatch Range of its trees. Worry over erosion that might destroy the watershed above Salt Lake City was the early impetus for land preservation.

Wildflowers brighten the slopes of the Mount Timpanogos Wilderness.

A bull moose grazes in the Lone Peak Wilderness.

There are both natural lakes within the wilderness areas and man-made reservoirs on their boundaries. Both are popular destinations for hikes. The more ambitious hikers make bagging the various impressive summits a goal. Winter use centers around the ski resorts, including Snowbird, Alta, Brighton, Solitude, and Sundance—all located just outside wilderness boundaries. Some climbing clubs practice ice climbing in the Wasatch Range, usually in February and March. Highways into most of the canyons are kept open year-round, but the Alpine Scenic Loop around the eastern edge of the Mount Timpanogos Wilderness normally closes from December to April. Heavy snowfall also forces the Nebo Loop to close for part of the winter season.

Mount Olympus Wilderness 4

The view from Desolation Trail

GREEK MYTHOLOGY IDENTIFIES Olympus as the home of immortals such as Zeus, Hera, Hephaestus, and Aphrodite: thunder, marriage, fire, and sex. A tall order for a wilderness area. There's another Mount Olympus in Greece, where the hike to the peak begins near a topless beach. As far as I know, the citizens of Salt Lake City do not condone topless females, but when we hiked the area, topless males were out in force.

Mount Olympus rises to 9,026 feet and Mount Raymond is 10,241 feet. Just outside the wilderness boundary, the highest nearby peak, Gobblers Knob (10,246 feet), is home to a helicopter-skiing enterprise.

LOCATION: Central Utah
SIZE: 15,300 acres
ELEVATION RANGE: 5,000 to 10,241 feet
ECOREGION: Middle Rocky Mountain
MILES OF TRAIL: About 28.5
ADMINISTRATION: Wasatch-Cache NF, Salt Lake Ranger District
MAPS: Trails Illustrated: Map #709. Wasatch-Cache NF: Salt Lake District. USGS 1:24,000: Sugar House, Mt. Aire.

Here are the various access routes:

I-215 runs along the eastern edge of Salt Lake City. Coming from the south on I-215, take exit 4, and drive east on 3900 South to Wasatch Blvd. (If you are driving south on I-215, you must take the 4500 South exit in order to intersect Wasatch Blvd.) Wasatch Blvd. parallels I-215. Drive north and watch for a small brown-and-white sign for Mill Creek Rd., where you will turn east. Mill Creek Rd. is the access point for all hiking trails on the northern edge of Mount Olympus Wilderness; it also provides access to numerous picnic sites in Mill Creek Canyon but no campgrounds. There are a few inns on private land. All of the trailheads and picnic areas are signed, but user-created social trails can cause some confusion. Pet owners, take note of the hike to Dog Lake, a popular trail that allows a rarity in the Wasatch Range: hiking with pets. Dogs are prohibited on all other trails.

To access the trailhead for Mount Olympus, drive south on Wasatch Blvd. beyond exit 4 for 2.3 miles and look for a paved parking lot and the "Mt. Olympus Trailhead" sign.

Big Cottonwood Canyon Rd. serves the southern edge of Mount Olympus Wilderness and the northern edge of Twin Peaks Wilderness. Continue driving south on Wasatch Blvd. to intersect Big Cottonwood Canyon Rd., 2.6 miles south of Mount Olympus Trailhead.

> **DAY HIKE:** MOUNT OLYMPUS SOUTH SUMMIT
> One-Way Length: 3.2 miles
> Low and High Elevations: 4,830 and 9,026 feet
> Difficulty: Strenuous

A very good trail leads to the south summit of Mount Olympus, but steep terrain still forces hikers to use their hands for the last 0.1 mile. Although this is a short hike (6.4 miles round trip), it earns its strenuous rating with 4,200 feet of elevation gain.

The trail crosses private property via an easement in the first 0.5 mile, then begins to climb through a desert environment. The hike can be extremely hot in the afternoon when the sun heats up the hillside. Take plenty of water.

Where the trail enters Tolcat Canyon, hikers get some relief from the sun. A seasonal stream runs in Tolcat in the spring. Recently constructed switchbacks lead hikers up through juniper-piñon woodlands, Gambel oak, and mountain mahogany. A good place to stop for a rest is at the first grove of Douglas fir in a saddle 0.2 mile below the peak. The trail turns north at the saddle and the rocky scramble for the peak begins. Enjoy the views of Salt Lake City and return the way you came.

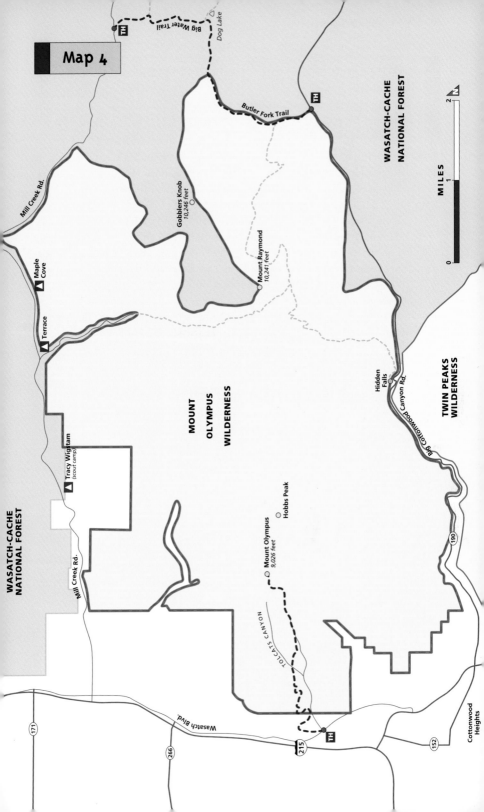

Map 4

WASATCH-CACHE
NATIONAL FOREST

Big Water Trail

Dog Lake

Butler Fork Trail

Gobblers Knob
10,246 feet

Mount Raymond
10,241 feet

Mill Creek Rd.

Maple
Cove

Terrace

Tracy Wigwam
(scout camp)

Mill Creek Rd.

WASATCH-CACHE
NATIONAL FOREST

MOUNT
OLYMPUS
WILDERNESS

Hidden
Falls

Canyon Rd.

Big Cottonwood

TWIN PEAKS
WILDERNESS

Hobbs Peak

Mount Olympus
9,026 feet

TOLCATS CANYON

190

Wasatch Blvd.

171

266

215

152

Cottonwood
Heights

MILES

0   1   2

SHUTTLE DAY HIKE: BIG WATER TRAILHEAD TO BUTLER FORK TRAILHEAD
One-Way Length: 5.2 miles
Low and High Elevations: 7,120 and 8,740 feet
Difficulty: Moderate

At the end of Mill Creek Rd., hike steeply uphill and south on Big Water Trail (this is the route that is open to dog owners, so expect canine company). There are so many trails and loops of trail in this area that you might need Trails Illustrated Map #709 to figure things out—or just follow all the dogs to Dog Lake.

From Dog Lake, hike west on Butler Fork Trail (Trail 012). The trail splits where Mill A Basin leads to Gobblers Knob (Desolation Trail on Trails Illustrated map). Keep left on Butler Fork. The view from Butler Fork served up the best fall color we saw in the Mount Olympus Wilderness. From Dog Lake at 8,740 feet, you'll descend to 7,120 feet at Butler Fork Trailhead on Big Cottonwood Canyon Rd. The last 2 miles of hiking along Butler Fork are spectacularly scenic.

Your shuttle vehicle should be parked at the signed Butler Fork Trailhead in Big Cottonwood Canyon, 19 miles from Salt Lake City. Big Cottonwood Canyon Rd. can be accessed by driving south on Wasatch Blvd. from Mill Creek Rd., or take the 6200 South exit off I-215 and drive east on 6200 South, which then becomes Wasatch Blvd.

Twin Peaks Wilderness 5

Mountain maples in an aspen grove

THE TWIN PEAKS FROM which this wilderness derives its name are glaciated crags of quartzite and granite shouldering 11,328 and 11,330 feet into the sky. O'Sullivan Peak and Dromedary Peak also top 11,000 feet. Lake Lillian and Lake Blanche are popular destinations for both hiking and trout fishing.

This small wilderness area is bounded on the north by Big Cottonwood Canyon (see Chapter 4, Mount Olympus Wilderness) and on the south by Little Cottonwood Canyon. The city of Salt Lake sits at the western base. The southern edge of Twin Peaks Wilderness is so steep

LOCATION: Central Utah
SIZE: 11,334 acres
ELEVATION RANGE: 5,039 to 11,330 feet
ECOREGION: Middle Rocky Mountain
MILES OF TRAIL: About 15
ADMINISTRATION: Wasatch-Cache NF, Salt Lake Ranger District
MAPS: Trails Illustrated: Map #709. USGS 1:24,000: Mount Aire, Draper, Dromedary Peak.

that no hiking trails lead up the cliffs. For trailheads on the northern edge, take the 6200 South exit from I-215 and drive east-southeast about 1.8 miles. 6200 South becomes Wasatch Blvd. At the intersection with Fort Union Blvd., at a stoplight, turn left on Fort Union and drive into Big Cottonwood Canyon. The road is paved.

For visitors who want to spend several days in the canyon, Redman and Jordan Pines Campgrounds are fee-based facilities. Unfortunately, the Forest Service starts closing campgrounds when cold nights threaten to freeze the water supply, which means that campgrounds close right at the peak times for viewing fall color. One option is to book a room at a nearby ski resort. Having no place to camp presents serious logistical problems when planning multiple or extended hikes.

Here is an excerpt from my travel diary: Sunlight slices through the aspen groves in late September. Every color of aspen is on display in Twin Peaks Wilderness—lemon juice, new gold, antique gold, orange juice, apple cider, strawberry. You can tell one aspen family from another by its colors. Cirrus clouds roll in slowly from the west, climbing the Wasatch Front to mount a blue-and-white show over the aspens. We humbly work our way uphill along the trails as locals from the city jog past us—no daypacks, no gear of any kind, sometimes no shirts—though we could smell snow on the air.

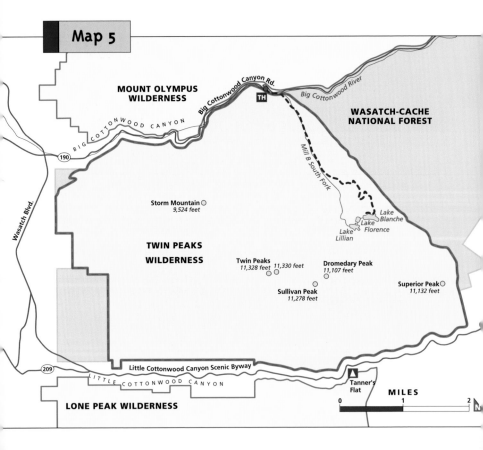

DAY HIKE: LAKE BLANCHE
One-Way Length: 2.8 miles
Low and High Elevations: 6,320 and 8,900 feet
Difficulty: Moderate

Drive 4.3 miles up-canyon on Big Cottonwood Canyon Rd. (see directions in the introduction to this chapter). Drive cautiously, as the turn to the trailhead is located on a curve with short sightlines. Watch for a brown-and-white sign for Mill A Basin.

From the parking area, hike along a paved walkway that parallels a stream. The miniature waterfalls are a delight. Where the paved trail ends, the footpath begins to climb immediately.

You'll soon come to the wilderness boundary sign as the trail climbs through a beautiful setting. Groves of aspen, a few conifers, and many mountain maples stand out against smooth and rough-cut cliffs. The trail to Lake Blanche is steep but well maintained. Campfires are not permitted.

Near the lake a signature rock bears the names of Salt Lake basin residents. Some signatures date as far back as 1924, but most cluster around 1933–1949. A stone dam, now breached, sits at the western end of the lake.

From the shores of Lake Blanche you'll find excellent views of Dromedary Peak and partial views of Twin Peaks. The rocks around the edge of the lake betray their origin as part of a former ocean bottom. The layers, folds, and reddish colors add to the photographic opportunities.

Elevation gain from the trailhead to the lake is 2,580 feet, and it shows in the vegetation. By late September, battered alpine flowers, sumac, and rose hips have been frostbitten by the cold nights. On your return, stop and look back for views of Sundial Peak.

6 Lone Peak Wilderness

Red Pine Lake

LOCATION: Central Utah
SIZE: 30,088 acres
ELEVATION RANGE:
5,140 to 11,326 feet
ECOREGION:
Middle Rocky Mountain
MILES OF TRAIL: About 31.5
ADMINISTRATION: Wasatch-Cache NF,
Salt Lake Ranger District;
Uinta NF, Pleasant Grove Ranger District
MAPS: Trails Illustrated: Maps #701
and #709.
USGS 1:24,000: Draper, Dromedary Peak,
Lehi, Timpanogos Cave, Brighton.

TWO ACCESS ROUTES FROM Salt Lake City–Provo flank Lone Peak Wilderness: on the north, Little Cottonwood Canyon, and on the south, American Fork Canyon. In addition to the dirt road to Silver Lake, narrow paved roads lead to wilderness trailheads.

Lone Peak Wilderness was designated in 1978. It was the first and in many ways is still the best of the trio of wilderness areas southeast of Salt Lake City. Sharply defined canyons cut through thick, scrubby brush at lower elevations. Rocky peaks such as Little Matterhorn (11,326 feet) and Lone Peak (11,253 feet) can be seen from all over the Great Salt Lake Basin.

Water is not a problem on most of the hikes in Lone Peak Wilderness. Trails follow streams, with lakes as destinations. Even drier routes such as the Box Elder Trail (Trail 044) frequently cross creekbeds. Snow is more likely to put a damper on hiking. Most of the highcountry does not melt out until late June, and even then you will come across snow in shaded and sheltered areas.

DAY HIKE: RED PINE LAKE
One-Way Length: 3.5 miles
Low and High Elevations: 7,580 and 9,620 feet
Difficulty: Moderate

See Chapter 5 for directions to Big Cottonwood Canyon. From the entrance to Big Cottonwood Canyon, continue south on Wasatch Blvd. to Little Cottonwood Canyon and turn left (east); the turn is also signed for Snowbird and Alta ski resorts. Drive 5 miles up Little Cottonwood Canyon to White Pine Trailhead, signed for White Pine/Red Pine/Maybird Gulch.

This trailhead is 1.2 miles past Tanner's Flat Campground, a fee-based facility that was full when we were there. A river of cars and trucks flowed up paved Little Cottonwood Canyon Rd. from 4 a.m. to midnight, the inevitable fallout from having two famous ski resorts at the end of the road.

Begin the hike on an old jeep road that the Forest Service now uses as a service road. It is closed to other vehicles. The trail climbs up the side of White Pine Canyon to a junction with Red Pine Lake Trail. Cross the footbridge over the White Pine Fork and follow the lesser-used trail west. Elevation gain from the parking lot to this junction at mile 1 is about 450 feet.

The eastern end of Red Pine Lake harbors a lush assortment of plants.

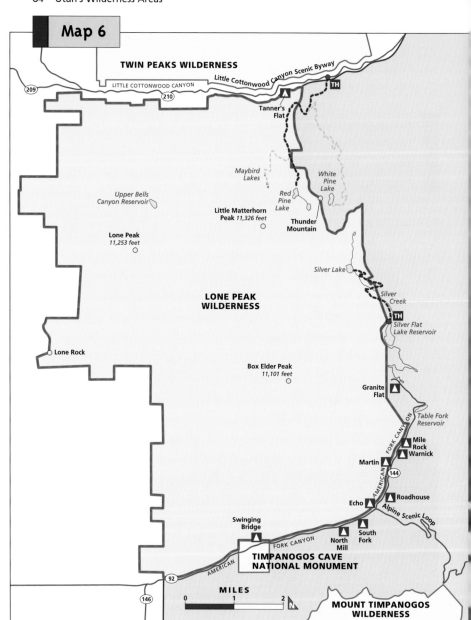

Map 6

TWIN PEAKS WILDERNESS

Little Cottonwood Canyon Scenic Byway

209

LITTLE COTTONWOOD CANYON

210

Tanner's Flat

TH

Maybird Lakes

White Pine Lake

Upper Bells Canyon Reservoir

Red Pine Lake

Little Matterhorn Peak 11,326 feet

Thunder Mountain

Lone Peak 11,253 feet

Silver Lake

Silver Creek

LONE PEAK WILDERNESS

TH

Silver Flat Lake Reservoir

Lone Rock

Box Elder Peak 11,101 feet

Granite Flat

Table Fork Reservoir

AMERICAN FORK CANYON

Mile Rock Warnick

Martin

144

Roadhouse

Echo

Alpine Scenic Loop

Swinging Bridge

FORK CANYON

North Mill

South Fork

TIMPANOGOS CAVE NATIONAL MONUMENT

AMERICAN

92

146

MILES

0   1   2

N

MOUNT TIMPANOGOS WILDERNESS

As you make your way up the trail to Red Pine Lake, you can see and hear the highway. Occasionally, the cityscape where Salt Lake City blends into smaller cities can be seen framed in the V-shaped cliffs of Twin Peaks Wilderness on one side and Lone Peak on the other. As far as city views go, it's a winner.

Once you enter Red Pine Canyon, you leave the sights and sounds of highway and city behind. At mile 2.5 you come to a signed junction with the trail to Maybird Lakes. For Red Pine Lake, keep left at this junction. (Maybird Lakes Trail crosses to the east side of Red Pine Creek.) This section of trail might not melt out until late July. A shaded and protected spot, it holds snow long into summer. Most of the time, it's possible to hike over the patches of snow.

Beyond the junction with Maybird Lakes Trail, the path to Red Pine Lake gets steeper as it continues to climb in the canyon. The trail flattens at the top of the canyon, about 0.25 mile from the lake. Like most alpine lakes in the Wasatch Range, Red Pine is framed by a beautiful setting of glacier-carved crags.

> **DAY HIKE: SILVER LAKE TRAIL**
> One-Way Length: 1.75 miles
> Low and High Elevations: 7,560 and 9,000 feet
> Difficulty: Easy

There's more than one Silver Lake in the Wasatch Range, so check the directions and map carefully. To get your bearings on the map, look for Granite Flat Campground on American Fork Canyon Rd., on the eastern edge of Lone Peak Wilderness. A maintained trail leads to Silver Lake, and hikers can continue cross-country to Silver Glance Lake.

UT 92 and UT 146 meet near the entrance to American Fork Canyon between the smaller towns of Alpine and American Fork, southeast of Salt Lake City. There are several exits off I-15 that will get you there, but exit 287 is probably the easiest. From exit 287, drive directly east on UT 92 to American Fork Canyon. Timpanogos Cave National Monument and trailheads related to Timpanogos Wilderness are also accessible from American Fork Canyon Rd. (also called Alpine Scenic Loop).

At mile 11.8 from the entrance to American Fork Canyon, the gate for Granite Flat Campground comes into view. Immediately before the gate, turn right onto a dirt road. This is Silver Lake Flat Rd., which is a 2WD (in good weather) road for about 3 miles. Park where the road crosses the creek (4WD vehicles can drive through the creek and continue up the road to access a few unimproved camping areas). Granite Flat Campground has groomed cross-country skiing trails for winter use.

Silver Lake Trailhead begins at the parking area near the creek crossing and parallels the west bank of the creek. A section of old mining tailings pushes the trail to one side. One switchback leads up and over a steep section to a dam at the foot of Silver Lake. Black and white limestone layers embrace the small lake, but the best view is to the south, as the lake's cirque lines up perfectly with Mount Timpanogos.

7 Mount Timpanogos Wilderness

Mount Timpanogos from the Lone Peak Wilderness

LOCATION: Central Utah

SIZE: 10,750 acres

ELEVATION RANGE:
6,850 to 11,753 feet

ECOREGION:
Middle Rocky Mountain

MILES OF TRAIL: 18.6

ADMINISTRATION: Uinta NF,
Pleasant Grove Ranger District

MAPS: Trails Illustrated: Maps
#701 and #709.
USGS 1:24,000: Timpanogos Cave,
Aspen Grove, Bridal Veil Falls,
Orem.

FROM TIMPOONEKE TRAILHEAD we set off
for a long day hike in the Mount Timpanogos
Wilderness. In June the flowers and aspen trees
at the middle elevations were in their prime, but
Mount Timpanogos' snowy head was still releasing avalanches. Far below were the aquamarine
swimming pools of the well-to-do. We were in
the wilderness, but right next door to a mountain community and Robert Redford's Sundance
ski resort.

There are two main trailheads, Aspen
Grove and Timpooneke, that provide access to
the highest summit of Mount Timpanogos. Aspen
Grove, the most frequently used, is at about the
midpoint of UT 92 (Alpine Scenic Loop), north of
Sundance Resort. Timpooneke is at the northern
end of the Alpine Scenic Loop.

With an elevation gain of 1,300 feet in the last 0.5 mile to the Timpanogos Summit, the hike definitely rates as "strenuous." It is, nevertheless, the most popular peak to bag in the whole range. The distance to the peak is 9.1 miles from Aspen Grove and 9.5 miles from Timpooneke. At a junction below the north summit ridge, the two trails join, making it convenient to plan a shuttle hike, with a 0.5-mile scramble to the peak in the middle of the hike.

Actually, there is more than one "peak" on Mount Timpanogos, and there are seven glacier-carved cirques. The peaks and cirques are the main destinations for hikers. Pleistocene glaciers retreated about 12,000 to 10,000 years ago, leaving only one permanent snowfield in the Wasatch Range, above Emerald Lake on Mount Timpanogos.

From I-15, take exit 275 at Orem and drive east on UT 52 to a junction with US 189. Drive northeast on US 189 through Provo Canyon for about 12 miles to the junction with the Alpine Scenic Loop, the narrowest paved road in the state. Stick to the speed limit of 20 miles per hour and sneak around the corners like a wary animal or you might end up in a head-on collision. The scenic loop is open from May to mid-October and is not suitable for trailers.

If you are approaching from the north, from I-15 take exit 287 and drive east on UT 92 (11000 North St.) into American Fork Canyon. Mount Timpanogos is about 45 miles south of Salt Lake City.

There are several no-fee camping spots along Cascade Scenic Drive (FR 114) and some commercial campgrounds on the main Alpine Scenic Loop. There are winter snowmobile trails on Cascade Scenic Drive.

DAY HIKE: ASPEN GROVE TO TIMPANOGOS SUMMIT
One-Way Length: 9.1 miles
Low and High Elevations: 6,850 and 11,750 feet
Difficulty: Strenuous

The trailhead is off the Alpine Scenic Loop, at the northwestern end of the small community of Aspen Grove. The trail looks like a road where it takes off from a large parking lot visible from the loop road. Near the first two waterfalls, the trail narrows and begins to climb toward Hidden Lakes Cirque. The hike to Timpanogos Summit is the most scenic route in the whole mountain range, according to most Wasatch aficionados. It has a perfect combination of flower-filled meadows, waterfalls, snowfields, and glaciated peaks.

Stay on the trail if you're hiking early in the season when there are still some snowfields to cross. Four hikers have died after falling through snow crusted over ravines. Rangers check the route and purposely destroy the dangerous snow bridges. Staying on the trail also diminishes the problem of erosion. The trail zigzags to keep the grade shallow enough to prevent erosion, so don't cut the switchbacks.

Finding drinking water is not a problem. Depending on the season, there are about a dozen waterfalls on the Aspen Grove Trail. Bring a water filter or other water

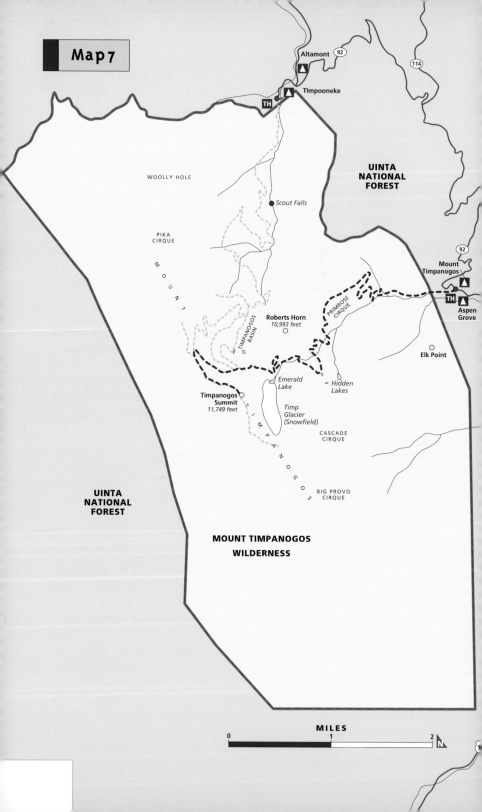

treatment method. Hikers should also bring a jacket, even on the warmest days. The temperature on the summit, combined with wind, can make it chilly.

Strong, experienced hikers can reach the summit in about four hours, but most people take five or six hours. Allow three to four hours for the descent, plus an hour for a break at the summit. An early start and long daylight hours are best for a day hike. Of course, hard-body types run the round trip in about two and a half hours just to make the rest of us look bad.

Although most hikers cover the 18.2 miles of this round trip in a single day, camping is allowed near Hidden Lakes Cirque and other areas. Rangers suggest you choose previously used campsites. Allow more time for the ascent if you are loaded down with a backpack. If you're short on time or physical fitness, the 2-mile round trip from the trailhead to First Falls is a nice stroll.

There are several options for descending once you have reached Timpanogos Summit. First, you could go back the way you came. Or you can descend 0.5 mile northwest along the ridge, then follow the trail as it swings back to Emerald Lake. Finally, you can follow the ridge northwest, but instead of going back toward the lake, take the trail to Timpanogos Basin and then down to the Timpooneke Trailhead. This last option requires a shuttle car. It's 6 miles along the Alpine Scenic Loop from Timpooneke Trailhead to Aspen Grove Trailhead. If you decide to ascend to the summit from the Timpooneke Trailhead instead of from Aspen Grove, you'll hike about 0.5 mile farther, but the climb is less steep.

Other Excursions

Cascade Springs: Near milepost 18 on UT 92 (Alpine Scenic Loop), turn northeast on FR 114 and drive about 7 miles to Cascade Springs; the road to the springs is paved. At Cascade Springs, groundwater surfaces through coarse glacial sediments. The rest of Utah can be bone-dry, but everything at Cascade will be wet. Aquatic songbirds walk along the bottom of the stream while eating insects. Cattails, yellow columbines, monkshood, monkey flowers, Scouler's willows, river birches, box elders, and canyon maples thrive next to the springs. Deposits from minerals that precipitate from the springs' waters form a series of basins for the pure, clear water. In the fall, the reds and yellows of the surrounding trees are reflected in the pools.

Timpanogos Cave National Monument: Timpanogos Cave is part of the same system of watery tunnels and weeping limestone that makes up Cascade Springs. Access is via UT 92 in American Fork Canyon. Three small but intricately decorated limestone caves are open for viewing whenever snow depths allow access to the 1.5-mile hiking trail. The trail is paved but rises 1,065 feet in elevation, so the climb is relatively strenuous. Pets and wheeled vehicles (including baby strollers) are not allowed. Cave temperatures are cool so bring a jacket, even during hot weather. Purchase tickets at the visitor center.

8 Mount Nebo Wilderness

Mount Nebo, the highest peak in the Wasatch Range

LOCATION: Central Utah

SIZE: 28,000 acres

ELEVATION RANGE:
5,300 to 11,928 feet

ECOREGION:
Middle Rocky Mountain

MILES OF TRAIL: About 24
(many more miles in adjacent
roadless area)

ADMINISTRATION: Uinta NF,
Spanish Fork Ranger District

MAPS: Trails Illustrated: Map #701.
Forest Service: Uinta NF.
USGS 1:24,000: Santaquin, Payson
Lakes, Birdseye, Mona, Nebo Basin,
Spencer Canyon, Nephi, Fountain
Green North.

THE NEBO SCENIC LOOP, the prime access
for trailheads in Mount Nebo Wilderness, is the
best introduction to this wilderness. Snow usually
closes the road in late October and it opens again
in June or July. Take exit 225 off I-15 in the small
town of Nephi (south of Provo and Utah Lake).
Drive 6 miles east on UT 132 to Nebo Loop Rd.
(FR 15). Another approach, from the north, is
accessible at exit 248 in Santaquin.

At 11,928 feet, Mount Nebo is the highest
peak in the Wasatch Range. Early Mormon pioneers
named the peak as a reference to Mount Nebo
in Palestine. The meaning roughly translates as
"Sentinel of the Gods." American Indians used
the peak to light signal fires, so it played the part

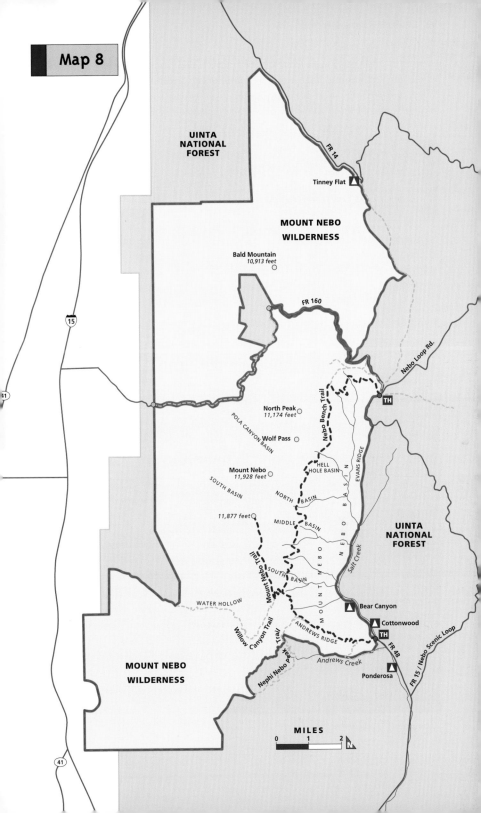

Map 8

UINTA
NATIONAL
FOREST

MOUNT NEBO
WILDERNESS

Bald Mountain
10,913 feet

FR 14

Tinney Flat

FR 160

Nebo Loop Rd.

Nebo Bench Trail

TH

North Peak
11,174 feet

POLA CANYON BASIN

Wolf Pass

EVANS RIDGE

HELL
HOLE BASIN

Mount Nebo
11,928 feet

SOUTH BASIN

NORTH   BASIN

N E B O   B A S I N

11,877 feet

MIDDLE   BASIN

UINTA
NATIONAL
FOREST

SOUTH BASIN

M O U N T   N E B O

Salt Creek

Mount Nebo Trail

WATER HOLLOW

Bear Canyon

Cottonwood

TH

Willow Canyon Trail

ANDREWS RIDGE

Andrews Creek

FR 48

FR 15 / Nebo Scenic Loop

MOUNT NEBO
WILDERNESS

Nephi Nebo Peak Trail

Ponderosa

15

11

41

MILES
0   1   2

of sentinel for them as well. They carried wood on their backs up Nebo's long flanks to the notched summit, and there they communicated with their gods or friends. When we hiked the Nebo Bench Trail, sun dogs flared in feathery cirrus clouds over Mount Nebo, a spot of colored fire from a completely different kind of signal flare.

SHUTTLE DAY HIKE: MONUMENT TRAILHEAD TO NEBO BENCH TRAILHEAD
One-Way Length: 13 miles (4.5 additional miles to Mount Nebo Summit)
Low and High Elevations: 9,216 and 9,826 feet (11,928 for summit)
Difficulty: Moderate to Strenuous

Most hikers out to bag the summit of Mount Nebo begin the trek at Nebo Bench Trailhead at 6,480 feet in elevation, near Ponderosa Campground. Beginning the hike at Monument Trailhead instead serves several purposes: You drive your car up to 9,216 feet to begin, eliminating 2,736 feet of climbing; the northern section of Nebo Bench Trail (Trail 117) offers solitude not found on the busy lower trail; and you can enjoy a truly spectacular hike in terms of scenery, even if you opt not to go for the summit.

View from the northern end of Nebo Bench Trail

From the intersection of UT 132 and Nebo Loop Rd., drive about 12 miles north to Monument Trailhead. You'll pass Devil's Kitchen Geologic Interest Site. Several trails depart from Monument Trailhead, including Trail 117 into Mount Nebo Wilderness and other trails into surrounding roadless areas.

The northern end of Nebo Bench Trail does not melt out completely until the end of July, so August and September are good months for the hike. Earlier in the season, avalanche danger and fragile snow bridges over the many streams prevent access. The trailhead and trail are signed. There are flat spots for unimproved campsites on the east side of Nebo Loop Rd.

A few hundred yards below and west of Nebo Loop Rd., the trail crosses the marked wilderness boundary. There are gentle ups and downs in elevation as the trail makes its way along Nebo Bench, but mostly you just hike north to south through an impressive array of aspen trees, firs, and waterfalls, with panoramic views to the south.

Boulder hopping over small watercourses is the greatest difficulty you'll encounter. At some turns in the trail there are good views of Nebo Ridge, and all three "summits" can be seen. At the intersection with Nebo Summit Trail (about mile 11) you can choose to go for the south summit (a gain of more than 2,000 feet) or continue on Nebo Bench Trail.

Leave a shuttle vehicle at Nebo Bench Trailhead. The lower trailhead is north of Ponderosa Campground, on a paved spur road at mile 3.3 on Nebo Loop Rd., signed for Ponderosa Campground.

Option: Backpackers can turn this into a two-day hike. There are campsites near the summit, but only hikers acclimated to the altitude will be comfortable there. Most hikers choosing to overnight on the trail camp in the area of Andrews Ridge, about 1.4 miles west of the junction where the Nebo Summit Trail meets the Nebo Bench Trail, and about 3 miles below the south summit of Mount Nebo. Few hikers choose to carry their backpacks all the way to the summit.

West-Central Utah

Somewhere west of I-15, down an unsigned dirt road, we set up camp. Juniper-piñon woodlands surrounded a long-abandoned log and stone building, but that was not the oldest sign of human habitation. The remains of a Fremont Indian site included dirt darkened by charcoal from past fires, a couple of arrowheads, and potsherds. As night fell, the Milky Way was as plain as a silk scarf arcing across the sky.

For that feeling of truly being away from it all, there's nothing like the wilderness study areas in west-central Utah. We did see one jeep at a trailhead in the Deep Creek Range, but we never saw the owner. We were more likely to see traffic in the sky. West-central Utah is part of the U.S. Air Force's Utah Test and Training Range. In 1984 a cruise missile crashed in the Fish Springs WSA. Low-level flights continue regardless of land status.

Statistics tell the story of human traffic on the ground. As part of its environmental impact statements, the Bureau of Land Management estimates the number of visitors per year to each WSA:

> **Cedar Mountains:** 384
> **Conger Mountain:** 163
> **Deep Creek Mountains:** 5,600
> **Fish Springs:** 50
> **Howell Peak:** Under 50
> **King Top:** 300
> **North Stansbury Mountains:** 300
> **Notch Peak:** 250
> **Rockwell:** 3,960
> **Swasey Mountain:** Under 50
> **Wah Wah Mountains:** 155

If you add up all the visitors for an entire year, the total is less than 1% of the visitors to just one of Utah's five national parks. Plus, the counts from the two wilderness study areas with higher visitor numbers are misleading because Rockwell siphons ORV users from the adjacent Little Sahara Recreation Area and Deep Creek numbers represent two hunting seasons but not much in the way of other recreation.

Tunnel Springs tuff in the Wah Wah Range

In west-central Utah, there's one designated wilderness, Deseret Peak. This wilderness looks like a slightly dried-out version of its Wasatch sisters to the east. It has the high peaks (11,031 feet), the steep-walled canyons, fir and aspen groves, and signed and visible trails. Water is not absent, just noticeably less. People are not absent, just very noticeably less.

Seeing how few visitors the west-central areas attract, especially the wilderness study areas, it looks like most people think the best season to visit is *never*. All of the west-central areas can be classified as cold deserts characterized by extreme weather and temperatures. Winter exploration is out of the question for all but the lowest elevations of areas accessible by plowed roads. Summer expeditions are not advisable because of intense heat that becomes more deadly when coupled with the lack of water. (The exceptions to this rule are the highest elevations of Deseret Peak and of the Deep Creek Range, which are comfortable summer hiking destinations.)

The Basin and Range gets most of its precipitation in the form of snow during the winter months, so spring is usually dry, but with enough residual moisture to support desert flowers and blooming shrubs—a good time to visit. Late spring (late May and June) is also dry and is an optimum time for those with only a 2WD vehicle to drive the approach roads. Early September is usually still too hot, but mid-September through early October can be beautiful. The desert is high in overall elevation, so cold temperatures, with accompanying rain or snow, can descend suddenly from late September on. Be prepared with a 4WD vehicle if you plan a late-season foray. In dry years, you can hike into November.

While water is available in Deseret Peak Wilderness and in the Deep Creek Range, it's completely missing in some of the other areas. The BLM describes the water sources in some of the west-central WSAs as "…no perennial streams, springs, or groundwater aquifers." Well, that's definitive. There's no water. Howell Peak, King Top, Notch Peak, Rockwell, Cedar Mountains, and Wah Wah Mountains WSAs are that dry. There are one or more intermittent springs in Fish Springs, Conger Mountain, Swasey Mountain, and North Stansbury Mountains WSAs. Deep Creek Mountains WSA is an exception, with six perennial streams on its eastern slopes. Even so, the Deep Creek Range felt powder dry when we were there, and the creeks, though welcome, were far from deep.

Plan for long day hikes from a base camp stocked with lots of water. Land administrators and the locals (mostly ranchers) extend their range with 4WD pickups, horses, four-wheelers (an all-terrain vehicle that's open and smaller than a jeep), and specially equipped motorcycles. Some visiting hikers and rock climbers add a mountain bike to their arsenal of approach vehicles. Note that the vehicles, even if rated as "off-road," are *not* used off the roads. Ditto for mountain bikes. These wilderness and wilderness study areas are surrounded by rough dirt roads, and many have trailhead access roads cherry-stemmed into their interiors. Hiking the dry terrain is difficult enough—you don't want to add road walking because there's not enough water to support it.

Towns with gasoline and other services can be as distant as 70 miles, so bring extra cans of gas, spare tires, and extra water and food supplies. Traveling with two or more vehicles is recommended.

Here are the main highways and roads that lead to access points (see individual area descriptions for more detail):

Deseret Peak: I-80, UT 36, UT 138, or UT 199; small town of Grantsville

North Stansbury Mountains: Same as Deseret, plus UT 196 (Rowley-Dugway Rd., exit 77 off I-80)

Cedar Mountains: I-80 (exit 70), Hastings Pass Rd.; no towns

Deep Creek Mountains: Pony Express Rd., US 93; village of Callao (no services), town of Wendover

Fish Springs: Pony Express Rd., UT 174; village of Callao (no services)

Rockwell: US 6; town of Nephi

Wah Wah Mountains: UT 21, UT 257; town of Milford

King Top: US 50/US 6, Blind Valley Rd.; town of Delta, village of Border Inn, Nev.

Conger Mountain: US 50/US 6, Notch Peak Loop Rd., Cowboy Pass Rd.; town of Delta

Notch Peak: US 50/US 6, Notch Peak Loop Rd., Miller Canyon Rd.; town of Delta

Howell Peak: US 50/US 6, Notch Peak Loop Rd., Marjum Canyon Rd.; town of Delta

Swasey Mountain: US 50/US 6, Notch Peak Loop Rd.; town of Delta

Deseret Peak Wilderness, North Stansbury Mountains WSA, and Cedar Mountains WSA

9

Deseret Peak

LOCATION: West-Central Utah

SIZE: Deseret Peak Wilderness: 25,212 acres
North Stansbury Mountains WSA: 10,480 acres
Cedar Mountains WSA: 50,500 acres

ELEVATION RANGE: 5,000 to 11,031 feet

ECOREGION: Basin and Range

MILES OF TRAIL: 24 in Deseret Peak Wilderness;
no official trails in WSAs

ADMINISTRATION:
Wasatch-Cache NF, Salt Lake Ranger District;
BLM, Pony Express Resource Area

MAPS: USGS 1:24,000: Deseret Peak East,
Deseret Peak West, North Willow Canyon, Salt
Mountain, Timpie, Flax, Aragonite, Hastings Pass,
Hastings Pass NE, Aragonite SE, Quincy Spring,
Hastings Pass SE.

MOST OF THE AREA west of Salt Lake City is blasted by summer heat, a blank canvas for winter winds, and largely waterless (except for the enormous, shallow saline pond of Great Salt Lake, three times saltier than the ocean). No streams reach the sea from this area. The Stansbury Mountains are a 30-mile-long oasis of rugged beauty in this salt desert, especially in the spring. The mountains are named after U.S. Army Capt. Howard Stansbury, who led a surveying party around Great Salt Lake in 1849. Deseret Peak, 11,031 feet high, dominates the skyline for hundreds of miles. From its crest, the Skull Valley Indian Reservation and the military's Dugway Proving Grounds are visible. The Stansbury Mountains, and Deseret Peak in particular, create their own weather systems and are sometimes shrouded with clouds while the Bonneville Salt Flats to the northwest (famous as a site for setting land speed records) bake under a clear sky. North Stansbury Mountains Wilderness Study Area is about 5 miles north of the designated Deseret Peak Wilderness; Cedar Mountains WSA is about 14 miles to the west.

The old Pony Express Route wisely skirted well to the south of this high country. The ill-fated Donner party of 1846 passed through Skull Valley, most perishing later in the snows of the Sierra Nevada. A weathered note had been left for the emigrants by Lansford Hastings, promoter of the shortcut to California known as Hastings Cutoff. He left the note by a spring in Skull Valley, "Two days—two nights—hard driving—cross desert—reach water." The wagon train, steering by sighting on Pilot Peak in what is now Nevada, drove hard day and night. As they lightened their loads, they left a trail of belongings that future adventurers were still finding a hundred years later. Hastings Pass in the Cedar Mountains WSA is named after the giver of questionable advice.

Deseret Peak Wilderness

Deseret Peak Wilderness is 47 miles southwest of Salt Lake City. I-80 provides convenient access. From I-80, drive south on UT 36 and then southwest and west on UT 138 to Grantsville. Or take exit 88, Burmester Rd., south from I-80 to Grantsville. In Grantsville, turn right (west) on Main St., then south on West 400, following Forest Service signs for trailheads in North Willow and South Willow Canyons.

There are six campgrounds along South Willow Creek. A trail from the last of the campgrounds leads about 3.5 miles to the top of Deseret Peak. There are two routes to the peak from this eastern side of the wilderness.

In North Willow Canyon, the O.P. Campground is the end of the road for 2WD vehicles. High-clearance 4WD jeep-type vehicles can continue a bit farther. O.P. Campground is the access for the northern terminus of Stansbury Crest Trail and for Willow Lakes Trail.

From the western side of the wilderness, the main access trails are the Indian Hickman and Antelope Canyon Trails, both accessible from Rowley-Dugway Rd., exit 77 from I-80. These two trails also access Deseret Peak.

The best hiking weather is in the late spring and early summer. Autumn can present opportunities to enjoy the first snowfall and autumn colors. Backpackers can explore the entire area without permits or reservations. Off-trail hiking is the best way to be certain of finding solitude. High-topped hiking boots are a must for off-trail hiking. Snowmobiles are allowed on some trails during the winter months.

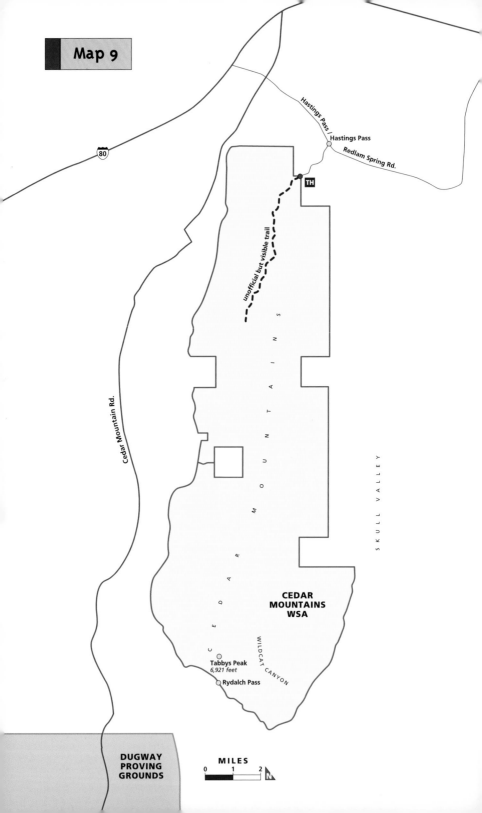

Map 9

80

Hastings Pass

Hastings Pass

Redlam Spring Rd.

TH

unofficial but visible trail

C E D A R   M O U N T A I N S

Cedar Mountain Rd.

S K U L L   V A L L E Y

CEDAR
MOUNTAINS
WSA

WILDCAT CANYON

Tabbys Peak
6,921 feet

Rydalch Pass

DUGWAY
PROVING
GROUNDS

MILES

0   1   2

N

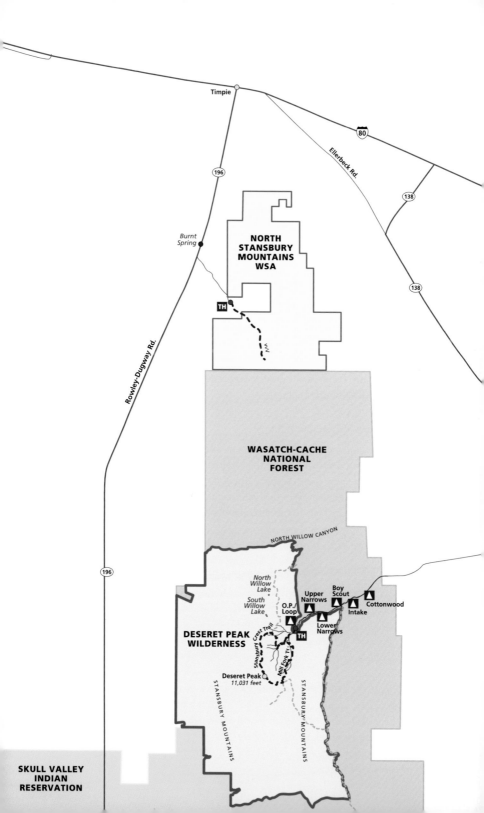

LOOP HIKE: MILL FORK TRAIL/DESERET PEAK/STANSBURY CREST TRAIL
One-Way Length: 8.4 miles
Low and High Elevations: 7,418 and 11,031 feet
Difficulty: Strenuous

See the directions in the Deseret Peak Wilderness introduction for the road to South Willow Canyon. The Mill Fork Trailhead at the last campground gives access to Deseret Peak via two routes. To make a loop, hike up Mill Fork Trail to the Stansbury Crest Trail, which takes you to Deseret Peak, then return via the northern portion of Stansbury Crest Trail (descending northward from Deseret Peak). At the intersection of Stansbury Crest Trail and Pockets Fork Trail, bear right (southeast) to intercept the Mill Fork Trail and return to Mill Fork Trailhead. All of the trails and intersections are signed.

In 3.5 miles, this route climbs 3,600 feet, making its way through stands of aspen trees, grassy meadows, and a few conifers. If you hike in early spring or early summer, you'll find running water in all the streams. Views from the crest of the Stansbury Mountains are spectacular, including 10,305-foot Victory Mountain, the Great Salt Lake and its surroundings, Pilot Peak in Nevada, and the Wasatch Range east of Salt Lake City. On the way down, you'll cross one perennial stream in a meadow where the trail forks to provide access to Willow Lakes. Keep right at this fork to return to Mill Fork Trailhead.

North Stansbury Mountains WSA

This wilderness study area is 40 miles west of Salt Lake City and is a continuation of the steep ridges and deep canyons of the Deseret Peak Wilderness, though its highest elevation is considerably lower, topping out at 8,800 feet near its southern boundary. A lack of water also distinguishes this WSA from its southern neighbor: There's only one intermittent spring high in the cliffs above Muskrat Canyon, so visitors are advised to bring their own water.

The entire WSA is only 6 miles long and about 3 miles wide, so day hiking in this extremely rugged terrain will take you just about everywhere you can go. There are about 2 miles of 4WD vehicular way in Muskrat Canyon (west side of the WSA) that can also be used as a hiking route. Deer hunting, upland game hunting, and a small amount of day hiking in the WSA center around Muskrat on the west and Miners Canyon on the east.

Take exit 77 (Rowley-Dugway Rd.) south from I-80. Bring a very detailed map with you, preferably the USGS topographical map Timpie, because some access roads are not signed. Drive about 6 miles south to where the paved road bends gently westward, note the bend, and continue another 0.5 mile, then turn left on an unsigned gravel road. Drive southeast on this road, passing a power substation. The road is passable for 2WD vehicles in good weather, though it deteriorates to dirt past the substation. Keep right where the road forks. Park about 2.5 miles from where you turned off the pavement. 4WD vehicles with a short wheel base and higher clearance can proceed a little farther.

Hike up the two-track toward the mouth of Muskrat Canyon, negotiating an intervening stock fence. The trail is pleasant once you enter the Douglas fir forest, a gain of about 800 feet in elevation from the parking area. The canyon is not very impressive or narrow until it turns east at about 6,800 feet in elevation. Onaqui Peak shows between bare ridges of limestone rock where the canyon narrows. The basin will be the end of the trek for most day hikers. It's a green world that is pleasant by virtue of its contrast with the surrounding terrain.

More intrepid hikers (carrying lots of extra water) can negotiate an off-trail route up the north wall of upper Muskrat Basin. The ridge above is 8,800 feet in elevation. Onaqui Peak is south of the high ridge, and extremely fit hikers can bag the peak in a long and rugged day hike (10 miles round trip).

Cedar Mountains WSA

The Cedar Mountains WSA stretches from Hastings Pass in the north to Rydalch Canyon in the south. Cedar Mountains is about 52 to 65 miles west of Salt Lake City, depending on the route you choose. Take exit 70 off I-80 at Delle to access the eastern side of the WSA or exit 56 to visit the west side of Cedar Mountains. You'll need detailed maps to negotiate backroads, and a 4WD vehicle is recommended. See the last six maps in the map list at the beginning of this chapter.

A spring storm lifts in Deseret Peak Wilderness, leaving a dusting of snow and watering a field of arrowleaf balsamroot.

This is a dry mountain range, so bring your own water. (Quincy Spring is a perennial water source, but it is outside of the WSA and is associated with private land.) Sheer limestone cliffs provide opportunities for technical rock climbing. There are no official trails, but there are several day-hiking opportunities that begin where 11 rough access roads end. In Wildcat Canyon, about 3 miles of unofficial vehicular way penetrate the WSA and can be used as a hiking route. Roads cross the mountain range at Hastings Pass and at Rydalch Canyon; from these two locations, you can work your way up and down both sides of the WSA, trying every dirt road until you find something you like for exploration.

Wild horse trails cross the spine of the mountains in the southern portion of the range. The BLM estimates that about 200 wild horses populate Cedar Mountains WSA on a seasonal basis, with only about 20 of them staying in the WSA through the summer. Raptors, including golden eagles and Swainson's hawks, are common.

No cedar trees grow in the Cedar Mountains. "Cedar" is local slang for the junipers that are scattered over the mountains from where the alkaline soils of the lower elevations end to the crest of the range.

DAY HIKE: RIDGEWALK SOUTH OF HASTINGS PASS
One-Way Length: 3–5 miles
Low and High Elevations: 5,780 and about 6,600 feet
Difficulty: Easy

From exit 70 off I-80, turn west on a gravel frontage road and drive 2 miles to Hastings Pass/Redlam Spring Rd. Turn left (south) on this improved dirt/gravel road. At an unsigned junction 7 miles down the road, turn right (northwest) up a rough road to Hastings Pass. You can park and walk south from the pass into the WSA, or drive south a short distance if you have a 4WD vehicle.

An unofficial but visible trail takes off from the 4WD two-track near an intersection with the old Hastings Cutoff wagon train route. Follow the trail as it climbs to the south to gain a ridgeline that offers good views of the distinctive Basin and Range topography. The trail peters out, but hikers can continue along the ridgeline for many miles, limited only by the amount of water they can carry. Lower elevations and very little snowfall make this a good early spring day hike or horseback ride.

Deep Creek Mountains, Fish Springs, and Rockwell WSAs

10

Mining ruins in the Deep Creek Mountains

DEEP CREEK MOUNTAINS and Fish Springs Wilderness Study Areas are about 90 miles from Nephi, on I-15, and about 50 miles from Wendover, on I-80. The Rockwell WSA is less isolated, only about 28 miles from Nephi and adjacent to the Little Sahara Recreation Area.

For all three wilderness study areas, exit from I-15 at Nephi (exit 225), or at Santaquin (exit 248), or at Lehi/American Fork (exit 282). Drive west on UT 132 from Nephi, or on US 6 from Santaquin, or on UT 73 from Lehi. The routes from

LOCATION: West-Central Utah

SIZE: Deep Creek Mountains WSA: 68,910 acres
Fish Springs WSA: 52,500 acres
Rockwell WSA: 9,150 acres

ELEVATION RANGE: 5,000 to 12,087 feet

ECOREGION: Basin and Range

MILES OF TRAIL: No official trails, but some jeep tracks

ADMINISTRATION: BLM, Pony Express and House Range Resource Areas

MAPS: USGS 1:24,000: Ibapah, Clifton, Goshute, Goshute Canyon, Ibapah Peak, Indian Farm Creek, Partoun, Trout Creek, Fish Springs SW, Sand Pass NW, Cherry Creek, Lynndyl NW.

Santaquin or Lehi are more convenient for intercepting the Pony Express Rd. to Deep Creek and Fish Springs. UT 132 from Nephi is the shortest route to Rockwell WSA. A combination of US 6 and UT 36 west of I-15 can be used to intercept all possible routes, getting you where you want to go no matter what exit you take.

If you're driving from the west, exit I-80 at Wendover on the Nevada-Utah border and drive south on US Alt. 93 about 27 miles to approach the Deep Creek Range and the Pony Express Rd. The old Pony Express route goes up Dead Cedar Wash and then dives south toward the settlement of Ibapah, near the northern border of the Goshute Indian Reservation. Before you get to Ibapah, turn east on Deep Creek Mountains Rd. (still following the Pony Express route) and cross a low spot in the northern end of the mountain range. This will take you to the east side, where all of the trailheads are located. From the point where you leave US Alt. 93, it is about 52 miles of dirt road to the village of Callao. Woe to all who venture forth unprepared, as there are no services in Callao.

If the Pony Express riders could find their way with no signs and no roads, then you've got a good chance of getting it right. We drove the Pony Express Rd. in early August and it was 2WD all the way, though rough in spots. Most of the route is improved gravel, with only a few areas where infrequent rains turn it into 4WD-only mush. The Pony Express stations along the way make for interesting stops. Fresh mounts, jerky, miniature bibles, and ammunition for the riders' Navy Colt revolvers were stocked at each station. The Pony Express only ran from 1860 to 1861 before the telegraph put it out of business. The riders made big history in a small stretch of time, once riding 2,000 miles in 10 days to carry messages designed to keep California in the Union at the outbreak of the Civil War.

When we were there, we encountered one battered and dusty pickup truck (local rancher) in the entire 70 miles of Pony Express Rd. from Fairfield to Callao. The drive was spectacularly scenic—there was nothing to obstruct the sweeping vistas.

Rockwell WSA is a different world altogether. Little Sahara Recreation Area is ORV/ATV heaven. Parts of the recreation area are set aside for horse and foot travel only, but most of it is a playground for off-road vehicles. Rockwell WSA shares the recreation area's defining characteristic of free-moving open sand dunes. Free-moving sand dunes are a rare commodity, so their presence earns the Rockwell WSA a "Class A Scenery" rating from the BLM.

There are no water sources in Rockwell WSA. There's one spring and one well in Fish Springs WSA. Deep Creek Mountains boasts six perennial springs, glacial cirques, alpine meadows, and a smattering of ecosystems that better match the Rocky Mountain region than the Basin and Range. The Deep Creeks are the highest block-faulted range in western Utah.

Deep Creek Mountains WSA

The most wilderness-like hiking routes are southwest of the village of Callao. From the junction of the Pony Express Rd. and Deep Creek Mountains Rd., drive south about 3 miles and turn west on an improved dirt road signed "Toms Creek, Middle and Goshute Canyon." This is the access to Scotts Basin (about 7 miles, 4WD recommended), which is technically not within the boundaries of the WSA, but the water sources and alpine meadow surrounded by rocky peaks make it a popular destination. The Nature Conservancy acquired more than 3,000 acres in Scotts Basin and might transfer the land to the BLM for inclusion in a wilderness proposal. When we were there, we enjoyed the scenery, but didn't camp in the basin because it was full of cows. Down on the main road, there's a campground south of the turn for Toms Creek.

Eroded jeep trails lead up many of the canyons north of the Callao intersection. For the most part, the tracks are more suitable for hiking than for jeeping. The reason for their existence becomes clear when you pass debris from now-defunct gold and silver mining operations. Views out over the salt flats are stunning.

DAY HIKE: GRANITE CREEK CANYON
One-Way Length: 5–6 miles
Low and High Elevations: About 6,000 feet and about 10,400 feet
Difficulty: Strenuous

The rock formations in Granite Creek Canyon were the most striking we saw in the Deep Creek Range. The sheer cliffs have attracted a few rock climbers and will no doubt see more technical climbing as word gets out.

Drive about 13 miles south of Callao on Deep Creek Mountains Rd., then turn west toward the high peaks on your right. A gravel road parallels an aqueduct

The Deep Creek Mountains are the highest block-faulted range in western Utah, and the third-highest range in the entire Basin and Range province. From the summits, a hundred miles or more of basins and ranges can be seen.

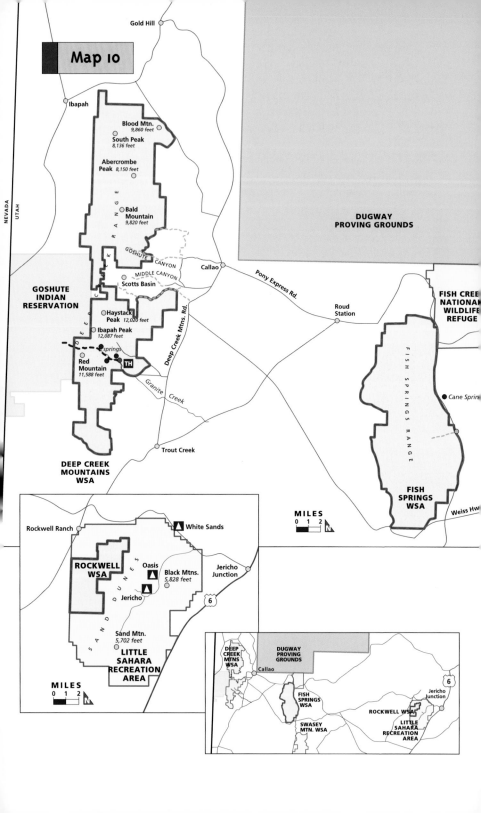

Map 10

Gold Hill

Ibapah

Blood Mtn.
9,860 feet

South Peak
8,136 feet

Abercrombie
Peak 8,150 feet

DEEP CREEK RANGE

Bald
Mountain
9,820 feet

GOSHUTE CANYON

MIDDLE CANYON

Callao

Pony Express Rd.

DUGWAY
PROVING GROUNDS

Scotts Basin

GOSHUTE
INDIAN
RESERVATION

DEEP CREEK RANGE

Haystack
Peak 12,020 feet

Ibapah Peak
12,087 feet

Deep Creek Mtns. Rd.

Roud
Station

FISH CREE
NATIONA
WILDLIFE
REFUGE

Red
Mountain
11,588 feet

springs

TH

Granite   Creek

Trout Creek

FISH SPRINGS RANGE

Cane Spring

DEEP CREEK
MOUNTAINS
WSA

FISH
SPRINGS
WSA

MILES
0 1 2   N

Weiss Hw

Rockwell Ranch

White Sands

ROCKWELL
WSA

Oasis

SAND DUNES

Black Mtns.
5,828 feet

Jericho

Jericho
Junction

6

Sand Mtn.
5,702 feet

LITTLE
SAHARA
RECREATION
AREA

MILES
0 1 2   N

DEEP
CREEK
MTNS
WSA

DUGWAY
PROVING
GROUNDS

Callao

FISH
SPRINGS
WSA

SWASEY
MTN. WSA

Jericho
Junction

6

ROCKWELL WSA

LITTLE
SAHARA
RECREATION
AREA

NEVADA

UTAH

plainly shown on the Indian Farm Creek topographical map. The road forks, with one branch leading to Granite Creek Canyon and the north fork leading to a ranch at the foot of Cottonwood Canyon. The Granite Creek Rd. is 2WD to the mouth of the canyon, then swiftly disintegrates into a rough 4WD track. There are several unimproved campsites within the canyon and on the alluvial fans near the mouth of the canyon.

The two-track becomes so rough that even jeeps park and everyone hikes the remainder of the pleasant, streamside climb to the head of Granite Creek and beyond. An old pack trail goes over the spine of the mountains and down into the Goshute Indian Reservation, but it's hard to find after the trail tops out in a saddle northwest of Red Mountain. Hikers should not enter reservation lands without permission from the Goshute Tribe. Depending on how far you drive up the jeep road, you'll begin hiking at 6,000 or 7,000 feet in elevation, and climb to about 10,400 feet in 5 to 6 miles. It's a strenuous and long day hike if you go all the way to the top and then return the way you came.

Bristlecone pines, ponderosa pines, and Douglas-fir are some of the more impressive conifers at the higher elevations.

Eroded sandstone on the eastern slopes of the Deep Creek Mountains

Fish Springs WSA

Fish Springs Wilderness Study Area is southwest of Fish Springs National Wildlife Refuge. The refuge—an enormous wet spot that's on the migratory route for thousands of birds—is worth a side trip.

The Pony Express Rd. rounds the northern end of the WSA, and the Weiss Highway (84 miles from the town of Delta) rounds the southern end. Between these two good roads, jeep tracks run north-south along both sides of the Fish Springs Range. In several places, spur tracks lead a short way into the WSA. A jeep trail about 2 miles south of Cane Springs on the east side of the range is a good bet for a jumping-off spot to explore. Hike west on the jeep track as far as the terrain allows.

No official trails exist in this extremely rugged, very dry, quite rocky area. The only gentler terrain is on the benches of the outskirts, where some cattle and sheep graze. The herders haul water in for the stock.

Rockwell WSA

This area of sand dunes is bordered on the east and north by the Tintic and Sheeprock Mountains. Desert Mountain to the west, the Black Mountains to the east, and Sand Mountain to the southeast make up the rest of the topographical fence around the dunes. Large juniper trees, both living and dead, rise from the sand dunes to create a visually arresting scene.

Cattle are sometimes trailed through the WSA en route to other grazing allotments, and there's a small amount of grazing on leased land in the northern end of the study area. The WSA is named for a ranch outside the northwestern border. Orin Porter Rockwell was one of Brigham Young's bodyguards, a stalwart of the Church of Jesus Christ of Latter-Day Saints.

The Little Sahara sand dunes that are within the WSA are off-limits to motorized recreation, but are still affected by the adjacent high-use area. Although this is a wilderness study area, the BLM chose not to include it in the 1991 proposal to Congress because of the limited opportunities for solitude and the difficulty of managing it for wilderness values. The Utah Wilderness Coalition disagrees and has recommended 11,000 acres for wilderness designation.

There are no water sources in the WSA, so hiking is limited by the amount of water you can carry. There are no official hiking trails. Access roads to Little Sahara Sand Dunes are from the intersection of US 6 and UT 132. Follow the BLM signs. There are three BLM campgrounds on the eastern edge of the adjacent Little Sahara Recreation Area.

Wah Wah Mountains, King Top, Conger Mountain, Notch Peak, Howell Peak, and Swasey Mountain WSAs

A playa, or dry lake bed, near the Wah Wah Mountains

BEFORE MY BROTHER AND I BEGAN our hiking tour of these wilderness study areas, we got gas in Milford. The road sign said, "No services for the next 70 miles." Dry lakebeds, reminders of ancient Lake Bonneville, dot the desert east of King Top, Notch Peak, and the Wah Wah Mountains. Sevier Dry Lake is the largest of these playas. In 1872 it had a surface area of

LOCATION: West-Central Utah

SIZE: Wah Wah Mountains WSA: 42,140 acres
King Top WSA: 84,770 acres
Conger Mountain WSA: 20,400 acres
Notch Peak WSA: 51,130 acres
Howell Peak WSA: 24,800 acres
Swasey Mountain WSA: 49,500 acres

ELEVATION RANGE: 4,590 to 9,669 feet

ECOREGION: Basin and Range

MILES OF TRAIL: No official trails, but jeep tracks
and wild horse trails may be used for hiking

ADMINISTRATION: BLM, House Range Resource Area

MAPS: USGS 1:100,000: Wah Wah Mountains North,
Wah Wah Mountains South, Tule Valley.
USGS 1:24,000: Crystal Peak, Pine Valley Hardpan North, Grassy Cove,
Fifteenmile Point, Pine Valley Hardpan South, Wah Wah Summit,
Wah Wah Cove; Thompson Knoll, Bullgrass Knoll, Pyramid Knoll,
King Top, The Barn, Warm Point; Cowboy Pass, Knoll Hill, Conger Mountain;
Notch Peak, Miller Cove, Hell'n Moriah Canyon, Skull Rock Pass;
Sand Pass SE, Swasey Peak NW, Swasey Peak, Whirlwind Valley NW,
Swasey Peak SW, Marjum Pass, Whirlwind Valley SW.

188 square miles. When the Sevier River was diverted for irrigation, the shallow lake dried up in less than 10 years. After a rain, or in a wet year, the lakebed may still hold sheets of water. When we passed the dry lakebeds, dust devils stirred a fine grit into the air, and a dead cow was lying on its bloated side with stiff legs sticking out to make a perch for a black crow.

Water is scarce, people are scarce, road signs are scarce. Official hiking trails are nonexistent. To prepare for an expedition to the Wah Wah Mountains, House Range, and Confusion Range, use the BLM 1:100,000-scale maps for overviews, and the 1:24,000 maps if you plan to do a lot of hiking off the jeep trails.

We visited in March, but that's really pushing it. Snowstorms are still common in March and April. Late April and May, or late September and October, are good months to visit. There's very little shade or water in these areas, so you want to avoid the hottest months. Many access roads close in the winter.

All six wilderness study areas in this chapter are located west of I-15, near the Nevada border, in the Great Basin Desert. Highways and dirt roads separate them from each other. Two highways cross the area, US 50/US 6 to the north and UT 21 in the middle. Other than those two highways, there's no pavement for approximately 150 miles.

Wah Wah Mountains WSA

Near Crystal Peak we came upon a BLM sign that said "Crystal Peak." You have to arrive at your destination before you can see how to get there on the mostly unsigned roads. Drive west on UT 21 from I-15 at the small town and historic site of Beaver. Continue west on UT 21 to Minersville, then northwest on UT 21 to Milford. West of Milford, UT 21 crosses the Basin and Range area of the San Francisco Mountains and the Wah Wah Valley. The BLM has proposed only the northern section of the range as wilderness, but citizen groups would like to include the Wah Wahs south of UT 21 as well.

To get to the northern end of the WSA, turn north at Milford on UT 257. Drive to Black Rock (a one-house, one-corral intersection of roads) and turn left (west) on Black Rock Rd., which crosses south of the Sevier Lake playa. From the Black Rock intersection, it's about 30 miles to Crystal Peak. You can see the glittering peak long before you arrive. The roads are rough but suitable for 2WD vehicles in good weather. In bad weather there are plenty of opportunities to get stuck in the mud. Bring extra gas, water, and food.

Several 4WD tracks lead south from Black Rock Rd., offering opportunities to explore the eastern side. Explore the jeep track into Grassy Cove, then drive south down the Wah Wah Valley to explore Lawson Cove and Long Valley. (The road south through the Wah Wah Valley connects to UT 21. Going north along the Tule Valley Rd. gives you access to the east side of King Top WSA and connects to US 50/US 6.) You are now only 20 miles from the Utah-Nevada border, in a section of the Wah Wah Mountains that is about 20 miles long and 5 miles wide.

There are unimproved campsites in a stunted piñon-juniper woodland at the base of Crystal Peak. This is one of the best places in Utah for stargazing. The air is usually dry and exceptionally clear. There's no light pollution. The pale, whitish volcanic tuff of the peak changes color with the progression of the day—from a blanched yellow like clotted cream, to ash gray, to white in moonlight. Crystal Peak has texture like nobody's business. All of it is intricately pocketed, carved, and eroded.

Crystal Peak is a leftover from Tertiary volcanoes that preceded block-faulting in the area. This 42-acre chunk is the thickest, most prominent example of Tunnel Spring tuff in western Utah. The Tunnel Spring Mountains, a short range northwest of the Wah Wah Mountains, have given their name to volcanic ash that has hardened into rock over a period of 30 million years.

To scramble up Crystal Peak, approach along tree-studded ridges from either the northwest or the southeast. Both are long approaches, but both get you at least two-thirds of the way up the peak before you ever have to start using your hands to climb. The longer approaches would be the way to go if you want to traverse the entire north-south ridgeline, looking at the view and not suffering too much rock bite. At the top of the peak (7,106 feet) there are keyhole arches worn in the rock. The view eastward extends to the Tushar and San Pitch Mountains; westward views include Nevada's Great Basin National Park.

No official hiking trails exist here, but the open nature of the country is conducive to cross-country travel. A 190-acre stand of bristlecone pine trees that are exceptionally large grows along the center ridgeline of the Wah Wah Mountains. Seek and ye shall find.

There are no water sources other than lingering snowbanks in early spring.

King Top WSA

King Top WSA is very narrow at its southern tip and broad in the north. See the road descriptions for the Wah Wah Mountains in the previous section for directions to the southern end of King Top. It's directly north of Crystal Peak and south of Notch Peak. On the north side of King Top WSA, US 50/US 6 crosses the Confusion Range through Kings Canyon. This is the best access route for a day hike. Between mile markers 26 and 27, park at the unsigned mouth of Cat Canyon. A brown carsonite post marks the WSA boundary about three car lengths from the highway. US 50/US 6 stays open year-round and provides paved access to this little-used wilderness.

For the Cat Canyon hike, follow the dry streambed and the canyon floor. You can hike about 4 miles in the canyon, or leave the canyon to explore Horse Heaven and Little Horse Heaven (marked on USGS map Bullgrass Knoll). The eroded limestone walls narrow and then widen again as you hike up-canyon. The shapes of weathered stone and niches where spring flowers find just enough soil and water to survive echo the sandstone canyons of south-central and southeastern Utah. There are no perennial streams or springs in the WSA, but annual snowfall is enough to support grassy areas in Cat Canyon that are a magnet for wild horses and cougars. You'll see signs of both animals if you hike the canyon and the surrounding plateaus. Elevation gain from the mouth of Cat Canyon to as high as you can go in a single day hike is about 2,000 feet.

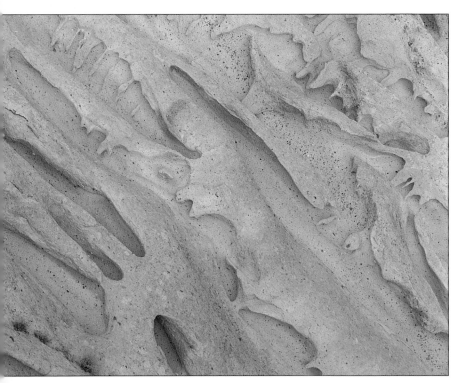

Textured sandstone on Crystal Peak in the Wah Wah Mountains

The BLM rates fossil collecting here as excellent. Fossil Mountain on the east side of the southern tip is the only good spot for fossil collecting. Access is from Tule Valley Rd. on a spur road that leads to Warm Point and Fossil Mountain.

Conger Mountain WSA

Whereas King Top WSA is the southern end of the Confusion Range, Conger Mountain is the range's northern end. Hundred-mile-long Snake Valley begins west of Conger Mountain and stretches all the way to the salt desert near Callao (see Chapter 10). The Border Inn on the Utah-Nevada border is a miniscule gas-food-lodging establishment about 20 miles west on US 50/US 6. The nearest large town is Delta, Utah, 50 miles to the east. This remote locale purportedly supports a community of religious groups that practice plural marriage.

The BLM posted Conger Mountain as a wilderness study area, but did not include it in the 1991 proposal to Congress because "about 30% of the area lacks outstanding opportunities for solitude due to sparse and low vegetation and relatively flat terrain." The Utah Wilderness Coalition has proposed 19,760 acres for wilderness designation. There are no official trails, but jeep, livestock, and wild horse trails can be used for day hiking. A spring in the northeastern tip, in Willow Spring Canyon, is the only water source within the WSA. Conger Spring is just outside the southern border of the WSA.

On the eastern flank, access is from numerous jeep roads in the northern end of Tule Valley. At the southern end, use jeep roads that enter Little Valley north of US 50/US 6. To the north, access is via the road over Cowboy Pass, which is a westward extension off the Notch Peak Loop Rd.

Notch Peak WSA

Notch Peak WSA is a semicircle of highcountry that encompasses most of the southern half of the House Range. US 50/US 6 runs along its southern edge and the highway corridor is the WSA boundary. A road running through Marjum Canyon is its northern boundary, and Notch Peak Loop Rd. runs up both the west and the east sides. Notch Peak Loop Rd. also includes the Howell Peak WSA in its embrace.

You can see the landmark of Notch Peak all the way from Delta, some 45 miles to the east. As you drive the highway toward Notch Peak, you can easily identify the distinctive notched outline. Some sources claim this is the largest limestone monolith in Utah, with an absolute elevation of 5,000 feet above Tule Valley (9,665 feet above sea level). The steep western face, of interest to geologists, displays a layer cake of sedimentary rock.

There are no official, maintained trails, but many miles of jeep roads and ORV tracks give access to the WSA and can be used as hiking routes. In addition, there are three informal hiking approaches to Notch Peak: Amasa Valley, Hell'n Moriah Canyon, and Sawtooth Canyon. There are no springs or streams within the WSA, so take your own water, as well as the appropriate topo maps if you plan to hike cross-country.

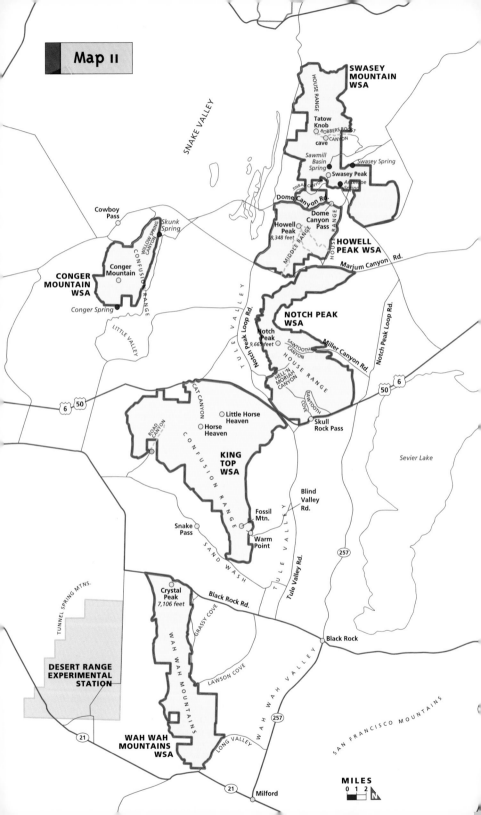

Map 11

SWASEY MOUNTAIN WSA

HOUSE RANGE

Tatow Knob
ROBBERS ROOST
CANYON
cave

Sawmill Basin Spring
Swasey Spring

SINBAD CANYON
Swasey Peak
Antelope Spring

SNAKE VALLEY

Dome Canyon Rd.

Dome Canyon Pass

Cowboy Pass
Skunk Spring

WILLOW SPRING CANYON
Howell Peak
8,348 feet
MIDDLE RANGE
HOUSE RANGE

HOWELL PEAK WSA

CONFUSION RANGE

CONGER MOUNTAIN WSA

Conger Mountain

Marjum Canyon Rd.

Conger Spring

LITTLE VALLEY

NOTCH PEAK WSA

Notch Peak Loop Rd.
Notch Peak Loop Rd.

TULE VALLEY

Notch Peak
9,665 feet

SAWTOOTH CANYON

Miller Canyon Rd.

HOUSE RANGE

HELL 'N MORIAH CANYON

SAWTOOTH COVE

50   6

6   50

CAT CANYON

Little Horse Heaven

Horse Heaven

Skull Rock Pass

Sevier Lake

ROAD CANYON

CONFUSION RANGE

KING TOP WSA

Blind Valley Rd.

Fossil Mtn.

Snake Pass

Warm Point

SAND WASH

TULE VALLEY

Tule Valley Rd.

257

Crystal Peak
7,106 feet

Black Rock Rd.

GRASSY COVE

Black Rock

TUNNEL SPRING MTNS.

WAH WAH MOUNTAINS

DESERT RANGE EXPERIMENTAL STATION

LAWSON COVE

WAH WAH VALLEY

257

SAN FRANCISCO MOUNTAINS

21

WAH WAH MOUNTAINS WSA

LONG VALLEY

21

Milford

MILES
0 1 2
N

Howell Peak WSA

Howell Peak WSA is directly north of Notch Peak WSA, separated from its southern neighbor only by the Marjum Canyon Rd. Notch Peak Loop Rd. runs around the northern tip of Howell Peak WSA and separates it from its northern neighbor, Swasey Mountain WSA.

See the road descriptions in the previous section. There are no perennial streams, springs, or groundwater aquifers in the WSA. Dry, dry, dry. Jeep roads, ORV tracks, and cross-country trekking are the options for hikers. One attraction for visitors is the huge entrance to Council Cave, near Antelope Peak, which is visible for more than 50 miles.

From Notch Peak Loop Rd. on the east, drive west on Marjum Canyon Rd., then turn north on a 2WD dirt road that skirts the Howell Peak cliffs on the east side. This road reconnects to Notch Peak Loop Rd. again near Dome Canyon Pass, and it is the eastern boundary of the WSA. It provides access to three unofficial vehicular ways that lead west into the WSA, with the most southern way being the best access to climb Howell Peak. From where the way ends to the top of Howell Peak is about 1 mile, all cross-country. Elevation gain from the end of the way to the peak (8,348 feet) is about 1,000 feet. If you hike the way instead of using an ORV for access, the elevation gain will be about 1,500 feet over about 3 miles. The route is steep, rocky, and strenuous in places.

Swasey Mountain WSA

The next stop going north in the House Range is Swasey Mountain, directly across Notch Peak Loop Rd. from Howell Peak WSA. As Notch Peak Loop Rd. goes through Dome Canyon, it is also called Dome Canyon Rd. As we've worked our way north in this chapter, we've been slowly getting closer to the town of Delta, and are now about 35 miles from that full-service community. US 50/US 6 is still the major paved access route.

There are five springs in Swasey Mountain WSA, but no perennial streams. Additional springs lie just outside the WSA boundary. A herd of about 80 wild horses grazes grassy areas and makes use of the springs. A jeep track leads up Sawmill Basin to Sawmill Basin Spring, and this makes a good day-hiking route. If you park where the road begins to get rough, you'll walk about 4 miles to the spring. If you drive a 4WD or ORV up the track, you should be able to get close to the spring. Sawmill Basin Spring is north of Swasey Peak, at 9,669 feet the highest peak in the WSA.

There are about 150 acres of trilobite fossil beds within Swasey Mountain WSA. The BLM estimates that 200 to 300 visitors per year come to this nationally significant fossil bed. The spur road to the Antelope Spring trilobite bed is off the Dome Canyon Rd., about 1 mile east of Dome Canyon Pass.

On the southwest end of the WSA, Sinbad Overlook Rd. (near Sinbad Canyon) climbs to good views of this WSA and of distant mountains such as the Deep Creek and Confusion Ranges. Sinbad Spring, at the head of Sinbad Canyon, is the easiest start for bagging Swasey Peak.

Near Tatow Knob there are several wild horse trails. A wild horse trail along a ridge north of Robbers Roost Canyon can be followed for several miles.

Southwest Utah

Utah's "Dixie" is hot and dry for most of the year. The city of St. George in the heart of Dixie is the supply source and the starting point for three designated wildernesses and seven wilderness study areas. The areas described in this southwestern section are islands of wilderness that are grouped here because they share access roads and supply points.

October is fine for hiking in all of the designated and proposed wildernesses, with the exception of the highest elevations in Pine Valley Mountain and Ashdown Gorge Wilderness Areas. With elevations over 10,000 feet, they often receive their first dusting of snow in late September or early October. Springtime in the desert is also a good time for hiking expeditions because water is easier to find and the desert flowers are in bloom. But if you're looking for solitude, late fall is the best bet. One of the enduring charms of southwestern Utah is its mild, short winter. When cold weather makes it hard to hike anywhere else, Dixie beckons. Hiking season extends into March and November.

Water is scarce in the Beaver Dam Mountains, Red Mountain, Cottonwood Canyon, Moquith Mountain, Canaan Mountain, and Parunuweap areas. Plan to take your own water. With adequate preplanning, you won't find water to be a problem in Ashdown Gorge and Pine Valley Mountain Wilderness Areas. In areas where water is scarce, we have emphasized day hiking; where water sources are plentiful, we suggest multiday expeditions or longer day hikes.

Joshua Trees form a brilliant green foreground for the red sandstone of eroded rock formations in the Beaver Dam Mountains Wilderness.

12 Ashdown Gorge Wilderness

A bristlecone pine on the Markagunt Plateau

LOCATION: Southwest Utah

SIZE: 7,043 acres

ELEVATION RANGE:
8,000 to 10,400 feet

ECOREGION: Middle Rocky Mountain

MILES OF TRAIL: About 12

ADMINISTRATION: Dixie NF, Cedar City Ranger District

MAPS: Trails Illustrated: Map #702. Dixie NF: Dixie NF Travel Map. USGS 1:24,000: Flanigan Arch, Brian Head.

ASHDOWN GORGE IS A SMALL but unique wilderness area next door to Cedar Breaks National Monument. Locals use the area during the hunting season, but otherwise it receives few visitors. You're more likely to share the trail with yellow-bellied marmots, Clark's nutcrackers, mule deer, and Steller's jays. Bristlecone pines, Douglas fir, and lodgepole pines are the dominant flora. High elevations mean long winters with deep snow. The lower portion of Ashdown Gorge melts out at least a month before the highest elevations. Access roads to the highcountry usually open in May and close in October.

A private inholding takes a big chunk out of the lower elevation of the gorge, but it's possible to hike across the private land to link Rattlesnake Trail to Potato Hollow Trail. In addition to those two trails, a short trail leads through the Twisted Forest of bristlecone pines.

Deer Creek, portions of Ashdown Creek, and Shooting Star Creek are in the Ashdown Gorge Wilderness. These and other tributaries from Cedar Breaks join to become Coal Creek, which has carved an impressive canyon through layers of many-colored stone. The gorge cannot be accessed from the Cedar Breaks rim, and that's where Ashdown Gorge Wilderness comes in. It wraps around the west side of the monument and is rich in hiking opportunities.

The nearest town is Cedar City on I-15. From Cedar City, go east on UT 14 to access both Ashdown Gorge Wilderness and Cedar Breaks National Monument. See the following trail descriptions for more road access information.

DAY HIKE: POTATO HOLLOW TRAIL TO ASHDOWN CREEK
One-Way Length: 4 miles
Low and High Elevations: 7,320 and 8,950 feet
Difficulty: Moderate

The trailhead for Potato Hollow Trail is at the end of Crystal Spring Rd. (FR 301 on the Dixie NF Travel Map and 30361 on the Trails Illustrated map). The turn is about 0.5 mile east of Cedar Canyon Campground on UT 14. Early spring is not a good time for this hike, as the water coming down Ashdown Creek will be cold, deep, and dangerously swift. The gorge is also susceptible to flash flooding, so watch the weather when you plan your hike.

Potato Hollow Trail is officially only 2.5 miles long. It supposedly ends where it meets private property. However, property owners allow hikers to cross and continue about another 1.5 to 2 miles. Be respectful and do not camp on private property.

Potato Hollow Trailhead is at 8,950 feet, and hikers will lose 1,630 feet of elevation in a relatively short distance. The steep hike down makes its way through aspen and fir trees, crosses a jeep road, and eventually intercepts Ashdown Creek. During low-water times, you can explore the gorge, which has been intricately carved and eroded. Bring footwear that will stand up to a lot of wading. A hike upstream will take you to the border of Cedar Breaks National Monument. Most visitors never see the impressive pinnacles of the Breaks from below. Return the way you came, up Potato Hollow Trail.

> **DAY HIKE: TWISTED FOREST TRAIL**
> One-Way Length: 1–2 miles
> Low and High Elevations: 9,200 and 9,500 feet
> Difficulty: Easy

In the northern tip of Ashdown Gorge Wilderness, an exceptionally beautiful forest of weathered bristlecone pines clings to a rocky slope. The elevation at the trailhead (about 9,200 feet) makes this a good summer hike. It's possible to hike well beyond the marked trail by continuing to explore along the ridges. Navajo Point to the northeast is 10,575 feet in elevation.

Unimproved camping is available in meadows on adjacent Forest Service lands, just off the approach road. There's a mix of private property and public lands along FR 265 (30265 on the Trails Illustrated map). Camp only on public lands. To get to the access road, drive down the steep part of Parowan Canyon (below the ski resort) on UT 143 to Dry Lakes. Turn southwest onto Dry Lakes Rd. (FR 265) and drive about 7 miles to the Twisted Forest Trailhead. We've given directions here as if visitors were coming from Cedar Breaks or from Rattlesnake Trailhead, but it's also possible to drive into the mountains on UT 143 out of the town of Parowan, situated on I-15.

> **SHUTTLE DAY HIKE: RATTLESNAKE TRAILHEAD TO POTATO HOLLOW TRAILHEAD**
> One-Way Length: 9.5 miles
> Low and High Elevations: 7,320 and 10,500 feet
> Difficulty: Easy

Rattlesnake Trailhead is just outside the northern boundary of Cedar Breaks National Monument, on UT 143. Look for the sign and a parking area. This hike starts in alpine terrain and descends more than 3,000 feet to Ashdown Gorge. It crosses about 2 miles of private property in the lower gorge (see the previous description of Potato Hollow), then climbs about 1,600 feet to the Potato Hollow Trailhead. You'll need a shuttle vehicle where Potato Hollow meets Crystal Spring Rd.

The Rattlesnake Trail quickly descends from an alpine meadow into fir forests. As you continue to descend along Rattlesnake Creek, the forest changes to aspen trees and even some sagebrush-grass flats. This 5-mile section of trail doesn't get a lot of traffic, and the terrain screens hikers from the many visitors to Cedar Breaks.

After the second major ford of Rattlesnake Creek (not counting any minor hops over meltwater in early spring), watch carefully for the turn to the east, above and along the slopes north of Ashdown Gorge. You will parallel the gorge, hiking upstream above steep cliffs for about 0.25 mile before the trail descends to cross Ashdown Creek. The creek cannot be safely crossed at high-water times in early spring. Wade the creek and proceed across private land. (At low-water times, hikers can explore a short distance down the gorge.) Intercept first a jeep road and then the Potato Hollow Trail. Hike 2.5 miles up the Potato Hollow Trail to the trailhead.

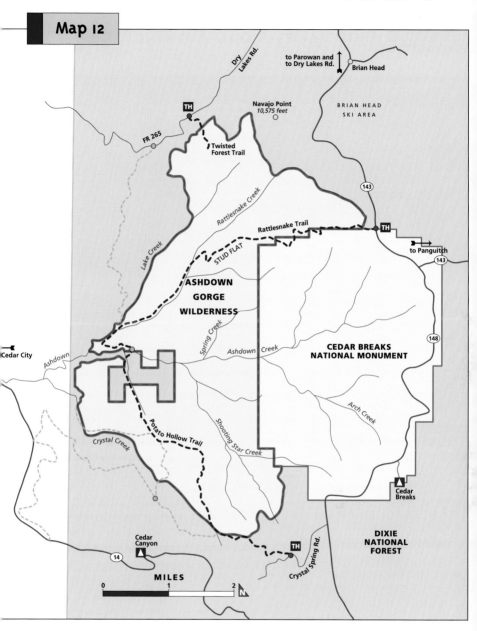

Map 12

Dry Lakes Rd.

to Parowan and
to Dry Lakes Rd.

Brian Head

TH

Navajo Point
10,575 feet

BRIAN HEAD
SKI AREA

FR 265

Twisted
Forest Trail

143

Rattlesnake Creek

Rattlesnake Trail

TH

Lake Creek

STUD FLAT

to Panguitch

143

ASHDOWN
GORGE
WILDERNESS

Spring Creek

148

Cedar City

Ashdown

Ashdown Creek

CEDAR BREAKS
NATIONAL MONUMENT

Potato Hollow Trail

Arch Creek

Crystal Creek

Shooting Star Creek

Cedar
Breaks

DIXIE
NATIONAL
FOREST

Cedar
Canyon

14

TH

Crystal Spring Rd.

MILES

0   1   2   N

13 Pine Valley Mountain Wilderness

Lynna Howard takes a break near Signal Peak.

LOCATION: Southwest Utah

SIZE: 50,000 acres

ELEVATION RANGE:
4,500 to 10,360 feet

ECOREGION: Colorado Plateau

MILES OF TRAIL: About 90

ADMINISTRATION:
Dixie NF, Pine Valley Ranger District

MAPS: Trails Illustrated: Map #702.
Dixie NF: Pine Valley Ranger District.
USGS 1:24,000: Grass Valley,
New Harmony, Saddle Mountain,
Signal Peak, Pintura.

PINE VALLEY MOUNTAIN IS a laccolith that bulged upward in Tertiary time. The mass of igneous rock broke through lower sedimentary layers, but never made it all the way to the surface as magma. The bulge now rises 3,500 feet above the surrounding terrain, making for some lung-busting, quad-burning hiking opportunities.

Pine Valley Mountain Wilderness is 10 miles north of St. George. The small community of Pine Valley is a welcome summer retreat from the heat of St. George. At 6,630 feet, the cool evenings and shade from ponderosa pines seem like a little piece of heaven, especially if you've been hiking in the surrounding deserts. The early Mormon settlers must have thought so, too. They arrived in 1855 and some of their descendants are still there. The Whipple Trail is named after Patience F. Whipple, one of the town's early midwives. Ebenezer Bryce, a shipbuilder from England, was the architect of the Pine Valley Church, which was put together with wooden pegs and rawhide strips. Bryce Canyon National Park bears his name.

Although it looks like a large enough resort to spawn all manner of yuppie amenities, the town of Pine Valley has no gas station and only limited supplies in one small restaurant-store. The community of Latter-Day Saints is a palpable presence. The nearest gas station is in Veyo on UT 18, 15 miles to the southwest. The town of Central at the intersection of UT 18 and the Pine Valley Rd. also has no gas station.

Neat-as-a-pin campgrounds, many with special accommodations for horses, are lined up along the Clara River, right on the wilderness border. There are six developed campgrounds (with more than 70 campsites) and four trailheads in the forested area east of the town. I wish I could say the campsites on the wilderness trails were as good, but along Summit Trail we found considerable amounts of trash and multiple fire pits that were full to running over with debris and ashes. Please follow Leave No Trace guidelines when you visit.

Oak Grove Campground and trailhead on the southeastern edge of the wilderness offers a less crowded atmosphere. Oak Grove is 15 miles west of I-15. Take the Silver Reef exit at Leeds. Three trails, one of them extremely steep, depart from the campground. The eastern face of the laccolith looks like a very unlikely spot for a trail, but there's a switchbacking trail from the desert environment at the bottom to the pines at the top. The climb is dauntingly hot in spring and summer, and if you go in early spring, the highcountry will be snowed in—so the best time for climbing the Oak Grove Trail is late autumn. Mountain maples show their candy red colors in autumn. Two lower-elevation trails from Oak Grove, both just outside the wilderness boundary, are desert hikes that are relatively flat and easy—good early springtime hikes. Wear cactus-proof boots.

To access trailheads near the town of Pine Valley, drive north from St. George via UT 18, and then easterly on FR 035, the Pine Valley Rd. Alternatively, from Cedar City, take UT 56 to Newcastle, where you turn southwest to Enterprise, then south on UT 18 to FR 035.

With so many trails and trailheads around what is essentially one big chunk of rock, there are at least a dozen possible loop hikes. July, August, and September are the best months for hiking from the northwestern trailheads to any number of destinations along the Summit Trail. A very early morning start is recommended. Temperatures cool dramatically as you climb. With only a couple of exceptions, approach routes to the crest follow streams, all of them perennial, so lack of water is seldom an issue. Treat all water before drinking.

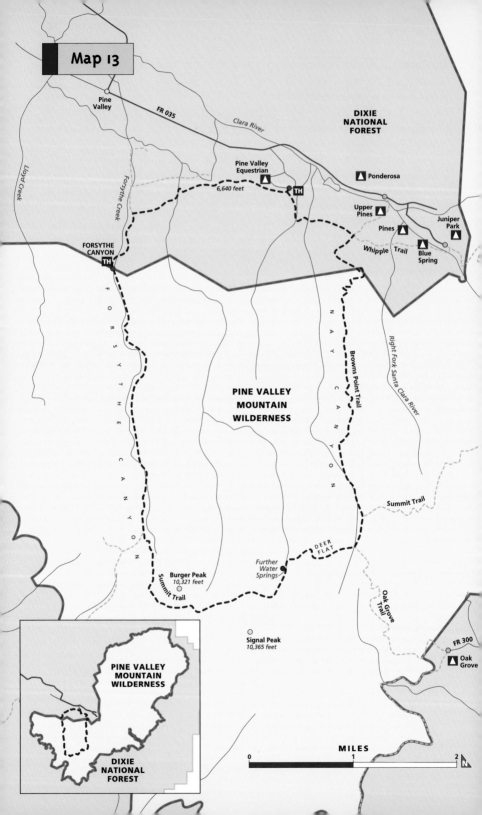

Map 13

Pine Valley

FR 035

Clara River

DIXIE
NATIONAL
FOREST

Lloyd Creek

Forsythe Creek

Pine Valley
Equestrian

6,640 feet

TH

Ponderosa

Upper
Pines

Pines

Juniper
Park

FORSYTHE
CANYON

TH

Whipple   Trail

Blue
Spring

F
O
R
S
Y
T
H
E

C
A
N
Y
O
N

N
A
Y

C
A
N
Y
O
N

Browns Point Trail

Right Fork Santa Clara River

PINE VALLEY
MOUNTAIN
WILDERNESS

Summit Trail

DEER
FLAT

Oak Grove
Trail

Burger Peak
10,321 feet

Summit
Trail

Further
Water
Springs

FR 300

Oak
Grove

Signal Peak
10,365 feet

PINE VALLEY
MOUNTAIN
WILDERNESS

DIXIE
NATIONAL
FOREST

MILES

0   1   2

N

DAY HIKE: EQUESTRIAN CAMPGROUND TO FORSYTHE CANYON
One-Way Length: 1.75 miles
Low and High Elevations: 6,640 and 6,750 feet
Difficulty: Easy

This day hike just outside the wilderness boundary is an easy stroll that's most pleasant in the spring when wildflowers such as lupine and larkspur are blooming. For a 3.5-mile hike, follow the trail to the Forsythe Canyon entrance and then return the way you came. (This is also the starting point for a backpacking trip up Forsythe Canyon to the Summit Trail; see the following hike.)

The trailhead is on the south side of the Equestrian Campground. Park in an open spot near the corral. The trail is shown accurately on both Trails Illustrated Map #702 and the Dixie National Forest Pine Valley map. Bear right at the first fork. A sign noting the distance to Forsythe Canyon as 1 mile is incorrect (should be 1.75 miles). The path gradually loses about 300 feet in elevation as it takes you through shrubby oak groves and grassy meadows. Fences and gates mark cattle and horse control areas. There are some unsigned trail intersections, so you might want to carry a map.

The trail passes through one wire gate and hops three creeks. After the third creek crossing and at a four-way intersection of foot/horse paths, bear sharply left (south). You'll soon come to the entrance of Forsythe Canyon. If time and energy allow, continue up the canyon, enjoying the shade and rock formations along Forsythe Creek. This is a good hike for families with children. Remember to step well off the trail when meeting horses.

LOOP BACKPACK: SUMMIT TRAIL SAMPLER
One-Way Length: 16.25 miles
Low and High Elevations: 6,640 and 10,165 feet
Difficulty: Strenuous

For the first 1.75 miles of this loop hike, see the day hike described previously. From the Forsythe Canyon Trailhead, the trail is serious about climbing up the canyon for 5 miles. The upper sections of Forsythe Creek dry up in midsummer, so be certain that your water bottles are filled in the lower canyon. Much of the canyon is shady as you hike past rock walls and through pine and aspen groves. Some of the aspen trees are like historical markers, bearing carved names and dates from the 1920s and '30s.

This is Trail 021 (Trail 3021 on the Trails Illustrated map), identified on all maps as the Summit Trail. The entire Summit Trail is 35 miles long within the wilderness, plus another 10 miles for most exit points. This hike samples the Summit Trail by beginning at the southwestern end on a popular approach route, traveling along the ridge to intercept the Browns Point Trail, and then descending to Pine Valley.

The relatively short mileage of 16.25 is deceptive. This hike is strenuous, skirting two peaks over 10,000 feet (Burger and Signal), gaining 3,460 feet, and then losing 3,460 feet on the descent. However, the trails are generally easy to find and well cut, which helps considerably. There are a few places east of Signal Peak where trail tread disappears or is faint and you have to follow tree blazes. Do not plan to complete this hike in a single day. There are good campsites in the meadows of Deer Flat. Refill water bottles at Further Water Springs, west of Deer Flat. Earlier in the season, at the tail-end of snowmelt, you may find running water in Deer Flat (10,000 feet).

Near Burger Peak and Signal Peak, vertical cliffs look out over St. George, Cottonwood Canyon, Snow Canyon, and beyond. On clear days, you can easily see into Arizona and the Virgin River Gorge. Climb about 200 feet above the trail to top Signal Peak (10,365 feet).

The Summit Trail intersects the Browns Point Trail in Nay Canyon (9,600 feet), 1.5 miles east of Further Water Springs. This is where you turn north to descend 4 miles to complete this loop hike. The upper portion of Browns Point Trail parallels the creek in Nay Canyon, then leaves the steep creekbed to travel along the ridge to the east. At Browns Point Trailhead in the valley, turn left (west) to hike about 1.25 miles to the Equestrian Campground, where this loop hike began.

The foothills of Pine Valley Mountain Wilderness are mirrored in the ponds of Grass Valley.

Beaver Dam Mountains Wilderness, Red Mountain WSA, Cottonwood Canyon WSA, and Cougar Canyon WSA

14

The rugged landscape of the Beaver Dam Mountains Wilderness is warmed by the glow of a springtime sunset.

Beaver Dam Mountains Wilderness

Beaver Dam Wash is the lowest point in Utah, making it a good bet for early season hiking. Spring was in full force when we visited in April. Prickly pear cactus was in bloom, and even the Joshua trees were softened by spring green.

The only improved campground is at the Virgin River Gorge Recreation Area, right off I-15, about 15 miles south of St. George. Primitive camping along Cedar Pockets Rd. and along dirt roads that flank the northern border is available wherever you can find a flat spot. Bring your own water.

From the Virgin River Campground, many paths, some of them marked simply as "trail," lead to the river. These obvious trails bordered with rocks disappear in a few hundred yards, as soon as they reach the flash-flood plain.

The Virgin River is full of silt. It's mud with a current. The current is swift and at least knee-deep at its lowest level. Quicksand is common. Hikers accustomed to the Virgin River nearer its source in Zion National Park won't recognize this raucous,

LOCATION: Southwest Utah
SIZE: Beaver Dam Wilderness: 2,600 acres in Utah (plus 17,000 acres in Arizona)
   Red Mountain WSA: 18,290 acres
   Cottonwood Canyon WSA: 11,330 acres
   Cougar Canyon WSA: 10,568 acres in Utah (5,400 acres in Nevada)
ELEVATION RANGE: 2,200 to 6,784 feet
ECOREGION: Great Basin Desert, Colorado Plateau, and Mojave Desert
MILES OF TRAIL: None; washes, canyons, and ridgelines are unofficial routes
ADMINISTRATION: BLM, Dixie Resource Area
MAPS: Trails Illustrated: Map #702.
BLM: Arizona Strip District.
USGS 1:24,000: Jarvis Peak—UT, White Hills—UT, Littlefield—AZ, Pintura—UT, Mountain Sheep Spring—AZ; Veyo—UT, Gunlock—UT, Santa Clara—UT, Shivwits—UT, Harrisburg Junction—UT, Washington—UT, Water Canyon Peak—UT, Pine Park—UT/NV, Goldstrike—UT, Docs Pass—UT/NV, Signal Peak—UT.

opaque flow. In early spring, when snowmelt rushes down from the highcountry, kayakers and rafters play in the dangerous rapids.

Hiking south into Arizona's Paiute Wilderness requires only one ford of the river, but hiking upstream into the Beaver Dam Mountains Wilderness requires multiple fords. Both hikes are impossible during high water. The trail south into Sullivan Canyon, Ariz., is more frequently used and has good, potable water sources. There's no trail upstream into Utah, and apart from the undrinkable river, the route is waterless.

The Jedediah Smith Trail appears on the BLM's Arizona Strip District map, along with other historic routes such as the Mormon Wagon Road and the Spanish Historic Trail, but these historic routes are not hiking trails.

In Beaver Dam Mountains Wilderness, there are no beavers and no dams. Beaver Dam Wash, which is west of the wilderness area and close to the Nevada border, is marshy, and the mountain range is much larger than the designated wilderness area. Here, the western edge of the Colorado Plateau meets the southern edge of the Great Basin and the northern extremes of the Mojave Desert. There's a 2,000- to 3,000-foot difference between the wilderness heights and the low wash to the west.

One wash, Cedar Pockets, boasts a piñon-juniper forest and a very precious commodity: shade. A circuitous driving route takes you west, over the mountains via the Cedar Pockets dirt road. The road is directly across the freeway from the campground and is cherry-stemmed through the wilderness. This road exists to serve a mining area, a few water tanks for cattle and sheep, a power line, and hikers.

In good weather you can negotiate Cedar Pockets Rd. with a higher-clearance 2WD vehicle, but 4WD is recommended. If you pull off the road and day-hike to the south, you can enjoy the delicate desert environment and mellow terrain. Carry plenty of drinking water and wear cactus-proof boots. Poisonous snakes, scorpions, and Gila monsters hide from the heat of the midday sun, so don't put any of your body parts into a shady place without checking for other occupants first.

The wilderness area is so small that Cedar Pockets Rd. crosses it in less than 5 miles. To continue your exploration and to camp, drive west to the highway, then turn north for a few miles. Watch for the "Woodbury Desert Study Area" signs, where you turn east and approach the wilderness again via the dirt road up Bulldog Canyon. Woodbury Desert Study Area is a fenced, 3,040-acre area managed to protect the desert tortoise. The tortoises only come out briefly in the spring and fall—good advice for hikers in this area. The road passes through the Woodbury Study Area and continues up the canyon, but it is signed neither for Bulldog Canyon nor for Bulldog Pass.

Soon after the road enters the canyon, various 4WD tracks lead south toward the wilderness boundary. These unofficial ways do not appear on any maps, but they offer the best opportunity for viewing desert bighorn sheep. You can 4WD about 0.25 mile off the main road, camp in the desert, and watch for sheep in early morning and late dusk. The dust-colored bighorns are hard to spot and are relatively shy. Mule deer graze some of the same areas. No campground noises, no road noises, and no light pollution impede the ability to stargaze in peace.

Farther up Bulldog Canyon, the road skirts the northern border of a thumb-shaped section of the wilderness. The most prominent feature, visible for miles, is a metal colossus of a power line that marches across the landscape. Caterpillar scrapes or 4WD roads lead to the base of each tower. Power lines, roads, and freeways besiege the small wilderness.

At the apex of the thumb, a rough dirt road leads south into the unsigned Cedar Pockets Wash. Drive a few hundred yards down this road to find good, unimproved camping in the shade of juniper and piñon trees. Hike down Cedar Pockets Wash. You'll pass a couple of water tanks that deer and bighorn sheep use, as well as cattle. Where the road ends, signs mark the wilderness boundary. As we hiked down the wash, it looked as if no human activity of any kind had taken place since the signs were erected in 1984. There are no maintained trails.

Cedar Pockets Wash splits, with one section going to the river and crossing under I-15, and the other tributary meeting Cedar Pockets Rd. Take USGS maps Jarvis Peak and Mountain Sheep Spring with you so that you can end up where you want to be. You can hike the entire wash one way in half a day, and round trip in one day.

Red Mountain WSA

Red Mountain is the big block of Navajo Sandstone 8 miles northwest of St. George. UT 18 and the Santa Clara River Rd. encircle the area. Day hiking and horseback riding are the most frequent pursuits. A complete lack of perennial water sources discourages backpacking. Pockets in the slickrock might hold water after a rainstorm.

The plateau rises to about 5,000 feet and provides views of the Pine Valley Mountain Wilderness, Snow Canyon, and the city of St. George. Snow Peak doesn't look like much of a peak, but at 5,570 feet, it is the high point on the plateau. The popular Snow Canyon Trail, in the adjacent state park, runs outside the eastern edge of the WSA.

One jeep trail is cherry-stemmed into the northeastern edge of the plateau, and this makes a good beginning for a plateau hike. From St. George, drive north on UT 18 about 12 miles. Watch for the Red Mountain sign on your left, just past

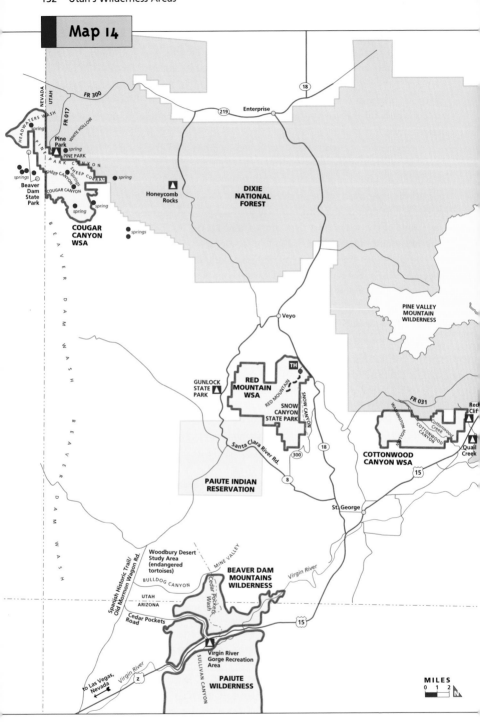

Map 14

milepost 15. There is a rat's nest of dirt roads here, but the main road leads west to a parking lot. The jeep road into the wilderness study area is rough, so parking in the lot and hiking on the sandy, rocky road is advised. The track will take you about 5 miles onto the plateau, with a gain of about 400 feet in elevation. Cactus-proof boots are recommended. Where the jeep track ends, you can turn around and go back the way you came, or wander off-trail to explore the plateau. Use the Santa Clara and Veyo maps and a compass to make sure you can get back to the jeep track.

Sand flies are a nuisance from June to November, so enjoy this hot desert area in the early spring and winter months.

Cottonwood Canyon WSA

The small wilderness study area of Cottonwood Canyon is northeast of St. George. I-15 runs along its eastern edge. The Pine Valley Mountain Wilderness is only 6 miles north. The area appears on Trails Illustrated Map #702, though it is not outlined as a wilderness study area.

Utah boasts several features named "Cottonwood Canyon," so don't confuse this one with the similarly named canyons in the Wasatch Range. This WSA gets about 3,000 visitors per year, thanks to the long hiking season and close proximity to St. George.

More than 10,000 visitors per year use the adjacent Red Cliffs Recreation Site on Quail Creek, but most of them have no idea they are next to a wilderness study area with about 13 miles of hiking on the canyon floor. No maintained trails exist beyond the Red Cliffs Recreation Site. Rock shelters and pictographs from Anasazi prehistoric cultures have been vandalized near Quail Creek—one of the hazards of easy access from a freeway. Red Cliffs Campground is accessed via the Harrisburg exit off I-15. A freeway underpass with an 11-foot overhead clearance and a narrow opening poses an obstacle to larger vehicles.

FR 031 (or 30031 on the Trails Illustrated map) on the WSA's northern boundary offers more solitude. There are no trails from the road, but primitive camping is possible in many spots. Bring your own water, and use topographical maps Pintura and Signal Peak to find washes leading into the heads of Cottonwood Canyon and Heath Hollow. There's some ORV use in Washington Hollow.

You can drive north from Red Cliffs Campground to FR 031, but a much more direct route is to take exit 23, Silver Reef, off I-15. (This is the same exit that you take to get to the Oak Grove Trailhead at the southeastern base of the Pine Valley Mountains.)

Cougar Canyon WSA

This wilderness study area is at the headwaters of Beaver Dam Wash, near Clover Mountain, about 30 miles northwest of St. George. Beaver Dam State Park borders the WSA. There are no roads or unofficial vehicular ways in the Cougar Canyon WSA, but there are about 6 miles of perennial streams that support trout fishing. These are the only native reproducing fisheries in the area.

The WSA gets its name from the area's most prominent mammal, the cougar. These big cats roam Pine Park Canyon and the adjacent rock formations. Elevations range from 5,000 to 6,700 feet, and most of it is rugged, with steep-walled canyons and ridges cut with drainage patterns. There are no official trails within the WSA. Dense vegetation makes hiking in the narrow riparian areas in Sheep Corral, Sheep, and Cougar Canyons difficult. Headwaters Wash and Pine Park Canyon are broader and usually have braided cattle trails that you can use for hiking. Pine Park Canyon is easier to access from Beaver Dam State Park.

Pine Park Campground on adjacent Dixie National Forest land is open from Memorial Day to about the first week of October. This primitive campground has no water source. Hiking trails lead from the campground into White Hollow and Pine Park Canyons and then disappear. You will need the Pine Park and Water Canyon Peak USGS topo maps.

Getting to the area by car requires a lot of driving on dirt roads, but they are suitable for 2WD vehicles in good weather. Drive west on UT 219 from the small town of Enterprise. Eight miles west of town, the pavement ends. After about 15 miles of gravel and dirt road, turn left on FR 017, which is signed as "Pine Park 10 miles." There are several more intersections, but they are all marked with Pine Park signs.

The Beaver Dam Mountains Wilderness on the Utah-Arizona border occupies a unique eco-zone where Great Basin, Mojave Desert, and Colorado Plateau ecoregions meet.

Canaan Mountain and Parunuweap Canyon WSAs

15

A touch of green against Parunuweap Canyon's cliffs

CANAAN MOUNTAIN AND PARUNUWEAP Canyon Wilderness Study Areas are extensions of the slickrock plateaus and deep canyons of their neighbor, Zion National Park. Canaan Mountain is south of Zion and Parunuweap is east of it.

The Canaan Mountain plateau is high enough to support scattered groves of aspens and ponderosa pines, in addition to the usual piñon-juniper woodlands. South of Canaan Mountain, in Arizona, lies the Cottonwood Point Wilderness.

Roughly half the length of Parunuweap Canyon is inside national park boundaries. The eastern half is in Parunuweap WSA, managed by the BLM. *Parunuweap* was John Wesley Powell's

LOCATION: Southwest Utah

SIZE: Canaan Mountain WSA: 47,170 acres
Parunuweap Canyon WSA: 30,800 acres

ELEVATION RANGE: 4,400 to 7,427 feet

ECOREGION: Colorado Plateau

MILES OF TRAIL: About 22, plus jeep trails

ADMINISTRATION: BLM, Dixie and Kanab Resource Areas

MAPS: BLM: Arizona Strip District. USGS 1:100,000: St. George and Kanab.
USGS 1:24,000: Springdale West, Springdale East, Hildale, Smithsonian Butte, Mount Carmel, Elephant Butte, The Barracks, Yellowjacket Canyon.

version of a Paiute word meaning "roaring water canyon." Numerous archaeological sites have been found in the canyon, 88 of them within Zion National Park.

There are no official trails into Parunuweap Canyon within the national park. On Zion's backcountry trip planning guide, the entire canyon is marked "Closed to Entry." There's also no legal entry into the wide mouth of Parunuweap Canyon at its western end. There's no legal entry to the head of the canyon at the Foote Ranch on the eastern edge of the wilderness study area, either. It's possible to enter the canyon legally, staying entirely on public land, but it's difficult. See the Parunuweap descriptive section at the end of this chapter.

Several jeep trails and unofficial ways extending into the southern portion of Parunuweap Canyon WSA can be used as day-hiking trails. A lack of water precludes backpacking. Water is a problem in a different way when it comes to flash-flood danger. July through December is the wettest season. In the narrow sections there's no way to escape the rush of water, so be sure to check the weather forecast before you enter a canyon.

Canaan Mountain WSA

The main highways for access are UT 9 and UT 59 from St. George (35 miles from St. George); from Kanab via US 89; and AZ 389 and AZ 377 to the south. Canaan Mountain Trailhead (Squirrel Canyon) is off of UT 375 east of Hildale–Colorado City. Hildale is in Utah and Colorado City is in Arizona—the two are twins with the state border between them. Both are religious communities that practice plural marriage.

Canaan Mountain rises 2,000 feet above the surrounding desert, so expect to do some uphill hiking to take advantage of the sweeping views from the top. Developed trailheads include Canaan Mountain and Cottonwood Canyon on the south; Eagle Crags on the northwest boundary; and Broad Hollow on the northeast. Trails make use of old logging and livestock paths. Visible tread often disappears on slickrock. Watch for rock cairns or scout for a reappearance in softer soil. Pine tree limbs that have been trimmed out of the way with a saw are also a clue to the routes.

The BLM notes, "Drinking water for hikers within the WSA is unpredictable both to source and quality. During the spring, tanks and seeps are plentiful. During the summer, water sources become scarce and difficult to locate. Potability is often questionable."

> **DAY HIKE:** SQUIRREL CANYON
> One-Way Length: About 5–6 miles
> Low and High Elevations: 5,100 and 6,800 feet
> Difficulty: Moderate

To find the Squirrel Canyon Trailhead (Canaan Mountain Trailhead on the BLM Arizona Strip map), make your way to the northeast side of the town of Hildale. Turn right on Utah Ave. and follow it until it becomes Canyon St. Keep right at an intersection where the pavement ends. Drive 1 mile into the canyon and turn right on a BLM road to the trailhead. If you don't turn right here, you end up in Water Canyon, at the town reservoir, another possible day-hiking trailhead, or the end point for a loop hike that includes both Squirrel Canyon and Water Canyon. The road distance between the two trailheads is about 0.5 mile.

The trail for Squirrel Canyon follows Short Creek to the northeast, then turns northwest to enter Squirrel Canyon. There's also an ATV trail in the Short Creek wash. In Squirrel Canyon the trail is an easy stroll through grassy areas and along a stream for about 0.5 mile, then it climbs steeply, gaining about 600 feet in 1 mile.

Once on top of the plateau, you can see the Navajo Sandstone formation called The Beehive and the sharp lines of the Vermilion Cliffs. The various shapes and textures encountered on this hike are a major source of its charm.

Join an old pack trail and follow it northwest toward Spring Birch Creek. Now is a good time to look at the Hildale topographical map so that you don't get lost in a maze of ATV tracks and slickrock. (ATVs used to come up a jeep trail, now closed to vehicles, from Broad Hollow on the east side of the WSA.) The pack trail is on the south side of Spring Birch Creek. Climb to the saddle above Water Canyon and enjoy the varied and beautiful views, about 5 miles from the trailhead. Wandering around on the plateau a bit before you head back is a good idea. Waterfalls in Water Canyon, groves of ponderosa pines, and views of Zion and of Eagle Crags can all be had by climbing to one rise in the terrain or another.

Return the way you came, or, for a loop hike option, continue to follow the pack trail west of Water Canyon, watching for a faint footpath that leads south. From here on, the trail becomes more difficult to find and to negotiate.

The trail climbs gradually through sand and slickrock. The footpath you're looking for passes through a dip in a ridge. Watch for trimmed limbs on pine trees as indicators of the trail route. Hike about 0.5 mile from where you left the pack trail to a stream that creates a waterfall. The trail descends sharply to cross the stream, then climbs the opposite slope. About 0.5 mile of climbing brings you to a flatter area where rock cairns and a path can be seen. Follow the path along the rim of the canyon.

From the rim of Water Canyon, the path switchbacks down through pines and firs. In Water Canyon, follow the trail for about 1.75 miles, bouldering and climbing down rock chimneys. Hikers spend about 3 miles above and in Water Canyon. The trail gets wider and easier to see as you near the reservoir.

Parunuweap Canyon WSA

This wilderness study area is about 25 miles northwest of Kanab. Activity is concentrated around the southern part of Elephant Cove, where ORV enthusiasts cruise the jeep tracks and trails. Coral Pink Sand Dunes State Park is southeast of the WSA, and portions of it are also open to ORV use.

Four miles of jeep road are cherry-stemmed through Elephant Cove. Three additional miles of road, going northeast to the Foote Ranch, are classified as an unofficial way by the BLM, which means that the user-created route evolved by 4WD vehicles driving over the same path. The BLM prefers that the route be used as a foot/horse path instead of as a road. Unless the way is closed by the BLM, it will still be drivable with a 4WD vehicle. Other jeep trails lead into The Barracks area south of the East Fork of the Virgin River, onto Harris Mountain, and into canyons north of Block Mesa. These southern jeep roads are accessible from UT 237 through Yellowjacket Canyon (named Sand Dunes Rd. on some maps). There are no official hiking trails in this WSA. If experienced jeep drivers find their way to The Barracks, there is a Class II scramble that follows deer trails to the bottom of the canyon.

The East Fork of the Virgin River and its tributaries are the most impressive terrain features. These watercourses have carved canyons in Navajo sandstone. The East Fork of the Virgin River runs from east to west down Parunuweap Canyon, and in places it has carved a gorge several hundred feet deep and only 10 to 12 feet wide.

Naturally, some hardy souls have found a way into the canyon. A route down the West Fork of Misery Canyon to Parunuweap is recommended only for those experienced in technical canyoneering. Such a difficult technical route is beyond the scope of this book, but you can find more information on websites devoted to technical climbing in Utah.

DAY HIKE: CHECKERBOARD MESA AREA TO PARUNUWEAP CANYON
One-Way Length: About 4 miles
Low and High Elevations: 4,800 and 6,000 feet
Difficulty: Extremely Strenuous

For mere mortals, there is an approach to Parunuweap Canyon across the upper plateau, but it presents navigational challenges and is not recommended for beginners. Drive 0.7 mile into Zion National Park from the east entrance on UT 9. Checkerboard Mesa is your stopping point. Park west of the mesa in one of the pullouts south of the highway, elevation 5,540 feet. Hike south up the first canyon west of Checkerboard Mesa. This canyon enters the White Cliffs and is an interesting day hike on its own. You don't need a Zion National Park permit to day-hike in this area. The route soon exits the park and enters the WSA. This is not an official trail, but a user-created foot-path exists for most of the way. You need Springdale East and The Barracks USGS maps and good map-reading skills.

Rock art captures everyone's imagination in Utah's desert canyons.

From the saddle (6,000 feet) at the top of the canyon west of Checkerboard Mesa, descend a gully, using the trail on the right side. As the gully flattens, follow the footpath east and cross another, shallower gully. In this second gully, watch for a junction of footpaths (N37°12.283', W112°52.283'). The junction is about 2 miles south of the highway. The east fork leads to Misery Canyon (for canyoneering experts only); the southeasterly fork stays on the sand and slickrock plateau as it makes its way to the canyon rim at the National Park–BLM border. Follow rock cairns and user-made trails southeast. A Class IV scramble down a steep gully is the last leg into the canyon.

The hike is dry all the way, with no water until you reach the East Fork of the Virgin River (about 4,800 feet), approximately 4 miles south of the highway. In the bushes above the river, a plaque commemorates the 1872 Powell Expedition. Like everything else on this hike, the plaque is hard to find. Hiking downstream into Zion National Park is prohibited. You can explore upstream in the forbidding but beautiful canyon. Some swimming or wading might be required to explore the canyon. Return along the same route to UT 9 for a round trip of about 8 miles.

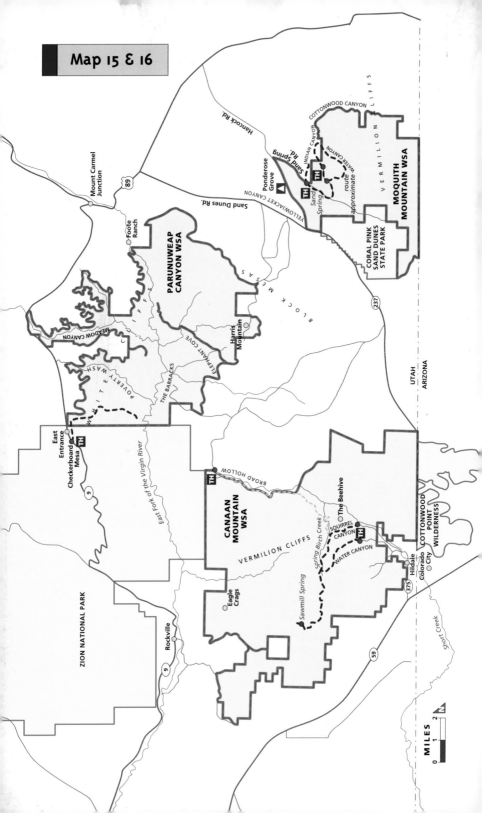

Map 15 & 16

Moquith Mountain WSA 16

A piñon pine stump pokes up from the sand.

THREE MAIN ROADS PROVIDE access to Moquith Mountain WSA, US 89 and Hancock Rd. to the northeast, and UT 237 on the west side. On some maps UT 237 is identified as Sand Dunes Rd. and the canyon it runs through is identified as Yellowjacket. From Kanab, drive 7.25 miles northwest on US 89 to an unsigned intersection with Hancock Rd. Turn southwest on paved Hancock Rd. and drive about 6 miles to a Y intersection. At the intersection you can continue on Hancock to the Ponderosa Grove Campground (no water, no fees, BLM-maintained), or take the left fork onto Sand Spring Rd. The trailhead at Sand Spring is the access point for viewing a panel of rock art in the South Fork of Indian Canyon (see details in the following day hike).

LOCATION: Southwest Utah
SIZE: 14,830 acres
ELEVATION RANGE: 5,000 to 7,050 feet
ECOREGION: Colorado Plateau
MILES OF TRAIL: About 0.5 mile of constructed trail; plus unofficial ways and tracks
ADMINISTRATION:
BLM, Kanab Resource Area
MAPS: BLM: Arizona Strip District.
USGS 1:100,000: Kanab.
USGS 1:24,000: Yellowjacket Canyon, Kanab.

Moquith Mountain WSA is small, about 6 miles by 5 miles, so it's more suited to day hiking than to backpacking. The WSA's eastern boundary is Cottonwood Canyon. ("Cottonwood Canyon" and "Water Canyon" are names frequently used in Utah. This is not the Cottonwood Canyon near Pine Valley Mountain, nor the one near Salt Lake City. This is not the same Water Canyon as the one in nearby Canaan Mountain WSA.) The northern boundary is Hancock Rd. and private land. The southern boundary is the Utah-Arizona border. Coral Pink Sand Dunes State Park is the western boundary. The state park has a campground and picnic area.

The delicate coral colors of the sand dunes extend into Moquith Mountain WSA. A section of Vermilion Cliffs forms the highcountry. These red sandstone summits are cut by Cottonwood Canyon, where there is no official trail. Citizen groups would like to see a roadless area east of Cottonwood Canyon included in the wilderness proposal.

Ponderosa pine trees in dune areas and uplands add to the beauty of this area. From Ponderosa Grove Campground to Sand Spring Trailhead is only 3 miles. But if you prefer even more primitive camping than at the BLM campground, set up your base camp at Sand Spring, which is also in a grove of ponderosa pines. Campfires are prohibited at Sand Spring. A 4WD vehicle is recommended for Sand Spring Rd. A 4WD road extends from Sand Spring into adjacent Coral Pink Sand Dunes State Park.

DAY HIKE: INDIAN CANYON AND SOUTH FORK PICTOGRAPH
One-Way Length: About 3.5–4 miles, depending on route taken
Low and High Elevations: 5,960 and 6,220 feet
Difficulty: Easy to Moderate

Park at Sand Spring Trailhead (see directions in the previous section). You can hike along an ORV track into the head of Indian Canyon for 0.5 mile before a 40-foot pouroff stops you. This is a good mini-hike for children. Return the way you came and continue to the second part of this hike, the pictograph panel.

The easiest route to the pictograph panel in the South Fork of Indian Canyon is to follow the 4WD road south of Sand Spring for about 1 mile until you come to a Y intersection where another road (South Fork Pictograph Trail Rd.) leads northeast to the panel. These 4WD roads are cherry-stemmed into the wilderness study area.

Where South Fork Pictograph Trail Rd. ends, an improved trail switchbacks down into the canyon. Hikers will descend about 300 feet in 0.5 mile. The trail ends at the pictograph panel. Return the way you came.

For a longer hike, return to the rim of the South Fork of Indian Canyon, and from the top of the switchbacking trail, turn southwest on South Fork Pictograph Trail Rd. Hike about 1 mile on the road, then turn south to hike through grass and pine groves in the wash that is the head of the South Fork of Indian Canyon (refer to the Yellowjacket Canyon USGS topo map). After you cross the wash, turn southeast and hike upslope to the ridge above Water Canyon. You can see into the canyon, where a moist environment supports hanging gardens and Douglas fir trees. Return to Sand Spring via the 4WD Sand Spring Rd.

Moquith Mountain Wilderness Study Area is adjacent to Coral Pink Sand Dunes State Park. Both regions are noted for the beautiful soft pink color of the dunes.

South-Central Utah, Designated Wilderness

Light courses gold, mauve, and blue down the water-carved sandstone. My brother counts the minutes when reflected sunlight finds us standing on the floor of Buckskin Gulch—four minutes. When the shadows return, we head for the trailhead. At the entrance to the slot, some amateur photographers have halted. They eye the mud caked up to my knees and decide not to go farther. I can't find the words to tell them how wrong they are.

There are two designated wilderness areas in south-central Utah: Paria Canyon–Vermilion Cliffs and Box–Death Hollow. We have included the Phipps–Death Hollow Instant Study Area in the Box–Death Hollow chapter because not only are the two cheek-by-jowl, but hiking routes traverse both areas.

Paria Canyon is farther south and at a lower elevation, so its plateaus can be hiked in March and its canyons in May. The fall hiking season extends into early November. Box–Death Hollow starts high on the shoulder of the Aquarius Plateau and ends low, so beginning a hike where snowdrifts remain and ending up in a hot desert is the norm. Either late May and June or late September and October are good hiking months for Box–Death and Phipps–Death.

Don't let all the "death" in the names scare you off. The names refer to the untimely demise of horses and mules that took a wrong step and ended up at the bottom of a ravine. (To make matters confusing, there's more than one Death Hollow, and there's even a Little Death Hollow in Grand Staircase–Escalante National Monument. So many opportunities to tempt fate, so little hiking time!)

Speaking of repetitive names, all across south-central and southwest Utah you'll see bands of cliffs identified on maps as Vermilion Cliffs. Sections of disconnected plateaus and cliff formations run from Utah into Arizona, and they share the same name because it's a geological description of similar sandstone rock formations. See Geology and Ecosytems in the Along the Trail section at the beginning of this book for more information. Box–Death Hollow is at the top of the "Grand Staircase" and Paria Canyon is at the bottom. Box–Death Hollow is on the northern boundary of Grand Staircase–Escalante National Monument and Paria Canyon is on its southern border.

A ponderosa pine in the Navajo Sandstone above Death Hollow

Paria Canyon is one of the most heavily used areas in southern Utah. Reservations are required for backpacking or horsepacking expeditions, and fees must be paid even for day use.

Some printed and website information says that there are no trails in Box–Death Hollow Wilderness—not true. There's an 8-mile trail down The Box, though it's lightly used. It's true that there's not a trail in upper Death Hollow, but intrepid hikers make their way cross-country from Hell's Backbone Rd. to Mamie Creek. Eventually, you end up in the BLM-administered Phipps–Death Hollow ISA and intercept the Boulder Mail Trail or a primitive trail down-canyon to join the Escalante River.

Even though these two designated wilderness areas differ dramatically in number of visitors and established trails, they do have some things in common. Each features hikes in spectacular canyons that cut through layers of sandstone, and both carry warnings that "trails" may be streambeds that require wading and swimming. Both wilderness areas have dense patches of poison ivy along their streams and in the hanging gardens that flourish where water seeps from canyon walls.

Flowers thrive in riparian areas of the Phipps–Death Hollow proposed wilderness.

Paria Canyon–Vermilion Cliffs Wilderness **17**

Sand reflects the light from sunset clouds.

THE PARIA RIVER RUNS through Paria Canyon, carving a scenic route that is one of the most popular hiking-backpacking destinations in Utah. Buckskin Gulch is a tributary to Paria Canyon, and at 16 miles, it is said to be the longest slot canyon in the world. Wire Pass is a short tributary of Buckskin Gulch. Canyons that do not house a permanent stream nevertheless have "tributaries" formed by flash floods and seasonal meltwater. Buckskin Gulch runs roughly southeast to meet the Paria River and is entirely in the Utah portion of the designated wilderness. (For information on the Arizona portion of the wilderness, see *Guide to Arizona's Wilderness Areas* from Westcliffe Publishers. It's possible to

LOCATION: South-Central Utah

SIZE: 20,000 acres in Utah
(plus 92,500 acres in Arizona)

ELEVATION RANGE: 3,200 to 7,300 feet

ECOREGION: Colorado Plateau

MILES OF TRAIL: 55.7

ADMINISTRATION:
BLM, Vermilion and Kanab Resource Areas and Arizona Strip Office in St. George; NPS, Glen Canyon NRA

MAPS: BLM: Arizona Strip District and Hiker's Guide to Paria Canyon.
USGS 1:100,000: Kanab, Smokey Mountain.
USGS 1:24,000: Pine Hollow Canyon—UT, West Clark Bench—UT, Bridger Point—UT, Coyote Buttes—AZ, Poverty Flat—AZ, Wrather Arch—AZ, Water Pockets—AZ, Ferry Swale—AZ, Lees Ferry—AZ.

hike 38 miles south to the Colorado River in Arizona. A couple of miles before hikers reach Lees Ferry, they cross the wilderness boundary and enter the Glen Canyon National Recreation Area.)

Access to Paria Canyon–Vermilion Cliffs Wilderness is from US 89 on the northern edge, and from US Alt. 89 along the base of the Vermilion Cliffs on the south and east edges. House Rock/Coyote Valley Rd. (BLM Rd. 1065) is the access route along the west side. House Rock Rd. is dirt, sand, and gravel, but is passable via 2WD in good weather. It quickly becomes 4WD when wet and is impassable in winter.

The nearest towns are Kanab, Utah, 44 miles west of the Paria Contact Station on US 89; and Page, Ariz., 30 miles to the east. The closest airports are in Flagstaff, Ariz., about 135 miles from Page; and St. George, Utah, about 100 miles west of Kanab.

Reservations are required for overnight hikes and are limited to 20 persons per day. Day hikers may come and go as they please, as long as group sizes are kept to 10 persons or less. Fees are $5 per person (or dog) daily for day hiking. See Appendix B for permit contacts.

The best season to visit for canyon hiking is in May, when the weather is warm and the flash-flood potential is low. Next best are April, June, and October. Flash floods increase in July, August, and September, with a dramatic spike in August. Daytime temperatures in the desert can top 100 degrees in July and August; 80s and 90s are common in April and May. The deeper slot canyons stay as cold as a refrigerator throughout the hiking season. Temperatures plunge by 30 degrees at nightfall.

Hypothermia is a threat in deep slot canyons. Bring an extra pair of boots and warm, dry clothes. Wear footwear that protects your feet and can also be worn in water. Old boots that lace up tightly are good because the mud can't suck them off. Slot canyons change every year, so descriptions from previous seasons are just a general guideline. Be prepared to climb, wade, or float your pack on longer expeditions. If you hike alone, bring 20 feet of rope to hoist your pack over chock stones and down drop-offs. Check the weather forecast before entering a canyon. No potable drinking water is available in Buckskin Gulch or Wire Pass Canyon.

The Coyote Buttes area is an exception to every rule. It is such a desirable location for photography and day hikes that visits are limited to day-use only and to no more than 10 persons per day. Most of Coyote Buttes is in Arizona. This plateau of carved sandstone is covered with beehivelike sandstone formations and wave structures of stone, all containing many layers of color. Reservations are required. Access is from the Wire Pass Trailhead for the north section. The south buttes are seldom visited and a 4WD vehicle is required. Check with the BLM for road conditions. Coyote Buttes is plateau hiking, hot and dry even in the spring.

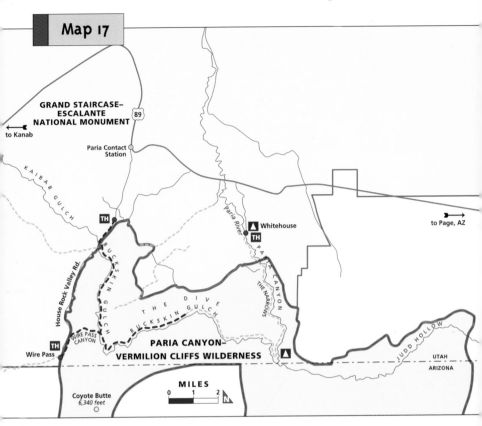

Map 17

GRAND STAIRCASE–
ESCALANTE
NATIONAL MONUMENT
← to Kanab

89

Paria Contact
Station

K A I B A B   G U L C H

TH

House Rock Valley Rd.

B U C K S K I N   G U L C H

Paria River

Whitehouse
TH

to Page, AZ

P A R I A   C A N Y O N

T H E   D I V E

B U C K S K I N   G U L C H

THE NARROWS

J U D D   H O L L O W

WIRE PASS
CANYON

TH
Wire Pass

PARIA CANYON–
VERMILION CLIFFS WILDERNESS

UTAH
ARIZONA

Coyote Butte
6,340 feet

MILES
0   1   2
N

DAY OR SHUTTLE HIKE: BUCKSKIN TRAILHEAD TO WIRE PASS TRAILHEAD
One-Way Length: About 6.75 miles
Low and High Elevations: 4,800 and 5,040 feet
Difficulty: Moderate

Those interested in an easier hike may day-hike from Buckskin Trailhead to the confluence of Wire Pass Canyon and Buckskin Gulch, then return the way they came. Buckskin is a little wider and a little easier in its upper portion. If hikers decide to exit through Wire Pass, they must be athletic enough to get over the 6-foot-high dry waterfalls and boulders.

Starting at the Buckskin Trailhead, which is located on House Rock Valley Rd., hike about 1 mile on relatively flat terrain in an open wash that leads to Buckskin Gulch. Enter the canyon and explore about 5 miles in Buckskin to the Wire Pass confluence. Exiting at Wire Pass requires a shuttle vehicle left at Wire Pass Trailhead. (See road directions in the next hike.) There is a developed campground near the Wire Pass Trailhead, with pit toilets.

> **DAY HIKE:** WIRE PASS TO BUCKSKIN GULCH
> One-Way Length: About 5–6 miles
> Low and High Elevations: 4,800 and 5,000 feet
> Difficulty: Moderate

If you are inexperienced at canyoneering, you should only attempt hiking the entire length of Buckskin Gulch in the company of a guide or skilled friends. A good alternative for beginners is to plan a day hike and turn around when the going gets rough. The intricate walls of slot canyons look different from every angle, so you won't be bored going back the way you came. Families with small children might find the Wire Pass approach too difficult because of 6-foot-high dry waterfalls and boulders. This hike used to be easier, before flash floods changed the contours of the canyon floor.

Five miles west of Paria Contact Station on US 89, turn south on House Rock Valley Rd. Begin at Wire Pass Trailhead, 8.3 miles south of US 89. Wire Pass Canyon is a 1.7-mile-long tributary of Buckskin that narrows to shoulder width at one point. Look for Anasazi rock art on the canyon walls near the confluence of Wire Pass and Buckskin. The floor of Wire Pass Canyon is sandy and usually dry.

Most hikers do not spend the night in the canyons. There's no high ground above flash-flood level, with the exception of a small shelf at the Wire Pass–Buckskin confluence. Buckskin Gulch is so narrow that it qualifies as a slot canyon for most of its 16-mile length. Many canyons have narrow sections (as does Paria Canyon), but only Buckskin remains so tightly closed for so many miles.

This day hike assumes that you will hike down Buckskin Gulch (a right-hand turn from Wire Pass Canyon) for about 3 miles, then turn around and return the way you came—that you'll backtrack long before you reach the confluence with the Paria River, and before you meet serious obstacles. Day hikers should turn back when they are faced with longer pools of muddy water, or boulder jams that require climbing. This hike is by far the best choice for photographers, and it is easier for everyone to carry only a daypack instead of a fully loaded backpack through the gulch.

Apart from wading through some muddy pools and working your way over mud shelves and short drop-offs, there are no real difficulties.

Box–Death Hollow Wilderness and Phipps–Death Hollow ISA

18

Iron oxides streak the banks of a creek rusty red.

DEATH HOLLOW IS IN THE highcountry where the Escalante River has its headwaters. The Escalante and all its tributary streams feed the Colorado River in Glen Canyon National Recreation Area. More than 6,000 feet in elevation change from the Aquarius Plateau to the Colorado River makes for some deeply incised canyons.

"The Box" of Box–Death Hollow Wilderness is a narrow canyon holding Pine Creek in its tight confines. In places the walls of The Box are 1,500 feet high. At its upper elevations, Douglas fir and ponderosa pine forests provide an almost impenetrable shade. Douglas firs give way to scattered ponderosas, aspens, wild roses, and finally sagebrush and cottonwoods as hikers descend along the creek. Hiking The Box

LOCATION: South-Central Utah

SIZE: Box–Death Hollow Wilderness: 25,751 acres Phipps–Death Hollow ISA: 42,731 acres

ELEVATION RANGE: 5,400 to 9,000 feet

ECOREGION: Colorado Plateau

MILES OF TRAIL: Box–Death Hollow Wilderness: 8 Phipps–Death Hollow ISA: 15.75

ADMINISTRATION: Dixie NF, Escalante Ranger District; BLM, Escalante Resource Area

MAPS: Trails Illustrated: Map #710. USGS 1:100,000: Escalante. USGS 1:24,000: Posy Lake, Rogers Peak, Escalante, Calf Creek, Boulder Town.

requires multiple creek crossings. In the spring, snowmelt swells the creek and boulder-hopping is much more difficult. The ability to walk narrow and shaky logs is helpful. Later in the season, when high water abates, the hike is easier and temperatures are still tolerable, especially in the shaded upper portion. This 8-mile day hike is the only official trail in Box–Death Hollow Wilderness.

The Box runs down the western side of the designated wilderness. The Death Hollow portion is the large central and eastern section that eventually drains into Phipps–Death Hollow Instant Study Area.

Thirteen miles of the Boulder Mail Trail and a 2.25-mile interpretive trail in the Calf Creek Recreation Area are the only maintained trails within Phipps–Death Hollow ISA. However, hikers use 14.9 miles of the Escalante River in the ISA as a hiking route and there are other unofficial routes in tributaries of the Escalante and on the slickrock plateau. Calf Creek is a special management area on the eastern edge of the proposed wilderness. Its two waterfalls are the main hiking destinations. The lower falls is 100 feet high and the upper falls is 86 feet high. (See the following day-hike descriptions.)

> **DAY HIKE:** UPPER CALF CREEK FALLS
> One-Way Length: About 1.2 miles
> Low and High Elevations: 5,900 and 6,400 feet
> Difficulty: Moderate

This hike begins on a spur road off UT 12 and drops 500 feet over slickrock benches into Calf Creek Canyon. The route is steep and is marked with rock cairns. Upper Calf Creek Falls is a day-use-only area, with no camping allowed within 0.5 mile of the falls. If you wish to camp in the canyon, remember to hike at least 0.5 mile away from the falls. This waterfall receives far fewer visitors than Lower Calf Creek Falls.

The turnoff to the trailhead for the upper falls is not marked. Drive 20 miles east of Escalante or 10 miles west of Boulder on UT 12. Between mileposts 81 and 82, watch for a dirt road leading into the junipers on the west side. Drive about 0.25 mile and park. There's a registration box but no sign at the trailhead. The trail forks before you reach the falls, with the right fork leading upstream to several deep pools. The left-hand, lower fork leads to the falls.

Signs warn visitors to leave any Indian ruins found in the alcoves undisturbed. The visible footpath disappears once you leave the canyon rim. Rock cairns have been placed on the slickrock incline.

The best hiking weather is in the spring. More intrepid travelers will find beautiful mists and low clouds filtering in and out of the canyon on mild winter days. Be prepared for mud in winter.

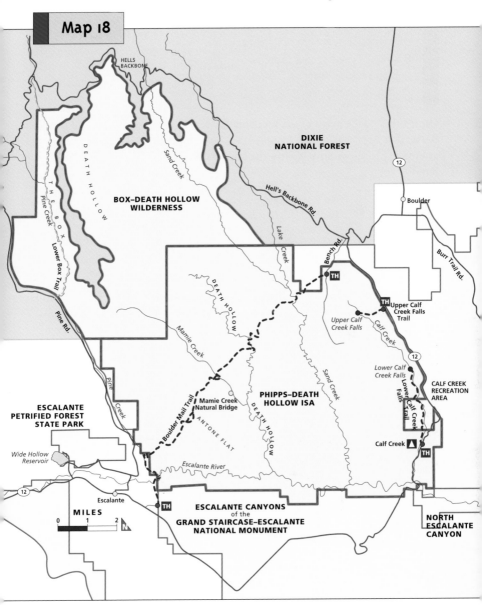

Map 18

HELLS BACKBONE

DIXIE NATIONAL FOREST

12

Boulder

DEATH HOLLOW

Sand Creek

Hell's Backbone Rd.

Lake Creek

Bench Rd.

Burr Trail Rd.

THE BOX

Pine Creek

Lower Box Trail

BOX–DEATH HOLLOW WILDERNESS

TH

TH Upper Calf Creek Falls Trail

Upper Calf Creek Falls

Calf Creek

DEATH HOLLOW

Mamie Creek

12

Pine Creek

Pine Rd.

Lower Calf Creek Falls

PHIPPS–DEATH HOLLOW ISA

Sand Creek

DEATH HOLLOW

CALF CREEK RECREATION AREA

ESCALANTE PETRIFIED FOREST STATE PARK

Boulder Mail Trail

Mamie Creek Natural Bridge

ANTONE FLAT

Lower Calf Creek Falls Trail

Wide Hollow Reservoir

Calf Creek

TH

Escalante River

12

Escalante

TH

MILES
0   1   2

ESCALANTE CANYONS
of the
GRAND STAIRCASE–ESCALANTE NATIONAL MONUMENT

NORTH ESCALANTE CANYON

DAY HIKE: LOWER CALF CREEK FALLS
One-Way Length: 2.5–2.75 miles
Low and High Elevations: 5,400 and 5,600 feet
Difficulty: Easy

On UT 12, 1 mile north of the Escalante River Bridge, watch for the Calf Creek Recreation Area sign. The 2.75-mile trail to the lower falls starts at the campground. This interpretive trail to the lower falls makes for an easy hike that families enjoy.

SHUTTLE BACKPACK: BOULDER MAIL TRAIL
One-Way Length: 16 miles
Low and High Elevations: 6,039 and 6,740 feet
Difficulty: Strenuous

Beginning in 1902, people used the Boulder Mail Trail route to carry mail and cans of cream between Boulder and Escalante. The trip was hard on the mules and horses, hence "Death Hollow." The Forest Service installed telephone lines along the route in the early 1900s. You can still see some remnants of the lines along the trail.

Near the intersection with UT 12, 0.2 mile up Hell's Backbone Rd., is the turnoff for the Boulder Mail Trailhead. When we were there, no sign marked the dirt road leading to the trailhead, but if you drive a short distance west, you'll see a "Boulder Mail Trail TRHD Parking" sign. On the Trails Illustrated map, this spur road is called Bench Road. Plan two to three days for this hike. There's a lot of climbing up and down as you enter and exit the various drainages.

The hike begins on the continuation of the road (now closed to vehicles). Where the trail leaves the road, it is signed. (A different branch of the road continues to an airstrip where a crashed airplane body is used as a windsock holder.) Cross the mesa on an obvious, sandy footpath. On slickrock the way is marked with rock cairns and occasionally with blazed junipers or ponderosa pines.

Where the trail crosses Sand Creek, a riparian area softens the landscape. Sand Creek is the only reliable water source before you drop into Death Hollow, so take advantage of it. Treat all water before drinking. The trail loses 700 feet in elevation as it drops into Death Hollow, switchbacking several times in the process. You can still see marks on the rocks where shod horses scraped and pawed for footing.

Once you reach the canyon floor the vegetation is thick: huge ponderosa pines, groves of box elder, water birches, willows, manzanita, and the lushest pockets of rosebushes and poison ivy I've ever seen—death by rose bushes and poison ivy. Long sleeves and long pants will help, but it's difficult to stay out of the noxious plants. The trail is not maintained, except by use, so you're in and out of the stream and up and down the banks to make your way either up- or down-canyon.

To stay on the Boulder Mail Trail, hike down-canyon for about 0.5 mile. There's a sandy trail on the west bank six bends downriver. It can be hard to spot the rock cairn that marks the exit because it has to be placed above the flash-flood line, at about eye level. Also, another trail continues down-canyon to meet the Escalante River; this trail has been getting more traffic lately, making it even easier to miss the turn for the Boulder Mail Trail.

Exit the canyon and follow rock cairns uphill and across another slickrock plateau. You'll cross Mamie Creek drainage, which may or may not have water in it. (For an interesting side trip, visit a 30-foot natural bridge in

Mysterious "Moki marbles" are created when desert varnish holds dry sand inside a ball-shaped concretion.

Mamie Creek Wash about 1 mile south of the Boulder Mail Trail. A pool below the bridge is usually full of water.) The trail climbs out of Mamie Creek, trending southwest as it heads for Antone Flat.

Antone Flat is, well, flat. The way is well marked with cairns. The route continues in gradual ups and downs past Antone Flat and then climbs over the top of a hill that has traditionally been used to mark an "E" for Escalante, a large whitewashed block letter. Beyond this last climb, follow the switchbacks down to Pine Creek. Hike along Pine Creek to the Escalante River. You'll come out on a dirt road. Follow the dirt road about 1.5 miles to UT 12.

To find the Escalante River Trailhead near the town of Escalante, the driver of your shuttle vehicle should go east of town on UT 12 past the high school, then turn left at a road junction signed "Escalante River Trailhead." Drive about 0.5 mile and turn left again. This turn is also signed. It's 1 more mile to the end of the road and the trailhead parking area.

Option: Note that this trailhead is the beginning point for a 15-mile hike down the Escalante River to the Escalante River Bridge (also on UT 12)—a popular and fairly easy shuttle/day hike through the southern edge of the Phipps–Death Hollow Instant Study Area. The hike passes Anasazi ruins, rock art, natural stone bridges, and arches. Pamphlets available at the trailhead describe the entire hike.

South-Central Utah, Grand Staircase– Escalante National Monument

Grand Staircase–Escalante is the largest national monument in the Lower 48. President Clinton established the Grand Staircase–Escalante National Monument (GSENM) on September 18, 1996, under the authority of the 1906 Antiquities Act. The monument is divided into three distinct regions: Grand Staircase, Kaiparowits Plateau, and Escalante Canyons. Monument administrators call the roadless areas a "Primitive Zone," and this zone is roughly analogous to proposed wilderness. The Utah Wilderness Coalition, a citizen group, has proposed an additional 100,000 acres as wilderness.

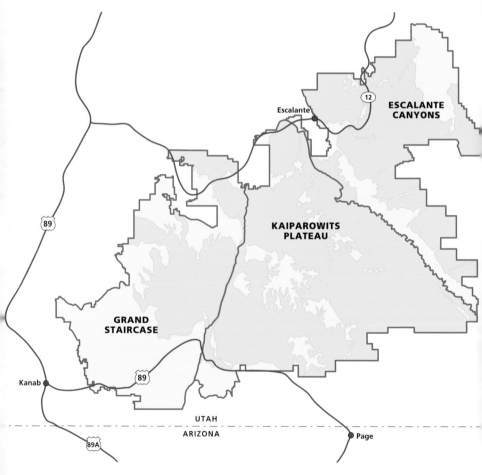

Grosvenor Arch, 152 feet off the ground and spanning 90 feet, is near the border of the Paria-Hackberry Wilderness Study Area.

Four wilderness study areas are in the Grand Staircase region: Paria–Hackberry, The Cockscomb, The Blues, and Mud Spring Canyon. There are five wilderness study areas in the Kaiparowits Plateau region: Carcass Canyon, Death Ridge, Fiftymile Mountain, Burning Hills, and Wahweap. Escalante Canyons is home to seven proposed wilderness areas: Phipps–Death Hollow, Steep Creek, North Escalante Canyons/The Gulch, Scorpion, Escalante Canyon Tract 1, Escalante Canyon Tract 5, and Devils Garden. Devils Garden is a borderline case because it's on the lower Kaiparowits Bench.

With the exception of Phipps–Death Hollow, all of the Grand Staircase–Escalante National Monument proposed wilderness areas are discussed in this section. Phipps–Death Hollow proposed wilderness and Box–Death Hollow designated wilderness are grouped together in Chapter 18 because they share boundary lines, road access, terrain similarities, and, most important, because some hiking trails and cross-country hiking routes include both areas.

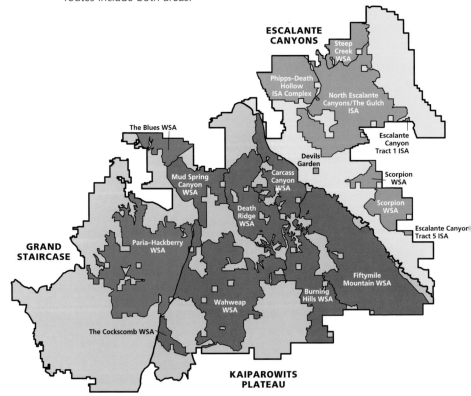

The full-service town of Kanab is located on US 89 near the southwestern corner of the national monument. Big Water is on US 89 south of the monument. Escalante and Boulder are on UT 12 on the northern border of the monument.

Escalante is the closest full-service town to the most frequently visited wilderness study areas. Escalante is also the organizational, operational center of the national monument. About 55 worker bees administer multiple layers of public land, including national forest, designated wilderness, Bureau of Land Management wilderness study areas, instant study areas (ISAs), national park lands, and national recreation areas (NRAs)—and how could we forget, a national monument!

In addition to offices in Escalante, a new visitor center was recently completed in Big Water, Utah. The Big Water Visitor Center, on US 89 near Lake Powell, focuses on paleontology and is built in the design of a spiral shell that mimics an ammonite, an extinct sea creature whose fossil remains are ubiquitous in the monument. Exhibits include most of the major fossil discoveries, including dinosaurs, found in the monument. At the time this book was written, a new visitor center had opened in Cannonville with an emphasis on human history; an improved visitor center opened in Kanab with an emphasis on geology and archaeology; an addition was being built in Escalante with an emphasis on biology and ecology; and a visitor center was planned for future construction in Glendale.

The GSENM has four distinct faces: frontcountry, passage zones, outback, and primitive zones. Most visitors never venture beyond the frontcountry, which is only about 4% of the monument. Passage zones are along major roadways and highways. "Outback" is a BLM term for zones that allow some motorized access to primitive areas. This book focuses on the primitive zones, where adventures that the BLM calls "self-directed" are virtually unlimited on 1,210,579 acres, or 65%, of the monument. The term "self-directed" hints at what backcountry visitors are in for: no facilities, few signs, and unmarked or only cursorily marked trails. Hiking in the primitive zones can range from easy to extremely strenuous, depending on the routes you choose. Good, detailed maps are essential for all hikes.

The strikingly beautiful geological features of the GSENM and its surrounding areas are its claim to fame. See the introductory material of this book for a description of the geology of the Colorado Plateau. In addition to the geological fantasia, a surprising variety of plants greets visitors to this mostly rocky land. In an area where elevations range from 4,000 feet to 10,188 feet, visitors see an impressive shift from desert to mountain forests. Adjacent to the GSENM borders, the Aquarius Plateau rises to more than 11,000 feet, and Lake Powell occupies the lowest elevations, at about 3,620 feet, giving nature an even broader palette.

Human History

The earliest human occupants were Fremont and Anasazi Indians. Some Anasazi rock art and rock shelters are easily accessed along the Escalante River not far from the town of Escalante. For more information on these Paleo-Indian cultures, see Human History in the Along the Trail section of this book.

In 1866, Captain James Andrus led a troop of Mormon cavalry into the valley during the Black Hawk War, a time of violent disagreement between Paiutes and Mormon settlers. Jacob Hamblin, explorer and Mormon missionary, passed through Escalante in 1871 to carry supplies for John Wesley Powell's second expedition. Powell had passed nearby on the Colorado River in 1869. However, it was two years later when Hamblin and Powell's brother-in-law, Almon Thompson, on separate attempts bumbled around the cliffs and canyons looking for a resupply route and finally figured out that the Escalante River was not the Dirty Devil River.

The deeply entrenched canyons and the rows of cliff-faced mesas slowed down exploration and settlement. Determined Mormons built roads through the most difficult terrain in Utah, using only manual labor and horsepower. Hole-in-the-Rock Road is named for one of these heroic road-building efforts, begun in 1879. The historic site of Dance Hall Rock dates from the era when the men and their families would meet to play music and dance together as a break from labor.

In 1934, Everett Ruess, an artist and memoirist, explored the canyons and mesas with two burros to carry his gear. Ruess disappeared, leaving no trace but his burros, later found in Davis Gulch. His legacy lives on through his writing. In this excerpt from a letter written by Ruess before he disappeared, he wrote, "I prefer the saddle to the streetcar and the star-sprinkled sky to a roof, the obscure and difficult trail, heading into the unknown, to any paved highway, and the deep peace of the wild to the discontent bred by cities."

The Civilian Conservation Corps, that governmental solution to out-of-work men during the Depression, built Hell's Backbone Rd. to connect the town of Escalante with Boulder. See Chapter 18 for historical information on the Boulder Mail Trail, a pack mule route that Hell's Backbone Rd. replaced.

Many of the lower-elevation canyons near the Colorado River were lost to view with the completion of the Glen Canyon Dam in 1964. Low water levels in 2003 and 2004 partially revealed canyons not seen for 20 years, including sections near the terminus of Hole-in-the-Rock Rd.

Various environmental groups, politicians, land managers, and local residents have been waging a war of words and conducting lawsuits over appropriate uses of the land. When we were there, we saw long banners hung on fences, with slogans like "S.U.W.A. OUT!" meaning "Southern Utah Wilderness Alliance, get out!" On the other side of the issue, register notebooks at trailheads had become suggestion boxes. If I recorded the suggestions here, we would have the first-ever R-rated wilderness guidebook. Once the rhetoric cools from flames to ashes, the opposing groups do get together and work out solutions. To present-day visitors, this means the monument is constantly being tuned in terms of regulations and road access. We suggest you stop at one of the visitor centers to get the most current information.

Highways and Roads That Access GSENM

US 89: A paved, two-lane highway connecting Page, Ariz., to Kanab, Utah (72 miles); serves the southwestern edge of the national monument. Chapters 17, 19.

Paria River Valley Rd.: 5 miles of dirt and gravel that are impassable when wet; a spur road off US 89 that serves the old Pahreah townsite, Western movie set, and Chinle Formation viewing area. Chapter 19.

Johnson Canyon Skutumpah Rd.: 46 miles of graded dirt, with upper section impassable when wet; traverses Grand Staircase section of the monument, from US 89 to Cottonwood Canyon Rd. Chapter 19.

Cottonwood Canyon Rd.: 46 miles of graded dirt and gravel, impassable when wet; serves The Cockscomb, Paria-Hackberry, and Mud Spring Canyon WSAs, as well as Kodachrome Basin State Park, and connects US 89 with UT 12. Chapters 19, 20.

UT 12: A paved, two-lane highway said by many to be the most scenic drive in Utah; connects the towns of Boulder and Escalante and offers access to trails and backcountry roads, including Hole-in-the-Rock Rd., Smoky Mountain Rd., Hell's Backbone Rd., and Burr Trail. Chapters 18, 20, 21, 22, 23.

Hole-in-the-Rock Rd.: 57 miles of graded dirt and gravel (hopefully recently graded if you don't want your teeth jarred out of your head), with the last 6 miles requiring a 4WD vehicle; leads southeast from the town of Escalante and provides access to famous slot canyons, as well as to hikes that continue into the Glen Canyon NRA. Chapter 22.

Smoky Mountain Rd.: 78 miles of graded dirt and gravel on top of the Kaiparowits Plateau, accessible from the town of Escalante in the north and from Big Water in the south; a remote, difficult drive that's rough and slow for long stretches (extra gas, water, emergency supplies, and 4WD are recommended, though some high-clearance, light-duty vehicles drive the road in dry weather). Chapter 23.

Hell's Backbone Rd.: 40 miles of dirt/gravel that loop onto the Aquarius Plateau from UT 12; freakishly narrow in spots, with dramatic dropoffs on both sides of the road, but provides access to Box–Death Hollow Wilderness and Phipps–Death Hollow ISA, as well as to the Boulder Mail Trail. Chapter 18.

Burr Trail Rd.: 31 paved miles in the monument, from Boulder to Capitol Reef National Park; 18 miles of steep, switchbacking dirt in Capitol Reef. Chapters 21, 40.

In addition to the main roads listed here, a network of 4WD roads leads to trailheads and canyon hiking routes. Numerous cattle-control gates on backcountry roads should be left closed or open, as you find them. Mountain biking is allowed on all secondary roads, but off-road travel by bike is prohibited. Off-road travel by ORVs is prohibited.

Paria-Hackberry and The Cockscomb WSAs

19

An old movie set in the Paria-Hackberry Wilderness Study Area. The colorful bands of rock in the background are mudstones about 220 million years old.

THESE TWO WILDERNESS STUDY AREAS OCCUPY a large expanse of terrain that is less often visited than most other sections of the Grand Staircase–Escalante National Monument (GSENM). Both The Cockscomb and Paria-Hackberry are southwest of the Kaiparowits Plateau, in the Grand Staircase. The "staircase" ascends from the Vermilion Cliffs to the White Cliffs to the Pink Cliffs. Nearby Paria Canyon–Vermilion Cliffs Wilderness receives such heavy use that reservations are necessary, but few people seem

LOCATION: South-Central Utah, Grand Staircase–Escalante NM

SIZE: Paria-Hackberry WSA: 136,222 acres
The Cockscomb WSA: 10,827 acres

ELEVATION RANGE: 4,700 to 7,271 feet

ECOREGION: Colorado Plateau

MILES OF TRAIL: No maintained trails; hiking routes are canyon floors and washes

ADMINISTRATION: BLM, Kanab Resource Area

MAPS: BLM: Arizona Strip District. USGS 1:100,000: Panguitch, Escalante, Smoky Mountain. USGS 1:24,000: Bull Valley Gorge, Slickrock Bench, Butler Valley, Horse Flat, Calico Peak, Skutumpah Creek, Deer Spring Point, Deer Range Point, Calico Peak, Nephi Point, Eightmile Pass, Fivemile Valley.

to cross to the north side of the highway to explore. (See Chapter 17 for the Paria Canyon designated wilderness.)

The Cockscomb actually looks like two cockscombs running parallel to each other for about 100 miles. Triangular piles and fins of rock stick up sharply like filed teeth with surprisingly uniform spaces between them. The giant fold in the earth's crust that forms The Cockscomb is part of the East Kaibab Monocline that runs from the Arizona border to Canaan Peak near Henrieville. The north-south flexure separates the Kaiparowits Plateau to the east from the Grand Staircase to the west. (See Geology and Ecosystems in the Along the Trail section of this book.)

US 89 runs along the southern edge of the terrain covered in this chapter. Kanab is the closest full-service town. Big Water is a small town with a big visitor center that focuses on fossils in the GSENM.

Paria River Valley Rd. is 5 miles of dirt and gravel passable only in dry weather. It provides access to Pahreah townsite (ghost town), a Western movie set, the colorful badlands near the townsite, and upper Paria River Canyon. The Chinle Formation, a Triassic mudstone about 220 million years old, is the most deeply colored formation in the Grand Staircase. Some of the best layers can be viewed near the old townsite north of US 89. The turnoff is signed between mileposts 30 and 31, and the area offers several easy day hikes that don't require directions. Watch for petrified wood deposits in the Chinle Formation.

Johnson Canyon Skutumpah Rd. provides access to Bull Valley Gorge from US 89 or from Cottonwood Canyon Rd. The northern section, where it connects to Cottonwood Canyon Rd., may be impassable when wet.

Cottonwood Canyon Rd. begins as pavement at Kodachrome Basin State Park in the north, then downgrades to dirt and gravel as it continues south to US 89. The dirt section is impassable when wet. It provides access to Grosvenor Arch, The Cockscomb, Round Valley Draw, and Hackberry Canyon. Morrison Formation badlands (having nothing to do with Jim Morrison of The Doors, but looking a similar bilious, drugged-out greenish gray) flank the road near the entrance to Round Valley Draw and Upper Hackberry Canyon. In places, Morrison Formation is the roadbed, which accounts for its slippery, ancient mud character when wet.

Because of its high sodium content, water from the Paria River is not potable, even after filtering. There are 24 undeveloped and six developed springs in the wilderness study area. These can be used for human consumption only after filtering or treatment.

Signs of human occupation include Fremont and Anasazi Indian ruins and rock art, pioneer cabins made of logs or stone, mining ruins, and 1950s–1960s Hollywood movie sets. Most modern-day uses revolve around ranching and recreation. Private ranchlands account for some of the oddities of the wilderness study boundary outlines. Respect private property and cattle control gates.

DAY HIKE: GROSVENOR ARCH AND COTTONWOOD NARROWS
One-Way Length: About 3 miles
Low and High Elevations: 6,000 and 6,500 feet
Difficulty: Easy (4WD recommended for access road)

Begin this trip on Cottonwood Canyon Rd., where the pavement ends near the entrance to Kodachrome Basin State Park (see road descriptions in the previous section). The state park offers improved camping and showers for a fee. The nearest town is Cannonville, at the intersection of Cottonwood Canyon Rd. and UT 12.

At mile 9.2, a short spur road leads to Grosvenor Arch. A picnic area and short hiking paths offer views of the arch. Grosvenor Arch consists of sandstone pillars capped with erosion-resistant conglomerate. If you were to stand on top of the arch, you would be 152 feet off the ground on a bit of rock about 4 feet wide that spans the 90-foot width of the space between the pillars. Viewing from the bottom is recommended—not climbing.

About 3.5 miles past Grosvenor Arch, just after the road dips into Cottonwood Canyon, a slot canyon is visible on the right (west). The narrows are not signed. Park alongside the road and hike down into the wash on a faint trail. Hike north (right-hand turn) where the canyon narrows dramatically. The section of narrows is about 0.25 mile long. Logs jammed in the canyon walls high over your head speak eloquently of the depth and force of past flash flooding. In hot weather, rattlesnakes take refuge in the shady canyon. Don't put your hands where your eyes can't see.

Turn around and hike south in the canyon. An amazing variety of plants survives here, including Mormon tea, prickly pear cactus, and juniper trees. The plants offer contrast to the deeply colored canyon walls. Cottonwood Narrows cuts through layers of sandstone associated with The Cockscomb and rejoins the road in 1.25 miles. Hike back up-canyon to return to your vehicle, or hike back on the road.

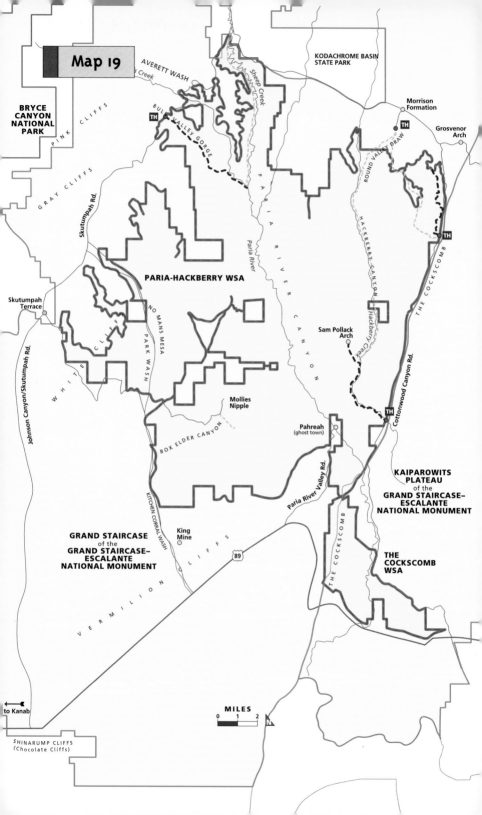

Map 19

BRYCE CANYON NATIONAL PARK

KODACHROME BASIN STATE PARK

AVERETT WASH

PINK CLIFFS

GRAY CLIFFS

Sheep Creek

BULL VALLEY GORGE

TH

Morrison Formation

TH

Grosvenor Arch

ROUND VALLEY DRAW

Skutumpah Rd.

PARIA RIVER CANYON

Paria River

HACKBERRY CANYON

TH

THE COCKSCOMB

PARIA-HACKBERRY WSA

Skutumpah Terrace

NO MANS MESA

PARK WASH

Sam Pollack Arch

Hackberry Creek

WHITE CLIFFS

Johnson Canyon/Skutumpah Rd.

Mollies Nipple

BOX ELDER CANYON

Pahreah (ghost town)

TH

Cottonwood Canyon Rd.

KAIPAROWITS PLATEAU of the GRAND STAIRCASE–ESCALANTE NATIONAL MONUMENT

KITCHEN CORRAL WASH

Paria River Valley Rd.

THE COCKSCOMB

GRAND STAIRCASE of the GRAND STAIRCASE–ESCALANTE NATIONAL MONUMENT

King Mine

89

THE COCKSCOMB WSA

VERMILION CLIFFS

← to Kanab

MILES
0   1   2

N

SHINARUMP CLIFFS (Chocolate Cliffs)

DAY HIKE: BULL VALLEY GORGE
One-Way Length: About 4 miles (longer with side trips and optional routes)
Low and High Elevations: 5,950 and 6,050 feet
Difficulty: Strenuous (4WD and rock-climbing ability recommended)

Bull Valley Gorge is a narrow slot that requires some climbing skills (one section might require a rappel) to negotiate dry waterfalls and boulders. Flash floods change the terrain of canyon floors on a seasonal basis.

From US 89, drive about 46 miles north on Cottonwood Canyon Rd. to Skutumpah Rd. (impassable when wet), or drive 2.7 miles south from Cannonville. At Skutumpah Rd. (signed for Bull Valley Gorge and Kanab), turn southwest and drive 7.8 miles to Bull Valley Gorge. Panoramic views of the White and Pink Cliffs are a highlight of the drive. The grave marker of Elijah Averett can be viewed along a 0.5-mile hiking trail at mile 4.5. At mile 5.9, there are good camping spots on Willis Creek. You can walk to a view of narrows in Willis Creek Canyon just a short distance from the camping area.

At about mile 7.8, park near a bridge over Bull Valley Gorge and walk 0.75 mile up-canyon along the rim to enter. Most day hikers enter the canyon and continue 2 to 3 miles down-canyon, then return the way they came. Bring 50 feet of rope, old hiking boots, and water. In striking contrast to the desert above, several Douglas-fir trees grow in the shaded canyon. Flash-flood danger is extreme.

DAY HIKE: LOWER HACKBERRY CANYON AND SAM POLLACK ARCH
One-Way Length: About 5.5 miles
Low and High Elevations: 5,360 and 6,000 feet
Difficulty: Easy (4WD required for approach road)

This narrow canyon in the Grand Staircase–Escalante National Monument never becomes a true "slot," but it is a beautiful, easy hike. See the previous directions for Cottonwood Canyon Rd. The unsigned trailhead is 12 miles north of US 89 and about 34 miles south of Cannonville. Take USGS 1:24,000 maps Calico Peak and Slickrock Bench for terrain details.

Hike west and then north on the canyon floor, through a Navajo Sandstone portion of The Cockscomb. The Cockscomb is almost 100 miles long, and Hackberry is one of the few canyons to cut through it. Navajo Sandstone gives way to Kayenta and Wingate Sandstone. The walls are saturated with red-orange color. Cottonwood trees and ponderosa pines, watered by a small stream, offer startling contrast. Wading shoes are useful for the many stream crossings and for sections where the stream is the easiest place to walk.

The first 2 miles as you hike up-canyon are the most narrow. The BLM prohibits camping in the narrows. Beyond that, backpackers can easily find places to camp. Watch for springs, which provide the area's best drinking water. Permits are required for overnight camping.

Sam Pollack Arch is located in a tributary of Hackberry Canyon. About 4 miles from the trailhead, note an old cabin on the west (left) side of Hackberry Creek. The cabin is partially hidden by sagebrush, so keep a sharp eye out for a bench that rises above the canyon floor about a dozen feet, with a dim trail leading onto it. Hike a few feet onto the bench and the Frank Watson cabin comes into view.

About 0.5 mile beyond this cabin landmark, hike northwest into the tributary for about 1.6 mile. Sam Pollack Canyon is strewn with rubble and requires some scrambling. A 20-foot dry waterfall blocks the way, but a path a couple hundred yards below it takes you up the east side of the canyon. Follow a ledge up-canyon until you are above the dry waterfall and can scramble back down into the canyon. The arch is about 1 mile up-canyon from the dry waterfall. Look high up on the north canyon wall. Cowboys of the Chynoweth family scratched their names into the rocks in several spots along Hackberry Canyon and its tributaries. In a cave north of the arch you can find "Art Chynoweth, 1912."

Return the way that you came, arriving back at your parking spot on Cottonwood Canyon Rd.

Kodachrome Basin State Park has a developed campground with showers. Some hikers use it as a base for exploring the Paria-Hackberry proposed wilderness just south of the state park.

Mud Spring Canyon and The Blues WSAs

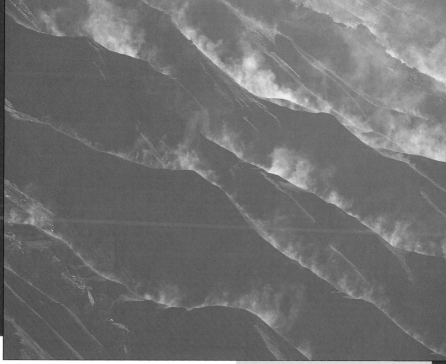

20

Tendrils of mist crawl up the folds of badlands.

MOST VISITORS TO the Grand Staircase–Escalante National Monument don't realize that Mud Spring Canyon and The Blues are part of the monument and are wilderness study areas. Mud Spring Canyon WSA is south of UT 12 and The Blues WSA is north of the highway. The closest towns are Henrieville, Cannonville, and Tropic—all small towns along the highway with limited but sufficient services for visitors to the monument and to nearby Bryce Canyon National Park. Escalante is the nearest town with a full array of services. See Chapter 38 for Bryce Canyon. See Chapter 19 for adjacent Paria-Hackberry WSA. See Chapter 23 for adjacent Death Ridge WSA on the Kaiparowits Plateau.

LOCATION: South-Central Utah, Grand Staircase–Escalante NM

SIZE: Mud Spring Canyon WSA: 38,075 acres
The Blues WSA: 19,030 acres

ELEVATION RANGE: 6,400 to 8,200 feet

ECOREGION: Colorado Plateau

MILES OF TRAIL: None; hiking routes are canyon floors and washes, and there are marked hiking trails in adjacent Dixie NF

ADMINISTRATION: Escalante Interagency Office

MAPS: Dixie NF: Powell, Escalante, and Teasdale Ranger Districts. USGS 1:100,000: Panguitch, Escalante. USGS 1:24,000: Tropic Canyon, Pine Lake, Cannonville, Henrieville, Canaan Peak, Butler Valley

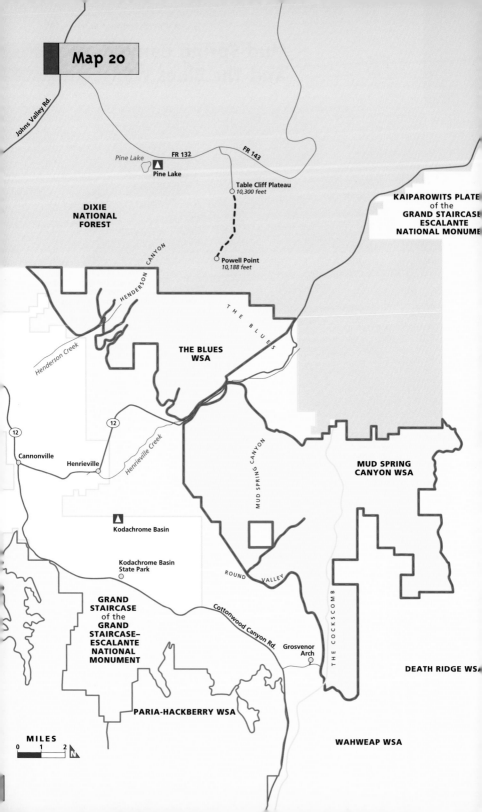

Map 20

Johns Valley Rd.

FR 132   FR 143

Pine Lake
▲ Pine Lake

Table Cliff Plateau
10,300 feet

**DIXIE
NATIONAL
FOREST**

KAIPAROWITS PLATE
of the
**GRAND STAIRCASE
ESCALANTE
NATIONAL MONUME**

Powell Point
10,188 feet

HENDERSON CANYON

Henderson Creek

THE BLUES

**THE BLUES
WSA**

12

12

Cannonville

Henrieville

Henrieville Creek

MUD SPRING CANYON

**MUD SPRING
CANYON WSA**

▲
Kodachrome Basin

Kodachrome Basin
State Park

ROUND   VALLEY

THE COCKSCOMB

**GRAND
STAIRCASE**
of the
**GRAND
STAIRCASE–
ESCALANTE
NATIONAL
MONUMENT**

Cottonwood Canyon Rd.

Grosvenor
Arch

DEATH RIDGE WSA

PARIA-HACKBERRY WSA

MILES
0   1   2   N

WAHWEAP WSA

The Bureau of Land Management (BLM) readily admits that "the most important recreational use of The Blues WSA is general sightseeing by tourists on Highway 12." Between the towns of Escalante and Henrieville, overlooks and pullouts from the highway offer views of the amphitheater of The Blues, and of the badlands and sandstone plateaus above Mud Spring.

From the town of Tropic, roads lead east and northeast into the Henderson Creek drainage of The Blues WSA, where 4WD jeep tracks are cherry-stemmed about 5 miles into the roadless area. In this section, noise from 4WD roads and from trucks on UT 12 can only be escaped by hiking farther into Henderson Canyon.

Cottonwood Canyon Rd. leads south from UT 12 at Cannonville, with access to Kodachrome Basin State Park, Round Valley, Mud Spring Canyon, Grosvenor Arch, and The Cockscomb. The dirt section can be impassable when wet. Day hikes that include Grosvenor Arch and The Cockscomb are described in Chapter 19. If you hike south and west of Cottonwood Canyon Rd., you are in the Paria-Hackberry or The Cockscomb WSAs. If you hike east or northeast of the road, you are in Mud Spring Canyon WSA. About 4,000 acres of The Cockscomb geological uplift are in Mud Spring Canyon WSA. The eastern section of the WSA is bluish-colored shale that forms eroded badlands similar to the Blue Hills next to Mount Ellen in the Henry Mountains.

Perennial streams in The Blues WSA and in Mud Spring Canyon WSA are not potable. Bring your own water and limit your explorations to day hiking or overnight backpacking.

Rock climbers make use of sheer cliffs along Henrieville Creek in both WSAs. Access is directly off UT 12 where it crosses Henrieville Creek.

Respect private property and cattle control gates.

DAY HIKE: TABLE CLIFF PLATEAU AND POWELL POINT
One-Way Length: About 2 miles
Low and High Elevations: 7,500 and 10,188 feet
Difficulty: Easy (4WD required for access road)

Most of the popular 4WD roads make their way through national forest lands outside the WSA boundaries, with Powell Point above The Blues WSA being the best jeep expedition. To visit 10,188-foot Powell Point, drive west on UT 12, past Tropic and through the northern tip of Bryce Canyon NP. Turn northeast on Johns Valley Rd. (UT 22), then turn east on FR 132 (signed for Pine Lake Campground) and drive about 13 miles to Table Cliff Plateau. Powell Point Trailhead at mile 14.4 is where the jeep track ends. FR 132 is graded gravel to Pine Lake Campground, then becomes rocky where seasonal high water from creeks washes over the road. A 4WD vehicle is recommended beyond the campground. Anglers and day hikers frequent Pine Lake. A fee is required for overnight camping.

On Table Cliff Plateau the road winds among trees; drive carefully to avoid vehicle damage. Unimproved camping spots are abundant on the plateau—no fee required, no crowds, less noise, but also no water source. Be prepared to practice Leave-No-Trace, high-desert camping.

Day hiking to the edge of the plateau for scenic overlooks is good all along the last 2 to 3 miles of FR 132. Look southwest to view the Henderson Canyon section of The Blues, and look southeast to see the gray-blue badlands that give this WSA its name.

Powell Point, part of the Pink Cliffs step of the Grand Staircase, bears the name of John Wesley Powell. From where the road ends, the point is about a 0.5-mile hike.

Chinle Shale, a Triassic mudstone about 220 million years old, is the most deeply colored formation in the Grand Staircase.

North Escalante Canyons/ The Gulch ISA, Steep Creek WSA, and Escalante Canyon Tract I ISA

21

Author Lynna Howard is dwarfed by the sheer walls of a canyon in the Grand Staircase–Escalante National Monument.

NORTH ESCALANTE CANYONS is a proposed wilderness that encompasses several tributary canyons on the north side of the Escalante River. The Gulch, Horse Canyon, Little Death Hollow, Wolverine Canyon, and Escalante Canyon are all excellent hiking routes. Of these, Little Death Hollow and Wolverine are true slot canyons for short distances. Most of the

LOCATION: South-Central Utah, Grand Staircase–Escalante NM
SIZE: North Escalante Canyons/The Gulch ISA: 120,204 acres
   Steep Creek WSA: 21,896 acres
   Escalante Canyon Tract 1 ISA: 360 acres
ELEVATION RANGE: 4,800 to 7,600 feet
ECOREGION: Colorado Plateau
MILES OF TRAIL: About 4
ADMINISTRATION: Escalante Interagency Office
MAPS: Trails Illustrated: Maps #213 and #710.
USGS 1:100,000: Escalante.
USGS 1:24,000: Steep Creek Bench, Lamp Stand, King Bench, Red Breaks, Pioneer Mesa, Wagon Box Mesa, Silver Falls Bench, Moody Creek.

other canyon routes can vary from easy strolls to strenuous hikes depending mainly on distance. When hiking routes include canyon floors, they are not considered "trails" because there's no way to maintain or mark a route that is altered and swept clean by seasonal flash flooding. There are many trailheads and almost no "trails." Hikes that extend into the Glen Canyon National Recreation Area are popular.

Spring and late autumn are the best times to visit. A lot of terrain is drained by the deeply entrenched canyons, so check the weather before you follow routes that include canyon floors where flash-flood danger is high.

One of the canyons we're exploring in this chapter is called The Gulch, but it has nothing to do with the Grand Gulch–Cedar Mesa complex of proposed wilderness areas, 75 miles east as the crow flies. (See Chapter 30 for Grand Gulch.)

Escalante Canyon Tract 1 ISA is a 360-acre chunk that doesn't show up on most wilderness study maps. It includes a trailhead right at the base of the Circle Cliffs for a hike down Silver Falls Creek. On its own, this ISA is not big enough to be a wilderness, but combined with Glen Canyon NRA, with which it shares a border, it becomes an important extension of protected lands.

Potable water supplies in perennial streams and springs make this an excellent location for extended day-hiking or backpacking. Careful planning for stops at known water sources is essential. Experienced hikers with a good set of maps can plan dozens of loop hikes that include crossing the benches between the many canyons. Benches near the Circle Cliffs are decorated with odd-shaped Kayenta Sandstone knobs that photographers find interesting.

Boulder, on UT 12, is the nearest town. Capitol Reef National Park shares the eastern border. Glen Canyon NRA lies to the south. Dixie National Forest lands are to the north, and to the west are more wilderness study areas (see Chapters 18 and 22).

Burr Trail is the main access road. It is paved for 31 miles as it leaves the town of Boulder, but at the Capitol Reef National Park border an unpaved section becomes rocky and sandy. (See Chapter 40 for the Capitol Reef section.) Large motor homes and vehicles pulling trailers might have difficulty negotiating Burr Trail Rd. because of tight switchbacks. Side roads off Burr Trail Rd. require 2WD high-clearance in dry weather, and 4WD at the least sign of moisture. Unimproved camping sites can be found in many places along Burr Trail Rd. One improved camping area is provided at Deer Creek, 6 miles southeast of Boulder.

From the town of Boulder to UT 276 (near the Bullfrog Marina on Lake Powell), Burr Trail Rd. is 63 miles of some of the most scenic driving in Utah. As it travels east and southeast from Boulder, Burr Trail Rd. winds around buttes of Navajo Sandstone patterned like muffins rising in irregular pans. Ponderosa pines grow in cracks in the sandstone. Where the road crosses The Gulch, Wingate Sandstone cliffs embrace it as it descends.

Just east of The Gulch, Burr Trail Rd. turns sharply northeast and enters Long Canyon, a narrow defile characterized by even higher and tighter red sandstone cliffs. This 7-mile-long section has fewer pullouts and camping areas.

Once you're out of Long Canyon, the Circle Cliffs dominate the view from Burr Trail Rd. Named by John Wesley Powell, this distinctive escarpment sports wildly colored Chinle Formation at its base, then rises in Wingate and Kayenta ramparts to surround the Escalante River basin and its many-branched canyons.

UT 12 offers limited access from the west. Calf Creek Recreation Area is next to the western border of North Escalante Canyons/The Gulch ISA. With its developed campground, interpretive trails, and short hikes to spectacular waterfalls, Calf Creek is a favorite spot for families. The campground can also be used as a base camp for short drives to hikes along the Escalante River and in Phipps Wash. For a full description of Calf Creek and associated hiking opportunities, see Chapter 18.

DAY HIKE: THE GULCH, UPPER SECTION
One-Way Length: 4–10 miles (may be extended to overnight backpack)
Low and High Elevations: 5,560 and 6,000 feet
Difficulty: Easy

At mile 9.6 from Boulder on Burr Trail Rd., trailheads for hiking The Gulch are signed, so keep a sharp eye out for miniscule parking areas that appear suddenly around curves. Drive carefully—sightlines along Burr Trail Rd. are too short for safe ingress and egress.

Even if you have precious little time, you'll still find a short day hike into the upper (north) section of The Gulch rewarding. Hiking is easy along a visible trail that frequently crosses a small stream. If you are not backpacking, the campground at Deer Creek is a good base camp location. This hike is entirely within the Steep Creek WSA.

From the trailhead, you can hike up or down The Gulch. We recommend the upper section for day-hiking because it narrows after about a mile to become a spectacular setting. In the spring, acid-green leaves contrast with vertical red cliffs. In the autumn, golds and yellows look like lamps lit in the shadows.

Steep Creek Canyon enters from the left at mile 1 and adds its trickle of a stream to the flow in The Gulch. A side trip of several miles is possible up Steep Creek, but The Gulch is a more scenic hike. Up-canyon from the confluence with Steep Creek, The Gulch narrows and hikers make their way around small waterfalls, through groves of cottonwood trees, and under the giant shell shapes of alcoves in the cliff walls. Scattered ponderosa pines add another element to the beautiful setting. The canyon looks best in low-angle light, in early morning or late afternoon/evening.

At mile 4, you reach the junction of Water Canyon and The Gulch, a good place for day hikers to head back to the trailhead. The hiking trail becomes rougher and sometimes disappears up-canyon from this junction.

At about mile 8, Indian Hollow Canyon provides an opportunity to view Lamanite Arch. Turn left into Indian Hollow and hike about 1.5 miles to the arch.

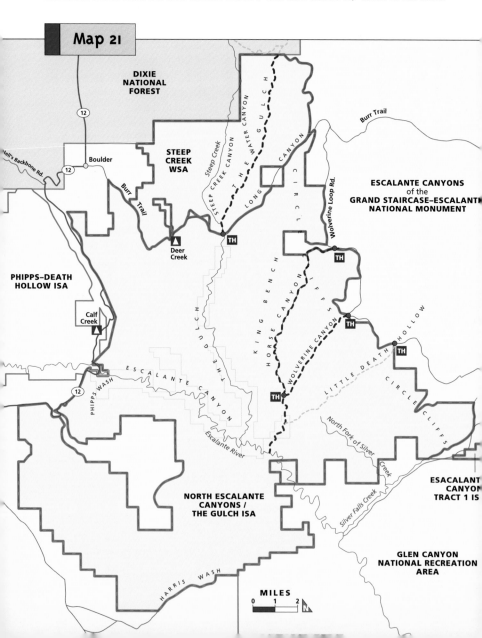

Hiking in Indian Hollow requires some bushwhacking. Long sleeves and long pants are recommended. Backpackers can camp in The Gulch and use the spring-fed stream of Indian Hollow as a water source. Treat or filter the water before drinking. There are no good camping spots in Indian Hollow Canyon, but the arch is worth the trip. It's a squarish bridge of stone whose opening frames ponderosa pines in the distance. The 10-mile hike (20 miles round trip) from the trailhead to Lamanite Arch is too much for most day hikers.

LOOP HIKE, SHUTTLE DAY HIKE, OR BACKPACK:
HORSE AND WOLVERINE CANYONS
One-Way Length: 6.5–20 miles
Low and High Elevations: 5,000 and 6,000 feet
Difficulty: Moderate (4WD recommended for access road)

The mileage estimate for this loop hike varies from 6.5 to 20 miles, depending on the condition of the 4WD track into Horse Canyon and on the availability of a shuttle vehicle to leave at Wolverine Creek Trailhead. When we were there, the 4WD track down Horse Canyon was open and dry; however, there was talk of closing it to vehicles, and wet weather may also close the track. If the Horse Canyon track cannot be driven for whatever reason, and you have no shuttle vehicle or mountain bike to leave at Wolverine Creek Trailhead, then the distance you'll walk on this loop is 20 miles. A shuttle vehicle will reduce the miles by 4.5 even if Horse Canyon is closed to vehicles. If the Horse Canyon track is open, you can drive about 9 miles down-canyon, subtracting another 9 miles from the total, leaving only 6.5 miles of hiking.

Narrow jeeps or ORVs might be able to drive even farther down Horse Canyon, but we discourage this even if the track is open. Hikers coming down Wolverine and Little Death Hollow Canyons will not appreciate the engine noise. Unlike the watery slot of Little Death Hollow, the Wolverine Canyon/Horse Canyon loop can be hiked in almost any weather. The usual warnings against hiking in flash-flood weather apply. The hike is entirely within the North Escalante Canyons/The Gulch ISA.

From the town of Boulder, drive about 18.5 miles on Burr Trail Rd. to Wolverine Loop Rd. (See the description in the introduction to this chapter for more details on Burr Trail Rd.) Wolverine Loop Rd. eventually makes a loop, joining with Moody Canyons Rd. to return to Burr Trail Rd. On this loop through the northeastern corner of the Grand Staircase–Escalante National Monument, there are a half-dozen prime hiking routes. Take the USGS 1:24,000 maps Lamp Stand, King Bench, Red Breaks, Pioneer Mesa, Wagon Box Mesa, and Silver Falls Bench if you'd like to spend several days exploring the terrain served by Wolverine Loop Rd. The Pioneer Mesa and King Bench maps cover the hike in Horse and Wolverine Canyons.

At mile 18.5 from Boulder, the turn onto Wolverine Loop Rd. is signed, with Capitol Reef, Horse Canyon, Wolverine Canyon, and Little Death Hollow noted as destinations. Turn south on this graded dirt road (suitable for high-clearance 2WD in dry weather) and drive about 5.7 miles to an intersection with the Horse Canyon 4WD track. Horse Canyon was signed when we were there. Although this is clearly a road intersection on the ground, the Horse Canyon track is not shown on maps. A large stand of cottonwood trees offers good unimproved camping spots where Horse Canyon cuts through the Circle Cliffs.

If the Horse Canyon track is open to vehicles and yours is equipped with 4WD, continue down-canyon. Large deposits of petrified wood are visible along the road. More camping spots and even a few trees line the wide canyon. The character of the canyon changes dramatically when it narrows and Wingate Sandstone cliffs rise hundreds of feet on either side.

Several line shacks of uncertain lineage are still used by local cowboys. Line cowboys lived in a cabin, camp, or shack in a remote part of a ranch and kept cows from ranging into territory belonging to other ranchers. The "line" was ridden as a sort of cow-policing operation before the installation of fences. Visitors to present-day proposed wilderness areas often come upon the ruins of line shacks from the late 1800s or early 1900s.

Close any cattle-control gates after passing through. A line shack near the south canyon wall at about mile 9 is a good place to stop. Springs that feed lower Horse Canyon begin near the shack. Seeps and springs support a population of birds, grasses, and willows. After passing a wire fence in a narrow section, and then also passing

In a canyon called The Gulch, creek waters mirror green foliage and the reflected light from canyon walls.

the line shack associated with springs in Horse Canyon, continue down-canyon for about 1.5 miles to the confluence with Wolverine Canyon. Wolverine Canyon opens on your left and is obviously a major tributary.

Wolverine Canyon is about 5 miles long. As you hike up-canyon, the narrowest and most impressive sections are in the first 3 miles, with the canyon closing in to about 5 feet wide in places. There are pools of water and boulders to skirt, but the hiking never becomes difficult. Wolverine Canyon widens and becomes shallow where it enters Wolverine Petrified Wood Natural Area. Petrified wood logs are abundant even before you enter the natural area, with entire logs strewn along the length of Wolverine Canyon. Hike through the natural area, enjoying more fossilized trees from Utah's distant past. Collecting petrified wood is prohibited. At the trailhead on Wolverine Loop Rd., hopefully you will have left a shuttle vehicle.

Wolverine Creek Trailhead is signed and is about 4.5 miles from the junction of Wolverine Loop Rd. and the 4WD track down Horse Canyon. If you don't have a shuttle vehicle, roadwalk to return to your starting point in Horse Canyon.

Option: Once you get started hiking down Horse Canyon, you might find it so charming that you decide to skip Wolverine Canyon and continue to the confluence with the Escalante River (see USGS map Red Breaks). If you hike all of Horse Canyon (not driving any of the 4WD track), it's about 13 miles to the Escalante River. There are plenty of campsites above the flash-flood plain. Springs and perennial streams provide water after about mile 9.

Option: An alternate loop hike in this area is Little Death Hollow to Horse Canyon to Wolverine Canyon. However, Little Death Hollow requires swimming, wading, Class V climbing, 40 feet of rope, and quite a bit of muscle and determination— and it can be impossible after a rain. Little Death Hollow Trailhead is signed, about 7.3 miles from Horse Canyon, and about 12.8 miles from the intersection of Burr Trail Rd. with the eastern half of Wolverine Loop Rd.

22 Scorpion WSA, Escalante Canyon Tract 5 ISA, and Devils Garden ISA

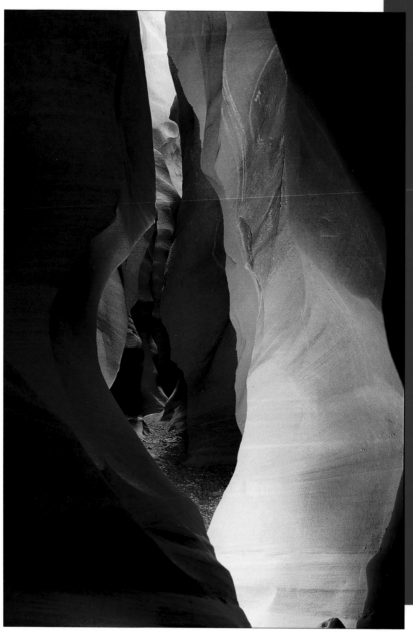

Brimstone Gulch's slot canyon eventually gets so narrow that you can't squirm through it.

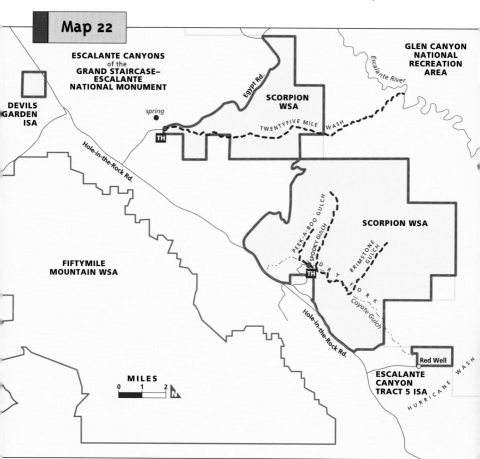

Map 22

ESCALANTE CANYONS
of the
GRAND STAIRCASE–
ESCALANTE
NATIONAL MONUMENT

DEVILS
GARDEN
ISA

GLEN CANYON
NATIONAL
RECREATION
AREA

Escalante River

Egypt Rd.

spring

Hole-in-the-Rock Rd.

TH

SCORPION
WSA

TWENTYFIVE MILE WASH

SCORPION WSA

PEEK-A-BOO GULCH

SPOOKY GULCH

BRIMSTONE GULCH

FIFTYMILE
MOUNTAIN WSA

DRY FORK

Coyote Gulch

TH

Hole-in-the-Rock Rd.

MILES

0   1   2

Red Well

ESCALANTE
CANYON
TRACT 5 ISA

HURRICANE WASH

LOCATION: South-Central Utah, Grand Staircase–Escalante NM

SIZE: Scorpion WSA: 35,884 acres
Escalante Canyon Tract 5 ISA: 760 acres
Devils Garden ISA: 638 acres

ELEVATION RANGE: 4,200 to 5,600 feet

ECOREGION: Colorado Plateau

MILES OF TRAIL: None; hiking routes are canyon floors and washes

ADMINISTRATION: Escalante Interagency Office

MAPS: Trails Illustrated: Map #710.
USGS 1:100,000: Escalante, Smoky Mountain.
USGS 1:24,000: Tenmile Flat, Seep Flat, Red Breaks, Big Hollow Wash, Scorpion Gulch, Egypt, Sunset Flat, Moody Creek, King Mesa, Sooner Bench, Davis Gulch.

HOLE-IN-THE-ROCK RD. IS about 55 miles of graded dirt and gravel connecting UT 12 near the town of Escalante to the Hole-in-the-Rock historical site and overlook on the shore of Lake Powell. The areas profiled in this chapter follow the corridor of Hole-in-the-Rock Rd. Most of the road is suitable for 2WD sedans. The last 6 miles, where the road enters the Glen Canyon National Recreation Area, are rougher, and 4WD with high clearance is required. Trailheads along the road are located on the Kaiparowits Bench. A few miles of hot, sandy walking are the norm before the canyons narrow and become more interesting. In addition to the otherworldly beauty of the canyons, archaeological sites—especially rock art of Anasazi and Fremont cultures— are prevalent.

About 56 miles of routes that begin in Scorpion WSA are canyon tributaries of the Escalante River. Where these canyons exit the Grand Staircase–Escalante NM, they enter Glen Canyon NRA. The Escalante River meets the backed-up waters of Lake Powell near Cow Canyon, where it proceeds to add its own load of silt to the reservoir.

Devils Garden is a picnic area at mile 12 on Hole-in-the-Rock Rd. Although this is an Instant Study Area, it is not considered a good candidate for wilderness designation owing to its proximity to the road. The setting is the base of the Straight Cliffs that edge Kaiparowits Plateau, a geologically and visually intriguing area. Eroded

Lynna Howard surveys a slickrock plateau near Harris Wash in the Grand Staircase–Escalante National Monument.

sandstone pockets, balanced rocks, arches, and knobs account for the "Devils Garden" name. There's no water source, so bring your own supply for short hikes in the area—excursions suitable even for small children. The BLM has provided tables, fire pits, restrooms, and footpaths.

Escalante Canyon Tract 5 ISA is too small to be a wilderness area on its own, but combined with land in Glen Canyon NRA, it is an important addition to the famous Coyote Gulch canyon system. Coyote Gulch is well known to photographers all over the world as one of the prime examples of the narrow and sensuously colored canyons of the Colorado Plateau: When the light is right, the cold stone takes on the warm colors of flesh or fruit, and the water-carved shapes in the canyon walls mimic the rounded shapes of living forms. About 0.5 mile of the 15-mile-long Coyote Gulch is in Escalante Canyon Tract 5 ISA. Spur roads to Red Well and Hurricane Wash Trailheads are signed at mile 30.4 and 33.5 on Hole-in-the-Rock Rd. Coyote Gulch deepens and boasts natural bridges, arches, and large waterfalls as it drains east toward the Escalante River and Lake Powell.

Potable water is scarce throughout the area, but does appear once you cross into Glen Canyon NRA from the Harris Wash access. Experienced canyoneers who are looking for a long excursion can begin at Harris Wash and hike/wade/swim/climb 43 miles to Lake Powell. Twentyfive Mile Wash hosts a perennial stream. With its riparian areas, entrenched canyon, and access to the Escalante River in Glen Canyon NRA, Twentyfive Mile Wash is also a popular hiking route.

BACKPACK: TWENTYFIVE MILE WASH
One-Way Length: 14 miles
Low and High Elevations: 4,500 and 4,960 feet
Difficulty: Moderate

At mile 16.3 on Hole-in-the-Rock Rd., turn east-northeast and drive about 3.5 miles to Twentyfive Mile Wash Trailhead (note that this spur road continues, providing access to Egypt Trailhead, and is signed "Egypt"). The name Twentyfive Mile is a relic of cowboy maps based on horseback distances from the town of Escalante.

From the trailhead, hike down the dry wash. Carry enough water to get you through the first 5 to 6 miles. As you proceed down-canyon, this hike becomes more interesting. You walk past and then down into various layers of rock, including Navajo, Kayenta, and Wingate Sandstones. Although there is a user-created trail all the way to the Escalante River, beaver ponds and seasonal flooding create areas where hikers might have to wade. Desert shrubs and cacti bloom from spring into fall, but late spring is the optimum viewing time for blossoming plants.

Choose campsites that are above the flash-flood plain. The confluence of Twentyfive Mile Wash and the Escalante River is brushy and not a good camping area. Filter or treat all water before drinking. Springs in Twentyfive Mile Wash are better drinking water sources than the Escalante River.

This hike is 14 miles (one way) to the Escalante River, but many excursions can be made into tributary canyons. If you want to explore side canyons, allow at least three days for the trip. If you want to explore up or down the Escalante River, add another day. About half of the hike is in Scorpion WSA and half is in Glen Canyon NRA. The boundary line is signed. Sunset Flat and Moody Creek USGS 1:24,000 maps cover the hike. Return the way you came.

Option: Experienced desert hikers can fashion a loop hike that includes Fence Canyon, which is accessible from the Egypt Trailhead. Getting from Egypt Trailhead to Twentyfive Mile Trailhead requires cross-country hiking or a shuttle vehicle.

DAY HIKE: PEEK-A-BOO, SPOOKY, AND BRIMSTONE SLOT CANYONS
One-Way Length: 4–10 miles
Low and High Elevations: 4,200 and 5,050 feet
Difficulty: Moderate to Strenuous

You can explore these three slot canyons in a single day. Turn southeast on the signed Hole-in-the-Rock Rd., 3.6 miles east of the town of Escalante. Watch for the Dry Fork Trail left-hand turn off the main road at about mile 24.5. Park at the trailhead 1.7 miles from Hole-in-the-Rock Rd.

Follow a rough path on the north edge that drops down into the Dry Fork section of Coyote Gulch. The Peek-a-boo slot canyon boasts a double natural bridge. Spooky Canyon starts out wide, but narrows to a slice so thin that you'll have to doff your pack and carry it sideways. Brimstone offers the best photo opportunities and the darkest passage. The narrow sections of Brimstone stay cool even on hot days, so you might want to bring a jacket. The sandstone walls of all slot canyons can be abrasive, so I prefer long sleeves, long pants, and a pair of thin gloves. It's hard to convince oneself to dress that way in the hot parking lot, so I carry at least a shirt and gloves in my daypack.

All three slot canyons are usually dry and sandy, but be aware of flash-flood danger, especially in Brimstone. The longest of the three canyons, Brimstone gathers more water during thunderstorms. Brimstone sometimes retains pools of water that hikers have to wade through. There are no reliable drinking water sources. Most of the hiking is relatively easy, though deep sand will slow you down as you hike from the mouth of one canyon to another. Fit and adventurous hikers can climb over chockstones and past dry waterfalls, exiting at the top of Spooky and then crossing the plateau to the top of Peek-a-boo.

Fiftymile Mountain, Death Ridge, Carcass Canyon, Burning Hills, and Wahweap WSAs

23

The Kaiparowits Plateau

"BURNING," "CARCASS," "DEATH"—the names alone alert visitors to the character of these wilderness study areas on the Kaiparowits Plateau. Water is scarce, and the vast landscape conceals dangers for both hikers and motorists. Dirt roads separate these WSAs from each other, but on the ground there's no way to really tell when you leave one WSA and enter another.

Fiftymile Mountain is the largest WSA in the Grand Staircase–Escalante National Monument. It gets its name from the approximately 50 miles of Straight Cliffs that mark the eastern edge of

LOCATION: South-Central Utah, Grand Staircase–Escalante NM

SIZE: Fiftymile Mountain WSA: 148,802 acres
Death Ridge WSA: 63,667 acres
Carcass Canyon WSA: 47,351 acres
Burning Hills WSA: 61,550 acres
Wahweap WSA: 134,400 acres

ELEVATION RANGE: 4,000 to 7,650 feet

ECOREGION: Colorado Plateau

MILES OF TRAIL: None; hiking routes are on vehicular ways, canyon floors, and washes

ADMINISTRATION: Escalante Interagency Office

MAPS: Trails Illustrated: Maps #710 and #213. USGS 1:100,000: Escalante, Smoky Mountain. USGS 1:24,000: Escalante, Dave Canyon, Death Ridge, Carcass Canyon, Petes Cove, Horse Mountain, Collet Top, Basin Canyon, Horse Flat, Fourmile Bench, Ship Mt. Point, East of the Navajo, Blackburn Canyon, Sooner Bench, Needle Eye Point, Lower Coyote Spring, Nipple Butte, Tibbet Bench, Smoky Hollow, Warm Creek Bay, Lone Rock.

Kaiparowits Plateau. The 1,000-foot-high cliffs are breached by only one 4WD road, Left Hand Collet Canyon Rd. off Smoky Mountain Rd. The road down Left Hand Collet requires a short-wheel-base, high-clearance 4WD vehicle and considerable driving skill. It is impassable when wet and does not appear on all maps. Some maps show a 4WD track in Hurricane Wash near the border of the proposed wilderness, but that road is now closed to motorized vehicles and is classified as an unmaintained hiking trail.

With 75 miles of graded dirt and gravel, Smoky Mountain Rd. is the longest backcountry byway in the national monument. For most of the hikes described in this chapter, begin in the town of Escalante and turn south on 500 West St., next to an RV park. At mile 2, the road leaves private land, becomes Smoky Mountain Rd., and enters GSENM. About 71 miles of Smoky Mountain Rd. are rough. High-clearance and 4WD vehicles are recommended. A detailed map is necessary for route-finding through many unmarked intersections. Trails Illustrated maps do not show all of the roads or the entire plateau. Bring USGS topo maps, extra gas, water, and spare tires.

From the town of Escalante, Smoky Mountain Rd. travels south across the Kaiparowits Plateau to Big Water on US 89. Near Big Water, the Kelly Grade section is a loop of steep switchbacks hung on the southern end of the Kaiparowits Plateau. The switchbacks serve up a grand, sweeping vista that includes all of lower Glen Canyon and Navajo Mountain.

There are literally hundreds of opportunities for primitive camping along Smoky Mountain Rd. and associated side roads. A thin cover of piñon-juniper woodlands across much of the plateau contrives to provide a bit of shade here and there. Hidden from view until you're right on top of them are canyons with remarkably varied ecosystems in their narrow confines.

Anasazi and Fremont ruins and rock art dot the Kaiparowits Plateau. Well-preserved red pictographs are painted onto the walls of Alvey Wash near the mouth of Coal Canyon, about 4 miles south of the town of Escalante, on the west side of Smoky Mountain Rd.

Burning Hills WSA is named for underground coal fires that have been burning for as long as a hundred years. This is not a good place to visit in the heat of the summer, as the fires raise the ground temperature. The BLM tried to put out the fires in the 1960s, but Smoky Mountain still smokes. There is little vegetation, no shade, and no water. The red-orange hills are tucked into the southeast corner of the Kaiparowits Plateau, and it can take a full day to drive about 60 miles to this unique area. See the following road directions for Left Hand Collet Canyon to find Collet Junction. Where you have the choice of turning left for Collet Canyon or right (south), turn right on Croton Rd. (signed as "Big Water 69 miles") and drive southeast about 8 miles to a Y intersection. Take the right fork (signed as "Big Water 61 miles") and drive about 4 to 5 miles to explore Burning Hills.

> **DAY HIKE:** TRAP CANYON
> One-Way Length: 3 miles
> Low and High Elevations: 6,800 and 7,100 feet
> Difficulty: Easy (4WD required for approach road)

Trap Canyon in Death Ridge WSA is one of the hidden jewels on the Kaiparowits Plateau. Cowboys used the narrow canyon as a corral, trapping horses and other stock in its narrow confines by placing fences across the ends. At a spring near the head of Trap Canyon, we saw the paw prints of a black bear mother and cub. There are several springs in the area, but they are unreliable and difficult for humans to use, so bring your own water.

In the canyon, the odd sights of mature Douglas fir trees, ponderosa pines, and wild roses create an environment completely different from the plateau. Deer and other wild animals use the canyon and feed on plants near hanging gardens. One dry waterfall near the entrance forces hikers to scramble, but it's an easy detour. Trap Canyon narrows to about 4 feet in one spot and is relatively narrow for about a mile. Ice and snow linger in the shadows into late May. The best Trap Canyon has to offer can be hiked in 3 miles, 6 miles round trip. Turn around where the canyon widens.

The canyon is easy to hike, but finding it is difficult. From the town of Escalante, drive south on Smoky Mountain Rd. for about 8 miles. Take the right (west) fork at the junction with Death Ridge Rd. (signed) and drive southwest about 3 miles, watching for a dirt road on your left that descends steeply into Trap Canyon Wash (not signed). If you come to an orange-and-black "Lease Road" sign, you have missed the Trap Canyon turnoff. Drive 1 mile down the steep road into Trap Canyon Wash and park there. The USGS 1:24,000 map Death Ridge is a helpful guide to the roads.

> **DAY HIKE:** LEFT HAND COLLET CANYON
> One-Way Length: 3–5 miles
> Low and High Elevations: 5,400 and 6,410 feet
> Difficulty: Moderate

This hike is in Carcass Canyon WSA. As noted in the introduction to this chapter, a 4WD road leading from Smoky Mountain Rd. down to Hole-in-the-Rock Rd. runs through this canyon. However, the road is so rough and so seldom driven that it works better as a hiking trail or mountain-biking trail. Left Hand Collet Canyon is about 800 feet deep and is decorated with tiny riparian areas, seams of black coal in multicolored sandstone walls, and rock ledges over which seasonal waterfalls make their ephemeral way. A balanced rock near the confluence with Willard Canyon, as well as the ruins of old corrals, add to the scenic value.

To access the upper end of Left Hand Collet, drive south from the town of Escalante on Smoky Mountain Rd. to mile 30.5 and Collet Junction (signed). A large corral at Hardhead Water Spring serves as a landmark to alert drivers to the upcoming junction.

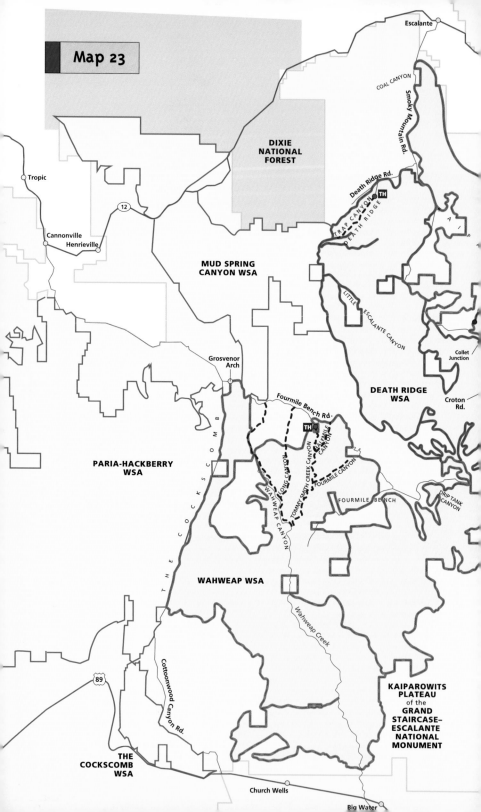

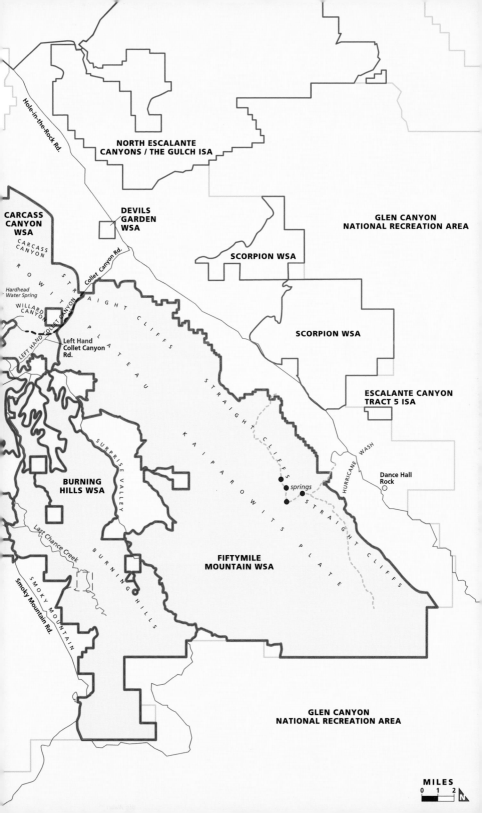

NORTH ESCALANTE
CANYONS / THE GULCH ISA

CARCASS
CANYON
WSA

DEVILS
GARDEN
WSA

GLEN CANYON
NATIONAL RECREATION AREA

CARCASS
CANYON

SCORPION WSA

R O W I T

S T R A I G H T

Hardhead
Water Spring

WILLARD
CANYON

Left Hand
Collet Canyon
Rd.

Collet Canyon Rd.

COLLET CANYON

LEFT HAND

SCORPION WSA

P L A T E A U

C L I F F S

ESCALANTE CANYON
TRACT 5 ISA

S U R P R I S E   V A L L E Y

K A I P A R O W I T S

S T R A I G H T   C L I F F S

H U R R I C A N E   W A S H

Dance Hall
Rock

BURNING
HILLS WSA

springs

Last Chance Creek

B U R N I N G   H I L L S

FIFTYMILE
MOUNTAIN WSA

P L A T E

S T R A I G H T   C L I F F S

S M O K Y   M O U N T A I N

Smoky Mountain Rd.

GLEN CANYON
NATIONAL RECREATION AREA

Hole-in-the-Rock Rd.

MILES
0   1   2

N

Watch for Fremont Indian ruins near the junction. Flat spots near the top of Collet Canyon can be used as primitive camping sites for modern humans as well.

Turn east at Collet Junction, drive about 2 miles to an intersection, and take the left fork into Lower Trail Canyon. Park where the road drops into the canyon and walk down Lower Trail Canyon to its confluence with Left Hand Collet Canyon.

To access Collet Canyon from the lower end, drive about 13 miles down Hole-in-the-Rock Rd. (From UT 12 the turnoff for Hole-in-the-Rock Rd. is 3.6 miles east of the town of Escalante.) Turn onto Collet Canyon Rd. about 1 mile south of Devils Garden (see Chapter 22 for Devils Garden). Drive about 5 miles to the base of the Straight Cliffs. Park and walk up the road.

Option: The lower section of Carcass Canyon can also be accessed near the lower end of Collet Canyon. Drive about 2.5 miles up Collet Canyon Rd. from Hole-in-the-Rock Rd. Park and walk northwest up a shallow wash to the mouth of Carcass Canyon. You can also hike into Carcass Canyon from the Devils Garden picnic area.

DAY HIKE: TOMMY SMITH CREEK CANYON
One-Way Length: 2–7 miles
Low and High Elevations: 5,300 and 5,600 feet
Difficulty: Easy (4WD required for approach road)

The Wahweap WSA, where this hike takes place, does not appear on Trails Illustrated maps; use the USGS Horse Mountain and Fourmile Bench maps. Numerous 4WD roads and tracks stem from Fourmile Bench Rd. Go south on Cottonwood Canyon Rd. to Grosvenor Arch (see Chapter 19) and turn left (east) on Fourmile Bench Rd. Continue past the arch and cross The Cockscomb, Wahweap Creek, and Blue Wash. About 5.5 miles from Grosvenor Arch, and about 1.5 miles past Blue Wash, an unsigned spur road leads to Tommy Smith Creek Canyon. Park where the road ends at a corral.

The canyon's small stream, springs, hanging gardens, and cottonwood trees make for a pleasant change in this dry country. It doesn't look promising from the parking area at the corral, where the wash is shallow and uninteresting, but down-canyon the creek cuts into the sandstone. March and April, when water is more plentiful, are good months for this hike.

Halfmile Canyon is worth a side trip to see the groves of super-sized cottonwood trees. Day hikers short on time can explore Halfmile Canyon and then return to the parking area.

Continue downstream in Tommy Canyon about another 2 miles to the confluence with Fourmile Canyon. As time permits, explore Fourmile Canyon or continue down Tommy Canyon to the wide opening where Tommy, Long, and Wahweap Canyons meet. The meeting of the three canyons is about 3 miles beyond Fourmile Canyon. Hikers with a shuttle vehicle can return to Fourmile Bench Rd. by hiking up Long or Wahweap Canyons.

A lone Douglas fir barely finds room to grow in Trap Canyon.

Southeast-Central Utah

"I'm just damned glad to be alive," announced Robert Howard, my brother. On one of our research expeditions for this book, we took along some of our relatives visiting from Alaska. Our guests were hardened outdoors enthusiasts. Nevertheless, after exploring parts of southern Utah, we ended up with the quote above.

It was early April and we were alternately fried and frozen as we hiked from the floors of 800-foot-deep canyons, to wind-blasted moonscapes of mesas, and onto snow-draped peaks. The terrain is so varied that one really can't choose a single "best season" to visit, but here are some suggestions:

Henry Mountains (peaks northwest of UT 276):
Late June, early July, October

Dirty Devil River: Early April to late May, late autumn

Horseshoe, French Spring, and Happy Canyons:
May, autumn

Little Rockies (peaks southeast of UT 276):
March, April, November

Fiddler Butte: Late April, May, late September

At Hanksville, the rare sight of water appears in the form of the confluence of Muddy Creek and the Fremont River, which drain into the Dirty Devil River, which, in turn, flows into the Colorado River. Sounds like lots of water, but until you get to the Colorado River and the northern end of Lake Powell, all those "rivers" look more like streams for most of the year. Utahans have a habit of calling anything that flows, even intermittently, a "river." Hanksville is an important water-replenishment site. Our advice is not to venture into the backcountry without at least 5 gallons of water per person stowed in your vehicle, but use the outdoor hose at the Sinclair Station, not the river water.

Hanksville is also the intersection of UT 95 and UT 24. Despite this apparently central location, Hanksville looks and feels like a temporary Western movie set. Real outlaws from the Wild Bunch, including Butch Cassidy, used Hanksville and nearby canyons as hideouts. The expeditions described in this region include a modern-day visit to Robbers Roost Canyon and to the Wild Bunch stomping grounds of Horseshoe Canyon.

A dead juniper pitchforks the sky on Bull Mountain,
one of four major peaks in the Henry Mountains WSA.

Near Hanksville, sandstone cliffs and isolated rock towers dominate the landscape. There is very little greenery, as most of the land is nude under a dry sky. But an impressive backdrop, the large forested island of the Henry Mountains, is snowcapped and altogether different from the desert. Herds of wild buffalo graze the lower slopes of the Henry Mountains.

All of the areas described in this region are wilderness study areas, administered by the Bureau of Land Management. There are no designated wildernesses. A limited amount of cattle grazing occurs in and around all of the study areas. Mining activity stretched into the 1950s, and many of our modern-day access roads to hiking trailheads were once mining roads. Archaeological sites include historic cowboy-related ruins from the early 1800s. Archaeological remains of Archaic peoples (Paleo-Indians) abound in the canyons.

Deeply incised canyons that cut through layers of colorful sandstone formations offer the best opportunities to view archaeological remains. Hiking routes that include lots of wading to access views of rock art in the Dirty Devil River Canyon are described in detail. Drier hiking routes in the Horseshoe Canyons can be extended to include famous rock art panels in Canyonlands National Park. French Spring–Happy Canyon, Horseshoe Canyon South, and Horseshoe Canyon North derive their value as proposed wilderness in part from proximity to other public lands, most notably Canyonlands NP, Glen Canyon NRA, and Dirty Devil WSA.

Mount Ellen–Blue Hills, Bull Mountain, Mount Pennell, and Mount Hillers WSAs

24

Rust-colored lichen on eroded mudstones

AN ARTICLE IN a Hanksville newspaper about the bison in the Henry Mountains described the herd as previously "reduced almost to distinction [sic] by indiscriminate hunting." The real distinction of the Henry Mountains bison is that they are now the largest herd of free-roaming buffalo in the nation. In 1941, 3 bulls and 15 heifers were shipped from Yellowstone National Park to the San Rafael Desert. In the early 1960s the herd moved to the Henrys and stayed there. The herd now numbers about 425 to 450 after calving season. An annual buffalo hunt keeps the numbers within limits set by a Division of Wildlife Resources

LOCATION: Southeast-Central Utah

SIZE: Mount Ellen–Blue Hills WSA: 81,726 acres
Bull Mountain WSA: 13,620 acres
Mount Pennell WSA: 74,300 acres
Mount Hillers WSA: 20,000 acres

ELEVATION RANGE: 4,600 to 11,615 feet

ECOREGION: Colorado Plateau

MILES OF TRAIL: About 9, but many unofficial routes and old mining roads

ADMINISTRATION:
BLM, Henry Mountains Resource Area

MAPS: Trails Illustrated: Map #213.
USGS 1:100,000: Hanksville, Hite Crossing.
USGS 1:24,000: Cass Creek Peak, Copper Creek Benches, Ant Knoll, Turkey Knob, Raggy Canyon, Mount Ellen, Mount Pennell, Bull Mountain, Black Table, Town Point, Steele Butte, Stevens Mesa.

agreement with the BLM. Spotting the bison is one of many unique scenic draws for visitors.

There are four wilderness study areas along the main spine of the Henry Mountains: Mount Ellen–Blue Hills, Bull Mountain, Mount Pennell, and Mount Hillers. They're separated by ribbons of dirt/gravel access roads, and by a few pockets of private land used for mining or ranching. Hanksville is the nearest town. Capitol Reef National Park is along the western border. The Little Rockies WSA is basically across the street, southeast of UT 276. San Rafael Swell is a few miles to the north. The Glen Canyon National Recreation Area and Lake Powell are near the southeastern edge.

The Henry Mountains exhibit a lot of what geologists call "absolute elevation." A great deal of their height springs up suddenly above relatively flat surroundings. In the Mount Ellen–Blue Hills WSA, elevations range from 4,600 feet to 11,615 feet, with the peak of Mount Ellen being the highest point in the Henry Mountains. The best times to visit the lower elevations are March, April, and early October. The best times to visit the higher elevations are late June through July, as well as September. Roads that access the higher passes are usually clear of snow by mid- to late June.

The Henry Mountains are named after Joseph Henry, who worked for the Smithsonian Institution. It was his friend, John Wesley Powell, who named the mountain range after him. The mountains are so isolated that they were the last in the Lower 48 to be explored and named by white men. Geologist Grove Karl Gilbert surveyed the mountains in 1875 and noted the impressive height of the peaks, and their likely origin as intrusions of igneous rock, or laccoliths.

Perennial streams and springs are scattered throughout the Henry Mountains, but the area is generally arid to semiarid. Hikers should bring plenty of water and plan ahead to use the accessible water sources.

A long history of mining for gold, silver, lead, and uranium has left a legacy of abandoned claims, tunnels, cabins, and stone huts. Butch Cassidy and the Wild Bunch also made use of the area during their infamous outlaw days. The weathered remains from these human activities add a unique cultural flavor to the roads and trails, whose most common modern-day uses are ranching and hunting. Remember to leave all cattle-control gates as you find them, closed or open, as necessary. Some active mining claims lie just outside the wilderness study area boundaries. Respect private mining property.

Mount Ellen–Blue Hills WSA

This wilderness study area presents visitors with the most dramatic topographical differences of any area in Utah. The blue clay badlands of the Blue Hills portion are a desert of shale, alkali flats, and incised erosional patterns. More barren badlands and mesas occupy the western and southwestern sections of the WSA.

In direct contrast to the badlands is the 50- to 70-million-year-old intrusion of Mount Ellen, a combination of diorite porphyry stocks and laccoliths bursting up through sedimentary layers. The strength and depth of the sedimentary layers kept the Henry Mountains from becoming full-fledged volcanoes. Mount Ellen's higher elevations receive about four to five times the precipitation of the desert, enough to support pines, firs, mountain mahogany, scrub oak, aspen groves, and grassy meadows.

> **JEEP TRIP/DAY HIKE/BACKPACK:** BLUE HILLS, MOUNT ELLEN SUMMIT
> One-Way Length: About 54 miles driving; about 7–9 miles hiking
> Low and High Elevations: 4,600 and 11,615 feet
> Difficulty: Moderate, 4WD required

This expedition samples all the varied terrain that Mount Ellen–Blue Hills WSA has to offer. Plan for at least one overnight camp, preferably at McMillan Springs Campground. Well-maintained gravel roads prevail, but it will be slow going on the steeper roads that climb into the mountains. There are lots of opportunities for short day hikes, so if you have time, plan to camp for two nights and hike two to three days. In good weather most 4WD vehicles can make it all the way to Bull Creek Pass.

The first stop is in Upper Blue Hills for a day hike. About 9.2 miles west of Hanksville, on UT 24, watch for an unmarked dirt track leading south between mileposts 106 and 105. Park where the short track ends. Follow a faint trail south to the river. Wade the Fremont River and explore about a mile into the Upper Blue Hills. No official trails and no potable water sources exist here. The landscape of Mancos Shale looks bluish in the right light. Selenium-tolerant plants offer the only other spots of color in the highly eroded hills. Fossilized shark teeth found here testify to a past far different from today's desert. This hike is not possible in wet weather because the clay will quickly build up a pound of goop on your shoes.

From your Upper Blue Hills exploration, return to UT 24. About 24 miles west of Hanksville, at the eastern border of Capitol Reef National Park, turn south on Notom Rd. The road is paved to the old townsite of Notom, formerly a uranium mining boomtown. At mile 4.7 from UT 24, continue south across Notom Bench on a gravel road, ignoring all side roads and jeep tracks. The Waterpocket Fold of Capitol Reef National Park will be on your right.

At mile 12.8 from UT 24, at Sandy Ranch Junction, turn left (east) to climb into the foothills of Mount Ellen and access McMillan Springs Campground. About 2 miles east of Sandy Ranch Junction, the road is rougher where it descends to cross Blind Trail Wash (not signed). Having a high-clearance 4WD vehicle is recommended. Keep left at a major road junction to continue to McMillan Springs. At the developed campground, ponderosa pines create welcome shade, a water source is available, and the views westward to Capitol Reef are spectacular. Bison often frequent the meadows around McMillan Springs.

Above McMillan Springs, the road gets rockier and steeper as it climbs to Bull Creek Pass. A primitive hiking trail leads from Bull Creek Pass to the summit of Mount Ellen. At 10,485 feet, the pass is the highest point for driving. The summit hike gains another 1,130 feet in about 2.7 miles. Panoramic views from the summit include the Dirty Devil River Canyon, portions of Canyonlands and Capitol Reef National Parks, and the Circle Cliffs of Grand Staircase–Escalante National Monument.

Driving beyond Bull Creek Pass, keep left to descend past Lonesome Beaver Campground and Dandelion Flat Picnic Area. Bull Mountain WSA is on your right as you descend. You can stay on backroads all the way to UT 24 or turn right at Halfway Wash and connect with UT 95. Hanksville sits at the intersection of UT 95 and UT 24.

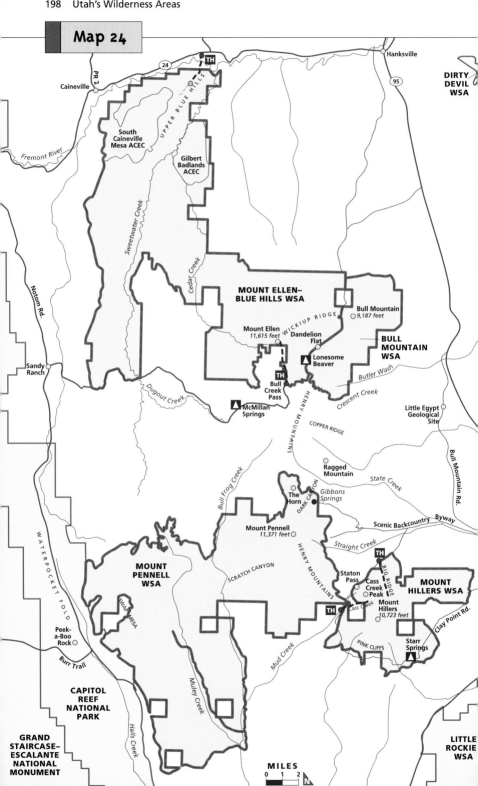

Map 24

Hanksville

DIRTY
DEVIL
WSA

Caineville

PR 2

24

95

Fremont River

TH

UPPER BLUE HILLS

South
Caineville
Mesa ACEC

Gilbert
Badlands
ACEC

Sweetwater Creek

Cedar Creek

Notom Rd.

MOUNT ELLEN–
BLUE HILLS WSA

Bull Mountain
9,187 feet

Mount Ellen
11,615 feet

Dandelion
Flat

WICKIUP RIDGE

BULL
MOUNTAIN
WSA

Sandy
Ranch

Lonesome
Beaver

Dugout Creek

Butler Wash

Bull
Creek
Pass

Crescent Creek

HENRY MOUNTAINS

McMillan
Springs

Little Egypt
Geological
Site

COPPER RIDGE

Bull Mountain Rd.

Bull Frog Creek

Ragged
Mountain

State Creek

The
Horn

Gibbons
Springs

DARK CANYON

Scenic Backcountry   Byway

Mount Pennell
11,371 feet

Straight Creek

TH

WATERPOCKET FOLD

MOUNT
PENNELL
WSA

SCRATCH CANYON

HENRY MOUNTAINS

Staton
Pass

BIG RIDGE

Cass
Creek
Peak

MOUNT
HILLERS WSA

SWAP MESA

TH

Cass Creek

Mount
Hillers
10,723 feet

Clay Point Rd.

Peek-
a-Boo
Rock

Burr Trail

Mud Creek

PINK CLIFFS

Starr
Springs

CAPITOL
REEF
NATIONAL
PARK

Muley Creek

Halls Creek

GRAND
STAIRCASE–
ESCALANTE
NATIONAL
MONUMENT

LITTLE
ROCKIE
WSA

MILES
0   1   2

N

A Utah juniper has a tentative hold on the steep terrain of Bull Mountain.

Option: Other routes also descend from the Bull Creek Pass area. At 2.6 miles northeast of the pass, a road intersection at Wickiup Pass (9,360 feet) offers the option to descend along Crescent Creek, past the ghost town of Eagle City, to Little Egypt Geologic Site next to UT 95. Entrada Sandstone formations at the Little Egypt site have been compared to the shape of the Sphinx of Egypt. Turn left (north) on UT 95 to go to Hanksville, or south to go to Lake Powell.

Option: Below and west of McMillan Springs Campground, dirt roads lead southeast to The Horn in Mount Pennell WSA. See the Mount Pennell description, which follows.

Option: If you continue south on Notom Rd. instead of turning east at Sandy Ranch Junction, you will enter Capitol Reef National Park, view the Oyster Shell Reef, and eventually connect with the Burr Trail (see Chapter 21).

Mount Pennell WSA

At 11,371 feet, Mount Pennell is the second-highest peak in the Henry Mountains. Perennial streams and 16 springs provide adequate water sources for hikers, but all sources require filtering.

From UT 276, 4.4 miles south of the junction with UT 95, turn west on the signed Scenic Backcountry Byway. Old log cabins and the remains of Trachyte Ranch are worth a stop at mile 3.3. You will pass several side roads, but stay on the main road until you come to a signed intersection for The Horn. Turn right (north-northwest). The Horn presents several solid granite faces, nearly vertical, that tempt technical climbers. Rock climbers frequently use the two undeveloped camping areas near The Horn. Water is available in Gibbons Springs between the two dry campgrounds. There are no official trails but you can easily make your way through boulders and brush to the base of The Horn. Nontechnical climbers can scale The Horn from the northern or western sides. Long pants and hiking boots are recommended for off-trail hiking and moderate bushwhacking. Large ponderosa pines and the distinctive shapes of The Horn make for Class A scenery.

For another approach via dirt roads from the west, turn southeast near Blind Trail Wash (not signed), about 2.5 miles east of Sandy Ranch Junction. From this Y intersection, the left fork leads to McMillan Springs Campground and the right fork heads to Mount Pennell.

Mount Hillers WSA

Mount Hillers is the peak between Mount Pennell and Little Rockies WSA. The sides of Mount Hillers are so thickly vegetated that they present an impenetrable obstacle to off-trail hiking. Mountain mahogany and Gambel oak predominate, but pine and aspen groves offer a few unimproved camping spots along the dirt access roads.

Starr Springs Campground is the only developed camping area in this WSA. It makes an excellent base camp for exploration and has a reliable water source. About 16 miles south of the intersection of UT 95 and UT 276, turn west from UT 276 on Clay Point Rd., signed for Starr Springs Recreation Area. The road to the campground is graded and suitable for 2WD vehicles in good weather. Beyond Starr Springs, we recommend 4WD, although high-clearance, light-duty vehicles can negotiate the rocky road if it is dry.

The road climbs to Stanton Pass (7,470 feet). Old mining roads in the Cass Creek and Big Ridge areas can be used as hiking trails. About 0.5 mile below Stanton Pass, a jeep track on the right can be used as the beginning of a hike to the summit of Mount Hillers. The USGS topo Cass Creek Peak is helpful for finding old roads and for choosing a route to the summit. There are no marked trails.

As you might have figured out by now, the roads in the Henry Mountains connect to each other in a bewildering array of loops. About 0.5 mile below Stanton Pass, a left fork leads to Mount Pennell and The Horn, and on to Bull Creek Pass.

The Dirty Devil River below sandstone cliffs

HIKING IN THE DIRTY DEVIL RIVER corridor gets a lot easier when the water level is low. The year we hiked the canyon, irrigation water was withdrawn from the river beginning April 1, so our early springtime expedition worked out well. In April, the canyon floor was warm, cacti and desert flowers were in bloom, and the muddy river warmed up enough by afternoon to make our numerous fords pleasant. Steep, sheer canyon walls force hikers first to one side of the river, then to the other. When the river is running high, kayaking and inner-tubing the river are popular forms of recreation, with Lake Powell as the destination. Anyone hiking or floating along the river should be certain to

LOCATION: Southeast-Central Utah

SIZE: 61,000 acres

ELEVATION RANGE: 4,000 to 5,600 feet

ECOREGION: Colorado Plateau

MILES OF TRAIL: More than 100 miles of routes, but only about 2.5 miles of marked trail

ADMINISTRATION: BLM, Henry Mountains Resource Area

MAPS: Trails Illustrated: Map #213. USGS 1:100,000: Hanksville. USGS 1:24,000: Point of Rocks West, Point of Rocks East, Angel Cove, Angel Point, Robbers Roost Flats, Whitbeck Knoll, The Pinnacle, Burr Point, Baking Skillet Knoll.

camp well above the flash-flood plain. Seventy percent of the Dirty Devil WSA is classified as barren rock, a fact that will give you some idea of the intense contrast between the riparian areas and the Sonoran Desert zone.

Dirty Devil River water is not potable, but there are springs from which water can be filtered for drinking. Springs are more reliable as water sources in April and May. John Wesley Powell dubbed the river Dirty Devil and it lives up to its name, with a muddy bottom that will suck the tightest wading shoes off your feet. After digging my wading shoes out of their muddy grave several times, I finally resorted to wading the Dirty Devil barefoot, putting my footgear on when exiting the river. In autumn, the Dirty Devil diminishes to a dirty trickle.

The closest town is Hanksville, about 5 miles west of the wilderness study area border. Nearby wilderness study areas include Fiddler Butte, French Spring–Happy Canyon, Little Rockies, and those in the San Rafael Swell and Henry Mountains. The Dirty Devil WSA is about 15 miles north of the most northerly extension of the Glen Canyon National Recreation Area, and about 24 miles from Lake Powell. Proposals backed by citizen groups suggest a larger tract of wilderness here.

BACKPACK: DIRTY DEVIL, ROBBERS ROOST, AND BUCK CANYONS
One-Way Length: About 6–25 miles (less or more, as desired)
Low and High Elevations: 4,000 and 4,900 feet
Difficulty: Moderate to Strenuous

The most popular access for backpacking trips in the Dirty Devil WSA is Angel Trailhead. Drive south on UT 95 from Hanksville. Just past milepost 5, watch for an unsigned dirt road (there is a stop sign, but no road name). The road is 2WD in good weather, with the exception of two sandy spots that might require 4WD. Drive east about 12 miles to a junction of dirt roads marked with a faded orange post. Turn left at the post and drive less than 0.25 mile to the Angel Trailhead. Trails Illustrated Map #213 is good for an overview, but it's not detailed enough to show the dirt roads and the trail. Hikers should take the USGS 1:24,000 maps Angel Cove and Angel Point. The trail is depicted as a pack trail on the USGS Angel Cove map.

Allow three days to explore the Dirty Devil river canyon and two tributary canyons. You can easily spend 5 to 6 days in the canyons if you wish to extend the trip to include No Mans and Larry Canyons. If you only have time for an overnight backpacking trip, set up base camp in Angel Cove and hike/wade to the mouth of Robbers Roost Canyon, then return.

From the Angel Trailhead, hikers quickly drop down about 800 feet in elevation. The trail begins as an obvious footpath on the plateau, but where it crosses solid rock, the "trail" is marked only with rock cairns. This is the route, minus the cairns, that Butch Cassidy and the Wild Bunch used to escape the law. As you're hiking over the steep Navajo slickrock benches, it is hard to believe that this is the place where outlaws rode and herded horses down to the Dirty Devil River in the late 1800s. Hiking sandals are not a good choice here. You need supportive hiking boots or shoes with soles that allow maximum contact with the slickrock. Some of the distinctive rock on top of the sandstone is volcanic, rained from an ancient sky; other bits are agate or jasper.

Follow the rock cairns as the trail trends southeast, then arcs east toward the river. The tributary canyon that you can see entering from the southwest is Beaver Wash Canyon, an optional side trip of this hike. A colony of beavers has erected several dams in the canyon, creating pools and an extended riparian area that is unique to this desert river system. Hiking in Beaver Wash requires scrambling over rocks, climbing in and out of side gorges, and bushwhacking through tall reeds.

About 1.5 miles of descent from the Angel Trailhead bring hikers to a broad bench above the river. At a Y intersection on the bench, take the right fork to go to Angel Cove and Angel Spring, or take the left fork to continue hiking along the bench to Robbers Roost Canyon. From the Y intersection, the right fork of the trail curves around a cliff of pink Navajo Sandstone to enter Angel Cove, where a reliable spring and an area shaded with trees make for a popular camping spot.

Angel Cove has obvious advantages, but a great view at sunrise and sunset is not one of them. The enclosed cove limits the sightlines for the canyon version of alpenglow, the distinctive flush of otherworldly color that seems to emanate from the cliffs themselves when the horizon holds just a hint of the invisible sun. Both for the views and for the sake of solitude, we camped on a bench above the eastern riverbank, about a mile north of the mouth of Robbers Roost Canyon. I followed the prints of mule deer to a spring about 100 yards from the river. The spring does not appear on the USGS topo map. The Bureau of Land Management notes that there are many undocumented springs along the river and in the tributary canyons. Springwater comes right out of the sand, and if you find a damp spot, a little digging will usually result in a pool deep enough for filtering.

Petroglyphs and cowboy glyphs can be found all over the Dirty Devil WSA. Scan the cliff walls and alcoves for examples as you hike. Look for petroglyphs and pictographs near the entrance of Robbers Roost Canyon.

Robbers Roost Canyon is north of Angel Cove. You can get there by hiking along and in the river from Angel Cove; or you can hike along the western bench above the river. In the early spring, I prefer the hike along the bench. An obvious hiking path makes for easy going through a variety of desert flowers, blooming cacti, and low shrubs. The path does not appear on topo maps, but is easy to find on the ground. Rock cairns mark the way where the route crosses solid rock. The path descends from the bench and skirts a nameless cove with an unreliable water source. Across from this cove, as you look northeast, is the opening to Robbers Roost Canyon. Several older guidebooks for this area incorrectly identify in their textual descriptions the location of Robbers Roost in relation to Angel Cove. Trust the USGS map.

Beautiful cliffs 300 to 800 feet high are a given in the Dirty Devil River canyon, but the penultimate example of conch-shell pink Navajo Sandstone in monolithic size is the cliff opposite the mouth of Robbers Roost. That view alone is worth the sweat it takes to get there.

About a mile up Robbers Roost Canyon, the canyon splits where the South Fork bends sharply south. About 4.5 miles from the mouth, the main Robbers Roost Canyon splits again. South Fork Robbers Roost Canyon is about 10 miles long; you'll

Map 25

BUCK CANYON

PASTURE CANYON

no name canyon

WHITE ROOST CANYON

NORTH FORK

MIDDLE F

ROBBERS ROOST CANYON

SOUTH FORK

ANGELS POINT

Angel Cove

Angel Spring

TH

BEAVER WASH CANYON

NO MANS CANYON

LARRY CANYON

Dirty Devil River

95

Burr Point

Burr
Pass

Silvertip
Spring

Robbers
Roost
Spring

RK

DIRTY

DEVIL

WSA

TWIN CORRAL MESA

SAMS MESA

MILES

0   1   2

N

need about 25 feet of climbing rope to get into and out of the dropoffs. The main canyon, including Middle Fork Robbers Roost, is about 8.5 miles long. Add to this about 3 miles of White Roost and about 4 miles of North Fork Robbers Roost and you quickly come to the conclusion that you could spend a week in Robbers Roost and its tributaries and still not see it all. Whichever fork you choose to hike, you're sure to enjoy an astonishing variety of rock alcoves, ephemeral waterfalls, slots that narrow to the width of one human, wide spots where cottonwood trees and Gambel oak proliferate, and even a few hardy Douglas-firs hogging an oasis of water and shade. Water from occasional springs in all the forks of Robbers Roost can be filtered for drinking. Fill up every chance you get because you might have to hike/climb for several hours between springs.

North of Robbers Roost Canyon, there are two more canyon openings before you get to Buck Canyon. The first is nameless. When we hiked into the nameless canyon, we wore long pants to protect us from the creeping Oregon grape plants, with their wicked, hollylike leaves. We stopped at a slot featuring a chest-high pool of water. Pasture Canyon, true to its name, is grassy and wide, narrowing only as you near its head. Buck Canyon is a 3.25-mile walk/wade up the meandering Dirty Devil River from the mouth of Robbers Roost Canyon. Buck Canyon splits in its upper reaches and also sports numerous, tentacle-like tributaries along its main spine. There's a natural arch in the largest right-hand fork. Narrows and more narrows are par for the course in the upper reaches of Buck and its tributaries. Flash-flood danger is extreme.

To extend this backpacking trip, hikers can go south along the Dirty Devil to explore No Mans and Larry Canyons. No Mans Canyon is about 5.5 miles south of Angel Cove. It's closer as the crow flies, but hikers have to follow the meanders of the river, wading it many times. The primary allures of No Mans are pools filled by waterfalls and a suite of Fremont Indian ruins. The ruins are near the mouth, about a mile up-canyon. Springs in No Mans Canyon provide filterable water.

Larry Canyon is about 4 miles south of No Mans Canyon, about 9.5 river miles south of Angel Cove. Solitude, deep narrows, and a hanging garden in the left fork are the main attractions. Obstacles in all the forks of Larry Canyon prevent hikers from penetrating more than 2 to 3 miles up-canyon. Campsites and water sources in the accessible sections increase opportunities for solitude.

Horseshoe Canyon South, Horseshoe Canyon North, and French Spring–Happy Canyon WSAs

26

Handprints of prehistoric people who lived in the Horseshoe Canyon region. Archaeological sites like these are easily damaged and should never be touched.

LOCATION: Southeast-Central Utah

SIZE: Horseshoe Canyon South WSA: 38,800 acres
Horseshoe Canyon North WSA: 20,500 acres
French Spring–Happy Canyon WSA: 25,000 acres

ELEVATION RANGE: 4,200 to 6,500 feet

ECOREGION: Colorado Plateau

MILES OF TRAIL: None; unofficial routes along eroded roads and canyon floors

ADMINISTRATION: BLM, Henry Mountains and San Rafael Resource Areas

MAPS: Trails Illustrated: Maps #210, #213, and #246.
USGS 1:100,000: Hanksville.
USGS 1:24,000: Keg Knoll, Bowknot Bend, Sugarloaf Butte, Head Spur, Gordon Flats, The Pinnacle.

HORSESHOE CANYONS SOUTH AND NORTH ARE proposed wilderness areas that bracket the Horseshoe Canyon detached unit of Canyonlands National Park. The famous rock art panel "Great Gallery" is the centerpiece of a canyon system that boasts the greatest concentration of Barrier Canyon–style art in the San Rafael Desert. In places, art as old as 5,000 years bears an overlay of more recent rock paintings.

Hiking the national park section of the canyon and then continuing south or north into Bureau of Land Management areas offers several advantages. The signed, easy access and marked trail provided by the national park gets you off to a good start, and you are guaranteed a view of some of the best rock art. Leaving the park boundaries means leaving most of the crowds behind—solitude and unimproved campsites that don't require fees or reservations are the reward for those willing to backpack, or to take longer day hikes. There are no marked trails in the BLM wilderness study areas.

Horseshoe Canyon drains north-northeast into the Green River, and into the deep cut of the justly famous Labyrinth Canyon. Contrary to what you might think, Labyrinth Canyon is not famous for whitewater, but for its scenery and its no-rapids, easy paddle for beginners. Horseshoe Canyon is deepest, more than 1,000 feet deep, where it meets Labyrinth Canyon. River rafters and kayakers can access the canyon at its mouth, and this is a section that is heavily used. River runners have created primitive trails and campsites in the area. Intermittent running water, pools, and springs make it an ideal spot to stop on a long river trip.

The emphasis in this book is hiking and solitude seeking, so our backpacking trip will lean toward the lesser-used Horseshoe Canyon South, but that's not meant to diminish the charms of Horseshoe Canyon North as a hiking or river travel destination. River access for a float trip is from the town of Green River, at Green River State Park. Permits are available free of charge from the BLM in Price or Moab, and at Green River State Park. River travel rules for Leave-No-Trace camping are strict, so check with administrators to make sure you have all the equipment you need to comply. See Appendix B for contact information.

French Spring–Happy Canyon is seldom visited, and yet, it is just across Hans Flat Rd. from the southern end of Horseshoe Canyon South WSA. Some of the rangers at the Hans Flat Station have explored Happy Canyon and its northernmost fork, French Spring. If solitude is your idea of heaven, French Spring is the place to go. French Spring–Happy Canyon is a tributary of Dirty Devil Canyon, but few hikers brave the canyon floors all the way to the Dirty Devil River. A lack of reliable water sources is the main obstacle to long backpacking trips.

Access to these wilderness study areas requires a lot of backcountry driving (34 to 70 miles of gravel and dirt road), but most of the driving is on the 2WD Hans Flat Rd. If the weather is dry, sedans can negotiate the roads, but wet weather can turn clay-based sections into slime that troubles even 4WD vehicles.

From UT 24 about 18 miles north of Hanksville, near the turn to Goblin Valley State Park, go southeast on a graded dirt road that is signed as access to The Maze (a Canyonlands National Park area). This road is identified in the DeLorme *Utah Atlas & Gazetteer* as Lower San Rafael Rd. (CR 1010) at its northern end, but is identified as Recreation Rd. 633 at its southern end in the Glen Canyon NRA. Other maps and most locals and land administrators call it Hans Flat Rd., after the

Hans Flat Ranger Station. There are a lot of dirt roads in this area, so you might want to take the 1:100,000 Hanksville map for an overview and the 1:24,000 maps listed in the beginning of this chapter for details. Trails Illustrated maps also provide good overviews, but they do not show all the 4WD side roads. Trails Illustrated maps are more up-to-date when it comes to trails and campgrounds.

The closest town, Hanksville, is about 51 miles from Horseshoe Canyon and about 75 miles from Happy Canyon. Be sure you are well equipped with a good spare tire, lots of water, food, and other emergency supplies. Cell phones do not work in the canyons.

> **BACKPACK: HORSESHOE CANYON SOUTH, HORSESHOE CANYON UNIT OF CANYONLANDS NATIONAL PARK**
> One-Way Length: About 13 miles (less or more, as desired)
> Low and High Elevations: 5,800 and 6,200 feet
> Difficulty: Moderate to Strenuous

See the road access description in the previous section for the turn off UT 24. About 23 miles from UT 24, at a signed intersection, turn north to the Horseshoe Canyon detached unit of Canyonlands National Park. Drive to the signed trailhead, about 33 miles from UT 24.

Hike southwest on the 3-mile-long Horseshoe Canyon Trail. It's difficult to do justice in words to the ghostly rock art on the canyon walls, especially the Great Gallery. Most visitors go silent before the life-sized images. Signs of modern man are not absent in the park. In a few places, thoughtless visitors have defaced the rock art. Gates near the unit's border block 4WD tracks leading to the eastern edge of the canyon.

As you continue southwest, 0.4 mile beyond the Great Gallery, you'll come to Deadman's Trail, which ascends the east side of the canyon and meets a jeep road spur from Hans Flat. Don't exit at Deadman's Trail. Continue to hike southwest along the canyon floor to reach the park boundary about 2 miles from the Great Gallery.

Hike south into the wilderness study area, Horseshoe Canyon South. The canyon floors are sandy, and if you add a backpack to the drag of the sand, you can expect to hike about 1.5 to 2 miles per hour.

Seeps and springs in Horseshoe Canyon South feed a smattering of grasses, willows, and cottonwoods. Barrier, Bluejohn, and Spur Creeks are all ephemeral. In dry years water can be scarce, so carry plenty of your own. Backpackers can carry enough water for an overnight stay, but if you plan a longer excursion, be sure to take the USGS 1:24,000 maps Sugarloaf Butte and Head Spur. These maps plainly show the locations of springs. Wild burros and cattle graze some of the WSA, so be prepared to filter or treat drinking water.

As you hike farther up-canyon, you'll find the scenery varied and magnificent. Enjoy a steep-walled canyon that ranges in width from a few feet to about 0.5 mile, more unique rock art of the Barrier Canyon style, plus cave sites. Cowboy Cave, near Spur Fork of Horseshoe Canyon, is an archaeological site of great importance. The cave seems to have been used by mammoths, bison, horses, camels, and sloths about

13,000 to 11,000 years ago, and by human occupants from about 6,800 years ago. This is one of two rock shelters listed on the National Register of Historic Places, the other one being Jim Walter's Cave, which has been seriously vandalized. Now the exact location of both caves is restricted information. More recent cultural remains are cabins used by Butch Cassidy and the Wild Bunch. Some of the named springs reflect this heritage. Look for Outlaw Springs on the eastern edge of the WSA.

Option: If you hike all of Horseshoe Canyon South from the national park boundary to Twin Corrals on Hans Flat Rd., you'll traverse about 20 miles of canyon floor (not including Spur Fork, which is about an additional 10 miles). This is certainly doable if you're confident of your map-reading abilities and are an experienced desert hiker. A shuttle vehicle can be left at the end of a spur road leading north from Hans Flat Rd. at Twin Corrals. The spur road is about 4 miles west of Hans Flat Ranger Station and leads to Trail and Wildcat Springs. To exit near the head of Horseshoe Canyon, follow cattle trails up to the springs, and from the springs to the spur road. Horseshoe Canyon South is difficult to get into and out of at any other point, so it's a good idea to reconnoiter the exit point when you leave a shuttle vehicle.

Option: Hike down-canyon from the Trail and Wildcat Springs area (see previous description) through Horseshoe Canyon South; continue through Horseshoe Canyon North all the way to the Green River, a distance of about 35 miles. Arrange for a raft or kayak shuttle from the canyon mouth. Some commercial outfitters will provide both vehicular and river shuttles.

Bluejoint marsh grass can grow 5 to 6 feet high along riverbanks.

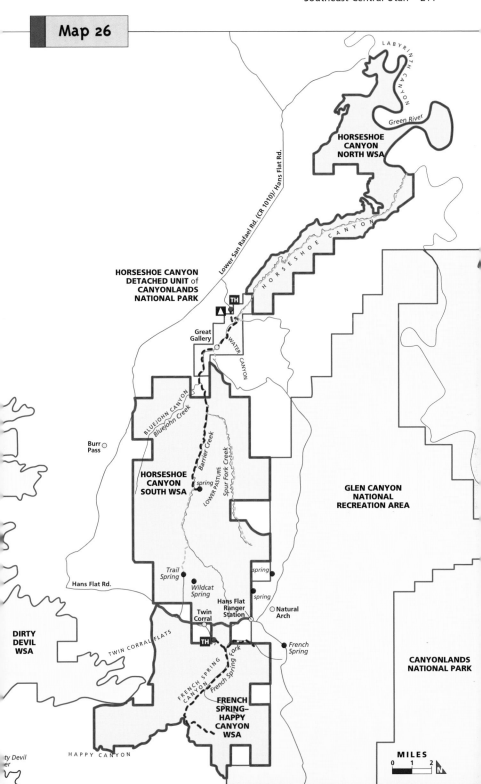

Map 26

LABYRINTH CANYON

Green River

HORSESHOE CANYON NORTH WSA

Lower San Rafael Rd. (CR 1010)/ Hans Flat Rd.

HORSESHOE CANYON
DETACHED UNIT of
CANYONLANDS
NATIONAL PARK

TH

Great
Gallery

HORSESHOE CANYON

WATER CANYON

BLUEJOHN CANYON

Bluejohn Creek

Burr
Pass

Barrier Creek

Spur Fork Creek

LOWER PASTURE

HORSESHOE
CANYON
SOUTH WSA

spring

GLEN CANYON
NATIONAL
RECREATION AREA

Hans Flat Rd.

Trail
Spring

Wildcat
Spring

spring

spring

Hans Flat
Ranger
Station

Natural
Arch

DIRTY
DEVIL
WSA

Twin
Corral

TH

TWIN CORRAL FLATS

French
Spring

CANYONLANDS
NATIONAL PARK

FRENCH SPRING CANYON

French Spring Fork

FRENCH
SPRING–
HAPPY
CANYON
WSA

HAPPY CANYON

ty Devil
er

MILES

0   1   2

N

DAY HIKE: FRENCH SPRING FORK OF HAPPY CANYON
One-Way Length: About 6 miles (less or more, as desired)
Low and High Elevations: 4,800 and 6,400 feet
Difficulty: Moderate to Strenuous

See the access road description in the introductory section of this chapter for the first 23 driving miles. In Antelope Valley, where the north turn to Horseshoe Canyon is marked, continue southwest on Hans Flat Rd. toward Hans Flat Ranger Station. About 2 miles west of the ranger station, on the south side of the road, there is an unsigned dirt track leading to an old drill pad. This road is not shown on the Trails Illustrated map, but it does appear on USGS maps. Turn south and drive about 1.5 miles, or until you see a good camping spot in the trees (any flat spot equals "good").

From wherever you park on the spur road, make your way southwest into a shallow finger of French Spring Canyon. There's no trailhead and no official trail, but you can follow cattle trails into the canyon and then along the canyon itself. At the junction of the finger of the canyon you entered and the main fork of French Spring, turn sharply left and hike up-canyon to see some interesting narrows. Return to the canyon-finger junction and, if you have time, hike about 1 mile farther south to explore Happy Canyon Main Fork. Hike up-canyon in Happy Canyon Main Fork as time and your water supply allow.

At about 600 to 1,000 feet deep, French Spring Canyon is the deepest for its width in the area. Sheer cliffs of colorful sandstone, stone alcoves, narrows, and log-jams from past flash floods make for an interesting hike with a whiff of danger. Temperatures can reach 95 degrees Fahrenheit on the canyon floor during the summer. Late spring and fall are better times for a trek.

Water in French Spring Fork is intermittent. Depending on the time of year, there may or may not be water sources you can filter, which is why we recommend limiting this to a day hike, about 6 miles in and then 6 miles to return to your starting point. Solitude is so likely here that it's wise to err on the conservative side for the sake of safety. Turn around at midday, or earlier if you are tired or low on water.

Little Rockies and Fiddler Butte WSAs

27

Fishook cactus and a small Gambel oak

TWO PEAKS FORM the southeastern terminus of the Henry Mountains, Mount Holmes and Mount Ellsworth. Separated from the rest of the Henry Mountains by an intervening plateau and UT 276, these peaks constitute the Little Rockies WSA. Both the Little Rockies WSA and Fiddler Butte WSA are east of UT 276 in arid terrain that abuts Glen Canyon National Recreation Area. When combined with a visit to proposed wilderness in Glen Canyon NRA, Little Rockies and Fiddler Butte WSAs are well worth the trip.

LOCATION: Southeast-Central Utah

SIZE: Little Rockies WSA: 38,700 acres
Fiddler Butte WSA: 73,100 acres

ELEVATION RANGE: 3,700 to 8,235 feet

ECOREGION: Colorado Plateau

MILES OF TRAIL: No official trails, but about 40 miles of unofficial routes

ADMINISTRATION:
BLM, Henry Mountains Resource Area;
NPS, Glen Canyon NRA

MAPS: Trails Illustrated: Map #213.
USGS 1:100,000: Hanksville, Hite Crossing.
USGS 1:24,000: Ticaboo Mesa, Mount Holmes, Hite North, Stair Canyon, Fiddler Butte.

A thick finger of Lake Powell extends north, near the eastern border of the Little Rockies and near the southern portion of Fiddler Butte. The lake is difficult to access and is not a potable water source. We suggest carrying your own water and planning for day-hiking, as opposed to backpacking expeditions. Hikers with a lot of desert experience, canyoneering skills, and topographical map reading skills will find opportunities for extended hikes.

The nearest town, Hanksville, is about 35 miles north of the Little Rockies and about 25 miles from Fiddler Butte WSA. Clean, dry air and no human settlements make for long-distance views and excellent stargazing. The BLM's wilderness study reports note that these WSAs are "near the center of the area with the highest visual range (70+ miles) in the United States."

Little Rockies WSA

> **DAY HIKE:** MOUNT ELLSWORTH
> One-Way Length: About 3.6 miles
> Low and High Elevations: 5,400 and 8,235 feet
> Difficulty: Strenuous

This desert hike begins in a parking area about 500 feet north of milepost 20 on UT 276. Motorcycles and other ORVs can negotiate a rough dirt road that leads from the parking lot about 2 miles to the base of Mount Ellsworth, approximately 6,000 feet in elevation.

From the parking area near the highway, follow the dirt road to a granite outcropping. There are no maintained trails, but user-generated trails work their way along a southeasterly network of ridges to the main ridge, then turn south-southwest to lead to the peak at 8,235 feet.

There are many ups and downs on this route, so expect to climb more than 3,000 feet before you top out next to a solar-powered radio transmitter. (The transmitter is serviced by helicopter, with no road access.) This is not a hike you'll want to attempt on a hot day. There's no water, and the only sparse shade comes from scattered juniper and piñon trees. The hike is best in early spring when the cacti are in bloom. Wear sturdy boots impervious to cactus spines. Thanks to nonexistent or light snowfall amounts, the hike can even be done in the winter months. Watch for bighorn sheep at the higher elevations.

Views of the rest of the Henry Mountains to the northwest, and of the desert surrounding Lake Powell, are vast. UT 276 and the inevitable traffic noise preclude a true wilderness experience during the hike to the top of Mount Ellsworth. Seekers of solitude will have to make their way into canyons such as Ticaboo, Fourmile, Trachyte, and Twomile—east of Little Rockies WSA. See the overnight backpacking trip described in the following section.

> **BACKPACK: FOURMILE CANYON**
> One-Way Length: About 11.2 miles
> Low and High Elevations: About 3,700 and 5,660 feet
> Difficulty: Moderate

As noted in the previous excursion, choosing a route along and in the canyons east of the Little Rockies WSA will reward hikers with solitude. The hike down Fourmile Canyon is marked as a trail on Trails Illustrated Map #213, but don't expect a maintained trail.

This hike begins at the same parking area described in the previous section, but as you hike toward the base of Mount Ellsworth, veer left (northeast), leaving the 4WD track at about its midpoint to head for the saddle between Mount Ellsworth and Mount Holmes. The pass or saddle between these two peaks is the highest elevation along the route. Once you're over the saddle, hike down the bed of Fourmile Creek. Usually dry, this drainage provides a relatively easy walk east to Lake Powell. The length of the hike will vary depending on the water level in Lake Powell. In cool weather, a strong hiker could complete the 22-mile round trip in one long day.

Water is scarce, and the best plan is to carry all the water you will need for one and a half days. You might be able to filter water from Fourmile Spring, about 5.5 miles from the parking area, but the spring is more of a seep. As you near Lake Powell, you might find running water and potholes of water in Fourmile Canyon, but there are no guarantees.

Fourmile Canyon deepens as it nears Lake Powell, and there are a few narrow spots that are visually interesting. It's possible to climb out of the canyon to enjoy the views from the benches above, or to camp above the flash-flood plain. Complete solitude and stargazing are the main attractions. Hikers are unlikely to see other humans until they reach Lake Powell. The lake is the lowest elevation on this route.

Enjoy this hike in very early spring or very late fall to avoid the overwhelming desert heat and biting gnats.

Fiddler Butte WSA

The Dirty Devil River bisects Fiddler Butte WSA, located east of the junction of UT 276 and UT 95. The odd shape of Fiddler Butte WSA reflects the southern boundary it shares with Glen Canyon National Recreation Area. Dirty Devil WSA (see Chapter 25) is located several miles north of Fiddler Butte WSA.

In addition to the Dirty Devil River, this WSA includes eight slickrock canyons that drain into North Wash; a mesa named The Block; and benchlands east of the Dirty Devil River. The benchlands, an area of about 40,000 acres, do not measure up to most wilderness criteria. A lack of diversity and opportunities for solitude put the benchlands at the bottom of our list for hiking.

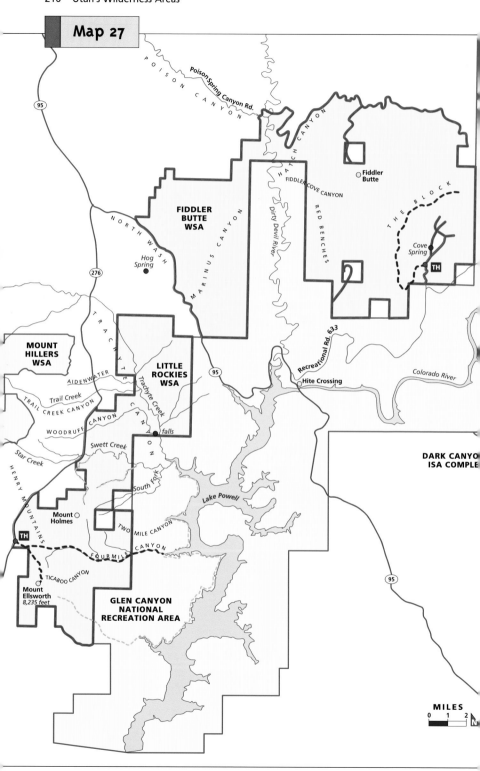

Map 27

POISON CANYON

Poison Spring Canyon Rd.

95

HATCH CANYON

Fiddler
Butte

FIDDLER COVE CANYON

THE BLOCK

FIDDLER
BUTTE
WSA

NORTH WASH

MARINUS CANYON

RED BENCHES

Cove
Spring

TH

Dirty Devil River

276

Hog
Spring

TRACHYTE

Recreational Rd. 633

MOUNT
HILLERS
WSA

LITTLE
ROCKIES
WSA

95

Hite Crossing

Colorado River

AIDENWATER

Trail Creek

TRAIL CREEK CANYON

Trachyte Creek

CANYON

DARK CANYO
ISA COMPLE

WOODRUFF

CANYON

Star Creek

Swett Creek

falls

HENRY MOUNTAINS

South Fork

Mount
Holmes

TWO MILE CANYON

Lake Powell

TH

FOURMILE CANYON

TICABOO CANYON

95

Mount
Ellsworth
8,235 feet

GLEN CANYON
NATIONAL
RECREATION AREA

MILES
0   1   2

N

The Block is an isolated mesa near the eastern edge of the WSA. At 6,805 feet in elevation, it is the highest point in Fiddler Butte WSA. The mesa is particularly difficult to access, so visitors are few. Even cattle do not wander the mesa top. Mining roads and unofficial ways find their way around the base of The Block, including about 8 miles of cherry-stemmed road in The Cove. At Cove Spring, the cherry-stemmed section of road splits and the left fork circles the base of South Block. From the left fork, a primitive trail leads to the top of South Block. From South Block, hikers can cross a narrow land bridge to North Block.

The remote nature of The Block, and the 360-degree views it affords, make for a stunning high-desert experience. Views from the top include Dirty Devil Canyon, Dark Canyon, Cataract Canyon, the Henry Mountains, Canyonlands National Park, and the Abajo Mountains. Juniper and piñon trees provide limited shade, but it is still best to choose cooler weather for hiking. There are no reliable water sources.

For access to The Block, begin near the large Hite Marina on Lake Powell, where UT 95 crosses the Colorado River. Just north of this crossing, Recreation Rd. 633 leads to the cherry-stemmed road into The Cove of Fiddler Butte WSA. From UT 95, it is about 18 miles of dirt road to Cove Spring. You will need Trails Illustrated Map #213 or the USGS map Fiddler Butte to find your way. Though 4WD is recommended, 2WD vehicles can negotiate most of the road; 4WD is required for about the last 1.5 miles.

On the western edge of Fiddler Butte WSA, day-hiking opportunities are excellent. Marinus is the longest canyon, at 6.5 miles, and is easily accessed from UT 95. Park between mileposts 34 and 35, about 14 miles north of Hite and south of the Hog Spring picnic site. Hike into the mouth of Marinus Canyon, whose elevation is about 4,000 feet. You will be hiking up-canyon, toward the cliffs that line the western edge of the Dirty Devil River canyon. Where Marinus canyon forks, keep left to explore the longer fork. A moderate amount of climbing over boulders and dry waterfalls where the canyon narrows could stop some hikers, but this can still be a pleasant out-and-back hike even if you turn around at the first obstacle. Take plenty of drinking water and choose cooler weather for your hike.

Southeast Utah

Other names for this area are the Four Corners, which refers to the meeting of the Utah, Colorado, Arizona, and New Mexico state boundaries; Cedar Mesa, which is usually applied only to the Grand Gulch section; Canyon Land, which is applied generally to the whole area; Canyonlands for the national park section; and Slickrock Country, a reference to the predominant sandstone formations.

Towns and cities are few and far between, with only Moab really qualifying for small city status. Monticello, Blanding, Bluff, and Mexican Hat are beads of civilization on the chain of US 191 and US 163 down the eastern edge of this area. The small town of Hanksville is the one-and-only outpost to the northwest. Lake Powell and the Glen Canyon National Recreation Area define the western edge (see Chapter 43 for a description of the NRA). Two national parks, Arches to the north of Moab, and Canyonlands to the town's southwest, attract the most visitors (see Chapters 37 and 39 for national park information). Natural Bridges National Monument has its own little circle of territory right in the middle of everything (see Chapter 42 for national monument information).

One designated wilderness, Dark Canyon, and 13 study areas are highlights of the varied, and less visited, portions of southeastern Utah. Dark Canyon, where it's possible to cross four land categories in a single expedition, is emblematic of the back-to-back public lands under various kinds of administration: Begin hiking in Manti–La Sal National Forest at the head of Dark Canyon, cross the boundary into the designated Dark Canyon Wilderness, continue down-canyon to the BLM-administered Dark Canyon Instant Study Area Complex (proposed wilderness), and even farther down-canyon, enter Glen Canyon National Recreation Area. Highways and towns are narrow corridors and islands in a huge chunk of wild lands roughly shaped like a right triangle whose hypotenuse is the Colorado River.

Water sources and the intense heat of the summer months are prime concerns when planning an expedition. Flash flooding and rough approach roads are also not to be taken lightly. The descriptions in each chapter outline the water sources and the roads, but be aware that these can change in exceptionally dry or exceptionally wet years. Optimal times to hike, as well as the weather you're likely to encounter, are described in each chapter.

The southeastern Utah chapters that follow are organized so that areas in proximity to each other, or that share a road access, are grouped together:

- **Chapter 28:** Dark Canyon Wilderness and adjacent ISA and WSA
- **Chapter 29:** Mancos Mesa WSA
- **Chapter 30:** Grand Gulch ISA Complex and nearby WSAs on Cedar Mesa
- **Chapter 31:** WSAs next to southeastern Canyonlands National Park
- **Chapter 32:** WSAs near Moab

Castle Butte and nearby formations in the Valley of the Gods are landmarks for hiking into the Road Canyon Wilderness Study Area.

Dark Canyon Wilderness, Dark Canyon ISA Complex, and Cheesebox Canyon WSA

28

Tall sagebrush, ponderosa pine forests, and piñon-juniper woodlands mix in the upper reaches of Dark Canyon, providing habitat for black bears, cougar, and mule deer.

LOCATION: Southeast Utah

SIZE: Dark Canyon Wilderness: 47,116 acres
Dark Canyon ISA Complex: 68,030 acres
Cheesebox Canyon WSA: 15,410 acres

ELEVATION RANGE: 3,700 to 8,500 feet

ECOREGION: Colorado Plateau

MILES OF TRAIL: About 56

ADMINISTRATION:
Manti–La Sal NF, Monticello Ranger District; BLM, San Juan Resource Area; NPS, Glen Canyon NRA; some weather and trail information available from Natural Bridges National Monument rangers: (435) 692-1234

MAPS: Trails Illustrated: Map #703.
USFS: Manti–La Sal.
USGS 1:24,000: Bowdie Canyon East, Bowdie Canyon West, Fable Valley, Indian Head Pass, Black Steer Canyon, Warren Canyon, Poison Canyon, Jacobs Chair, The Cheesebox, Woodenshoe Buttes, Kilgalia Point.

BOTH THE DESIGNATED WILDERNESS AND the adjacent instant study area (ISA) have the same name, Dark Canyon. The tributaries of Dark Canyon are Black Steer, Youngs, Lost, and Lean-To Canyons—all of which can be explored as side trips of a Dark Canyon expedition. Fable Valley is part of the Dark Canyon ISA Complex administered by the BLM, but it's a tributary of Gypsum Canyon, accessible from the Dark Canyon Plateau but not from the main canyon. Cheesebox Canyon, part of the White Canyon area near Natural Bridges National Monument, is separated from the Dark Canyon area by dirt access roads and a ridge of highcountry.

Most of the trailheads for Dark Canyon can be accessed only via driving over Bears Ears Pass, which tops out at 8,800 feet. High elevation, particularly when coupled with shade on north-facing slopes, makes for a late melt-out of snow. The road is usually open from May to October. A high-clearance vehicle is recommended and 4WD is required when the road is wet. Late spring or early fall are good times to hike the upper portions of Dark Canyon, but, thanks to the high elevation, even the summer months are bearable, especially if you hike early in the morning and in the evening. Be aware of flash-flood dangers when planning your hikes and campsites.

One trailhead usually remains open year-round, Sundance off UT 95, near Lake Powell. Low elevation makes this an excellent early season access point for lower Dark Canyon. However, the "trail" becomes extremely rugged once it leaves the plateau. Only hikers in good physical condition should attempt the descent into the canyon from the Sundance Trail. You'll want to pack as lightly as possible and have your hands free for working your way over the boulders.

It's hard to choose an ideal season for hiking the entire 40 miles of Dark Canyon from Big Notch Trailhead to the Colorado River (Lake Powell). We hiked the lower canyon in April and hiked the upper canyon on a later expedition in June.

Water is usually intermittent, but it is easy to find once you get to the floor of a canyon. Dry approach routes and exceptions are noted in the trail descriptions. Land managers have been discouraging campfires, though they are not forbidden.

BACKPACK: SUNDANCE TRAILHEAD TO DARK CANYON
One-Way Length: 8–10 miles (30 or more miles including side trips)
Low and High Elevations: 3,700 and about 6,200 feet
Difficulty: Strenuous

Allow at least three days to complete this strenuous hike: One day to get in, one day to explore, and one day to crawl out. Part of the approach requires Class III climbing on a 50-degree slope.

Sundance Trailhead appears on maps, but it is not signed on the ground. Access is from UT 95 about 36.5 miles northwest of Natural Bridges National Monument. About 1.4 miles west of the Glen Canyon NRA sign, turn northeast (a right-hand turn if you came from Natural Bridges) on a dirt road signed "San Juan County 208A—Horse Tanks." Drive 4.8 miles on Horse Tanks Rd. to an intersection with CR 213A—Brown Rim Rd. (another access point from UT 95 that is 1.2 miles from Hite Marina on Lake Powell). From the intersection, continue on Horse Tanks Rd.

as it turns southeast. Ignore the first opportunity to join CR 209A (7 miles from UT 95) as it's a rougher road. Stay on the main road until you come to the second intersection with 209A, at 8.2 miles from UT 95. In places, this road requires 6 inches of clearance, but it is usually passable for light-duty vehicles when conditions are dry; 4WD is required when wet. Follow 209A northeast for 2.5 miles. There are a few carsonite posts that say simply "trail." Although the turn to the Sundance Trailhead is not signed, it is marked with rock cairns. Turn left at the rock cairns, and it's 0.2 mile to a parking area (10.6 miles from UT 95).

The trail crosses the earthen dam of a stock pond and then begins its 2-mile trek across the plateau, not far from the rim of Dark Canyon. The approach to "Dark Canyon Wilderness/Dark Canyon Primitive Area" is signed. Where the trail splits a few hundred yards from the trailhead, keep right for Dark Canyon.

On the rim, the trail wanders over slickrock, through red sand, junipers, and cactus, sometimes descending or climbing very short sections of steep slickrock, and eventually losing about 300 feet in elevation. Rock cairns marking the trail are small and difficult to spot in some places; in other places the tread is obvious and easy to follow. There are no water sources on the plateau.

Where the trail leaves the rim and descends steeply (50 degrees) toward the canyon floor, the way becomes indistinct and difficult. It's a Class III scramble with misleading cairns and footpaths where unlucky hikers from the past have searched for a way down. *The best route down angles southwest.* The steepness is unrelenting for

From an overlook in the Abajo Mountains, Dark Canyon Wilderness stretches toward Lake Powell in southeastern Utah.

about a mile, and the elevation loss is about 1,120 feet. Before you descend, look into the canyon; if you can't see water in the bottom, you should not enter Dark Canyon.

Luckily, there's running water and a wide spot conducive to camping almost as soon as hikers reach the canyon floor. The stream usually flows year-round from a point 1 mile up-canyon from the Youngs Canyon confluence with Dark Canyon, all the way to Lake Powell. In extremely dry years, hikers might have to search for pools and springs.

An 8-mile up-canyon hike will take you across blue-gray limestone benches dotted with inclusions of mulberry-red chert—easy walking in some places, but in others requiring a bit of climbing and wading. It can be snowing on the rim while a delicate springtime blossoms on the canyon floor. You can spot the tracks of cougars and bighorn sheep in the wet sand at streamside.

Anywhere between Lean-To and Lost Canyons, there are plenty of spots wide enough to set up a tent well away from the water. From Lost Canyon to the Youngs Canyon intersection there are few camping spots, so plan accordingly. Going down-canyon toward Lake Powell, the canyon again narrows enough to eliminate campsites. A 3.5-mile hike down-canyon from the point where Sundance Trail reaches the floor of Dark Canyon will take hikers to Lake Powell.

If you hike far enough up-canyon you end up in the Dark Canyon Wilderness, the designated wilderness area in the Manti–La Sal National Forest. A much easier access point to this designated wilderness is via the Horse Pasture Canyon Trail off Elk Ridge Rd., or via the Woodenshoe Canyon Trail (see the next two hikes). It also makes more sense to hike from high elevation to lower elevation in upper Dark Canyon. The virtues of the Sundance Trailhead entrance are its year-round accessibility and the fact that it offers more opportunities for solitude and adventure.

> **BACKPACK: WOODENSHOE, DARK, AND PEAVINE CANYONS**
> One-Way Length: About 40 miles (more with side trips)
> Low and High Elevations: 5,900 and about 8,500 feet
> Difficulty: Strenuous

Woodenshoe Canyon Trail is the most popular access into Dark Canyon. The back-packing trip described here is a loop hike that takes five to seven days. It could be shortened by hiking the 13-mile length of Woodenshoe and then returning the same way for a total of 26 miles; by hiking to the first side trip described here and then returning (about 22 miles round trip); or by arranging for a 4WD vehicle shuttle out of Peavine Canyon via the Peavine Corridor Rd. (The Peavine Corridor Rd. is a motorized access that begins at Little Notch Trailhead and goes to the old drill rig in Rig Canyon. The extremely narrow road is seldom used and crosses several washouts. Only experienced drivers of short-wheel-base, high-clearance vehicles should attempt to drive it. It's actually a better hiking trail than a road.)

Trailhead access is 2WD in good weather, but snow can close it until mid-May. East of Natural Bridges National Monument, from UT 275, turn north on Elk Ridge Rd., also signed as CR 228. This graded dirt and gravel road takes you to FR 088,

In the Scorup Cabin in Dark Canyon a poem by Stephen Vincent Benet was copied onto a wall, "So I saddled a red unbroken colt/And rode him into the day there/But he threw me down like a thunderbolt/and rolled on me as I lay there...."

over Bears Ears Pass, and then down to an intersection with FR 108, Woodenshoe Rd. Turn left (west) on FR 108. After you drive 2 miles, FR 108 becomes FR 181, but it's the same road, still going west. Continue for another 1.6 miles on FR 181 to Woodenshoe Canyon Rd. Turn right (north) and drive 0.5 mile to the trailhead.

Register at the trailhead, then follow the trail through a gate on a jeep road that is now closed to motorized travel. The trailhead is at 8,040 feet and the ponderosa pines create a beautiful, parklike forest. An easy descent on the old road takes hikers through aspen groves, sagebrush, and scrub oak. The road eventually becomes a footpath.

You reach the Cherry Canyon confluence in about 4 miles; look for a seep of water where it joins Woodenshoe Canyon. It's possible to camp a short distance from the water source. Below Cherry Canyon, about a mile down Woodenshoe Canyon, look for petroglyphs and a cliff dwelling.

Option: About 2 miles below the Cherry Canyon confluence, a smaller, nameless canyon enters from the east. Watch for a stone arch near the canyon entrance, then take a side trip to view more cliff dwellings in the smaller canyon. Springs usually provide water about 2.5 miles up this nameless canyon.

Back on the main trail: About 8 miles from the Woodenshoe Canyon Trailhead, the canyon narrows and cuts through limestone. A lack of water and of camping sites will keep you hiking toward the confluence of Woodenshoe and Dark Canyons. One mile before the confluence, a spring and a hanging garden are a welcome respite. Campsites are easy to find in and around the confluence of the two canyons.

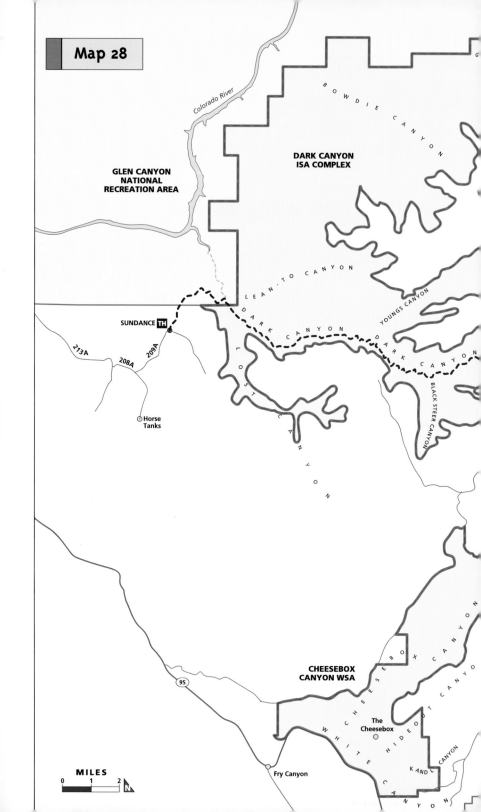

Map 28

GLEN CANYON
NATIONAL
RECREATION AREA

Colorado River

B O W D I E   C A N Y O N

DARK CANYON
ISA COMPLEX

L E A N - T O   C A N Y O N

YOUNGS CANYON

D A R K   C A N Y O N

D A R K   C A N Y O N

SUNDANCE TH

213A

208A

209A

Horse
Tanks

L
O
S
T

C
A
N
Y
O
N

BLACK STEER CANYON

95

CHEESEBOX
CANYON WSA

C H E E S E B O X   C A N Y O N

HIDEOUT CANYON

The
Cheesebox

W H I T E   H I D E O U T   C A N Y O N

K A N D   L   C A N Y O N

Fry Canyon

MILES
0   1   2
N

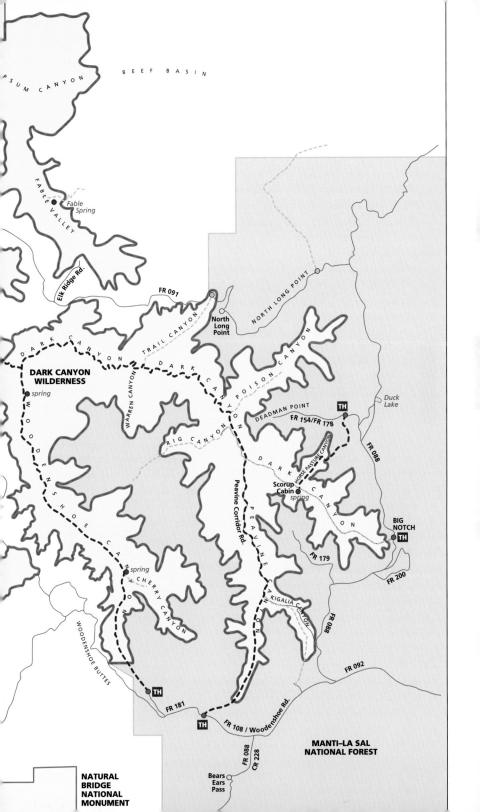

To continue this loop hike, turn right and hike up Dark Canyon. You'll gain about 500 feet in elevation as you hike past the entrances of Warren and Trail Canyons. A water source 6 miles after your turn up Dark Canyon shouldn't be skipped. Camping in the area around the water is pleasant, with the terrain dominated by sand, sagebrush, and grasses.

Another 5 miles (that's about 11 miles in Dark Canyon itself, 24 miles from the Woodenshoe Canyon Trailhead) brings hikers to Rig Canyon and signs of human activity: a corral, a dirt road, and fences. Rig Canyon gets its name from its status as a defunct oil-drilling site. One mile past Rig Canyon brings you to Peavine Canyon and your turn southeast on Peavine Corridor Rd. Hike up Peavine Canyon on the road about 4.5 miles. Where the road turns into Kigalia Canyon, leave the road and continue on Peavine Canyon Trail. Depending on the season, there's intermittent water in the streambed.

Another 5 miles of trekking up the Peavine Canyon Trail, with an elevation gain of about 1,000 feet, brings you to the corrals near Woodenshoe Rd. If you haven't arranged for a shuttle vehicle, you'll hike another 4 miles to return to Woodenshoe Canyon Trailhead.

> **DAY HIKE: HORSE PASTURE CANYON TO SCORUP CABIN**
> One-Way Length: 3.5 miles
> Low and High Elevations: 7,152 and 8,600 feet
> Difficulty: Easy

The destination, Scorup Cabin in Dark Canyon, is a holdover from a past era. J. A. Scorup was a local rancher who ran cattle in the canyons, beginning in about 1890. The Dutch Scorup family named nearby Woodenshoe Buttes. On one wall of this unattended museum, a poem by Stephen Vincent Benet has been copied: "So I saddled a red unbroken colt/And rode him into the day there/But he threw me down like a thunderbolt/And rolled on me as I lay there…And my youth returns like the rains of spring/And my sons like wild geese calling/And I lie and hear the meadowlark sing/And have much content in my dieing."

This cabin full of history and questionable spelling is not the only sign left of summer cow camps that remained in use until the 1970s. Now Forest Service property, the cabin is preserved for its historical value. It's fine to go in for a look, but don't camp in or around the building, and don't ruin this bit of the past by taking or moving any of the artifacts.

Horse Pasture Canyon Trail (Trail 025), a 3.5-mile access to upper Dark Canyon, joins the canyon near the Scorup Cabin. There are other ways to get to Scorup Cabin, but none are as pretty as the well-cut trail down from the aspen groves above to the green meadows and sandstone alcoves below. It's only 7 miles round trip, but you'll want to allow ample time for exploring and enjoying the surrounding area (there's a 1905 cow camp west of Scorup Cabin). And remember that you have a 1,448-foot elevation gain when you return to the trailhead.

See the road description in the previous hike for the route over Bears Ears Pass to the intersection of FR 088 and FR 108. At the intersection, turn right (east) on

FR 088. Stay on FR 088 for 17 miles, following it as it turns north. The road gets rougher and narrower as it goes north and is not suitable for towing trailers. It definitely requires 4WD when wet. You'll pass Big Notch Trailhead. Watch for Duck Lake on your right. Across from the lake, on the left, is FR 154 (FR 178 on Trails Illustrated map), which is signed as "Deadman Point/Horse Pasture." Recent logging to stop the spread of bark beetles makes the approach to the trailhead confusing, but persevere for 1.5 miles past an old corral on Deadman Point Rd.

The view from the rim includes white-and-pink cliffs that surround the pasture far below. For the first 1.5 miles, the trail descends gradually through groves of aspen, fir, and oak, with many more views of the canyon. Below the trees, the trail continues through a layer of cream-colored sandstone and is easy to follow as it makes its way down into the canyon. The visible trail peters out in the thick grass on the canyon floor, but you won't get lost. Just walk southwest through the grass, working your way down-canyon. Scorup Cabin sits at the confluence of Horse Pasture and Dark Canyons.

There's no water on this hike until you reach Scorup Cabin, where a stream flows over multiple ledges of erosion-resistant sandstone. A year-round spring near the waterfall provides the best drinking water.

Cheesebox Canyon WSA

There are no official trails in this area. Canyoneering is the best way to find solitude and screening from civilization. Pouroffs (dry waterfalls), plunge pools, and other rough terrain demand rock-climbing skills, swimming, and floating backpacks. Traveling in this area requires excellent route-finding skills with topographical maps.

Cheesebox Canyon WSA is accessed off UT 95. The one-building outpost of Fry Canyon, with its combined motel, cafe, gas station, and convenience store, offers the only services. Fry Canyon is a good place to inquire about the jeep roads in the area.

White, Hideout, and K and L Canyons are also within the boundaries of the WSA. White Canyon boasts a few cottonwood trees, with more vegetation around seeps. White Canyon is also the main feature of Natural Bridges National Monument. Many hikers headed for the 6 miles of White Canyon that are in the BLM-administered WSA begin in the monument and hike only those portions suited to their skills.

The infamous Black Hole (not to be confused with the Black Box in the San Rafael Swell) is in White Canyon, but is outside the WSA. Canyoneers who brave the Black Hole have to be prepared to swim a pool about 200 yards long in very cold water, with the surrounding rock walls narrowing to about 1.5 feet. Wetsuits are recommended for early season forays.

If this is your cup of cold tea, park at milepost 57 on UT 95 and make your way down a short side canyon. About 6 miles of the 7.5-mile route are moderately difficult canyon hiking. The most difficult spot is the Black Hole proper, which requires jumping, climbing, sliding, and maneuvering in addition to swimming. The exit from the Black Hole is a steep trail to milepost 55; you might want to scout this trail ahead of time to see if it is within your skill level. A few hardy souls continue beyond the Black Hole to Lake Powell and arrange for a boat shuttle near Copper Point.

29 Mancos Mesa WSA

Firecracker penstemon shows its brilliant red tubelike blooms in early spring.

MINERAL EXPLORATION HEAVILY IMPACTS about 10% of Mancos Mesa, but the remaining 90% is natural and offers both solitude and primitive recreational opportunities. No signs, no trails, no campgrounds. You will need the 1:24,000 topos listed in the maps section of this chapter to find roads, water sources, and routes into the canyons.

This remote area is 50 miles west of the small town of Blanding and lies north of UT 276, the border of the Red House Cliffs. To approach from the other direction, drivers have to take the ferry across Lake Powell at Halls Crossing.

Mancos Mesa is an enormous block of slickrock mesa surrounded by steep cliffs. Much of the mesa's highcountry is covered with windblown

LOCATION: Southeast Utah
SIZE: 51,440 acres
ELEVATION RANGE: 4,800 to 6,100 feet
ECOREGION: Colorado Plateau, northern limit of Sonoran Desert
MILES OF TRAIL: None; routes are in washes and canyon bottoms
ADMINISTRATION: BLM, San Juan Resource Area
MAPS: Trails Illustrated: Map #213.
USGS 1:100,000: Navajo Mountain.
USGS 1:24,000: Knowles Canyon, Mancos Mesa NE, Mancos Mesa, Chocolate Drop, Halls Crossing NE.

sand, a true desert environment. The mesa tilts to the west and its canyons drain into Lake Powell. The Glen Canyon NRA forms the WSA's western and northwestern borders (41,700 acres within the NRA have also been proposed as the Moki–Mancos Mesa Wilderness). The rim of Moki Canyon is the southern border. Red Canyon and the mining roads along its rim form the eastern border.

From UT 276 near milepost 81, an unsigned dirt road leads down Red Canyon, just outside the borders of the WSA. There are other canyons in Utah named Red Canyon, so make sure you've got the right one when you're planning an expedition. This particular Red Canyon is usually so dry that it has no reliable water sources and boasts only a single, lonely cottonwood tree. It's possible to hike or jeep the canyon all the way to Lake Powell. The road is 2WD for about 6 miles, then 4WD for the remainder of its length. Some sections of the Red Canyon Rd. offer views of Little Rockies WSA and of the Henry Mountains. The road becomes Recreation Rd. 650 where it enters the Glen Canyon NRA.

About 9 miles west of Clay Hills, a 4WD dirt road leads onto Mancos Mesa off UT 276, but it is not signed. Look for a mailbox that says "Wilderness Quest." There are 25 miles of ways open to ORV use within the WSA, but they are seldom used. The BLM does not maintain these ways and most of them are eroded or drifted over in spots and therefore not accessible to 4WD vehicles for much of their length. However, these old roads can be seen from the mesa top, and hikers can use them as trails.

Three major canyons and segments of two more canyons offer the best opportunities for solitude and for viewing interesting rock formations. The fact that there are no year-round streams and only a few springs limits backpacking and hiking possibilities (the springs are on the USGS 1:24,000 maps). Bring your own water and hike in the early spring when water is more plentiful. The few hanging gardens and seeps in the canyons offer striking contrast to the surrounding desert. North Gulch Canyon ranges from 450 to 800 feet deep and begins near the center of the WSA, then it trends southwest toward the Colorado River. Cedar Canyon begins near the eastern edge and trends northwest for 12 miles, where it also meets the Glen Canyon NRA and the Colorado River. Mancos Canyon, a major tributary of Cedar Canyon that occupies the northern tip of the WSA, is 8 miles long and about 250 to 450 feet deep. The BLM has recorded 17 archaeological sites in the WSA, 6 of which are Anasazi rock structures located in the canyons.

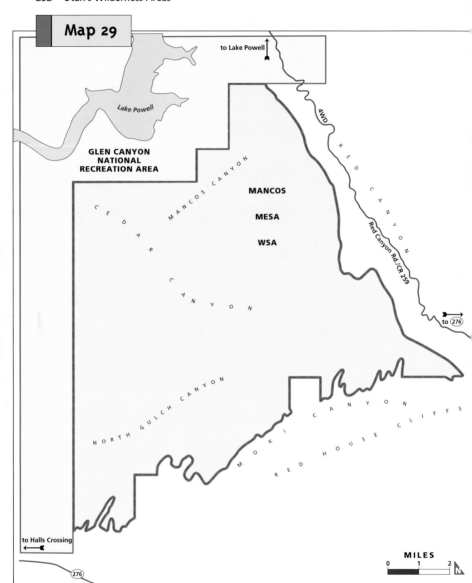

Map 29

to Lake Powell

Lake Powell

4WD

RED CANYON

Red Canyon Rd./CR 259

GLEN CANYON
NATIONAL
RECREATION AREA

MANCOS CANYON

MANCOS

MESA

WSA

CEDAR CANYON

to 276

NORTH GULCH CANYON

MOKI CANYON

RED HOUSE CLIFFS

to Halls Crossing

276

MILES
0   1   2

N

Grand Gulch ISA Complex, Fish Creek Canyon WSA, Road Canyon WSA, and Mule Canyon WSA

30

Barbara Howard admires the scenery in Kane Gulch, one of many tributary canyons to Grand Gulch.

LOCATION: Southeast Utah

SIZE: Grand Gulch ISA Complex: 105,520 acres
Fish Creek Canyon WSA: 46,440 acres
Road Canyon WSA: 52,240 acres
Mule Canyon WSA: 5,990 acres

ELEVATION RANGE: 4,000 to 7,000 feet

ECOREGION: Colorado Plateau

MILES OF TRAIL: About 75 miles of established routes, but few maintained trails

ADMINISTRATION: BLM, San Juan Resource Area

MAPS: Trails Illustrated: Map #706.
USGS 1:100,000: Bluff.
USGS 1:24,000: Moss Back Butte, Kane Gulch, South Long Point, Hotel Rock, Clay Hills, Red House Spring, Polly's Pasture, Cedar Mesa North, Snow Flat Spring Cave, Bluff NW, Slickhorn Canyon West, Slickhorn Canyon East, Cedar Mesa South, Cigarette Spring Cave, Bluff SW.

THIS CHAPTER COVERS the instant study and wilderness study areas in the Grand Gulch–Cedar Mesa region. Although road corridors separate these areas, they have the feel of one large chunk of backcountry. In addition to the four BLM study areas, an adjacent slice of the Glen Canyon NRA along the north side of the San Juan River has been recommended for wilderness.

"Cedar Mesa" refers to the Permian Cedar Mesa Sandstone that is the top layer of this broad uplift. The sandstone derives from dunes that drifted there about 300 to 230 million years ago. Many visitors assume the forest of short evergreens that covers much of the mesa are cedar trees, but the plants are actually junipers and piñons. True cedars (*Cedrus*) are not native to North America. (Trees of wet Northwestern forests that are called cedars are actually arborvitae of the genus *Thuja*.)

The nearest towns are Blanding, Bluff, and Mexican Hat. US 191 runs down the eastern side, several miles outside of the wilderness study areas. US 163 is a southern access; UT 95 and UT 276 are northern access routes; and UT 261 runs right down the middle. The Kane Gulch Ranger Station is on UT 261. In addition to these paved routes, several dirt roads provide access to trailheads and to cross-country routes:

• Valley of the Gods Rd. (CR 242) winds for 16.5 miles through the Valley of the Gods at the southern edge of Road Canyon WSA.

• Comb Wash Rd. (CR 235) connects US 163 in the south with UT 95 in the north, meeting up with Snow Flat Rd. (CR 237) along the way.

• Snow Flat Rd. (CR 237, or the Mormon Trail) divides Fish Creek Canyon WSA and Road Canyon WSA. A 4WD vehicle with high clearance and a short wheel base is required for negotiating Snow Flat Rd.

An April snowstorm blankets the West Fork of Lime Creek.

• Collins Spring Rd. or Gulch Creek Rd. (CR 260) leads from UT 276 to Collins Spring Trailhead.

• Owl Creek Rd. or Long Spike Rd. (CR 253) leads from UT 261 to the Owl Creek/Fish Creek Trailhead.

• Cigarette Springs Rd. (CR 239), off UT 261, leads to several mesa-top routes (unmaintained trails) that can be used to view the canyons and Anasazi ruins from above. Impassable when wet.

• Point Lookout Rd. (CR 203), directly across UT 261 from Cigarette Springs Rd., leads to several trailheads, each beginning at the head of a different fork of Slickhorn Canyon. Slickhorn Rd. (CR 245) is an offshoot of CR 203.

• CR 221A (off UT 261) is a rough track that leads to two access points for Johns Canyon, an area that receives very little use compared with the other major tributaries of Grand Gulch. Short day hikes can be made into its upper reaches.

• Experienced drivers might choose to negotiate other seldom-used routes that the BLM describes as "ways." You will need USGS topographical maps to locate these ways. Please observe all posted closures and check with the Kane Gulch Ranger Station before attempting to drive on an unofficial, unmaintained road.

Basketmaker peoples lived in Grand Gulch from about A.D. 200 to 700, and the Pueblo or Anasazi culture thrived as a large community from about A.D. 1060 to 1270. The cliff dwellings and other ruins that hikers see today are remnants from the Pueblo culture. For more information on these prehistoric cultures, see the introductory material in the front of this book and check the bibliography for further reading. To protect the fragile environment and the archaeological sites from the onslaught of 35,000 annual visitors, land administrators have limited recreational use and have requested that visitors follow "Ethical Backcountry Archaeology" guidelines:

1. Advance reservations are recommended for overnight use, and are required for groups of 8 to 12 people and for groups using horses. Groups of 1 to 7 persons are eligible for trailhead allocations held for walk-ins.

2. The total number of people per day is limited from 12 to 26 depending on the area, with the exception of Road and Mule Canyons, which receive less use, and where permits are not required.

3. Day users do not need a reservation but must pay a day-use fee.

4. Permits are issued at the Kane Gulch Ranger Station from 8 a.m. to noon each day. Day use passes are also available at designated trailheads, self-service mode.

5. Middens, ancient trash dumps near archaeological sites, are the main source of important artifacts. They are usually located in front of or to the side of the site. Avoid walking over middens as this will cause both damage and erosion.

6. Do not camp or cook in alcoves where ruins are located.

7. When viewing archaeological sites, keep impact as low as possible. Avoid touching or walking on any of the walls or roofs. Don't remove pottery or other artifacts. Don't touch rock art, as chalking, rubbing, tracing, or otherwise handling it will eventually cause it to disappear. Keep pets out of the sites.

8. Remember that visitors are given archaeological site stewardship and must take the responsibility seriously if the area is to remain open to hikers.

9. Follow all Leave-No-Trace hiking and camping guidelines.

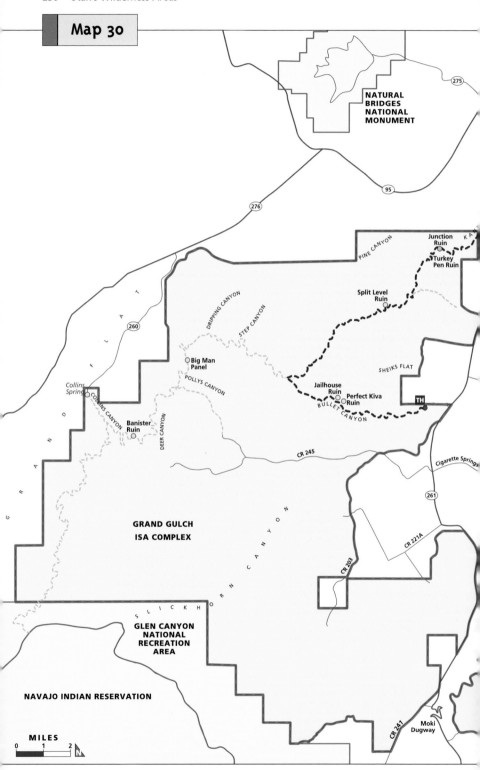

Map 30

NATURAL
BRIDGES
NATIONAL
MONUMENT

275

95

276

260

PINE CANYON

Junction
Ruin

Turkey
Pen Ruin

Split Level
Ruin

DRIPPING CANYON

STEP CANYON

SHEIKS FLAT

Big Man
Panel

POLLYS CANYON

Collins
Springs

COLLINS CANYON

Jailhouse
Ruin

Perfect Kiva
Ruin

BULLET CANYON

TH

DEER CANYON

Banister
Ruin

CR 245

Cigarette Springs

261

CR 221A

CR 203

GRAND GULCH
ISA COMPLEX

SLICKHORN CANYON

GLEN CANYON
NATIONAL
RECREATION
AREA

NAVAJO INDIAN RESERVATION

CR 241

Moki
Dugway

MILES
0   1   2
N

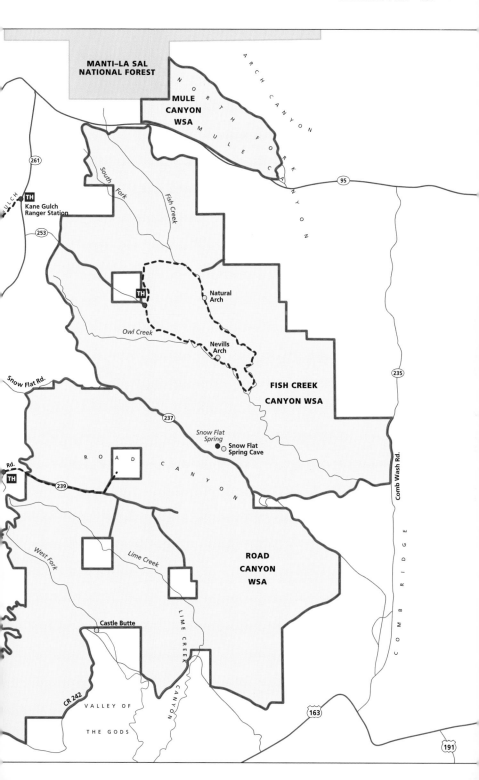

Grand Gulch ISA Complex

The Grand Gulch Complex is actually several WSAs grouped together with the Grand Gulch Primitive Area (or ISA): Pine Canyon, Bullet Canyon, Sheiks Flat, and Slickhorn Canyon. The most popular hikes are within the confines of the original BLM primitive area, where the greatest concentration of archaeological sites combines with canyon hikes that have reliable water sources.

> **DAY HIKE:** KANE GULCH TO TURKEY PEN RUIN
> One-Way Length: 4.7 miles
> Low and High Elevations: 5,840 and 6,400 feet
> Difficulty: Moderate

The trail begins directly across the highway from the Kane Gulch Ranger Station. Follow the signs and visible tread down Kane Wash to enter Kane Gulch. Hike down-canyon, making your way over slickrock benches, past scattered stands of aspen and cottonwood trees, and along the stream bank. The trail is marked with cairns in some places, but mostly follows the canyon floor in whatever way seems best. Junction Ruin is at mile 4, where Kane Gulch and Grand Gulch meet. Turkey Pen Ruin is at mile 4.7 on the south-facing wall of the canyon. Turn around here and go back the way you came for a 9.4-mile round trip.

> **SHUTTLE BACKPACK:** KANE GULCH TO BULLET CANYON TRAILHEAD
> One-Way Length: 23 miles
> Low and High Elevations: 5,360 and 6,429 feet
> Difficulty: Moderate

The most popular backpacking trip is the 23-mile hike from Kane Gulch to Bullet Canyon Trailhead, which still leaves you with about 7.5 miles of UT 261 for a shuttle back to your starting point. This route takes you past five of the most spectacular ruins: Junction Ruin (mile 4), Turkey Pen Ruin (mile 4.7), Split Level Ruin (mile 10), Jailhouse Ruin (mile 17.8), and Perfect Kiva Ruin (mile 18.3).

The hike begins at 6,400 feet in Kane Wash and descends as you work your way down the wash and into Kane Gulch (see the previous hike). The lowest point is the junction of Kane Gulch and Bullet Canyon. At the junction, you turn up Bullet Canyon and gain elevation as you approach the Bullet Canyon Trailhead.

About a mile of hiking in Kane Wash brings you to Kane Gulch, where the trail enters the canyon. There are fewer water crossings later in the season when the watercourse is dry in places. Seasonal flash floods alter the canyon floor so it's never quite the same from year to year.

Unnamed ruins await in many of the side canyons, and smaller ruins may not appear on any maps, so it can be a great adventure to go off the beaten path. South-facing alcoves are likely places to look for ruins. Overhangs with smooth sandstone walls below them are good spots to look for rock art.

Because this route is so heavily used, my advice is to day-hike to ruins in Kane Gulch one day, then day-hike to ruins in Bullet Canyon another day so as not to add to the backcountry camping use of an already overused area. Another option is to hike the route in mid- to late October when the crowds lessen.

Fish Creek Canyon WSA

The Fish Creek Canyon system includes four major canyons that are about 700 feet deep, as well as many more minor tributaries. Most of the hiking routes are not maintained trails. The high rock walls and the meanders of the canyons screen hikers from man-made sights and sounds.

> **LOOP BACKPACK: OWL CREEK CANYON TO FISH CREEK CANYON**
> One-Way Length: 15 miles (30 or more miles including side trips)
> Low and High Elevations: 4,800 and 6,200 feet
> Difficulty: Strenuous

Access to Owl Creek Canyon, the start of this three- to five-day loop hike, is via improved dirt CR 253 off UT 261. About 1 mile south of the Kane Gulch Ranger Station, turn left (east) onto CR 253 and drive about 5 miles to where the road ends at the trailhead.

The descent from trailhead to canyon bottom is difficult because there's no developed trail down the steep terrain. In a few places, visitors going over the same route have established a semblance of a trail. Some Class II and Class III climbing is required on steep rock pitches. Once you've made it to the canyon floor, the going is easier. Most hikers descend down Owl Creek, hike to the confluence, and return up Fish Creek.

Good water sources in both Owl and Fish Creek Canyons make this hike very pleasant. Reliable water sources also encourage numerous side trips up tributary canyons from several possible base-camp locations. The first good water source is about 1.6 miles from the Owl Creek Canyon rim. After you have made your way around two pouroffs (dry waterfalls), look for a spring and a good campsite near the bottom of the second pouroff. From this water source it is about 8.5 miles to the next water in Fish Creek Canyon. Pools of water are more frequent in early spring.

On your way up Fish Creek Canyon, the hiking is on solid slickrock for much of the way. Anasazi kiva, dwelling, and grain storage ruins are plentiful. Most of these are not marked on maps and it is easy to hike past them without seeing them. The locals who live in the canyon now include mountain lions and black bears.

At the first major junction in Fish Creek Canyon, keep left (west) to reach a spring about 0.5 mile from the junction. Ponderosa pines add to the beauty of the canyon here, and this is also a good place to set up a base camp for further explorations. From the spring in the left fork of Fish Creek, a user-created trail climbs 600 feet to the rim. It's a steep but short climb. Once on top, a visible trail takes you 1.5 miles back to the trailhead. This is a true loop hike, beginning and ending at the same trailhead.

Road Canyon WSA

Road Canyon WSA is bordered on the east by a section of the 90-mile-long, 600-foot-high escarpment of Comb Ridge. This monocline runs north-south, with its steep face on the west side. The dirt Comb Wash Rd. (CR 235) parallels the western face of the ridge and gives access to the wide mouth of Road Canyon.

In the southwestern section, the stone turrets and battlements of Valley of the Gods make for a very scenic approach route to Lime Creek Canyon. CR 242 (dirt road) from US 163 is the access to Valley of the Gods. Mexican Hat is the nearest town.

UT 261 is the western border of Road Canyon, and this route includes one of the most impressive stretches of road building in all of Utah, the Moki Dugway. Moki Dugway is a set of steep switchbacks that climbs a thousand feet up from the Valley of the Gods terrace to the top of Cedar Mesa. The terrace is, in turn, a thousand feet

Going with the flow—a cottonwood tree in the West Fork of Lime Creek shows the effects of having survived flash floods.

above the San Juan River, so the views from Moki Dugway, as you swing from horizon to horizon on the switchbacks, are spectacular. The Dugway was built during the uranium boom of the 1950s and has since been improved, but it is still a stretch of graded dirt that will trigger fear in most drivers. UT 261 is paved before and after the Moki Dugway, so a serious attitude adjustment is required when you hit the dirt section. Coming down from the mesa is a real brake-burner if you don't gear down—not recommended for trailers.

At the top of Moki Dugway, just before the pavement ends, dirt CR 241 leads to Muley Point, an overlook from which you can see The Goosenecks of the San Juan River and Arizona's Monument Valley. In a land of breathtaking overlooks, Muley Point ranks as one of the best, and I highly recommend that you don't pass it by. The overlook is on Permian rocks about 245 million years old, and it looks back in time to the older Pennsylvanian rocks. Northwest of the point lie portions of the Glen Canyon NRA that have been recommended for wilderness designation.

South of Kane Gulch Ranger Station and north of Moki Dugway, two dirt roads depart UT 261 to give access to the higher elevations of Road Canyon WSA: Snow Flat Rd. (CR 237) and Cigarette Springs Rd. (CR 239).

DAY HIKE: HEAD OF ROAD CANYON OVERLOOK
One-Way Length: 2–4 miles
Low and High Elevations: 6,000 and 6,400 feet
Difficulty: Easy

This mesa-top day hike has no official trail and no official trailhead. It is an easy hike, however, and it serves as a good example of the infinite opportunities for off-trail exploration in this area. You'll need the Trails Illustrated map or the USGS 1:24,000 Cedar Mesa North and Cigarette Spring Cave topographical maps. Remember to bring your binoculars.

About 10 miles south of the Kane Gulch Ranger Station, turn east on Cigarette Springs Rd. and drive about 3.25 miles to a spot just past the point where a nameless 4WD track enters from the right. Park just off the road in the junipers and start hiking on the left (north) side of the road, heading generally northeast toward the rim of Road Canyon, following the gently descending terrain for about 1 mile. Once you reach the rim, turn southeast and walk parallel to the rim. Another 0.5 to 1 mile of walking along the rim should bring you to a point from which you can see the Anasazi "Ceiling Ruin," a cliff dwelling in the south-facing wall of upper Road Canyon.

Cigarette Springs Rd. continues across the mesa to other canyon overlooks. A 4WD vehicle is required.

Mule Canyon WSA

There are two hiking routes (no official trails) about 5 miles long in this WSA. A reasonably fit hiker could explore both the North Fork and the main fork of Mule Canyon in one day, but there are also camping opportunities for an overnight back-packing trip. Snow melting off the Abajo Mountains, as well as seeps within the canyons, usually provide enough water for filtering, but bring your own water just in case. The canyon floors are the hiking routes, and they are open enough to also act as horseback routes for about half of their length. Cattle trails make for easy hiking to about the midpoint of each canyon. Beyond the midpoint, boulders and ponderosa pines combine with steep climbs to render progress through the narrow sections difficult. The overall elevation change is from about 6,000 feet to 7,000 feet. Mule Canyon's walls are 500 feet high where it cuts into the mesa, but only measure about 80 feet high where the hiking routes begin.

Drive about 25 miles southwest of Blanding on UT 95. Turn right (north) off UT 95 about 0.5 mile southeast of the Mule Canyon Ruins Rest Stop. Follow the road that heads west to cross both forks of Mule Canyon. This is CR 263 on the map and is the old Highway 95. Drive about 0.25 mile to the first canyon entrance, and 1 mile to the North Fork entrance.

In this small area, there exist 37 known archaeological sites, including Anasazi cliff dwellings and granaries in the south-facing sandstone alcoves. Archaeologists have speculated that some of the sites were built with holes in their walls that relate to changing seasons and to summer and winter solstices: Where light shines through a hole, it illuminates a petroglyph.

Thanks to the good road access, visitors can hike this wilderness study area in almost any season, including winter. Permits are not required. Nearby Arch Canyon is outside the boundary of the WSA, but it is listed in citizen proposals for wilderness to Congress.

River Travel

April and May are the best months to float the San Juan River from Bluff to Clay Hills Crossing. The 85 miles of river travel offer opportunities for numerous hikes up side canyons. A much shorter rafting or kayaking trip puts in at Bluff and makes use of the takeout at Mexican Hat, only 26.5 miles downstream. Class III rapids and access to Slickhorn and Johns Canyons, as well as Grand Gulch, are highlights of the longer float trip. With a steeper gradient than the Colorado in the Grand Canyon, the San Juan hurries its load of silt along toward Lake Powell. The strange sight of "sand waves" breaking upstream against the current attests to both the power and the silt load of the river.

Check with the BLM San Juan Resource Area for permits. The Navajo Indian Reservation begins in the middle of the river and takes in all the land you can see to the left as you head downstream. If you want to hike or camp on the south side of the river, obtain a permit from the Navajo Nation at least three weeks in advance (see Appendix B).

Butler Wash, Bridger Jack Mesa, and Indian Creek WSAs

31

The Needles Overlook reveals the tortuous path the Colorado River has cut through the plateau.

IN THIS CHAPTER WE VISIT three wilderness study areas attached to the southern and eastern sides of Canyonlands National Park. Adjacent lands within the national park are also being considered for wilderness designation, so these small parcels of BLM land are part of a larger picture. The nearest town is Monticello, at the intersection of US 191 and US 491 (formerly US 666). Moab is about 40 miles north of that.

All of these areas are typical of high desert environments on the Colorado Plateau. Water is very scarce, with the exception of Indian Creek.

LOCATION: Southeast Utah
SIZE: Butler Wash WSA: 24,190 acres
     Bridger Jack Mesa WSA: 5,290 acres
     Indian Creek WSA: 6,870 acres
ELEVATION RANGE: 4,000 to 7,200 feet
ECOREGION: Colorado Plateau
MILES OF TRAIL: None within WSA boundaries; routes are canyon floors and washes
ADMINISTRATION: BLM, San Juan Resource Area; NPS, Canyonlands National Park
MAPS: Trails Illustrated: Map #210.
USGS 1:24,000: Druid Arch, House Park Butte, South Six-Shooter Peak,
Harts Point South, Cathedral Butte, Lockhart Basin, North Six-Shooter Peak.

Piñon-juniper woodlands have a shaky hold on the higher elevations. Sagebrush and drought-resistant grasses grow wherever they can find a toehold in the rocks. Mule deer, bighorn sheep, and the usual cadres of lizards, snakes, and insects find these deserts to their liking. Elaborate and highly scenic sandstone rock formations are the biggest draw for human visitors. Mountain bikers, hikers, and jeep enthusiasts can find solitude if they work their way off the main roads. Indian Creek, with its riparian areas, offers contrast to the desert.

The best time to visit for hiking and backpacking is mid-March through May, and in October and November.

Butler Wash WSA

Butler Wash, as its name suggests, is a shallow canyon system. It drains northward, into The Needles region of Canyonlands National Park, and can be accessed either from the park side or from the south. Either way, a lot of driving on dirt and gravel roads is required to get to this remote location. The WSA is 55 miles by road northwest of the small town of Monticello, and about 31 miles from Dugout Ranch on UT 211. Equally long jeep drives through the park will take you to Butler Wash.

Boundary roads include a jeep trail into The Grabens (Hushaby Rd., or CR 119) and the road across Bobbys Hole on the northwest side of the WSA (suitable for mountain biking or 4WD vehicles); the Ruin Park/Pappys Pasture Rd. on the southwestern edge; and House Park Rd. to the southwest.

There are no official trails, but hikers use the bottoms of the washes as trails (as do some ORV users for a couple of miles before steep terrain stops them). Every time it rains, the signs of footprints or tire prints are washed away. Other hiking opportunities basically consist of parking anywhere it suits you along the boundary roads and wandering off to explore the rock formations or canyons.

House Park, a good destination, is relatively easy to find. From UT 211 on the east side of Canyonlands National Park, turn southwest on Beef Basin Rd. (CR 104). This road skirts the edge of Bridger Jack Mesa, so it serves as an access route for both Butler Wash and Bridger Jack. The highly scenic Salt Creek area and Cathedral Butte are also on the route. Butler Wash WSA shares the Salt Creek area with the national park. Road names and numbers around House Park Butte sound more confusing than they are on the ground. Trails Illustrated Map #210 clearly shows the dirt roads, though it doesn't list the numbers. FR 088 and FR 093 connect with Beef Basin Rd.; these are your House Park options.

Beef Basin Rd. continues its semicircle around the southeastern foot of the national park to connect to Hushaby Rd. and provide access to The Grabens, The Needles section of the park, and Bobbys Hole. There are two tent campgrounds just inside the park border at the northern end of the 4.7-mile Bobbys Hole section of Hushaby Rd. (from where Hushaby Rd. turns northwest in Bobbys Hole to the border of Canyonlands National Park): Horsehoof Arch Camp and Bobby Jo Camp. It's easy to hike into Butler Wash from these campgrounds. Permits are required for recreation in Canyonlands National Park (see Chapter 39 and Appendix B).

If you have hiked in the Dark Canyon Primitive Area and the Dark Canyon Wilderness, you might recognize Beef Basin Rd. as a northern access to hiking trails in Fable Valley and the North Long Point area. Turning south on FR 091 from Beef Basin Rd. takes you to the northern part of Elk Ridge—the escarpment of the Abajo Mountains and the eastern edge of Dark Canyon Wilderness.

Bridger Jack Mesa WSA

The sheer cliffs surrounding this narrow uplift 18 miles northwest of Monticello make access difficult. The mesa is about 10 miles long and only 1 mile wide, with cliffs about 800 feet high around most of its rim. There are no perennial streams or springs on the mesa. Such difficulties have their plus side for hikers: no ORV use and no current cattle grazing. Cattle grazed the area in the 1920s, and two old cattle trails (much eroded) lead onto the mesa. On top of the mesa, a plow and slip used to create now defunct water reservoirs are all that remain of these cattle-raising efforts.

At its southern end, Bridger Jack Mesa is 0.25 mile from the boundary of Canyonlands National Park. See the Butler Wash road descriptions in the previous section for 2WD gravel road access on the east side of the mesa. A jeep road in nearby Lavender Canyon provides access for viewing Anasazi and Fremont prehistoric rock art. The Anasazi people lived in every canyon and used every mesa in the vicinity, so it's reasonable to assume that Bridger Jack Mesa was no exception. Three archaeological sites have been recorded on the mesa, but no thorough survey has been done. Both Butler Wash and Bridger Jack occupy the transition zone between Fremont and Anasazi cultures (see Human History in the Along the Trail section of this book).

From the top of the mesa, UT 211 is both visible and audible as it leads into Canyonlands National Park. You can also see roads in Lavender and Cottonwood Canyons. The northern rim is less of a sanctuary from civilization than the southern section. The remnants of a cattle trail—now an eroded footpath—go up the southeast corner of the mesa, with access off Cottonwood Creek/Beef Basin Rd. (CR 104).

Note that there is another Bridger Jack Mesa closer to Moab, south of Behind the Rocks WSA. That's a different mesa entirely and it's not connected to this WSA.

Indian Creek WSA

BLM land along Indian Creek, east of the WSA, boasts one official trail, Trail 021. The trail follows Indian Creek and the narrow canyon that confines it. Access is from UT 211. About 3 miles before you reach the eastern boundary of Canyonlands National Park, turn right (north) on Lockhart Rd., also signed as "San Juan County 122." There are two BLM campgrounds on this improved dirt road, so it's an excellent opportunity for inexperienced adventurers to set up a base camp and take short hikes in a place that requires neither 4WD for access nor topographical map reading skills to find roads and trails.

From the turn off UT 211, it is about 2 miles on Lockhart Rd. to Indian Creek. Drive past both BLM campgrounds. The road gets a little rough after it crosses the creekbed, but it is still passable for 2WD vehicles. Drive about 1 additional mile, then turn left (west) on a short spur road that crosses a shallow wash. (Note that Lockhart Rd., the main road, continues past this point, eventually becoming a 4WD backcountry byway that passes directly under the famous Needles Overlook.) The spur road ends in about 0.2 mile. The trailhead is not signed.

To begin a hike that can range up to 50 miles, follow the trail southwest along a tributary canyon for 0.25 mile to Indian Creek. When you get to Indian Creek proper, look around and memorize the confluence with the tributary canyon so that you can find it again on your return. At this point, you are not yet within the border of Indian Creek WSA, but a hike of about 6 miles downstream will bring you to the WSA boundary. The elevation drop as you go downstream is very gradual. The first 3 miles of "trail" show some signs of ORV use. Hikers follow the motorized tracks and cattle trails along the stream. Some old mining debris slowly rusts and rots under the desert sun about 4 miles from the trailhead. Twelve archaeological sites have been identified within the WSA to date, so keep an eye out for rock dwellings, lithic scatter, and petroglyphs. The first good campsites appear about 5.0 to 5.5 miles into the hike. Visible trails, including cattle trails, become faint as you near the boundary of the WSA. If you turn around at the first good campsites, this round trip of 10 to 11 miles could be done as a day hike.

For a backpacking trip of about 35 to 50 miles, start at the same unsigned trailhead and continue to follow Indian Creek about 25 miles, almost to the confluence with the Colorado River in Canyonlands National Park. This longer trip is only for experienced backpackers with desert survival and topographical map reading skills. Indian Creek cuts a long, northwest-trending diagonal across the Indian Creek Wilderness Study Area. River rafters on the Colorado often stop at Indian Creek for overnight camping. Two pouroffs, or dry waterfalls, drop about 150 feet near the national park boundary (0.5 mile below the Rustler Canyon intersection); these obstacles will stop most hikers. You can return via the same route, or exit via 8-mile-long Rustler Canyon, a northern tributary canyon that conveniently intersects the 4WD road, Lockhart Basin Backcountry Byway. There is one pouroff in Rustler Canyon, but hikers can find a way around it. You'll need a shuttle vehicle parked at the unmarked entrance to Rustler Canyon. Rustler Canyon meets the road about 1 mile north of a landing strip. The Trails Illustrated map and the USGS topos show the terrain and roads clearly.

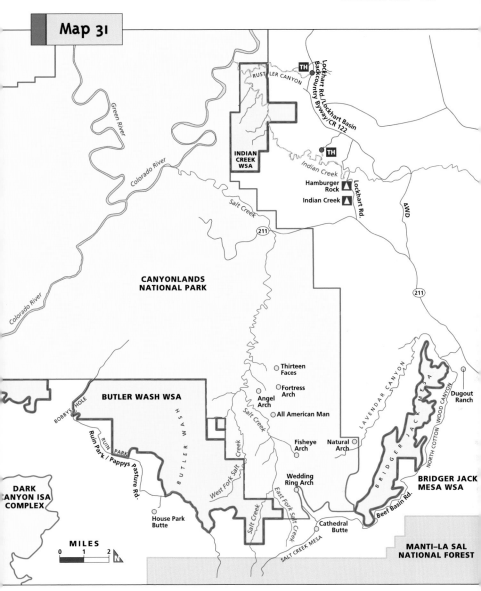

Map 31

Green River

Colorado River

Salt Creek

RUSTLER CANYON

TH

Lockhart Rd./Lockhart Basin
Back-Country Byway/CR 122

INDIAN
CREEK
WSA

Indian Creek

TH

Hamburger
Rock

Lockhart Rd.

Indian Creek

AWD

211

Colorado River

CANYONLANDS
NATIONAL PARK

211

Thirteen
Faces

Fortress
Arch

LAVENDAR CANYON

BUTLER WASH WSA

Angel
Arch

All American Man

BOBBYS HOLE

Ruin Park

Fisheye
Arch

Natural
Arch

Dugout
Ranch

NORTH COTTON WOOD CANYON

BRIDGER JACK MESA

RUIN PARK / Pappys Pasture Rd.

BUTLER WASH

Salt Creek

West Fork Salt Creek

Wedding
Ring Arch

BRIDGER JACK
MESA WSA

DARK
CANYON ISA
COMPLEX

House Park
Butte

East Fork Salt Creek

Cathedral
Butte

Beef Basin Rd.

Salt Creek

SALT CREEK MESA

MANTI–LA SAL
NATIONAL FOREST

MILES

0   1   2

N

32 Behind the Rocks, Mill Creek Canyon, and Negro Bill Canyon WSAs

Moab's redrock country is famous for hiking opportunities and mountain biking.

THREE BLM-ADMINISTERED WILDERNESS study areas are practically in the town of Moab's backyard. Behind the Rocks WSA is southwest of town, and as the name implies, it hides behind a band of rocky cliffs that parallel US 191. Mill Creek Canyon lies between Moab and Castle Valley, east of US 191. Negro Bill Canyon is Mill Creek Canyon's northern neighbor, northeast of Moab.

LOCATION: Southeast Utah
SIZE: Behind the Rocks WSA: 12,635 acres
Mill Creek Canyon WSA: 9,780 acres
Negro Bill Canyon WSA: 7,620 acres
ELEVATION RANGE: 4,000 to 6,530 feet
ECOREGION: Colorado Plateau
MILES OF TRAIL: About 6
ADMINISTRATION: BLM, Moab Ranger District, Grand Resource Area
MAPS: Manti–La Sal NF: Visitor Map.
USGS 1:24,000: Moab, Trough Springs Canyon, Kane Springs, Rill Creek.

All three areas are rich in two qualities: bare rock and excellent restaurants nearby. Raptors are as common over the rocky backcountry as mountain bikers are on the streets of Moab. Bikes and jeeps are not allowed within the boundaries of the WSAs, but traffic can be intense on surrounding bike trails and jeep roads. Some of the fins and buttresses within the WSAs are suitable for rock climbing, so expect to see rock-climbing species as well.

The best times to visit for hiking and backpacking are April through May and October and November. Avoid all holidays and college spring break times. The biannual Moab Jeep Safari takes place on Easter and on Labor Day weekends, which is great fun for jeep jockeys, but is noisy for those seeking a quiet backcountry outing. Avoid the furnace of the summer months.

Behind the Rocks WSA

The most impressive features of Behind the Rocks are the squadrons of red Navajo Sandstone fins, some of them 500 feet tall. Fins form when parallel joints in the sandstone split vertically and then weather into narrow slices of rock. Ridges as close together as a giant's version of corrugated cardboard contain arches and alcoves. Like nearby Arches National Park, Behind the Rocks is full of visually arresting openings, including about 48 stone arches (the number depends on how you define an arch).

The WSA is about 11 miles long and ranges from 0.5 to 3 miles wide, which is quite small for a wilderness area, but once you hike into the canyons and among the fins, you can actually get lost in there, not to mention finding quiet and solitude. The WSA lacks perennial streams and has only one spring. The developed spring provides water for irrigation of nearby private lands, so carry your own water for hiking. Hunter Canyon, which forms the WSA boundary on the southwestern side, does have some springs and seeps that feed hanging gardens on the canyon walls.

There are few footpaths within the WSA, but you can use the Moab Rim Trail and other jeep roads as hiking routes. Most visitors just pick a likely route and explore. Some quasi-visible hiking routes have been established through repeated use, including about 3 miles of trail associated with the Hidden Valley Trail, which begins outside the WSA (see the following day-hike description).

To access the Moab Rim Trail, look for Kane Creek Blvd. on the south end of Moab. Turn west and drive about 1 mile. A small turnoff on the left-hand side, just past the first cattleguard, is what you're looking for. This road runs along a rocky ledge

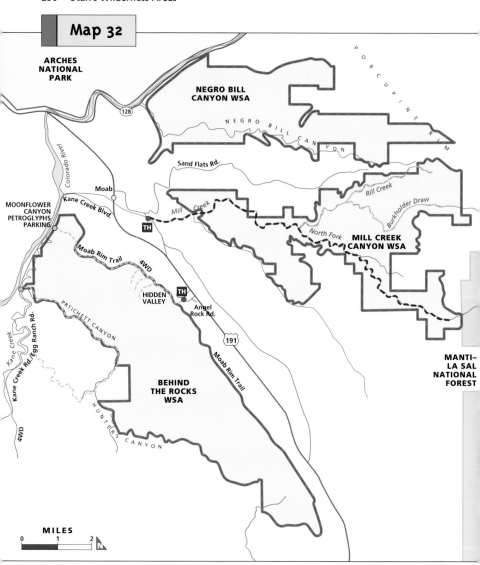

and is suitable for jeeping, hiking, or biking. Striking south or southwest off this road will take you into the wilderness study area. The WSA is closed to vehicular traffic, so plan on foot or horse travel only within the WSA.

Whether you're hiking, jeeping, or mountain biking, staying on the Moab Rim Trail as it rounds the study area and then bends southeast will connect you with Hidden Valley Trail, a foot trail up the cliff face on the east side. (See the following day hike.) Hiking all of Moab Rim and Hidden Valley Trails amounts to about 6 miles of walking (one way); add more miles and time for any side excursions. A shuttle vehicle at Hidden Valley Trailhead is the way to go.

Pritchett Canyon Trail is a 4WD jeep road that, like the Moab Rim Trail, takes off from Kane Creek Rd. on the northern edge of the WSA. Hiking east or northeast from Pritchett Canyon Trail takes you into the WSA. The road is in a slickrock gorge. Climbing some of the nearby slickrock ridges provides vistas that are particularly appealing in late afternoon and at sunset. Pritchett Rd. is about 10 miles long and offers access to Hunters Canyon, Halls Bridge, Pritchett Arch, and many unnamed stone formations. At its southern end, the road rejoins US 191.

> **DAY HIKE: HIDDEN VALLEY TRAIL**
> **(PLUS OFF-TRAIL EXPLORATION OF REDROCK FINS)**
> One-Way Length: About 3 miles
> Low and High Elevations: 4,590 and 5,270–6,000 feet
> Difficulty: Moderate

A popular day-hiking choice that measures more than 6 miles round trip is to access Hidden Valley Trail from its low point near US 191. Drive 3 miles south of Moab to Angel Rock Rd. (also signed "Hidden Valley"). Drive two blocks on Angel Rock Rd. to a T intersection and turn right on Rimrock Lane. The signed trailhead and parking area is 0.3 mile farther, where Rimrock Lane ends.

If you decide to hike just Hidden Valley Trail in order to avoid jeeps and bikes, it is a 5 mile round trip that begins at 4,590 feet, climbs to a pass at 5,270 feet, and then offers opportunities to climb higher on surrounding fins. User-created trails lead from the pass to panels of rock art that are well worth visiting. The main trail loses a little elevation as it drops into a valley beyond the pass. Where the trail meets the 4WD road (Moab Rim Trail), continue northeast for about 0.25 mile and then turn southwest whenever you feel the urge to explore the fins, a highly recommended activity. The canyons between each set of fins vary in size and in visual allure. Time and a lack of water will be limiting factors. Some canyons present obstacles such as pouroffs that require rock-climbing skills.

Mill Creek Canyon WSA

Sand Flats Rd. and a thin line of cliffs separate Mill Creek Canyon from Negro Bill Canyon WSA to the north. Access to Mill Creek Trail is via Power House Lane on the southeastern edge of the town of Moab. The trailhead is marked as #22 on the Manti–La Sal National Forest Visitor Map. Sandstone fins decorating the mouth of the canyon attract photographers.

Miles of perennial streams with waterfalls and swimming holes make Mill Creek Canyon a popular area for locals and visitors alike. The canyon floor is the trail in the North Fork of Mill Creek Canyon (the main branch of Mill Creek is outside of the WSA boundary). Depending on the water level, stream crossings vary from shallow to knee-deep wading.

About 2.5 miles up-canyon, Otho Natural Bridge can be viewed in a side canyon of the North Fork of Mill Creek (see the USGS topo map Rill Creek). In addition to scenic redrock formations, 25 pre-Anasazi sites and campsites add to the enjoyment of hiking in Mill Creek Canyon WSA.

Most visitors hike a few miles up the North Fork of Mill Creek and then return to the trailhead, but it's possible to hike more miles by continuing up Rill Creek or Burkholder Draw. If you hiked all of the North Fork, plus Rill Creek and Burkholder Draw, you'd end up with about 24 miles of hiking. Rill Creek has a seasonal stream and many seeps that support riparian areas. Caves and dry waterfalls are interesting destinations at the upper end of Rill Creek Canyon. Burkholder Draw branches off of Rill Creek Canyon and is an equally interesting hike. At its upper end it climbs to the Valley of the Gnomes. Rock pillars with erosion-resistant caps are the "gnome" shapes. Hike past the Valley of the Gnomes to intercept Sand Flats Rd., a good exit point to meet a shuttle vehicle. The upper reaches of Rill and Burkholder are steep enough to be rated strenuous, but the rest of the hike is only moderately difficult. Wear footgear suitable for wading.

Steep canyon walls screen parts of Mill Creek Canyon WSA from civilization, but housing developments in Moab come close to the western edge. Traffic on Sand Flats Rd. north of the WSA can sometimes be heard and seen. More secluded spots can be found deeper within the North Fork of Mill Creek and in Burkholder Draw.

A careful driver can negotiate Sand Flats Rd. to the head of Burkholder Draw with a 2WD vehicle in dry weather, but 4WD is definitely recommended.

Negro Bill Canyon WSA

This wilderness study area is just 3 miles north of Moab. From US 191, turn right (east) on UT 128, on the south side of the Colorado River. Drive 3 miles to a dirt parking area at the mouth of Negro Bill Canyon (3,995 feet in elevation). Off-road vehicle tracks and various forms of disgusting trash define the trail for the first 0.5 mile or more. Once you're past the debris at the entrance, the canyon is a joy to hike. One of the glories of Negro Bill Canyon is its perennial stream. Expect to hop and to wade the stream frequently.

About 2 miles up the main canyon, where a tributary canyon enters from the right, stop for a view of Morning Glory Natural Bridge. At 243 feet, the long rock span is hard to see until you're standing under it—then it is quite impressive. A spring and a pool of water complete the scene, but beware of the poison ivy! The bridge has been touted as both the fifth- and sixth-largest natural bridge in the United States. You can hike 10 miles or more into Negro Bill Canyon, but the stream is only reliable for about 6 miles. Seven springs feed the stream. One petroglyph panel and one "cowboy cave" in the canyon are of historical interest.

While the lower part of Negro Bill Canyon is a very pleasant and scenic hike, don't expect solitude. Local school groups hike the canyon on field trips and at least one commercial outfitter takes visitors in on horseback. If solitude ranks among the main criteria for your "wilderness experience," venture into the more secluded areas in the eastern section of the canyon, explore the fins near the western boundary, or try an early winter hike.

According to local history, the canyon was named after William Granstaff, a mulatto cattle rancher who lived in the area in the 1880s.

Red Navajo Sandstone erodes into fascinating shapes in Behind the Rocks and Mill Creek Canyon Wilderness Study Areas near Moab.

East-Central Utah

A broad swath of public lands in east-central Utah has been proposed or designated as wilderness. Included are the San Rafael Swell, the Book Cliffs region, and areas on the Utah-Colorado border. The descriptive chapters have been divided by region:

- **Chapter 33:** WSAs of the San Rafael Swell south of I-70
- **Chapter 34:** WSAs of the San Rafael Swell north of I-70
- **Chapter 35:** WSAs along or near the Green River (Book Cliffs, Desolation Canyon, plus Winter Ridge)
- **Chapter 36:** Black Ridge Canyons Wilderness and the adjacent Westwater Canyon WSA

With the single exception of the newer Black Ridge Canyons Wilderness, all of the areas described are wilderness study areas under the jurisdiction of the Bureau of Land Management.

On the map, the San Rafael Swell WSAs make a circle that almost encloses the uplift of the swell. The uplift rises a maximum of 1,500 feet above the surrounding terrain and is visible from as far away as 50 miles. The bulge in the earth's crust began about 60 million years ago and it now exposes older layers of sandstone and limestone, with the most rugged portion being the jagged San Rafael Reef along its eastern edge. The reef is cut by canyons formed by perennial and intermittent streams, and by the San Rafael River. I-70 runs east-west through the swell. Some citizen groups have recommended that the entire swell and its surrounding wilderness study areas be considered for designation as a national park. Other citizen groups have recommended a much larger wilderness area than the BLM has proposed.

The Book Cliffs region encompasses more than 956,000 acres managed as either "roadless" or as WSAs, but this figure includes some adjacent Indian reservation and state lands. On the map, a semicircle of wilderness study areas embraces the western, southern, and eastern borders of a big chunk of the Uintah and Ouray Indian Reservation. This book provides information on the WSAs, but keep in mind that more wild terrain nearby is worth exploring. Special permits are required for driving or hiking on

The San Rafael River cuts a canyon through the San Rafael Swell.

Indian lands (see Appendix B). The BLM usually lumps the following WSAs together as the Book Cliffs region: Desolation Canyon, Jack Canyon, Turtle Canyon, Floy Canyon, Coal Canyon, Spruce Canyon, and Flume Canyon. Each WSA is separated from its neighbor only by a road or by the Green River.

The Green River is by far the most frequently visited destination in the Book Cliffs region. A lack of water, trails, and 2WD access roads keeps visitors to a minimum beyond the river corridor. For adventurers comfortable with exploring unsigned jeep trails and skilled in cross-country or canyon hiking in dry terrain, the Book Cliffs can be a paradise of solitude. Reservations and permits are required for float trips on the Green River.

Black Ridge Canyons, a wilderness area designated in 2000, is mostly in Colorado, with only 5,180 acres in Utah. Moreover, private lands border the portion of the Colorado River that flows through the Utah section, and the wilderness doesn't touch the riverbanks there. Only the Jones Canyon Trailhead gives access to the Utah portion from the Colorado side. Having said all that, we still encourage you to visit the Utah area of the wilderness as it offers outstanding opportunities for solitude. Westwater Canyon WSA, which lies downstream on the Colorado River, is adjacent to Black Ridge Canyons Wilderness. Like Desolation Canyon, Westwater is most well-known for river-rafting and kayaking opportunities.

There's no best time to visit the San Rafael Swell, the Book Cliffs, and the Black Ridge Canyons/Westwater regions because river runners look for different conditions than do hikers, mountain bikers, and jeep travelers. Like all desert rivers, the San Rafael, the Green, and the Colorado run highest in the spring, with only intermittently increased flows later in the season, thanks to thunderstorms.

Hikers braving the extremes of the Black Box along the San Rafael River (not to be confused with White Canyon's Black Hole outside Cheesebox Canyon WSA) aim for warm-to-hot weather and low flows because they have to swim or wade frequently in a narrow, dark canyon. Whitewater aficionados run the Colorado and Green Rivers at peak flows in early spring. Most other visitors to the rivers like to be on the water in the hot summer months, when swimming—planned or unplanned—is pleasant. Hiking in the hot months of June, July, August, and part of September can be absolutely deadly. The question of when to visit for hiking gets more complicated when you look at the elevation ranges. It's possible to choose a higher-elevation camp in the Book Cliffs region above 9,000 feet, where aspen trees will mitigate the searing temperatures of the lower desert. If the roads aren't too muddy, early spring is a good time to hike. October and sometimes November can be great months to visit, with low water levels, dry roads, and comfortable daytime temperatures. Be prepared for cold autumn nights. See the individual description of each WSA for more tips on when to visit.

Potable drinking water is a problem in all of these areas. The rivers are too full of silt for drinking, and other water sources are scarce. Pay particular attention to notations in the trail descriptions for each area that steer you to reliable water sources.

The Green River is deceptively placid downstream of Nefertiti Rapid as it flows through the Desolation Canyon Wilderness Study Area.

33 San Rafael Reef, Crack Canyon, Muddy Creek, and Devils Canyon WSAs

"Swiss cheese" formations in Crack Canyon

LOCATION: East-Central Utah

SIZE: San Rafael Reef WSA: 59,170 acres
Crack Canyon WSA: 25,335 acres
Muddy Creek WSA: 31,400 acres
Devils Canyon WSA: 9,610 acres

ELEVATION RANGE: 4,700 to 7,400 feet

ECOREGION: Colorado Plateau

MILES OF TRAIL: 8 in Crack Canyon WSA

ADMINISTRATION:
BLM, San Rafael Resource Area

MAPS: Trails Illustrated: Map #712.
USGS 1:100,000: Salina, Hanksville, Loa,
San Rafael Desert.
USGS 1:24,000: Twin Knolls, Arsons Garden,
Greasewood Draw, Old Woman Wash,
Temple Mountain, Goblin Valley,
Little Wild Horse Mesa, Horse Valley,
Hunt Draw, Tomsich Butte, Ireland Mesa,
San Rafael Knob, Copper Globe.

THIS CHAPTER DESCRIBES the four San Rafael Swell wilderness study areas that are located south of I-70 (see Chapter 34 for San Rafael Swell WSAs north of I-70). Madame Curie's uranium came from nearby Temple Mountain. These ruins and other mining debris scattered around the swell are dangerous to explore. Signs warning of cave-ins and explosives are posted near some of the larger abandoned mines.

Drinking water is available at the Goblin Valley State Park Ranger Station. Take adequate drinking water with you for any expedition into the San Rafael Swell area. Even after filtering, some of the water sources in the wilderness study areas are not potable because of high mineral content.

A 4WD vehicle is not a must, but we highly recommend it. Many of the roads and unofficial ways are not signed. We also recommend that you carry Trails Illustrated Map #712 and/or the appropriate USGS 1:24,000 maps. You'll need detailed maps for the roads as much as for the hiking routes.

The entire San Rafael Swell offers excellent hiking opportunities in the cooler months of early spring and late fall, when more mountainous areas of Utah are snowed in. The exceptions to this "cool weather" rule are hikes that involve a lot of wading through narrow canyons—an activity that's pleasant on a hot day (see The Chute of Muddy Creek WSA).

Goblin Valley State Park receives about 5,000 visitors per year, and mountain bikers and ORV riders heavily use the public land outside the WSA boundaries. However, the wilderness study areas themselves average just a few hundred visitors per year, so you know where to go if you're looking for solitude.

San Rafael Reef WSA

I-70, UT 24, Temple Mountain Rd., Goblin Valley Rd., and CR 332 surround San Rafael Reef WSA. The town of Green River is about 8 miles east on I-70, and Hanksville is about 30 miles south on UT 24.

Canyons cutting through this section of the reef range from 200 to 1,000 feet deep. Pools of water gather at the bottom of enormous pouroffs in some of the canyons. There are no perennial streams, but there are 22 springs or water holes, and coming upon these in the arid landscape is a joy. No water sources should be used for drinking without filtering first. Stagnant water might have too high a saline content for human consumption. In addition to water holes, the other gemlike resource in San Rafael Reef WSA is grape agate, a rare form of agate that is found in Greasewood Draw.

DAY HIKE: STRAIGHT WASH, EARDLEY CANYON
One-Way Length: About 3 miles
Low and High Elevations: 4,800 and 5,200 feet
Difficulty: Moderate (4WD required for approach road)

The highlight of this hike is the largest perennial pool in the San Rafael Swell. Access is via an unnamed, unsigned 4WD road. About 12.5 miles north of the intersection of Temple Mountain/Goblin Valley Rd. and UT 24 (12.6 miles south of I-70), drive west on a dirt road that exits the highway at mile marker 148. A grove of cottonwood trees where the rough road ends, just 3.5 miles from UT 24, is a good place to camp. There are no recreational facilities here, but you will find plenty of flat spots for parking and setting up a tent.

Use the Arsons Garden and Greasewood Draw 1:24,000 maps to find your way, as there are no marked trails. Begin hiking west into Straight Wash/Eardley Canyon at a "Wilderness Study Area/No Vehicles" sign. When we hiked this route, we saw cougar tracks in the wash and peregrine falcons overhead.

Map 33

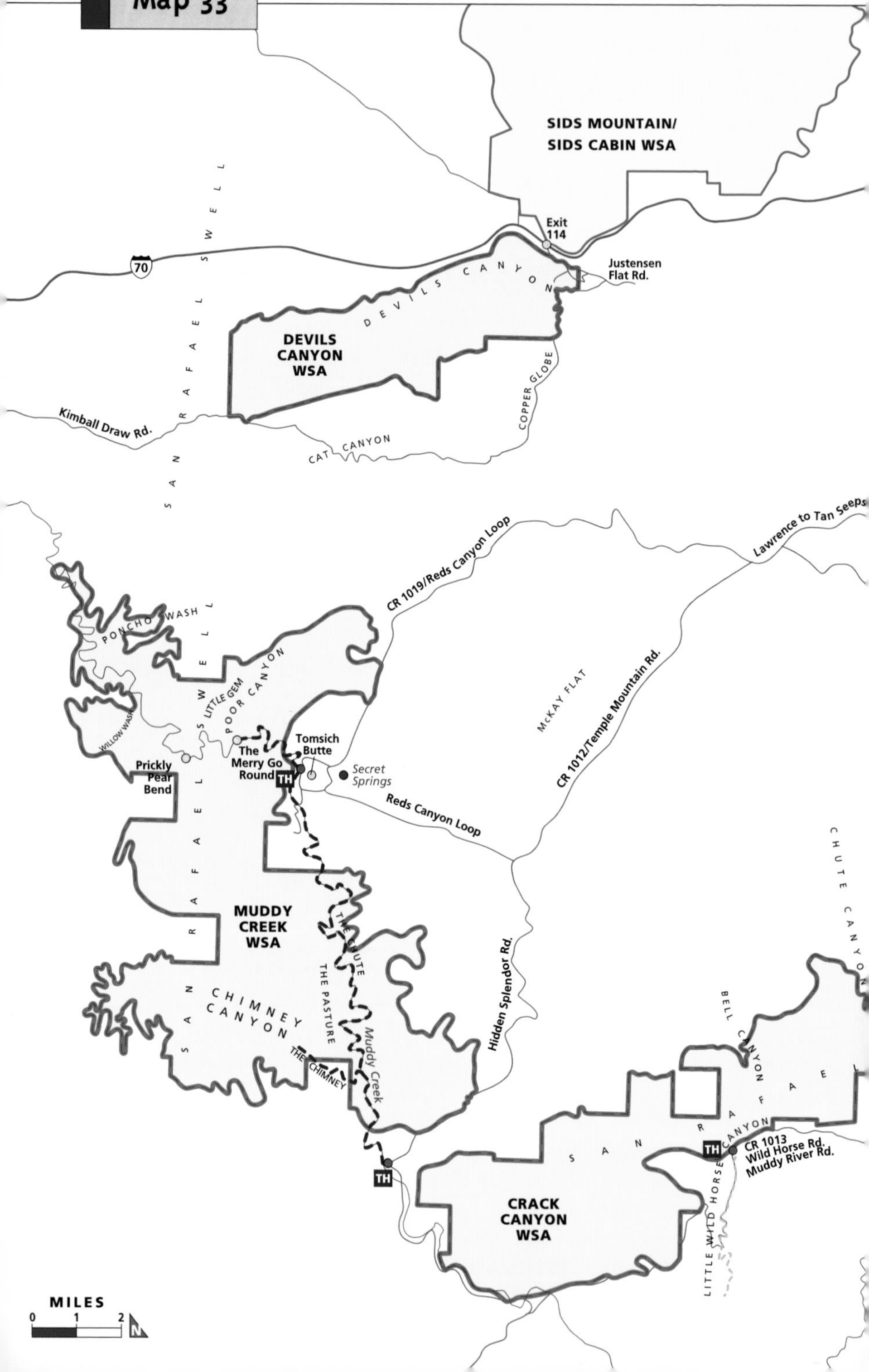

SIDS MOUNTAIN/
SIDS CABIN WSA

Exit
114

Justensen
Flat Rd.

70

S A N   R A F A E L   S W E L L

DEVILS   CANYON

DEVILS
CANYON
WSA

COPPER GLOBE

Kimball Draw Rd.

CAT   CANYON

CR 1019/Reds Canyon Loop

Lawrence to Tan Seeps

PONCHO WASH

S A N   R A F A E L   S W E L L

LITTLE GEM

POOR CANYON

WILLOW WASH

MCKAY FLAT

CR 1012/Temple Mountain Rd.

Tomsich
Butte

The Merry Go
Round

Secret
Springs

TH

Prickly
Pear
Bend

Reds Canyon Loop

MUDDY
CREEK
WSA

CHIMNEY   CANYON

THE CHUTE

THE PASTURE

Muddy Creek

Hidden Splendor Rd.

CHUTE   CANYON

BELL   CANYON

THE
CHIMNEY

S A N

R A F A E L

TH

TH

CR 1013
Wild Horse Rd.
Muddy River Rd.

CRACK
CANYON
WSA

LITTLE WILD HORSE CANYON

TH

MILES
0   1   2

N

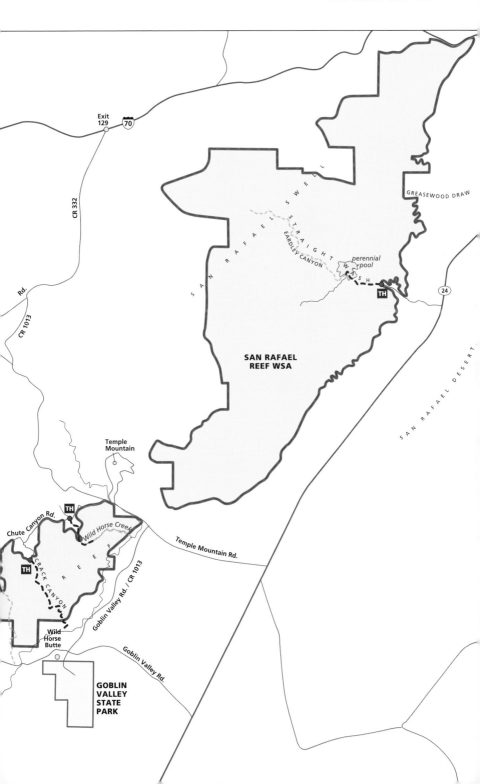

Straight Wash belies its name: It is not straight. The twists and turns make for a visually interesting hike. The hike up-canyon gains about 300 feet in elevation, but is relatively easy, with only a mild bit of bouldering required here and there.

After passing an area of white slickrock, the canyon constricts but doesn't form a true slot. Keep track of your hiking time once you exit the narrowed part of the canyon. Hiking for about 15 minutes at a moderate pace beyond the narrow section brings you to the entrance of the side canyon that boasts the enormous pool of water.

Boulders nearly block the entrance to the canyon on your right that holds the pool. An intermittent stream of water, which might be running in early spring, supports a necklace of grasses and shrubs in and among the boulders. Climb a few hundred yards up this unpromising rock jumble and round a corner to find a pool lying like a 30-foot-diameter mirror at the base of an impassable pour-off. This pool is not shown on any maps.

Return the way you came, or extend this hike by returning to Straight Wash and hiking farther up-canyon.

Crack Canyon WSA

Occupying the southeastern flank of the San Rafael Swell, Crack Canyon WSA is 2 to 3 miles wide and 16 miles long. The portion of the northeast-to-southwest-trending San Rafael Reef included in this WSA crosses several topo maps, extending from a few miles south of Temple Mountain all the way to Muddy Creek. To explore the entire Crack Canyon WSA, refer to USGS 1:24,000 maps Temple Mountain, Goblin Valley, Little Wild Horse Mesa, and Hunt Draw. If you just plan to hike Crack Canyon itself, use the Temple Mountain and Goblin Valley maps.

> **DAY HIKE:** CRACK CANYON AND ENVIRONS
> One-Way Length: About 6–14 miles (depending on routes chosen)
> Low and High Elevations: 4,700 and 5,400 feet
> Difficulty: Moderate

About 21 miles north of Hanksville (about 29 miles south of I-70), turn west off UT 24 at mile marker 137 onto Temple Mountain/Goblin Valley Rd. Continue west about 6.5 miles to Chute Canyon Rd. (CR 1016). Note that the DeLorme *Utah Atlas & Gazetteer* identifies Chute Canyon Rd., but on the ground the road was not signed when we were there, and it is not named on USGS topos. It is the first dirt road to your left (south) after you pass the intersection with the Temple Mountain Rd., which leads north. Drive southwest (turn left) on Chute Canyon Rd.

The first canyon you come to is nameless, but it houses a fork of Wild Horse Creek and is worth a short hike. A short jeep track leaves the main road and ends at the head of the canyon. Unimproved campsites abound.

You can explore the canyon in an hour or two: an hour to meander a mile east, half an hour or so to return. Intermittent water sources surrounded by tall grass, and a couple of narrow sections in the canyon, are the primary visual attractions. Moderate bouldering and climbing slows you down. It's possible to hike farther, to the eastern side of the reef, but the hike becomes less interesting as the canyon widens.

At Crack Canyon—the next stop on your tour along Chute Canyon Rd.—a short spur road leads directly south from the main road to end in the wide canyon head. Shade and water are scarce. Par for the course in the San Rafael Swell, there's no sign identifying Crack Canyon, and no sign identifying the spur road. Trash from previous campers festoons the opening, but once you're in the canyon proper, the setting is pristine. Park where the jeep track ends at a wilderness study area sign.

Crack Canyon is one of the most beautiful in the reef. Yellow and cream sandstone tops red and maroon layers that glow under the right conditions of reflected sunlight. The cross-bedded sandstone has been eroded into swirls of rounded, sensuous forms that delight the eye for about 3 miles. Swiss cheese–like sandstone formations abound. The canyon varies in width from a true shoulder-wide slot to wide enough for piñon pines or cottonwood trees.

When we hiked these two canyons, we handed our packs down and up to each other to free ourselves for climbing over dry waterfalls and other obstacles about 8 to 10 feet high. A person hiking alone would do well to take a rope for lowering and raising a daypack. None of the bouldering is difficult, but a moderate amount of flexibility and upper body strength is required. The hike is not suitable for small children, unless you are strong enough to lift them over obstacles. Retrace your route to the head of Crack Canyon. From there, Chute Canyon Road continues south.

About 4 miles south of Crack Canyon, the road officially ends in Chute Canyon, but 4WD, motorcycle, and ORV use is visible beyond. Old mining debris and buildings dot Chute Canyon and other areas adjacent to the WSA.

To explore the east side of Crack Canyon WSA, retrace your route on Chute Canyon Rd. to intersect the main road; turn right (east) to return to the intersection with the Goblin Valley Rd. Turn south toward Goblin Valley. Where the road forks left to enter Goblin Valley State Park, keep right to continue on CR 1013 (Wild Horse/Muddy River Rd.). A sign noting the end of Emery County road maintenance also notes that it's 14 miles to Muddy Creek and 5.3 miles to Little Wild Horse Canyon. The road is shown as 4WD on most maps, but is really 2WD to Little Wild Horse Canyon. Beyond Little Wild Horse Canyon, you will definitely need 4WD and high clearance.

Stop to hike Little Wild Horse Canyon, the only canyon named, signed, equipped with nearby latrines, and generally as much of a tourist hive as Goblin Valley State Park. The contrast between this canyon visit and the hikes beginning on the west edge of the reef could not be more dramatic. Do not expect solitude. Do expect human traffic jams in the narrowest slot canyon in the reef. Do expect to wade in shallow, muddy water. Carry a small, narrow pack, as a larger pack will not fit through the narrowest sections. Flash-flood danger is extreme.

The parking lot and trailhead for Little Wild Horse Canyon also serves Bell Canyon. An 8-mile-long loop trail that takes 4 to 6 hours to hike connects Little Wild Horse and Bell Canyons. This is the only official, marked trail in Crack Canyon WSA. There are no drinking water sources.

From Little Wild Horse Canyon, continue driving southwest on the 4WD road that skirts the edge of Crack Canyon WSA. (The road appears on some maps and not on others.) Bentonite hills riven with wrinkles and completely nude, their soil poisonous to almost all plants, dominate the horizon. Each mound is striated with colors: old blood, clotted cream, bile green, faded blueberry.

The southern border of Crack Canyon WSA is lower Muddy Creek. Tamarisk-choked banks and an abandoned pioneer cabin are a fitting end to the worst section of the road—but first you must cross one last dangerous ford of Muddy Creek. Check the water level before you drive across. The jeep track improves as it exits Crack Canyon WSA and nears UT 24, with the last 9 miles being graded and suitable for 2WD in good weather.

Muddy Creek WSA

When we explored Muddy Creek WSA, the creek itself was an ugly color reminiscent of Jabba the Hutt's skin, and completely opaque. It didn't look like water, but more like a flow of faded paint. A local tale involves a miner named Tomsich who, along with his dog, drank Muddy Creek water. The dog died. The miner survived and staked a uranium claim.

Our most moving (spiritually and literally) wildlife sighting was of a herd of wild horses. A black stallion with ropy muscles pushed his mares and one spindly colt into a run as they left the grasslands near the creek and headed up into the rocky hills. Their long tails and manes swept the tops of sagebrush and greasewood as they ran. The BLM estimates that 10 to 15 wild horses range over the wilderness study area.

Muddy Creek WSA is 8 miles south of I-70 and 12 miles northeast of Capitol Reef National Park, along the southwestern flank of the San Rafael Swell. This WSA is the most remote region of the Swell, with fewer access points and fewer visitors. The closest town is Emery on UT 10 (30 miles northwest of the WSA). In dry weather, and after a recent grading, both Reds Canyon and Hidden Splendor Roads can be negotiated in a 2WD vehicle—slowly. We recommend 4WD. Portions of Reds Canyon Rd.—a loop road listed as Red Canyon Loop Rd. on DeLorme maps—and all of Hidden Splendor Rd. are shown as 4WD on Trails Illustrated Map #712. Access

In the Crack Canyon Wilderness Study Area, Navajo Sandstone gives way to badlands of Morrison Formation mudstone. The soil chemistry does not support plant life.

is from ranch exit 129 off I-70, or from a continuation of the Temple Mountain Rd. off UT 24.

From ranch exit 129 on I-70, drive southwest along an improved, 2WD, nameless dirt road (CR 332 in the DeLorme atlas). Before you reach the Reds Canyon turnoff, you will pass several opportunities for exploration outside of the official WSA boundaries, most notably Earls Draw and Rods Valley Roads, both of which lead to Swasey's Cabin. The picturesque 1920s cabin is surrounded by unique rock formations. The Swasey family used a cave in the nearby rocks as a refrigerator. Rough tracks beyond the cabin lead to unimproved camping areas.

Reds Canyon Rd. provides access to (in order from north to south): Family Butte and a nest of mining ruins and mining roads; Sulphur Canyon and spur road; Lucky Strike Mine and spur road; mining ruins in a nameless, cliff-rimmed amphitheater and spur road; Tomsich Butte and Tomsich Trailhead on Muddy Creek; spur road north to The Merry-Go-Round; views of Hondu Arch; Hidden Splendor Rd. and Mine; and Chimney Canyon Trailhead. (All points of interest prior to Tomsich Butte lie outside the official WSA boundary.)

At a marked junction 13.5 miles southwest of I-70, turn right (west) onto Reds Canyon Rd. and drive to Tomsich Butte Trailhead. From this trailhead, you can hike/wade or float down Muddy Creek, or hike upstream into the area called The Merry-Go-Round.

Note that Reds Canyon Rd. is a true loop, so it's possible to skip the roughest part by staying on the graded dirt road across McKay Flats, returning to Reds Canyon at its southern end, where the road junction is also signed for Reds Canyon. Before you begin your expedition along or in Muddy Creek, you might want to allow some time to explore the area around Tomsich Butte. Sites worth visiting include corrals and cabins associated with abandoned mining claims; deeply coruscated Moenkopi cliff walls, looking like giant ribbon candy; and technical rock-climbing routes to the top of Tomsich Butte.

SHUTTLE DAY HIKE: MUDDY CREEK, THE CHUTE
One-Way Length: About 15 miles
Low and High Elevations: 4,700 and 5,200 feet
Difficulty: Moderate (with lots of wading, or floating at times of high water)

This is the most popular float/hike in Muddy Creek WSA. It begins at the Tomsich Butte Trailhead (see Reds Canyon approach described in the previous section) and ends near Hidden Splendor Mine, 15 miles downstream.

The Chute is the narrow section of Muddy Creek where the water cuts through several colorful layers of rock; the canyon's deepest point reveals strata of Coconino Sandstone about 250 million years old. At low water, the entire Chute can be hiked with occasional wading in knee-deep water. Take a trekking pole to probe for deep holes. At high water the entire trip can be kayaked or floated on an inner tube. Allow about 10 hours to hike 15 miles of Muddy Creek.

Flash-flood danger is extreme in The Chute. At high water, some technical maneuvering is required of kayakers and inner-tubers. In cool weather, an insulated wetsuit is recommended. At low water, a change of footwear and quick-drying shorts or pants will suffice. In drought years, there might not be a floating season.

As you hike down-canyon, the formation high on the cliff to your right is Hondu Arch. You can use the mining tracks that are no longer open to vehicles as hiking paths, frequently crossing Muddy Creek. The narrowest section of The Chute, about 9 miles down-canyon, is decorated with a logjam. The logs, about 25 feet overhead, amply illustrate the power and depth of flash floods.

The entrance to Chimney Canyon is about one hour of hiking down-canyon from the logjam. To explore Chimney Canyon, make a right (northwest) turn and hike a few hundred yards to a dry waterfall. If you are comfortable with Class IV climbing, you can scale both sections of the waterfall, about 8 feet for the lower section, and 20 feet for the upper section. A few hundred yards above the dry waterfall, a spring provides a good camping area.

Back in the main canyon, continue down Muddy Creek about 4 more miles from the intersection with Chimney Canyon to the take-out near Hidden Splendor Landing Strip. From Muddy Creek, you can see a 4WD track leading up the incline on your left (northeast). Follow this track to the parking area for shuttle vehicles.

Devils Canyon WSA

Because this wilderness study area is small (7.5 miles east-west, 2.5 miles north-south) and is adjacent to I-70, solitude can be hard to find. The best chance to escape the noise of I-70 and of ORV use on surrounding roads is to hike into Devils Canyon and its tributaries.

This area tops out at 7,921 feet on San Rafael Knob, a Carmel Sandstone peak that is the highest elevation in the Swell. The peak is outside of the BLM-proposed WSA boundaries. Even though it is relatively high country, the area is so dry that it can usually be hiked all year. If you visit before Easter or in very late fall, you will be less likely to run into crowds of ORV enthusiasts.

There are no official trails, but the Devils Canyon Trailhead off Justensen Flat Rd. offers easy access to find-your-own-way routes into the canyon and its tributaries. Take exit 114 off I-70 at the overpass for Moore Cutoff Rd.; turn south, then east along a paved frontage road. The road is paved for 2 miles, then improved gravel to the Devils Canyon Trailhead. Beyond the trailhead, the road becomes a 4WD dirt road. Short spur tracks leading off the main road are user-created accesses to camping spots.

There are no reliable water sources inside the WSA, but Devils Spring just outside the northwestern corner has a watering trough. Wild horses frequently use the spring. Distance from the trailhead to this spring is more than 8 canyon-hiking miles, so it's really not an option for day hiking. We recommend carrying your own water and hiking into the canyon for half a day and then returning to the trailhead. You will need Trails Illustrated Map #712 or USGS 1:24,000 maps San Rafael Knob and Copper Globe.

Some scrambling and climbing is required to find ways around dry waterfalls. There are dozens of side canyons, some very small and short, others longer. Impressive narrows alternate with wider sections.

Sids Mountain/Sids Cabin and Mexican Mountain WSAs

The San Rafael River

THIS CHAPTER DESCRIBES San Rafael Swell wilderness study areas that are north of I-70: Sids Mountain/Sids Cabin and Mexican Mountain. The Wedge Overlook on the northwestern border of Sids Mountain/Sids Cabin WSA looks down 600 feet to the San Rafael River. Even if you don't plan to hike in this area, the overlook is a must-see. The gravel road to the Wedge Overlook is accessible from the northwest by taking the Green River Cutoff Rd. (CR 401) from UT 10, 1.5 miles north of Castle Dale. Although

LOCATION: East-Central Utah

SIZE: Sids Mountain/Sids Cabin WSA: 80,970 acres
Mexican Mountain WSA: 59,600 acres

ELEVATION RANGE: 4,700 to 6,900 feet

ECOREGION: Colorado Plateau

MILES OF TRAIL: About 5; many routes in washes and canyon bottoms

ADMINISTRATION: BLM, Price River and San Rafael Resource Areas

MAPS: Trails Illustrated: Map #712.
USGS 1:100,000: Huntington, San Rafael Desert.
USGS 1:24,000: Spotted Wolf Canyon, Mexican Mountain, Devils Hole, Drowned Hole Draw, Bottleneck Peak, Sids Mountain, The Blocks, Sid and Charley.

the road is identified as Green River Cutoff on most maps, it is signed as "Buckhorn Draw, Wedge Overlook, Pictograph Panel" on the ground. From the south the road is identified as "Buckhorn Draw/Wedge Overlook" at exit 129 from I-70. On the Trails Illustrated map, the southern half of the road (everything south of the San Rafael Campground) is identified as "Cottonwood." It's all the same road, connecting I-70 with UT 10 via about 43 miles of backcountry road that is 2WD in all but the worst weather.

In addition to Wedge Overlook, Buckhorn Draw Rd. provides access to San Rafael Campground, multiple examples of rock art, cowboy rock art from the Butch Cassidy era, and a dinosaur footprint. Buckhorn Draw is the dividing line between Sids Mountain/Sids Cabin WSA and Mexican Mountain WSA. The road, the campground, and its immediate environs are not within the wilderness study areas, so vehicular traffic, including ORV use, is allowed. Some citizen groups have complained about the heavy ORV use in Buckhorn Wash, so if you prefer solitude and quiet, you might want to seek camping spots off the main drag. The road is worth driving if only for the access it provides to spur trails and to excellent views of rock art. Pictograph rock art painted by prehistoric cultures from about 5000 B.C. to A.D. 500 are found in many canyons and washes of the San Rafael Swell. Barrier Canyon–style rock art appears in Buckhorn Wash and Cane Wash.

New Mexicans traveling the Old Spanish Trail gave the San Rafael River its name, and the watercourse is still an artery of utmost importance in this dry land. Local ranchers water cattle along the more accessible portions of the river, and the river provides the most frequently used hiking routes. Any travel along the San Rafael also requires wading or swimming. There are about two weeks in May when the water is usually high enough for all float boating. Tubing and hiking/swimming are modes of travel that work throughout the season.

One unfortunate result of all the inner-tubing is that deflated tubes lie along the riverbank and the approaches. In a very real way, this trash destroys our freedom to have that ineffable wilderness experience we talk about so much but seldom enjoy. Trash deflates the spirit as well as being a physical obscenity.

About 34 miles of the San Rafael River flow through Mexican Mountain WSA, and about 18 miles are in the Sids Mountain/Sids Cabin WSA. The most popular float trip is the 18-mile stretch from Fuller Bottom to the bridge at the San Rafael Campground. Old hiking boots or wading shoes with ankle support are recommended for all routes, even those that include wading in the river. You'll need good footwear for approach routes where trails are primitive or nonexistent. Trekking poles or walking sticks are recommended.

The infamous Upper Black Box section of the San Rafael River is downstream from the San Rafael Campground, in Mexican Mountain WSA. The Lower Black Box is somewhat easier to negotiate, but still daunting. See the trip descriptions in the Mexican Mountain WSA section for more details.

Even though many of the hiking opportunities are along the river, take your own water. The mineral content of the San Rafael River is so high that it might give you cramps even if you filter it before drinking.

Sids Mountain/Sids Cabin WSA

DAY HIKE: SAN RAFAEL RIVER CANYON, CANE WASH,
LITTLE GRAND CANYON
One-Way Length: 3–7 miles (depending on turnaround point)
Low and High Elevations: 5,400 and 5,500 feet
Difficulty: Easy

Go 0.3 mile south of the San Rafael Bridge and Campground, turn right (west), and hike or drive about 0.1 mile on a dirt road signed "Corrals." This spur road off Buckhorn Draw Rd. ends at a no-vehicle sign. The trail along the river continues west-northwest, following cow/horse trails and user-created human trails. Cottonwood trees, flowering shrubs, and the remains of pioneer cabins flank both spur road and trail. Note the hand-hewn logs of the older cabin ruins.

About 3 miles upstream, Cane Wash enters from the left. Stop here and examine the low cliff walls about 100 yards up Cane Wash for pictographs. This is the first of several Barrier Canyon–style rock art panels accessible along this hiking route.

Option: If you have time, you might want to explore farther up Cane Wash. Flash floods have eroded the rock formations near the wash floor into interesting shapes. Seasonal springs and seeps harbor tiny gardens below towering Wingate Sandstone walls. Cane Wash is about 4 miles long and you can exit at its head across a dry plateau to Buckhorn Draw Rd. Our recommendation is to make a 0.5-mile excursion into Cane Wash from the San Rafael River, then return to the river to proceed upstream.

Continuing upstream, the San Rafael River bends sharply north, then south, making a U-turn. This is the entry to Little Grand Canyon. At high water flows, you might have to climb on the sidehill to get around the corner. At low water, there's plenty of room to walk along the riverbank, with minimal amounts of bush-whacking. In evening light, the cliff walls turn amazing shades of mauve, with the green stripe of the river course flowing at the bottom. This is the most scenic section that people floating the river on inner tubes from Fuller Bottom to the San Rafael Bridge will encounter.

After you round the U-turn corner, look up and to your left at a pale sandstone wall that has a smooth, inward-slanting section protected from the weather. Climb through a boulder-strewn foothill to the base of this wall to view an amazing panel of rock art paintings—seldom visited, seldom seen, and remarkably preserved. Do not touch the pictographs or the wall. After viewing the rock art panel, return the way you came.

Option: Continue hiking to Virgin Spring Canyon, about 4 miles upstream from Cane Wash. You will pass several smaller tributary canyons. Virgin Spring Canyon enters from the left (south). The entrance is distinctive because it is larger and is blocked by the river, but you can easily wade to enter. This tributary canyon is home to a perennial spring and to more Barrier Canyon pictographs. Hike about 0.25 mile up Virgin Spring Canyon to view the rock art. Bring along the Bottleneck Peak and Sids Mountain USGS 1:24,000 maps.

> **DAY HIKE: SIDS MOUNTAIN AND CABIN**
> One-Way Length: About 5–6 miles
> Low and High Elevations: 5,400 and 6,610 feet
> Difficulty: Moderate (4WD required for approach road)

From the Green River Cutoff Rd. (described at the beginning of this chapter), drive about 13 miles south to Fuller Bottom. The turn to Fuller Bottom is signed. Vehicles with 4WD can only cross the San Rafael River at low water. Once across the river, turn left (east) and drive Little Wedge Plateau Rd. to the Sids Mountain Trailhead. You can easily follow the 4WD roads with Trails Illustrated Map #712. You'll pass several side roads and unofficial 4WD tracks, all of which can be ignored.

From the river ford at Fuller Bottom, drive about 4 miles to Sids Mountain Trailhead. A trailhead for visitors on horseback is located another 2 miles down the road. The hiker version of the trail makes its way through a short slot canyon and then fords North Salt Wash before beginning the ascent to view Sids Mountain and two cabins. Foot and horse trails meet in North Salt Wash, near the confluence with Saddle Horse Canyon; from there, the trail is marked as it makes its way to the mesa top through juniper and piñon trees.

Where the trail meets a log fence, the terrain changes as you lose elevation to enter a meadow. The trail continues east between two slickrock domes to a historical cabin. Local lore has it that Sid Swasey—the same cowboy who jumped his horse across Swasey's Leap in Mexican Mountain WSA—followed a bighorn sheep onto the mesa and discovered the meadow. The cabin on stilts was built in the 1940s and served as a "line cabin." Line cowboys lived in a remote part of a ranch and kept cows from ranging into territory belonging to other ranchers. The "line" was ridden as a sort of cow-policing operation before the installation of fences. The ruins of a second cabin are also evident near Sids Mountain. The mountain is the high point on the mesa at 6,610 feet. The slickrock dome of Sids Mountain can be climbed most easily from the north side. Return the way you came for a round trip of 10 to 12 miles.

Mexican Mountain WSA

The large Mexican Mountain WSA east of Buckhorn Draw Rd. is known for its geological diversity. The oldest sandstone in the Swell, Coconino (about 250 million years old), is exposed at the bottom of the Black Boxes. Carmel and Entrada Sandstones are topped by Navajo Sandstone hummocks in the southeastern portion of the wilderness study area, where the San Rafael River cuts a cleft through the reef —that impressive-looking, jagged, up-thrust edge you see when you're driving from the town of Green River west along I-70.

A herd of about 15 wild burros uses the southeastern section near Jackass Benches, Lower Black Box, and Swasey's Leap. Excess burros have to be periodically rounded up and removed to prevent them from decimating the landscape.

You need detailed maps to find your way among all the dirt roads that branch off from Buckhorn Draw Rd. Trails Illustrated Map #712 shows most of the roads, or use USGS 1:24,000 maps Bottleneck Peak, Devils Hole, Mexican Mountain, Drowned Hole Draw, and Spotted Wolf Canyon.

> **DAY HIKE:** SWASEY'S LEAP
> One-Way Length: 2 miles
> Low and High Elevations: 5,000 and 6,600 feet
> Difficulty: Easy (4WD required for approach road)

This side trip off Buckhorn Draw Rd. begins about 5.6 miles north of I-70, or about 13 miles south of the San Rafael Bridge. The turn east is signed as "Sink Hole Flat/Jackass Bench." The road is 2WD in good weather for about 9 miles, and 4WD for the last 3.5 miles. Watch for wild burros on and near the road. For the first two road intersections, keep left. At mile 8.8 from Buckhorn Draw Rd., a sign at a fork reads "Swazys Leap and Lower Black Box." Keep left for Swasey's Leap (spellings of "Swasey" vary all over the map). Park where the road ends and hike 2 miles on a track now closed to vehicles.

All along the drive and the hike, there are panoramic views of pinnacles, buttes, and rolling plateaus. At Swasey's Leap, a dilapidated and unsafe stock bridge crosses the 14-foot-wide canyon. As local cowboy lore tells it, Sid Swasey jumped the chasm on his horse to win a bet with his brother—75 head of cattle being the payoff. The stock bridge was erected later. Drowned Hole Draw and Spotted Wolf Canyon USGS 1:24,000 maps cover this area.

> **LOOP HIKE:** LOWER BLACK BOX
> One-Way Length: 9 miles (about 5 miles in river, 4 miles out of river)
> Low and High Elevations: 4,418 and 5,000 feet
> Difficulty: Strenuous (4WD required for approach road)

In order for most semifit adventurers to enjoy this hike, water levels in the San Rafael River should be below 25 cfs (cubic feet per second). Even though you will only be in the river canyon for about 5 miles, you should allow six to eight hours. Swimming in chest-deep cold water and working your way around obstacles will slow you down. Flash-flood danger is extreme. Check the weather and the river water level before attempting this hike. In places the canyon is only 10 feet wide in the hiking corridor, limiting your options to escape or to get out of the cold water.

See the road directions for Swasey's Leap in the previous hike for the first part of the approach to the trailhead. About 4 miles from Buckhorn Draw Rd., the Sink Hole Flat/Jackass Bench Rd. splits to make a loop around Jackass Bench. Keep right, along the south side of Jackass Bench. At the next intersection, Black Dragon Rd., turn left (north). About 1 mile north of the Black Dragon intersection, watch for a fainter 4WD road on your right. Turn east on this road and drive about 3 miles to Lower Black Box Trailhead, the beginning and ending point for this hike. From the Lower Black Box Trailhead, it's about a 2-mile hike to the river.

The best plan is to backpack in and camp near the Lower Black Box Trailhead. Get an early start the next day by fording the river. On the east side of the river, hike upstream along the rim to a spot about 0.5 mile above Swasey's Leap. It's easier to hike on the east side of the river, and easier to enter the canyon from that side. Make

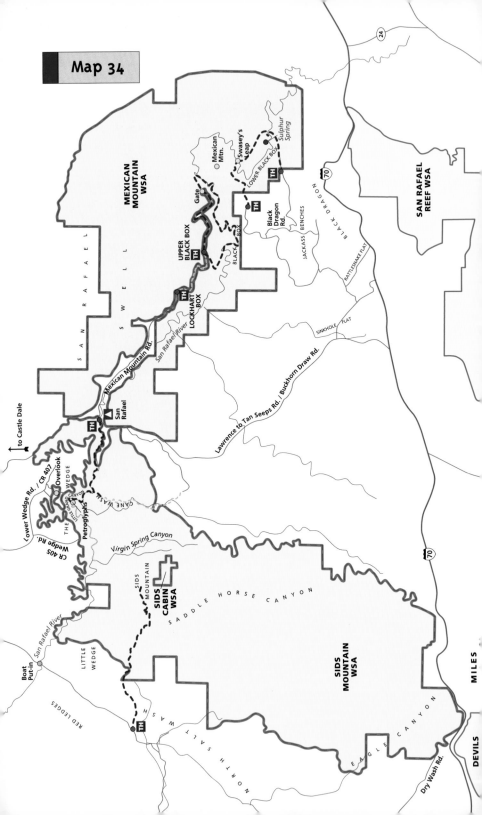

your way into the canyon and hike downstream. You'll hike/wade under Swasey's Leap. Below Swasey's Leap, some bouldering is required, both in and out of the water. Ten feet of rope to lower packs might prove helpful. Most hikers bring an inner tube to float their packs through the intermittent pools, and they also prepare their packs with waterproof liners. Waterproof "drybags" come in backpack versions with shoulder straps, and these are ideal. Hikers who are not confident in their swimming skills should wear a life vest. Wear a wetsuit or high-tech long underwear that retains some of its insulating qualities even when wet. This hike is not suitable for children, but teenagers on up will enjoy it.

If you have a GPS unit, carry it in a waterproof bag and confirm your exit point from the river as N38°58.39', W110°26.51'. The exit is about 0.5 mile below Sulphur Spring.

This makes for a long day, and the rim hike can be hot. Carry plenty of drinking water.

> **SHUTTLE DAY HIKE: UPPER BLACK BOX**
> One-Way Length: About 10 miles (add 4 miles if you don't have a shuttle vehicle)
> Low and High Elevations: 4,500 and 5,500 feet
> Difficulty: Extremely Strenuous (rock-climbing skills and swimming required)

The BLM notes that "every year several parties underestimate the difficulty of this trip and have to be rescued, sometimes not until 24 long, wet, and cold hours later." If you have the right canyoneering skills and equipment, this is a great adventure. If not, don't try it. In addition to all of the cautions listed for Lower Black Box in the previous hike, take the following into account:

• From the approach hike to the exit, you will be working hard, bouldering in and out of water, bushwhacking, swimming, jumping, and climbing. You will be moving about 1 mile per hour. If you're not physically fit enough to work that hard for 10 hours, this is not the expedition for you.

• No dogs. No children.

• Several vertical drops require climbing rope and a lot of upper body strength. You need 30 feet of rope or climber's webbing to set up for a maximum drop of 15 feet. Don't leave rope in the canyon. Don't use rope others have left—old rope is not reliable.

• Put your strongest swimmer in the lead to probe for deep holes and to guide others. Bring a floatation device for every hiker. Hike only at low water levels.

• There is no exit once you enter the Black Box, so everyone in your party must be strong enough to complete the entire hike.

• Park a shuttle car or mountain bike at the end of Mexican Mountain Rd. (mile 13.8 from San Rafael Campground) to save exhausted hikers a two-hour walk at the end of the day.

There are two trailheads on Mexican Mountain Rd., Lockhart and Upper Black Box. We suggest you use Upper Black Box Trailhead in order to shorten the hike. From near the swinging bridge and campground, drive southeast on Mexican Mountain Rd., an offshoot of Buckhorn Draw Rd. that is cherry-stemmed into the wilderness area. The road is 2WD, but you might need light-duty-truck clearance for some rocky areas and dips. Views and camping opportunities are good all along this road—an excellent drive even if you are not hiking. Black Box hikers often leave a shuttle vehicle where the road is blocked by a gate. This is the start of a pleasant 1.5-mile hike on the closed portion of the old road leading to Mexican Bend, an easy outing for those not fit enough to attempt the Black Box. Mexican Bend is rife with outlaw history, including shootouts between lawmen and the Wild Bunch. The remains of outlaw camps and horse corrals are still visible.

Upper Black Box Trailhead is signed at mile 10.1. This is where you'll start your hike. Cairns and an old cattle trail lead across the plateau and then down about 600 feet into the river canyon. The primitive and steep approach trail requires human four-wheeling in places, so allow about one hour. Boulder hopping, wading, and bushwhacking for about two hours once you are in the river canyon will bring you to the narrows for which the Black Box is famous. Once you enter the narrows, the largest drop is about another mile downstream, with a large pool beyond that requires swimming. After spending about three to four hours in the narrows, swimming frequently, you'll be happy to see the canyon widen near the exit point at Mexican Bend. Climb a gentle rise to Mexican Mountain Rd. (this is the portion of the road that is closed to vehicular traffic). Turn left on the road and walk back to your shuttle vehicle. If you don't have a shuttle vehicle, you have an additional 4 miles of roadwalking to return to the Upper Black Box Trailhead.

Sunset flares over the San Rafael River upstream of the Black Box. Cliffs pick up the colors from clouds above the Mexican Mountain Wilderness Study Area.

35 Desolation Canyon, Jack Canyon, Turtle Canyon, Floy Canyon, Coal Canyon, Spruce Canyon, Flume Canyon, and Winter Ridge WSAs

Meanders of the Green River leave a headland that will eventually become a rincon (an abandoned river channel) when the river cuts through the neck of the headland and takes a shorter path downstream.

THE WILDERNESS STUDY AREAS IN THIS CHAPTER are all located along or near the Green River, with the exception of Winter Ridge WSA. The Uintah and Ouray Indian Reservation separates Winter Ridge WSA from the Green River corridor. If you look at a Utah highway map, you'll notice that this entire area appears roadless. I-70 runs along the southern edge, with US 191 to the west and north. In places, Desolation Canyon (cut by the Green River) is 3,000 to 5,000 feet deep. This rugged canyon and its tributaries are not the only extreme terrain that limit access via paved highways. The 250-mile-long Book Cliffs divide the civilized world from this expanse of wilderness study areas. Frequently, boundary lines between wilderness study areas are rough dirt roads suitable for jeeps and other 4WD vehicles with high clearance.

LOCATION: East-Central Utah

SIZE: Desolation Canyon WSA: 290,845 acres
Jack Canyon WSA: 7,500 acres
Turtle Canyon WSA: 33,690 acres
Floy Canyon WSA: 72,605 acres
Coal Canyon WSA: 61,430 acres
Spruce Canyon WSA: 20,350 acres
Flume Canyon WSA: 50,800 acres
Winter Ridge WSA: 42,462 acres

ELEVATION RANGE: 4,150 to 9,510 feet

ECOREGIONS: Middle Rocky Mountain and Colorado Plateau

MILES OF TRAIL: About 35; other routes follow washes and canyon floors

ADMINISTRATION: BLM, Price River and Grand Resource Areas

MAPS: BLM 1:100,000: Price, Huntington, Seep Ridge, Westwater.
USGS 1:24,000: Duches Hole, Cedar Ridge Canyon, Firewater Canyon North,
Firewater Canyon South, Summerhouse Ridge, Steer Ridge Canyon,
Lighthouse Canyon, Chandler Falls, Turtle Canyon, Three Fords Canyon,
Jenny Canyon, Butler Canyon, Bobby Canyon North, Floy Canyon North,
Bogart Canyon, Tepee Canyon, Flume Canyon, Preacher Canyon,
Ten Mile Canyon South, Supply Canyon, Pine Spring Canyon, Wolf Point,
Agency Draw NE, Cedar Camp Canyon.

Desolation Canyon, Jack Canyon, and Turtle Canyon WSAs

Most visitors to Desolation Canyon WSA only experience the corridor of the Green River. Rafting and kayaking are the predominant forms of recreation. From Sand Wash in the north to Swasey's Rapid in the south, it is 84 miles (five to seven days) as the muddy, roiling river makes its way through Desolation and Gray Canyons. Most of the memorable rapids are rated Class II and Class III, making this a good learning river and a nice float trip for families. More rigorous float trips may continue south of the wilderness study area to the confluence with the Colorado River and beyond. Permits are required for river use, but not for hiking. Float trips are granted via a lottery system each January. Every year many launches awarded by lottery are cancelled when applicants fail to pay, so don't give up hope if you are planning a last-minute river trip. Commercial outfitters also often have openings.

In the busy river corridor, regulations are strict. A complete list of rules and requirements accompanies each permit granted. Fire pans, a means to carry out human waste and trash, along with other minimum-impact practices for travel along desert rivers, are required.

If you raft or kayak the Green River, day-hiking options are numerous. Most of the trails are no longer accessible except from the river, though the Wild Bunch and their horses used several of them in the late 1800s and early 1900s. A hike up Rattlesnake Creek on the east side of the Green River will take you to the spot where George Curry was shot by a posse in 1900.

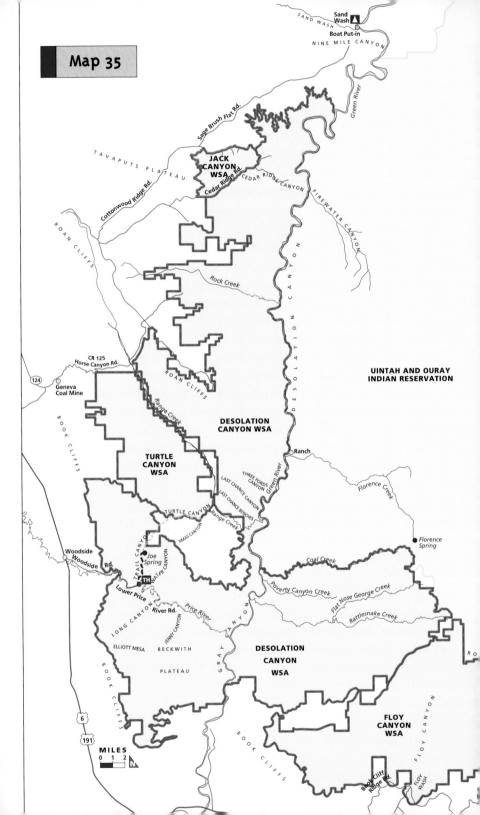

Map 35

Sand Wash

SAND WASH

Boat Put-in

NINE MILE CANYON

Green River

Sage Brush Flat Rd.

TAVAPUTS PLATEAU

JACK CANYON WSA

Cedar Ridge Rd.

CEDAR RIDGE CANYON

Cottonwood Ridge Rd.

FIREWATER CANYON

ROAN CLIFFS

Rock Creek

DESOLATION CANYON

CR 125 Horse Canyon Rd.

UINTAH AND OURAY INDIAN RESERVATION

124

Geneva Coal Mine

ROAN CLIFFS

Range Creek

DESOLATION CANYON WSA

BOOK CLIFFS

Ranch

TURTLE CANYON WSA

THREE FORDS CANYON

Green River

Florence Creek

LAST CHANCE CANYON

LAST CHANCE BENCHES

TURTLE CANYON

Range Creek

XMAS CANYON

Florence Spring

Woodside

Woodside Rd.

TRAIL CANYON

Joe Spring

TH

WATER CANYON

Coal Creek

Lower Price

Price River

Poverty Canyon Creek

Flat Nose George Creek

LONG CANYON

River Rd.

JENNY CANYON

Rattlesnake Creek

ELLIOTT MESA

BECKWITH

GRAY CANYON

PLATEAU

DESOLATION CANYON WSA

6

191

BOOK CLIFFS

BOOK CLIFFS

FLOY CANYON WSA

FLOY CANYON

Book Cliff Ridge Rd.

FLOY WASH

MILES

0 1 2

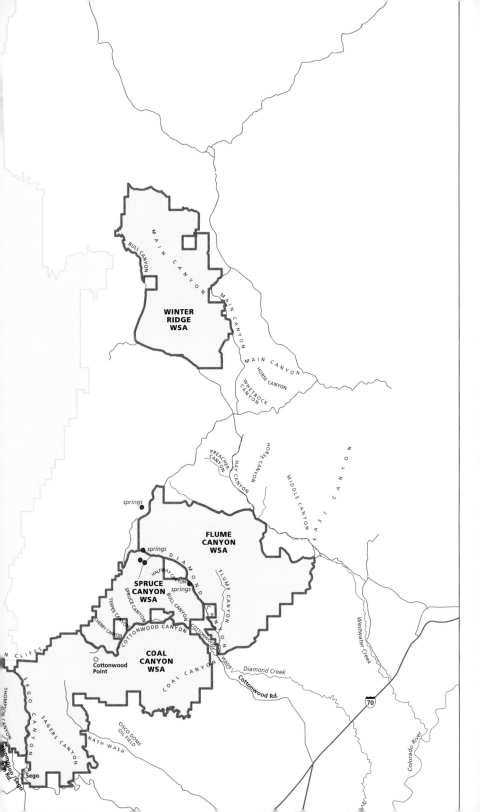

At Firewater Canyon, take a short hike to view the ruins of a cabin and moonshiner's still, and to fill water bottles at the spring. Watch out for poison ivy. The path to the moonshiner's place is just north of another path that leads up the main branch of Firewater Canyon. There are Paleo-Indian ruins in the main canyon.

At Florence Creek, a ranch built in 1890 nestles behind the more modern Ouray Lodge on the Uintah and Ouray Indian Reservation (east) side of the river. The stonework on the old buildings rates as a work of art. There's a potable water source near the lodge, and reservation administrators allow river rafters to stop there to replenish their water supplies.

Bald eagles, blue herons, desert bighorn sheep, black bears, cougars, mule deer, and midget faded rattlesnakes are common and most are likely to be seen by visitors. When we floated the Green River, we enjoyed sightings of all but the cougars.

In addition to the Green River and its immediate vicinity, Desolation Canyon WSA includes portions of the Tavaputs and Beckwith Plateaus; the Iron Cliffs; the Price River and its tributary drainages from where the river enters the Book Cliffs to its confluence with the Green River; and several canyons east of the Green River, including Rattlesnake, Flat Nose George, Poverty, and portions of Coal Creek.

Turtle Canyon WSA is tucked into the western midsection of Desolation Canyon WSA, with only dirt roads separating it from the surrounding arms of the larger study area.

Jack Canyon is a small wilderness study area just below the northwestern tip of Desolation Canyon WSA. There are no hiking trails in Jack Canyon. Cedar Ridge Rd. marks its south and east boundary, and Cottonwood Ridge/Sage Brush Flat Roads mark the north edge. Take the Cedar Ridge Canyon USGS topo map to explore a signless nest of unofficial ways and tracks in Jack Canyon WSA.

The nearest towns are Price and Green River, Utah. Green River is a full-service town about 5 miles south of Swasey's Rapid, the usual takeout for rafting trips. A dirt access road and a dirt landing strip serve Sand Wash near the northern end of the WSA. Small planes land on the plateau above Sand Wash, with service from Grand Junction, Colo., or from Green River, Utah. Grand Junction is about a two-hour drive from Swasey's Rapid takeout. To drive to Sand Wash, go south from US 40/US 191 on Nine Mile Canyon Rd., departing US 40/US 191 near the small town of Myton.

Four privately owned lodges near the borders of Desolation Canyon offer lodging, horseback riding, and river rafting. Many other outfitters offer kayaking and rafting trips on the Green River. See the list of outfitters in this book for more information (Appendix B).

There have been few fatalities on the Green River in the past 10 years, but medical evacuations for rock-climbing accidents and allergic reactions to poison ivy or bee stings average about one a month. Cell phones do not work in the canyons, and satellite phones only work in some areas. Though numerous, midget rattlesnakes seldom strike humans. Heat exhaustion is a problem in the summer months. All creek water must be filtered or treated before drinking. Some creek water might be chemically unpotable even after filtering. Published river guides for Desolation Canyon direct rafters to safe water sources. (See Canyonlands Natural History Association and Desolation Canyon River Information in Appendix B.)

DAY HIKE: TRAIL CANYON TO JOE SPRING

One-Way Length: About 2.5 miles (with options for continuing much farther)

Low and High Elevations: About 4,800 and 5,625 feet

Difficulty: Easy to Moderate (but route finding is sometimes difficult)

For those seeking solitude, the southwestern corner of Desolation Canyon WSA is about as good as it gets. A cherry-stemmed road leading up onto Elliott Mesa provides access to the heads of Long Canyon, Water Canyon, Jenny Canyon, and other drainages leading to the Price River. True to its name, Trail Canyon is served by a rough hiking trail leading to Joe Spring (about 2.5 miles) and beyond. This trail crosses the Price River—hikers wade the shallows. There's more than one Trail Canyon in this area, so please note that this is not the Trail Canyon off the Green River near the Iron Cliffs. Informal, primitive trails offer access to other canyons and washes. Be prepared to explore.

Leave US 6/US 191 near the non-town of Woodside. Drive east on the Woodside and Lower Price River Rd. about 7 miles. Trail Canyon is the first significant canyon north of the road. The trail begins near a sharp U shape in the gravel/dirt road, where Trail Canyon meets the Price River. There are no trail signs, and when we were there, no road signs. Hike up Trail Canyon for a pleasant desert hike. You can stop at Joe Spring, a small riparian area, or continue along the primitive path to cross a plateau and enter Turtle Canyon. Take your own water and the Jenny Canyon USGS topo map.

In good weather, Woodside and Lower Price River Rd. is 2WD for the first 8 miles or so. To continue another 10 miles to the end at a drill site, 4WD is recommended, though some light-duty trucks with high clearance have traveled the road in good weather. This 18-mile-long road provides access to three segments of primitive trail, including Trail Canyon, Owlhoot along the Price River, and Long Canyon. The access road ends near the head of Jenny Canyon.

Option: Hike downstream along the Price River to its confluence with the Green River (about 10 to 11 miles). The Owlhoot Trail begins on the north side of the Price River, near the Trail Canyon confluence, on the same U shape in the access road for the hike to Joe Spring. You'll know you're there when the access road comes close to the river's edge. Portions of Owlhoot Trail used to be a jeep trail. Tamarisk groves are thick along the riverbanks and might require occasional bushwhacking. Hikers will ford the Price River several times. About 1.5 miles into this hike, there's a photogenic old cabin. Fremont Indians left impressive petroglyphs on the canyon wall near the confluence of the Price and Green Rivers. At high water, the "hike" can be turned into a kayaking trip down the Price River. Potable drinking water is a problem —bring your own. Mosquitoes range from mildly annoying to deadly. Cool nights in late fall greatly reduce the mosquito population and increase a hiker's enjoyment.

Jeep/Hike Options in Turtle Canyon WSA

You will need the Turtle Canyon USGS map to find your way around 4WD roads, and to locate interesting hiking opportunities. Horse Canyon Rd. (CR 125), about 10 miles north of Woodside, is the starting point for a dirt road that leads southwest along the edge of Turtle Canyon WSA. From US 6/US 191, drive northeast on Horse Canyon Rd. toward the Geneva Coal Mine and aerial cableway (about 5 miles).

Beyond the coal mine, the road quality deteriorates. Continue east about 7 more miles to Range Creek. Turn right (south) on the dirt road that follows Range Creek. Now you are driving along the northeastern edge of Turtle Canyon WSA. There are no official trails, but user-created footpaths exist here and there. Six minor canyons can be explored to the right of the road before you arrive at the larger Turtle Canyon. Here a more obvious hiking trail appears (formerly a jeep route).

Refer to the day hike in Trail Canyon, described in the previous section, for hiking access to Turtle Canyon from Woodside Rd./Lower Price River Rd. (CR 129). That trail climbs out of Trail Canyon, crosses a plateau, and then drops down into Turtle Canyon.

In Desolation Canyon Wilderness Study Area, the Green River makes its way south toward the Colorado River. This area is a favorite for family rafting and kayaking trips.

Floy Canyon, Coal Canyon, Spruce Canyon, Flume Canyon, and Winter Ridge WSAs

Floy, Coal, Spruce, and Flume Canyon WSAs line up along the southern edge of the Uintah and Ouray Indian Reservation, and they do not abut the Green River. Their terrain and hiking opportunities are similar, and they are separated from each other by dirt and gravel roads. Winter Ridge WSA wraps around the eastern edge of the reservation.

The primary recreational use is by hunters who typically use 4WD vehicles and ORVs along the few roads and then hike or ride horseback into the surrounding canyons. There are some undeveloped springs in this mostly dry terrain; these springs serve as gathering places for both wild animals and grazing cattle.

These study areas are about 10 miles northwest of I-70 and about 20 miles west of the Colorado border. The Book Cliffs show an impressive 1,000 feet of their face on the southeastern edge of the WSA, but they top out at a relatively low 7,000 feet. The cliff wall is occasionally broken into hoodoos—pedestals of rock and soil that form when softer material erodes beneath a cap of harder rock. These pinnacles provide interesting photo opportunities.

The Cisco Dome oil field takes an irregular bite out of the south-central border of Coal Canyon WSA, but it also provides access to Nash Wash via a road over Windy Mesa. Part of the Nash Wash Rd. is cherry-stemmed into Coal Canyon WSA. Other major road accesses are Thompson Canyon/Sego Canyon Rd., Cottonwood Rd., and Book Cliff Ridge Rd., also called Hay Canyon Over the Top Rd. Various unnamed jeep trails also approach the Book Cliffs on the southern edge. A 4WD vehicle and USGS topographical maps are recommended. There are only about 8 miles of rough jeep trails that are actually within the boundaries of the WSAs—most roads skirt the edges. The nearest small town with services is Thompson, just off I-70. For more information, contact the Green River Visitor Center (see Appendix B).

Winter Ridge WSA on the east side of the Uintah and Ouray Indian Reservation is accessible via 4WD roads that intersect Book Cliff Ridge Rd./Hay Canyon Over the Top Rd. The BLM has written, "Day hiking and backpacking do not qualify as outstanding because the unit lacks a focal point of interest. No perennial streams, ponds, or lakes exist, and there are no prominent overlooks or high terrain which offer sweeping panoramic views." Birds and reptiles love Winter Ridge. If you are enraptured by red-tailed hawks, Cooper's hawks, American kestrels, and the occasional golden eagle, then you might like it, too. In spite of the lack of water, Winter Ridge also boasts a significant population of black bears and cougars. Access to Winter Ridge from the north is via UT 88 to Willow Creek Rd. See USGS topos Pine Spring Canyon, Wolf Point, Agency Draw NE, and Cedar Camp Canyon.

36 Black Ridge Canyons Wilderness and Westwater Canyon WSA

Kayakers and rafters enjoy the 13-mile-long series of rapids in Westwater Canyon.

BLACK RIDGE CANYONS WILDERNESS and Westwater Canyon WSA are both on the Utah-Colorado border, next door to each other. All of the wilderness study areas in the Green River Complex (see Chapter 35) are reasonably close. The closest large town is Grand Junction, Colo., about 10 miles from Black Ridge Canyons Wilderness. In Utah, the town of Moab is about 62 road miles away, and Green River is about 70 miles away. Access is from I-70 in Utah.

LOCATION: East-Central Utah
SIZE: Black Ridge Canyons Wilderness: 5,180 acres in Utah
(plus 70,370 acres in Colorado)
Westwater Canyon WSA: 31,160 acres
ELEVATION RANGE: 4,700 to 6,800 feet
ECOREGION: Colorado Plateau
MILES OF TRAIL: 77 (in Black Ridge Canyons Wilderness only)
ADMINISTRATION: BLM, Grand Resource Area, Utah;
Grand Junction Field Office, Colo.
MAPS: USGS 1:24,000: Bitter Creek Well, Westwater,
Agate, Marble Canyon, Big Triangle.

These wilderness areas are on the very edge of the terrain where the Rocky Mountains Ecoregion ends and the Colorado Plateau Ecoregion begins. Both areas are semiarid, but are cut by rivers and streams, with a moderately thick covering of piñon-juniper forest on the plateaus. Redrock canyons are incised into the plateaus, with seven major drainages in Black Ridge and three in Westwater. Alcoves, pinnacles, and other erosional features are displayed in the Wingate Sandstone cliffs.

Great blue herons nest along the Colorado River, and two endangered raptors cruise the skies, the bald eagle and the peregrine falcon.

Black Ridge Canyons Wilderness

Black Ridge Canyons became a designated wilderness area on October 24, 2000. Only a small portion of this wilderness is in Utah. For the Colorado portion, see *The Complete Guide to Colorado's Wilderness Areas* by Mark Pearson, published by Westcliffe Publishers.

Black Ridge Canyons Wilderness is second only to Utah's Arches National Park in the number of natural stone arches. Seasonal waterfalls and plunge pools distinguish Black Ridge from Arches. In Colorado, to visit this wilderness, drive south from Fruita on CO 340. Several well-signed roads announce access to the wilderness. The Loma Boat Launch west of Fruita is a put-in on the Colorado River for the Ruby–Horsethief Canyon run.

DAY HIKE: JONES CANYON TRAIL
One-Way Length: 4 miles
Low and High Elevations: 5,600 and 6,000 feet
Difficulty: Moderate

To explore the Utah section of Black Ridge Canyons Wilderness, begin at the Jones Canyon Trailhead in Colorado, 30 miles southwest of Grand Junction. Jones Canyon is one of the most remote areas in the wilderness, and it offers an excellent opportunity to enjoy the canyon in solitude.

From Grand Junction, travel west on Grand Avenue, which turns into Broadway. Cross two bridges and at the next stoplight, turn left on Monument Rd. Turn left at D Rd. Follow D Rd. until it ends at a fork; go right on Little Park Rd. to DS Rd.; and turn left on DS Rd. to Glade Park Store. At the store, turn right on 16.5 Rd. and drive 0.5 mile to BS Rd. Turn left and drive 14 miles to the trailhead.

From the trailhead, hike 4 miles to the canyon overlook. Take plenty of drinking water, as the hike is dry and can be very hot. From the overlook, you can choose to wander along the rim or across the mesa. The trail does not go to the floor of the canyon, but the views are spectacular from the rim.

Westwater Canyon WSA

In Westwater Canyon, the Colorado River slices through the Uncompahgre Uplift of the Colorado Plateau and dives into Utah. Recreational use mostly centers on the river, where kayakers and rafters enjoy the 13-mile-long concentration of rapids. A put-in at the confluence of Bitter Creek and the Colorado River serves up Class III and IV rapids such as Skull and Funnel Falls.

Take exit 225 off I-70, about 40 miles west of Grand Junction, and drive south on Harley Dome Rd. for about 12 miles. Cross the bridge and turn northeast where a road parallels the river to the Westwater Canyon put-in. In a two- to three-day trip, one day is usually spent running rapids; the river is calmer for the remainder of the trip. A popular take-out is at the ghost town of Cisco, exit 212 off I-70. Colorado River water is not potable, so take your own.

Rafters won't get through Westwater Canyon without getting wet. Where the Colorado River enters Utah, its gradient steepens, dropping an average of 11 feet per mile, and the canyon narrows. This area sees about 14,000 visitors per year, and this section of the Colorado has been rated as the river's best by many experienced rafters. The rafting season is from May to September, and permits are required. Commercial outfitters based in Green River and Moab, Utah, and in Grand Junction, Colo., offer guided float trips. Only experienced whitewater rafters and kayakers should try this on their own.

Side canyons to Westwater include Little Dolores, Marble, and Star. The mouths of these tributary canyons open onto Westwater Canyon 100 to 200 feet above the level of the Colorado, on a wide shelf that forms an upper canyon above the drainage of the Colorado. Marble Canyon boasts two rock formations worthy of photos: Smokey Bear Point and Wingate Arch. Little Dolores, Star, and Marble Canyons are easier to access from the Colorado side because the river cuts off access from the Utah side. You need a 4WD vehicle with high clearance to negotiate a nest of dirt roads that only appear on the USGS 1:24,000 maps Westwater, Marble Canyon, and Big Triangle. There are no official hiking trails, but 4WD access along Little Dolores River, along with the allure of a riparian area, have resulted in user-created trails into Utah.

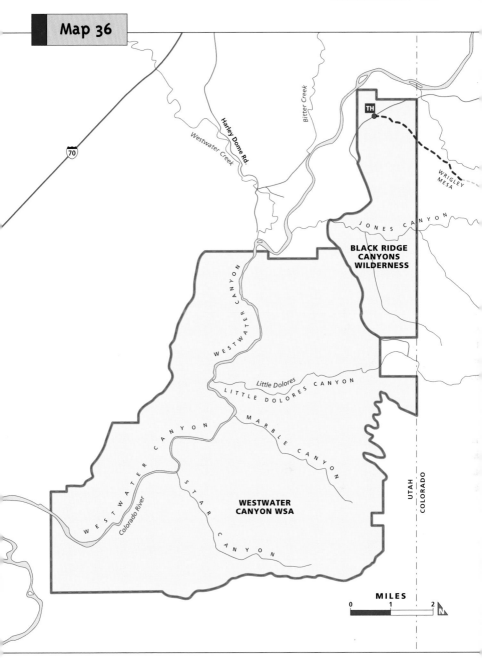

Map 36

East-Central Utah   287

70

Harley Dome Rd.

Westwater Creek

Bitter Creek

TH

WRIGLEY MESA

JONES CANYON

BLACK RIDGE
CANYONS
WILDERNESS

WESTWATER CANYON

Little Dolores

LITTLE DOLORES CANYON

MARBLE CANYON

WESTWATER CANYON

Colorado River

STAR CANYON

WESTWATER
CANYON WSA

UTAH

COLORADO

MILES

0   1   2

Recommended Wilderness in National Parks, Monuments, and Recreation Areas

In Utah's five national parks, in several of its national monuments, and in Glen Canyon National Recreation Area, more than 80% of the land has been recommended for wilderness designation, about 1.5 million acres. Congress has not acted on this recommendation, but the Park Service has continued to manage the lands for wilderness values. If Congress ever approves the recommended acres, the uses and administration of the land will change very little. Projects such as clearing brush and maintaining trails might take a little longer because chain saws and wheeled vehicles would be prohibited.

To hikers, this is a great boon. Utah's national parks, monuments, and recreation areas offer significant stretches of backcountry, enough to humble the most adventurous wilderness enthusiasts. More than 2 million people might visit Zion National Park each year, but few of those visitors explore the park's backcountry. Even in a busy national park, the lesson is don't let all those tour buses keep you from including it in your wilderness itinerary.

Countless guidebooks have been published for Arches, Bryce, Canyonlands, Capitol Reef, and Zion National Parks; the parks also publish a lot of useful hiking tips. The same is true for the national monuments: Cedar Breaks, Dinosaur, and Natural Bridges. The information presented for National Park Service lands in this book is only a summary of the recommended wilderness in each area, with a few suggestions for enjoying hiking opportunities. Visitors should supplement this information before heading into the backcountry. See the Bibliography (Appendix E) for further reading suggestions.

The 16 proposed wilderness areas in Grand Staircase–Escalante National Monument are covered in the chapters on South-Central Utah. Grand Staircase is the only national monument administered by the Bureau of Land Management, in cooperation with the National Park Service and the Forest Service, and we have presented its proposed wilderness areas separately.

Sandstone formations in the Needles District of Canyonlands National Park at sunset

37 Arches National Park

Double Arch frames a clear, blue desert sky.

ARCHES NATIONAL PARK is located 5 miles north of Moab. Of the five national parks in Utah, Arches is the one most dominated by domesticated "frontcountry." Nevertheless, park administrators now estimate that more than 70,000 acres have wilderness characteristics. The increase in recommended wilderness acreage comes from several sources, including the addition of Lost Spring Canyon's 3,140 acres, expiration of some mineral and grazing leases, and the exchange of school trust lands within the park for other lands.

LOCATION: East-Central Utah
SIZE: 80,490 acres (62,947 acres recommended as wilderness)
ELEVATION RANGE: 3,960 to 5,653 feet
ECOREGION: Colorado Plateau
MILES OF TRAIL: 18.5
ADMINISTRATION: NPS, Arches NP
MAPS: Trails Illustrated: Map #211.
USGS 1:24,000: Mollie Hogans, Klondike Buttes, Merrimac Butte, Big Bend,
The Windows Section, Cisco SW, Goldbar Canyon, Moab.

Natural stone openings are found all over the Colorado Plateau, and in other parts of the world where easily erodable stone weathers into semistable arches. But no place on earth can match Arches National Park for the dense concentration of these strangely graceful formations. Depending on what your criteria are for a measurable arch, there are about 900 stone windows, doorways, and eyes in the park. The best known and most frequently photographed arches are in the frontcountry section of the park, where paved roads and walkways, overlooks, and other amenities make some of them accessible to handicapped visitors. Delicate Arch, which appears on Utah license plates, and whose sunrise/sunset moments are accompanied by the cricketlike chorus of camera shutters, used to be called The Schoolmarm's Bloomers by local cowboys. It's a big pair of bloomers, 65 feet high and almost 35 feet wide. We recommend visiting when a dusting of snow contrasts with the salmon-colored rock.

Arches is in a "cool desert," with extremes of cold in winter and of heat in summer. To escape most of the crowds and sample the backcountry in Arches, try a long day hike into Lost Spring Canyon, or hike in Courthouse Wash, described in the following section. Backcountry permits are required. Inquire about special restrictions at the visitor center.

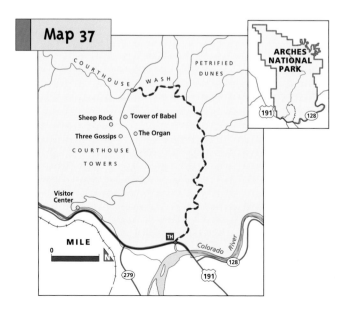

DAY HIKE: LOWER COURTHOUSE WASH
One-Way Length: 5.3 miles
Low and High Elevations: 3,960 and 4,140 feet
Difficulty: Easy

Begin your hike at a paved parking area 0.2 mile west of the spot where US 191 bridges the wash, about 2 miles northwest of the town of Moab.

A marked trail leads from the parking area to the wash. In the spring, thin veils of water decorate several stairstep sections of rocky ledges, and this water, combined with shade from the confining walls, makes for a welcome respite from the desert sun. Some hikers just go barefoot through both water and sand.

Near the miniature waterfalls there are several tributary canyons, and you can use the third canyon to access the Petrified Dunes. Do not attempt the side trip to the dunes area without a topographical map.

Extensive root systems of Fremont cottonwoods hold the soil in place along the main course of Lower Courthouse Wash, forming benches where overnight backpackers can pitch a tent. You can hike the 5.3 miles of Lower Courthouse Wash as a shuttle hike, ending at the main park road; or complete a 10.6-mile round trip as a day hike or as an overnight backpack trip.

Lower Courthouse Wash

Bryce Canyon National Park 38

Fresh snow dusts a balanced rock formation.

WHEN WE HIKED in Bryce Canyon, I frequently heard the distinctive rumble of a rock avalanche beginning and ducked under an overhang in time to escape a small shower of stones and dirt. Erosion! The major force at work was brought powerfully home.

Horizontal beds of limestone, sandstone, and shale on the eastern edge of Paunsaugunt Plateau are so erosion prone that a mind-numbing array of fins,

LOCATION: South-Central Utah

SIZE: 35,835 acres (20,810 acres recommended as wilderness)

ELEVATION RANGE: 6,620 to 9,115 feet

ECOREGION: Colorado Plateau

MILES OF TRAIL: 60

ADMINISTRATION: NPS, Bryce Canyon NP

MAPS: Trails Illustrated: Map #219. USGS 1:24,000: Podunk Creek, Rainbow Point, Bryce Point, Tropic Reservoir, Tropic Canyon, Bryce Canyon.

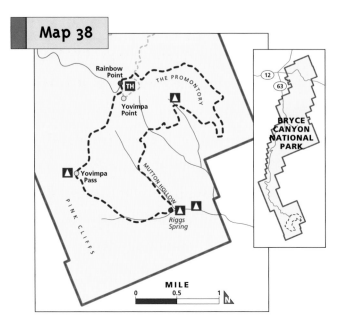

turrets, pinnacles, and spires has formed. Spires and pillars stand as tall as 1,000 feet and are surrounded by a wild architecture of natural forms resembling cathedrals, temples, ruins, dragons, gargoyles, and every other form that may come to the imaginative mind.

Many of the overlooks from the paved road on the rim are accessible to wheelchairs. A park concessionaire offers horseback rides from Sunrise Point and along Peekaboo Loop Trail. More than a million and a half visitors view the hoodoos from the rim road each year, and about 2,000 backpackers hike the trails.

White-throated swifts that can dive at up to 200 miles per hour are a common sight along the rim. Jet-black ravens cruise among the hoodoos and their calls echo eerily in the stone amphitheater. In 1996, six California condors were released near the park. The big birds have a 9-foot wingspan and can be seen perching on the rails at overlooks or flying below the rim. Four nesting pairs of peregrine falcons also live in the park. Humans have lived in the Bryce area for about 12,000 years, with the Fremont and Anasazi cultures pre-dating the Paiutes. Paiute tribes were living in the Bryce area when Captain Dutton explored the Colorado Plateau with John Wesley Powell in the 1870s.

The elevation of 8,000 to 9,000 feet at the rim usually guarantees cooler temperatures, seldom exceeding 80 degrees Fahrenheit in the summer. Precipitation averages 18 inches per year, so this park is not as dry and hot as Utah's other national parks. The North Campground at Bryce is open all year, but high winds and extreme cold make winter camping difficult. Intrepid winter campers will be rewarded with empty trails covered in creamy snow and mists that swirl around the eroded shapes, creating a mysterious landscape completely different from the crowded, noisy atmosphere that characterizes summer.

Most of the hiking trails are in good condition, but washouts in spring, or heavy snows in winter, mean that you need to wear sturdy hiking boots. Trails with mellow elevation changes are used as cross-country ski routes in the winter. Most of the hiking trails that dip below the rim are rated strenuous.

Backcountry permits, available at the visitor center, are required. Water availability and quality varies throughout the hiking season (May to October), so be sure to check the water chart at the visitor center before you go. There are springs along backpacking routes and near most of the designated camping sites. Nights are cool and campfires are prohibited, so be prepared with shelter and warm clothes. Group size is limited to six people.

The park's rim road, UT 63, is the access route for most trailheads. From US 89 (7 miles south of Panguitch and 61 miles north of Kanab), turn east onto UT 12. This highway takes you through scenic Red Canyon. The entrance to Bryce Canyon National Park is clearly marked, 7.5 miles west of the small town of Tropic. If you approach from the east, the distance from Escalante is 47 miles.

LOOP HIKE: RIGGS SPRING LOOP TRAIL
One-Way Length: 8.7 miles
Low and High Elevations: 7,440 and 9,115 feet
Difficulty: Moderate

This loop receives less use by park visitors and is more likely to feel like a wilderness excursion. The length of the trail is longer than most of the day hikes in Bryce, and the trailhead at Rainbow Point is at the extreme southern end of the park. Three distinct life zones are represented in the park's 2,500 feet of vertical relief. Riggs Spring Loop descends through two of the zones, fir forests and scrub oak woodlands, before the trail climbs back to the rim road over Yovimpa Pass. The forests, hoodoos, and views into Arizona are the scenic highlights. It's possible to do the loop as a day hike, but an overnight backpack is recommended. There are three campsites along the loop; two have a water source. Riggs Spring is a grassy, shady campsite with groves of pines and aspen trees. The aspen grove around the spring is particularly beautiful in the fall. The campsite at Yovimpa Pass boasts a reliable water source and grassy sites.

39 Canyonlands National Park and South Needles WSA

Grand View Point overlooks the confluence of the Green and Colorado Rivers.

ON A COLD SPRING EVENING, everything around Dead Horse Point turned rusty red and mauve as the sun dipped below the horizon. Birdcage evening primroses opened their delicate white faces at twilight. The Colorado River, wrapped into a tight gooseneck shape, was so far below us that it looked deceptively still. A tree, loosened from the bank and sent downstream on the silt-laden current, betrayed the river's motion and power.

With ample but inaccessible water in sight, a band of wild desert ponies died on Dead Horse Point after cowboys herded them into the natural corral but left the rejects to find their own way off. Overwhelmed by the topography, the ponies that were left behind failed to find the narrow exit over a land bridge and died of thirst.

From where I stood, I could see 5,000 square miles of the Colorado Plateau. Somewhere out there the Colorado and Green Rivers mingled. Between their arms was a rugged peninsula, the centerpiece of the Colorado Plateau, an area so difficult to access that it challenges drivers, rafters, and hikers alike.

In addition to park lands recommended for wilderness, there are several BLM-administered wilderness study areas adjacent to Canyonlands. Because South Needles WSA is too small to be a wilderness study area without its association with the national park, that area is described in this chapter. Butler Wash, Bridger Jack Mesa, and Indian Creek WSAs appear in Chapter 31.

LOCATION: Southeast-Central Utah

SIZE: Canyonlands NP: 337,570 acres (287,133 acres recommended as wilderness)
South Needles WSA: 160 acres

ELEVATION RANGE: 4,000 to 7,000 feet

ECOREGION: Colorado Plateau

MILES OF TRAIL: About 125

ADMINISTRATION: NPS, Canyonlands NP, Southeast Utah Group;
BLM, Monticello Field Office

MAPS: Trails Illustrated: Maps #210 and #246. USGS 1:24,000: Sugarloaf Butte,
Horsethief Canyon, Upheaval Dome, Musselman Arch, Shafer Basin, Turks Head,
Monument Basin, Lockhart Basin, Flaterite Basin, Spanish Bottom, The Loop, North
Six-Shooter Peak, Teapot Rock, Cross Canyon, Druid Arch, South Six-Shooter Peak,
Cathedral Butte. *See map, p. 11.*

For wilderness aficionados, the district of the park called The Maze offers the
best opportunities for solitude. With the nearest towns more than 100 miles away,
and a lot of the roads requiring 4WD, even accessing trailheads for hiking is an
adventure. Ernies Country is the least-visited section of The Maze. Seasonal potholes
hold the only water, and backpackers need desert hiking experience and some climbing skills before venturing into this unforgiving terrain. The rewards include solitude
and a combination of open spaces, slickrock, sand, and rugged canyons—and the
routes you take will be your own, not a maintained or signed trail. Deep sand and
lots of biting insects can slow you down and add to the irritation factor. Don't attempt
hiking this area in the heat of summer.

If you prefer to hike on a marked trail, try one of the trails leading from
The Doll House to the overlook above the Green and Colorado River confluence; to
Surprise Valley; or to Spanish Bottom. There's also a 1-mile-long Maze Trail from
Maze Overlook to the South Fork of Horse Canyon. The Maze Trail makes its way
over some very steep pitches of slickrock, some pockmarked with "Moqui steps,"
indentations carved into the sandstone as an aid to climbing. The 1-mile route is very
rugged, but it is still the easiest way into The Maze.

You can see the tempting Maze from The Needles and Island in the Sky areas
of Canyonlands, but it's a long and winding road to get to where the raptors fly with
such ease. From UT 24, about 21 miles north of Hanksville, turn east onto the signed
dirt road. Because the road is sometimes obscured with drifting sand, 4WD is highly
recommended. To your usual survival gear, add several extra gallons of water, extra
gasoline, and a tow rope. Experienced jeep drivers usually travel in teams, with at least
one vehicle outfitted with a winch. A sign at the turnoff from UT 24 tells you that it's
80 miles to The Maze and 100 miles to UT 95.

About 24 miles in, a signed junction directs you to either Horseshoe Canyon
Trail (see Chapter 26) or the Hans Flat Ranger Station. About 45 miles in, the ranger
station comes into view. Permits are required and reservations are recommended for
all visitors, and these can be obtained at the Hans Flat Ranger Station. A radio phone,
maps, and guidebooks are also available, assuming the station is open. (See Appendix
B for contact information.)

Policies and permit systems are always evolving in The Maze, so check with
the rangers for the latest rules.

South Needles WSA

The BLM frankly admits that they didn't know this little gem was theirs. They thought it was state land, but when that mistake had been corrected, recognizing the area's wilderness values was a no-brainer.

South Needles WSA is contiguous on two sides with The Needles section of Canyonlands National Park. It abuts 61,182 acres of recommended wilderness in the park, and it looks like it will be either added to the park's jurisdiction or managed as wilderness by the BLM. Within its tiny 160 acres, South Needles WSA boasts 100% Class A scenery, two archaeological sites, and a spring on the north edge. The spring is a great rarity in this dry land, and it supports a small riparian community of cottonwoods, scrub oak, and reeds. The eroded sandstone features include Vanhemert Arch and several sharp pinnacles.

There are no official trails. Several miles of walking from Butler Wash are required before you even get to the boundary of this WSA. There's no motorized access. An easier access is from the Upper Salt Creek Trail of The Needles district of the park. Elevations in South Needles range from 5,640 feet in the northeast where the canyons drain into the national park, to about 6,700 feet in the southwest corner.

This area is on Trails Illustrated Map #210, though it is not identified. You can find it by looking for Butler Wash WSA, then for the square between Butler Wash and the park that contains elevation point 6,764.

Other Excursions: Dead Horse Point/Dead Horse State Park/Potash Road

Take UT 313 west from US 191, 13 miles north of Moab. The best time to visit is from March to May and from August to October. If the weather remains dry, visiting in November and December can be an excellent experience as there are fewer visitors. The Needles Overlook, 32 miles south of Moab, is equally impressive and it can also be accessed in early winter.

The dirt road visible below Dead Horse Point is Potash Rd., a 4WD route that follows a bench 1,000 feet below the rim. Potash Rd. is an extension of UT 279 off of US 191. It passes large mineral evaporation pools and other signs of civilization before it enters the Island in the Sky northern section of Canyonlands National Park. This road, a good back door to the park, offers primitive camping along it, including a site directly below Dead Horse Point. The encircling, sun-warmed rocks embrace a pocket of warm air that is very pleasant in winter and unbearable in summer. Bring your own water. The steep drive out of the canyon via Shafer Trail Rd. is often used by mountain bikers. Drive with caution on the switchbacks.

Capitol Reef National Park and Fremont Gorge WSA

40

Sunset over Panorama Point

FROM INTERSTATE 70 in central Utah, take UT 24 south to Hanksville. Where UT 24 turns west, follow it to the Capitol Reef National Park entrance. The highway crosses the park and exits on the west near Torrey. Near the park entrance on the west side, there are motels, restaurants, gas stations, and other facilities, including horse and mountain-bike rentals.

The "frontcountry" of Capitol Reef National Park lies mostly along the access roads, with the backcountry being accessible only by hiking and, in some cases, by horseback. One "trail" from the visitor center in the park

LOCATION: South-Central Utah

SIZE: Capitol Reef NP: 241,671 acres (181,230 acres recommended as wilderness) Fremont Gorge WSA: 2,540 acres

ELEVATION RANGE: 3,900 to 7,600 feet

ECOREGIONS: Colorado Plateau

MILES OF TRAIL: 33.4, plus about 75 miles of principal routes (not maintained) along canyon floors

ADMINISTRATION:
NPS, Capitol Reef National Park;
BLM, Escalante Resource Area

MAPS: Trails Illustrated: Maps #213 and #707.
USGS 1:100,000: Loa.
USGS 1:24,000: Solomons Temple, Cathedral Mountain, Fruita NW, Twin Rocks, Fruita, Golden Throne, Bear Canyon, Sandy Creek Benches, Bitter Creek Divide, Wagon Box Mesa, The Post, Deer Point, Stevens Canyon North.

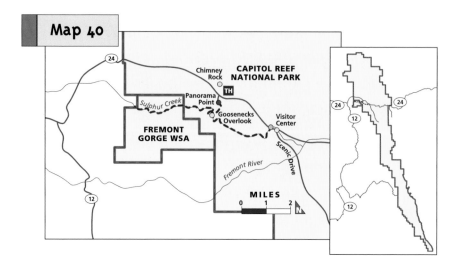

connects to a route in Fremont Gorge WSA. The trail is termed a route because it uses a canyon floor; therefore, flash floods periodically wash it out and alter it. See the day hike described in this chapter.

The small area of Fremont Gorge would not qualify as proposed wilderness without the adjacent proposed wilderness in Capitol Reef. Fremont Gorge WSA includes an extension of Sulphur Creek Canyon as it exits the park and portions of a tributary, Calf Canyon. Both canyons are about 200 feet deep at their deepest points within the WSA, as opposed to more than 600 feet deep inside park boundaries. Fremont Gorge WSA is about 3 miles east of the town of Torrey, near the intersection of UT 24 and UT 12.

Capitol Reef is hot desert for most of the year. Even sagebrush and roundleaf buffaloberry have a hard time finding nourishment. But for the human eye, the 165 million years of sedimentary "soft" rocks provide a feast that is unending. Wingate Sandstone, Navajo Sandstone, Carmel Formation, Dakota Sandstone, Chinle Formation—each has a distinctive character and color. Spring and summer thunderstorms sweep over Capitol Reef, dumping flash-flood waters into narrow canyons and leaving behind pools of captured water in hundreds of sandstone pockets that give this part of the plateau its name of Waterpocket Fold. The "fold" is a bulge in the earth that accounts for a difference in elevation of more than 2,500 feet from the low eastern side near Hanksville to the higher western rim near Torrey.

Even a short hike will be enough to carve this place into your memory. Several hiking trails are accessible from UT 24. Only 7 inches of rain fall here each year, so take plenty of water. Check at the ranger station for flash-flood warnings. The desert environment is unpleasantly hot in July and August. It's possible to visit in March and November if you want to miss the crowds and don't mind cold nights. For hiking, April, May, and October are best. More intrepid travelers will find that a dusting of snow in January and February accents the red rocks and leaves the air as clear as a flawless crystal.

There's only one developed campground in Capitol Reef National Park, Fruita Campground near the visitor center. A primitive camping area near the northern border of the park, Cathedral Camp, provides no amenities beyond a flat spot to set up your tent. Many of the best camping opportunities and services for visitors are outside the park boundaries. Visitors with 4WD vehicles can find more primitive camping sites in the adjacent Fishlake National Forest.

For an unusual and less-used approach to the Burr Trail at the southern end of the park, see the description of Notom Rd. in Chapter 24, in the Mount Ellen–Blue Hills expedition. From the intersection with Notom Rd., Burr Trail switchbacks up a precipitous 1,500 feet in 1 mile to offer one fine view after another. Picnic areas at pullouts near the top of the switchback section are also good overlooks.

Volcanic boulders below the sandstone cliffs of Capitol Reef National Park and Fremont Gorge WSA

SHUTTLE DAY HIKE: SULPHUR CREEK
One-Way Length: 6.2 miles (about 9.2 if you explore Fremont Gorge WSA)
Low and High Elevations: About 5,480 and 6,051 feet
Difficulty: Moderate

Despite the everpresent muddy streams and pools in Sulphur Creek, there is no potable water. This is a good hike for a relatively warm day, as it requires some wading and the narrow canyon provides intermittent shade.

Park a shuttle vehicle in the visitor center parking lot, or plan to walk 3 highway miles back to your starting point. Begin at the Chimney Rock Trailhead on UT 24, northwest of the visitor center. Cross to the south side of UT 24 and enter a shallow wash that leads down to the Sulphur Creek drainage. This route, although not an officially marked trail, appears on maps issued by Capitol Reef National Park.

As you proceed down the wash, you'll see ledges of Moenkopi Sandstone, some with ripple marks created by wind or water millions of years ago. You have to bypass dry waterfalls over erosion-resistant limestone by scrambling over rocks to one side or the other. At mile 1.7 you reach Sulphur Creek.

At this point you have the option of hiking up-canyon, a right-hand turn, to explore part of Fremont Gorge WSA. If you decide to make this side trip, you'll come to the park boundary 1 mile from the confluence of the wash and Sulphur Creek. Hike an additional 0.5 mile or so to get a sense of this proposed wilderness area. Return to the wash's confluence with Sulphur Creek to continue the hike.

After a brief exploration into the wilderness study area, hike down-canyon to enter The Goosenecks. The Goosenecks you hike into are twisting narrows visible from Goosenecks Overlook, about 600 feet above.

The canyon holds both Sulphur Creek and hikers in a narrowing grasp, with the narrowest section beginning about 3 miles from the highway. The down-cutting creek waters have exposed White Rim Sandstone, the park's oldest rocks. Where there is no other place to walk, hikers have to wade in the creek. Wading shoes or very supportive wading sandals are recommended. The highest pouroff encountered is about 8 feet. You can bypass it on the south side via a short climb down a rocky chute. A length of rope about 10 feet long might be helpful to lower your pack. It's easier to down-climb past dry or wet waterfalls without a pack. A moderate amount of upper body strength and flexibility is required. Tall, strong hikers can help others past the trickiest spots. Down-canyon from the 8-foot waterfall, a 5-foot pouroff will have you climbing again. At this waterfall, passage on either side is difficult, with a short Class IV climb on the south side.

At about mile 4.6 you exit the narrows. Where the canyon widens, benches above the flash-flood plain support piñon-juniper woodlands. If you wish to extend your trip to an overnight backpack, these benches are suitable camping spots.

The hike ends at the Sulphur Creek bridge on UT 24, close to the visitor center.

Zion NP and Red Butte, Spring Creek Canyon, The Watchman, Taylor Creek Canyon, Goose Creek Canyon, Beartrap Canyon, La Verkin Creek Canyon, Deep Creek, North Fork Virgin River, and Orderville Canyon WSAs

41

La Verkin Creek Canyon in the Kolob Canyons section of Zion National Park

IN ZION NATIONAL PARK, 91% of the land has been recommended for wilderness designation. In addition, there are 10 small parcels of adjacent BLM land that are wilderness study areas. These parcels would not normally qualify for wilderness designation because each is less than 5,000 acres in size. Their proximity to recommended wilderness within park boundaries justifies their inclusion in wilderness management plans. Most of these WSAs are access points or continuations of Zion National Park

LOCATION: Southwest Utah

SIZE: Zion NP: 147,000 acres (120,620 acres recommended as wilderness)
Red Butte WSA: 804 acres
Spring Creek Canyon WSA: 4,433 acres
The Watchman WSA: 600 acres
Taylor Creek Canyon WSA: 35 acres
Goose Creek Canyon WSA: 89 acres
Beartrap Canyon WSA: 40 acres
La Verkin Creek Canyon WSA: 567 acres
Deep Creek WSA: 3,320 acres
North Fork Virgin River WSA: 1,040 acres
Orderville Canyon WSA: 1,750 acres

ELEVATION RANGE: 4,270 to 9,000 feet

ECOREGION: Colorado Plateau

MILES OF TRAIL: About 85

ADMINISTRATION: NPS, Zion National Park; BLM, Dixie Resource Area

MAPS: Trails Illustrated: Map #214.
USGS 1:100,000: St. George, Kanab.
USGS 1:24,000: Kolob Arch, Kolob Reservoir, Smith Mesa, The Guardian Angels,
Temple of Sinawava, Springdale West, Springdale East, The Barracks,
Clear Creek Mountain. See map, p. 11.

hiking routes. Two significantly larger BLM wilderness study areas are adjacent to the southeastern and southern Zion borders: Parunuweap Canyon and Canaan Mountain. These WSAs are described in Chapter 15.

The main highway entrances to Zion National Park are manned by uniformed rangers wearing hats reminiscent of Saturday morning cartoons. These stylish rangers dispense information and collect fees. Pay the fees and you can drive on paved roads through mountain-long tunnels, hike on paved trails cunningly disguised to meld with the colors of the landscape, be advised by illustrated signs to avail yourself of the toilet facilities before hiking, and join tour buses at trailheads that resemble mall parking lots. With some determined hiking and backpacking, you can leave most of the crowds behind.

To stroll through the frontcountry of Zion and to access the visitor center, take UT 9 from Interstate 15; from the east take US 89 to Mount Carmel Junction north of Kanab, then continue on UT 9. Both Kanab and St. George are about 40 miles from the park. Frontcountry visits are most enjoyable in the off-season, late November and early March. The area around the visitor center is surrounded by bring-you-to-your-knees scenery, but it's nice to see it without a mob scene. During peak season, 3,000 cars per day jockey for 400 parking spots on Zion Canyon Rd. In May 2000, park managers began a mandatory bus system that moves visitors and hikers. The propane-fueled buses cease to be mandatory in the off-season and are not mandatory for lesser-used areas such as Kolob Canyons.

To camp in the park or to enjoy backcountry hikes, more fees must be paid and more forms filled out. Reservations are recommended for the more popular hiking routes, though it is sometimes possible to get a permit on a walk-in basis. Permits are required for day hikes as well as extended trips in the famous Zion Narrows. See Appendix B for contact information.

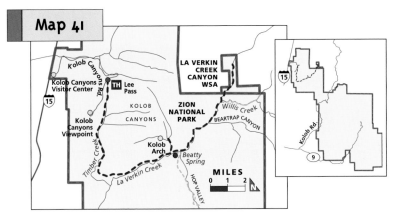

With the Virgin River carving a chasm 2,000 feet deep through the plateau, and many other canyons more than 1,000 feet deep, all the human activity is dwarfed by the grandeur of the setting. There are many deep, narrow canyons in Utah, but there are none that match Zion for beauty.

> *The surfaces of the world are aesthetically uneven. You come around a bend in the road, and the world suddenly falls open. When we come upon beautiful things…they act like small tears in the surface of the world that pull us through to some vaster space.*
>
> —Elaine Scarry, *On Beauty and Being Just*

As with many of Utah's remote wilderness locations, the first white explorers here were Mormons. From their cosmology, they drew the name "Kolob," meaning "the great one…nearest the throne of god." The Kolob Canyons section of Zion National Park has fewer visitors, fewer amenities, and greater opportunities to explore freely, to backpack, to enjoy the silence.

BACKPACK: KOLOB ARCH AND LA VERKIN CREEK
One-Way Length: About 12 miles
Low and High Elevations: 5,030 and 6,500 feet
Difficulty: Moderate to Strenuous

The highlights of this hike are Kolob Arch and an opportunity to really leave the crowds behind by continuing your hike into the upper reaches of La Verkin Creek, where the BLM has added proposed wilderness to that of Zion. Most hikers in this part of Zion explore a section of La Verkin Creek as part of their route to Willis Creek. At the Willis Creek confluence, this hike takes the canyon less traveled and continues north up La Verkin Creek. Strong hikers can choose a shortened day-hike version by trekking 7 miles to Kolob Arch and then returning to Lee Pass Trailhead. Be wary of hiking the Timber Creek section of the return trip in late afternoon. If the weather is hot, it will be scorching along Timber Creek. For the entire expedition, plan at least one overnight. Two nights and three days will give you time to explore along the way.

As with any hike that includes narrow canyons, flash flooding is a danger. As you hike, note places where you can climb above the flash-flood plain. Be aware of changes that precede a flood, including sudden changes in water clarity, rising water levels and stronger currents, distant sounds of thunder, and a roar of water coming from up-canyon. You can't outrun a flash flood. Climb above it and wait for it to subside (usually in 24 hours or less). If you can't climb above the water, shelter on the downstream side of a jutting rock so that the rush of water and debris will not knock you off your feet. The first half of the hike is easy, along a well-defined trail. After you enter the narrower sections of La Verkin, the going gets rougher and you must pay more attention to the weather.

Temperatures on Kolob Plateau can reach 105 degrees Fahrenheit in July and August. Creek waters can be too high to safely ford and wade in the spring, so an ideal hiking time is September through October. No matter what season you choose, you will be wading frequently, so bring appropriate footwear. Scrambling over rocks and jumping boulders to cross creeks are par for the course. Pets and campfires are not permitted. The Kolob Arch area is so heavily used that camping permits are limited for that section. Timber and La Verkin Creeks are perennial water sources, but filter or treat all water before drinking. You'll find insect repellent or protective netting necessary unless you are hiking so late in the autumn that cold nights have done the little biters in.

In the seldom-visited fingers of upper La Verkin Creek, the canyon walls are 700 to 900 feet high. This is not one of those places where all the prime scenery is in the national park and when you leave, you enter Class B scenery on BLM land. In this case, the goods are delivered all the way to the end.

About 18 miles south of Cedar City, take exit 40 off I-15, signed as "Kolob Canyons." Stop at the visitor center to inquire about trail conditions and to purchase a backcountry permit. Drive about 4 miles to Lee Pass, the trailhead for this hike. Hike south along Timber Creek. If you have gotten a late start, you can find camping spots along Timber Creek. You have to descend at least 2 miles from the trailhead before camping is allowed.

The trail ascends a ridge above Timber Creek at about mile 3, turning from its southerly direction to east-northeast. The trail gradually descends again into the La Verkin Creek drainage. Continue upstream. From the point where an old corral sits near the creek, it is about 2 miles to the junction with Kolob Arch Trail. Turn left (north) at the junction and hike 0.5 mile to view the 292-foot arch of Navajo Sandstone, said to be the world's largest freestanding arch.

Return to La Verkin Creek and continue up-canyon. The number of hikers on the trail will thin out after you pass Kolob Arch. You'll pass a junction with Hop Valley Trail (another trip for another time); stay on the Willis Creek Trail. As the canyon narrows, the cliff walls become more dramatic and the trail is more of a sketchy route than an actual trail. Frequent boulder-hopping and wading begins in the narrowed canyon. There are still campsites in wider sections.

A tributary canyon opens on your left (north) about 1 mile above the Hop Valley junction; stay right, in the main La Verkin drainage. From this tributary, it's about 0.5 mile to a major canyon junction, with Beartrap Canyon leading east (right fork) and La Verkin continuing north (left fork). If you have time, you can make a 1-mile side trip into Beartrap Canyon. A waterfall blocks further exploration for all but technical rock climbers. (The head of Beartrap Canyon is another BLM wilderness study area that begins where the park boundary ends.)

Back in La Verkin Creek Canyon, continue upstream through thick stands of foliage. Hanging gardens decorate the canyon walls. There's no room to camp until you reach the confluence with Willis Creek. Intermittent Willis Creek is not a reliable water source.

On this excursion we bypass Willis Creek and continue north along La Verkin Creek, exiting Zion National Park and entering the WSA. Solitude is almost certain, as few backpackers enter the branching fingers of upper La Verkin. The canyon remains narrow for about 1 mile. Make a short excursion into the WSA or a longer one, as time allows. Depending on the time of day, you might want to camp at the confluence of Willis Creek and La Verkin, saving your exploration of the WSA for a day hike from your base camp.

Return to Lee Pass Trailhead the way you came.

Shallow sheets of water cascade over a sandstone terrace in Taylor Creek Canyon, in the Kolob Canyons section of Zion National Park.

42 Cedar Breaks NM, Dinosaur NM and Daniels Canyon WSA, and Natural Bridges NM

Owachomo Bridge in Natural Bridges National Monument

THREE OF UTAH'S national monuments are large enough to include backcountry areas that have been recommended for wilderness designation: Cedar Breaks, Dinosaur, and Natural Bridges. In 1976, Cedar Breaks National Monument administrators recommended 4,840 acres (78.5%) as wilderness. The adjacent designated wilderness area, Ashdown Gorge (see Chapter 12), played a part in this decision. Normally, a 5,000-acre minimum is required for wilderness recommendation, but this requirement can be waived if adjacent land is wilderness or qualifies for wilderness designation.

With snow accumulations up to 10 feet deep, Cedar Breaks closes in winter to all but snowmobilers. The access roads open in May, and the visitor center normally opens on Memorial Day. Cedar Breaks National Monument is 2,000 feet higher than Bryce Canyon National Park, so the long winter and deep snows come as no surprise.

CEDAR BREAKS NATIONAL MONUMENT
LOCATION: Southwest Utah
SIZE: 6,154 acres (4,840 acres recommended as wilderness)
ELEVATION RANGE: 7,500 to 10,606 feet
ECOREGION: Colorado Plateau
MILES OF TRAIL: About 11
ADMINISTRATION: NPS, Cedar Breaks National Monument
MAPS: Trails Illustrated: Map #702. USGS 1:24,000: Flanigan Arch, Brian Head, Navajo Lake, Webster Flat. *See maps, pp. 11 and 123.*

Bristlecone pines 1,600 to 2,500 years old dot the western rim of the Markagunt Plateau. *Markagunt* means "highland of trees" in the language of Paiute Indians. There are no cedar trees in Cedar Breaks. Apparently, visitors in the 1930s mistook bristlecone pines for cedars.

A single paved road, with pullouts near the scenic points, curves around the eastern rim of the Breaks. Short trails lead from the highway to more scenic views and ponds. There's a 4-mile round-trip trail to Spectra Point, as well as a 2-mile loop to Alpine Pond. No developed trails lead down from the rim because the terrain is too steep and the formations are too fragile. Rattlesnake Trail in adjacent Ashdown Gorge Wilderness takes a circuitous route to the bottom of the Breaks.

From the top of the precipice, visitors can see most of the semicircular basins that make up the Cedar Breaks amphitheater. "Claron Formation" is the latest in geological name changing. The soft rock of the Cedar Breaks formations used to be called "Wasatch Limestone," a name you'll still see in many guide- and reference books. The top of the Breaks is also the top, and the youngest member, of the Grand Staircase (see Geology and Ecosystems in the Along the Trail section at the front of this book). From some of the scenic points, visitors can see the next step down in the staircase, the northern end of Zion National Park.

Take exit 59 off I-15 in Cedar City to intersect UT 14 through Cedar Canyon. Drive east on UT 14 to UT 148, which leads north to Cedar Breaks and also to Ashdown Gorge Wilderness.

DINOSAUR NATIONAL MONUMENT AND DANIELS CANYON WILDERNESS STUDY AREA

LOCATION: Northeast Utah
SIZE: Dinosaur NM: 225,156 acres; Daniels Canyon WSA: 2,496 acres
ELEVATION RANGE: 4,700 to 9,006 feet
ECOREGION: Great Basin Desert
MILES OF TRAIL: 16.25 in Dinosaur NM
ADMINISTRATION: NPS, Dinosaur National Monument; BLM, Book Cliffs Resource Area
MAPS: Trails Illustrated: Map #220.
USGS 1:24,000: Dinosaur Quarry—UT, Split Mountain—UT, Canyon of Lodore North—CO, Canyon of Lodore South—CO, Greystone—CO, Haystack Rock—CO, Hells Canyon—CO, Indian Water Canyon—CO, Jack Springs—CO, Jones Hole—UT/CO, Limestone Hill—CO, Stuntz Reservoir—UT/CO, Tanks Peak—CO, Zenobia Peak—CO. *See map, p. 10.*

IN DINOSAUR NATIONAL MONUMENT, administrators found 165,341 acres (mostly in Colorado) that met standards for wilderness designation in 1974. Later surveys increased potential wilderness acres to 180,899, but 210,727 acres and 186,114 acres are listed in other sources. The Park Service is working on a more formal wilderness management plan for Dinosaur National Monument, but at the time this book went to press, the plan was not complete.

The monument straddles a section of the Rocky Mountain Uplift that is actually a spur of the Uinta Mountains on the Utah-Colorado border. It was established in 1915 and contains the largest quarry of Jurassic dinosaur bones uncovered so far. Paleontologist Earl Douglass is credited with the discovery in 1909.

Most of the monument is extremely arid, a high desert, with riparian corridors along the Green and Yampa Rivers. Most visitors either frequent the museum or whoop it up on the whitewater rapids. Very few people hike the backcountry, and this is a good thing for those seeking solitude. The best month to hike is October, when access roads are likely to be dry, desert nights are cool, and hiking temperatures are bearable. Local rangers describe October as stunning, but I wonder if that admiration stems in part from a comparison with the Hades of July and August. Hordes of biting gnats make an appearance in June and don't abate until late September. If the roads are dry, a hike in early spring is also a treat: It's the only time the desert plants are in bloom.

For a description of numerous shorter day hikes, and of the river run from Gates of Lodore to Echo Park, see *The Complete Guide to Colorado's Wilderness Areas* from Westcliffe Publishers.

Daniels Canyon Wilderness Study Area is 2,496 acres of BLM-administered land on the southeast corner of Dinosaur National Monument (about 22 miles east of Vernal). The area is too small to stand by itself as wilderness, but might be considered if wilderness is designated in contiguous lands of the monument.

Daniels Canyon and Cub Creek on the edge of the Yampa Plateau both offer hiking opportunities. Access is from Cub Creek Rd., via a 12-mile drive east from the

Quarry Visitor Center. Paved for 10 miles and dusty dirt for 2 miles, the road is 2WD all the way in good weather. A visible trail begins at the Josie Morris Ranch, where the road ends. An easy hike of 1.1 miles brings you to Daniels Canyon. Views along the way include Split Mountain Gorge, the Green River, and red Moenkopi rock formations contrasting with white Weber Sandstone. Carry your own water, as the intermittent stream in Daniels Canyon disappears completely in dry seasons. A small stream issues from a spring in the lower canyon if you make it that far. Horseback excursions that include a ride to the top of Blue Mountain, east of the WSA, are another option. Sights and sounds from the nearby highways and the towns of Vernal and Jensen limit the possibilities for solitude and silence.

Fremont Culture archaeological sites from about A.D. 500 to 1250 are numerous, but most of these are just outside the WSA, downstream on Cub Creek. There are some cliff dwellings and storage pit ruins in Daniels Canyon.

NATURAL BRIDGES NATIONAL MONUMENT
LOCATION: South-Central Utah
SIZE: 7,435 acres (5,340 acres recommended as wilderness)
ELEVATION RANGE: 5,500 to 6,500 feet
ECOREGION: Colorado Plateau
MILES OF TRAIL: 12.8
ADMINISTRATION: Natural Bridges NM
MAPS: Trails Illustrated: Map #703.
NFS: Manti–La Sal.
USGS 1:24,000: The Cheesebox, Woodenshoe Butte, Moss Back Butte, Kane Gulch. See map, p. 11.

ACCESSIBLE VIA UT 275 from UT 95, Natural Bridges National Monument has been called "the undiscovered part of Utah." It's true that the nearest services are 43 miles away, but in recent years, the number of visitors has greatly increased. To accommodate visitors early and late in the season, the road to the visitor center is open from March to October. The paved access is plowed free of snow. Seventy-two percent of the monument has been identified as having wilderness characteristics and values—pretty much everything that is not paved, and not within sight of the road. Three trails lead to the natural bridges for which the monument is named. Without those trails, it would be difficult to get into or out of the steep canyons. Stairs, primitive ladders, and handholds have been added to the established routes. In addition to the trails to the bridges, the old entrance road into the monument has been converted into a foot trail across the mesa top, the Zeke Johnson Trail.

The bridges, named Owachomo, Sipapu, and Kachina, are monsters in the natural bridge category of sandstone monoliths. They span from 180 to 268 feet and range in height from 106 to 220 feet. Unlike an arch, a bridge forms when a meander, or curve, of a running stream tightens and the force of the water wears away the base of the remaining thin sandstone wall. The river breaks through the barrier and flows under the new bridge, slowly enlarging the hole in the rock.

The BLM administers lands surrounding the monument but has not recommended them for wilderness designation. However, the Utah Wilderness Coalition has included most of the BLM lands around Natural Bridges in its American Redrock Wilderness proposal.

For the time being, Natural Bridges National Monument shows signs of minor human impacts and does provide opportunities for solitude and for primitive recreation. Apart from the bridges, important archaeological sites within the monument are well worth visiting, including Basketmaker and Pueblo Anasazi ruins 700 to 2,500 years old. The dry climate has preserved the ruins, and overhanging canyon walls add to the protection of some cliff dwellings. As irreplaceable cultural resources, the archaeological remains should be viewed but not touched in any way. Do not enter the structures.

The monument offers a primitive campground but no other services. You can obtain drinking water at the visitor center. Flash floods, dehydration, and falling from rocks or narrow trails are the main hazards. The bridges are off-limits to climbing.

The "Horsecollar" Anasazi ruin in Natural Bridges National Monument

Glen Canyon National Recreation Area

Lake Powell holds back the Colorado River.

RISING FROM 3,116 FEET at Lees Ferry to 7,451 feet at Navajo Point on the Kaiparowits Plateau, Glen Canyon National Recreation Area offers no maintained trails. Lake Powell covers about 163,000 of its acres. After several years of drought, in 2003 and 2004 the level of Lake Powell dropped by 100 feet, opening up some canyons for exploration that had not been seen since 1980. Lake Powell, a man-made, 186-mile-long centipede of water, fills one main canyon and thousands of side canyons above its dam.

LOCATION: South-Central and Southeast Utah

SIZE: 1,250,000 acres
(668,670 acres recommended as wilderness)

ELEVATION RANGE: 3,116 to 7,451 feet

ECOREGIONS: Great Basin Desert and Colorado Plateau

MILES OF TRAIL: None

ADMINISTRATION: NPS, Glen Canyon NRA

MAPS: Trails Illustrated: Maps #213 and #710. USGS 1:100,000: Bluff, Navajo Mountain, Hite Crossing, Escalante. *See map, p. 11.*

Despite all the emphasis on boating in Lake Powell, a significant portion of the recreation area still has wilderness characteristics and values. In 1980, backcountry areas totaling 668,670 acres were recommended for wilderness designation.

The most popular "wilderness" hiking opportunities are those adjacent to Grand Staircase–Escalante National Monument (GSENM). Where Glen Canyon NRA meets GSENM along the Escalante River, several canyon hikes are world-famous for their scenic grandeur. (See Chapter 22.) Hikers begin their trek in the Grand Staircase and end up in Glen Canyon, with the distances traveled requiring at least an overnight backpack. Glen Canyon NRA administrators have identified 253,105 acres as suitable for wilderness along portions of the Escalante River that they manage.

Coyote Gulch is the most famous of the Escalante Canyons. Nearby canyons are similar in every way: hanging gardens around seeps, strikingly colored and steep canyon walls, lots of wading required in narrow sections, and reflected sunlight high-lighting water-carved walls. Consider taking the canyon less traveled.

Another popular approach to canyon hiking is by boat. Lake access to 90 named canyons exists within the NRA. In most cases, boaters travel partway up-canyon, moor the boat, and then day hike or backpack from there. At the time this book went to press, no permits were required for lake-access hiking.

Review the safety issues and Leave No Trace guidelines in the Along the Trail section at the front of this book as part of your planning for canyon hikes. In early spring and late fall, the days are warm and pleasant for hiking. All the areas around

The Goosenecks of the San Juan River in the Glen Canyon National Recreation Area

Lake Powell are searingly hot in summer, the surrounding desert is throat-gaspingly dry, and the lake sits like a piece of carved turquoise at the center of all that thirst. Summer is a good time to go swimming or wading: The intense heat makes wading in the cold water of the slot canyons more appealing. But summer is also the prime flash-flood season. Check the weather forecast before you venture out.

Rainbow Bridge National Monument is a 160-acre special-use area on the border of Glen Canyon NRA. There is no proposed wilderness within the monument. The spectacular natural bridge is popular with photographers, especially in winter, when 10,388-foot Navajo Mountain forms a snowy backdrop to the warm colors of the bridge. Most visitors access the bridge by boat from Lake Powell, with a 0.75- to 0.25-mile hike, depending on the lake's water level. There are also two hiking routes across the Navajo Indian Reservation. The monument is limited to day use only, so no overnight camping is allowed. Backpackers can hike across the reservation, camp outside the monument borders, and include Navajo Mountain in their trek. A one- or two-night backpack is the norm. Check with the Navajo Nation in Window Rock, Ariz., regarding permits and fees for crossing reservation lands (see Appendix B).

Muley Point, a spectacular overlook near the San Juan River's confluence with the Colorado, is described in Chapter 30, where the NRA is adjacent to the Valley of the Gods and Road Canyon WSA.

Glen Canyon NRA shares borders with many proposed wilderness areas managed by the Bureau of Land Management, and also with other National Park Service lands. See the following chapters for suggested hikes and access roads that include Glen Canyon NRA:

Paria Canyon–Vermilion Cliffs Wilderness: Chapter 17
North Escalante Canyons/The Gulch ISA: Chapter 21
Escalante Canyon Tract 1 ISA: Chapter 21
Scorpion WSA: Chapter 22
Fiftymile Mountain WSA: Chapter 23
French Spring–Happy Canyon WSA: Chapter 26
Horseshoe Canyon South WSA: Chapter 26
Little Rockies WSA: Chapter 27
Fiddler Butte WSA: Chapter 27
Dark Canyon ISA Complex: Chapter 28
Mancos Mesa WSA: Chapter 29
Road Canyon WSA: Chapter 30
Canyonlands National Park: Chapter 39
Capitol Reef National Park: Chapter 40

Appendix A Wilderness Areas

Designated Wilderness Areas

Name	Acreage	Established	Administration	Chapter
Ashdown Gorge	7,043	1984	FS	12
Beaver Dam Mountains	2,600 Utah*	1984	BLM	14
Black Ridge Canyons	5,180 Utah**	2000	BLM	36
Box–Death Hollow	25,751	1984	FS	18
Dark Canyon	47,116	1984	FS	28
Deseret Peak	25,212	1984	FS	9
High Uintas	456,705	1984	FS	3
Lone Peak	30,088	1978	FS	6
Mount Naomi	44,523	1984	FS	1
Mount Nebo	28,000	1984	FS	8
Mount Olympus	15,300	1984	FS	4
Mount Timpanogos	10,750	1984	FS	7
Paria Canyon–Vermilion Cliffs	20,000 Utah*	1984	BLM	17
Pine Valley Mountain	50,000	1984	FS	13
Twin Peaks	11,334	1984	FS	5
Wellsville Mountains	23,850	1984	FS	2

*Portions of these wilderness areas are in Arizona. Only the acreage in Utah is shown here.
**Part of this wilderness area is in Colorado. Only the acreage in Utah is shown here.

BLM Wilderness Study Areas (WSAs)

Acreage shown does not reflect citizen proposals. For example, Mount Pennell WSA is 74,300 acres according to the BLM, while the Utah Wilderness Coalition has proposed that 143,125 acres be designated as wilderness. "Administration" in this table lists the BLM resource office responsible.

Name	Acreage	Administration	Chapter
Beartrap Canyon WSA	40	Cedar City	41
Behind the Rocks WSA	12,635	Moab/Grand	32
Bridger Jack Mesa WSA	5,290	San Juan	31
Bull Mountain WSA	13,620	Henry Mountain	24
Burning Hills WSA	61,550	Escalante	23
Butler Wash WSA	24,190	San Juan	31
Canaan Mountain WSA	47,170	Kanab	15
Carcass Canyon WSA	47,351	Escalante	23
Cedar Mountains WSA	50,500	Pony Express	9
Cheesebox Canyon WSA	15,410	San Juan	28
Coal Canyon WSA	61,430	Price River	35
Conger Mountain WSA	20,400	House Range	11
Cottonwood Canyon WSA	11,330	Dixie	14
Cougar Canyon WSA	10,568 Utah*	Dixie	14
Crack Canyon WSA	25,335	San Rafael	33

BLM Wilderness Study Areas (continued)

Name	Acreage	Administration	Chapter
Daniels Canyon WSA	2,496	Vernal	42
Dark Canyon ISA Complex	68,030	San Juan	28
Death Ridge WSA	63,667	Escalante	23
Deep Creek Mountains WSA	68,910	Pony Express	10
Deep Creek WSA	3,320	Cedar City	41
Desolation Canyon WSA	290,845	Price River	35
Devils Canyon WSA	9,610	San Rafael	33
Devils Garden ISA	638	Escalante	22
Dirty Devil WSA	61,000	Henry Mountain	25
Escalante Canyon Tract 1 ISA	360	Escalante	21
Escalante Canyon Tract 5 ISA	760	Escalante	22
Fiddler Butte WSA	73,100	Henry Mountain	27
Fiftymile Mountain WSA	148,802	Escalante	23
Fish Creek Canyon WSA	46,440	San Juan	30
Fish Springs WSA	52,500	Pony Express	10
Floy Canyon WSA	72,605	Price River	35
Flume Canyon WSA	50,800	Price River	35
Fremont Gorge WSA	2,540	Escalante	40
French Spring–Happy Canyon WSA	25,000	Henry Mountain	26
Goose Creek Canyon WSA	89	Cedar City	41
Grand Gulch ISA Complex	105,520	San Juan	30
Horseshoe Canyon North WSA	20,500	San Rafael	26
Horseshoe Canyon South WSA	38,800	Henry Mountain	26
Howell Peak WSA	24,800	House Range	11
Indian Creek WSA	6,870	San Juan	31
Jack Canyon WSA	7,500	Price River	35
King Top WSA	84,770	Warm Springs	11
La Verkin Creek Canyon WSA	567	Cedar City	41
Little Rockies WSA	38,700	Henry Mountain	27
Mancos Mesa WSA	51,440	San Juan	29
Mexican Mountain WSA	59,600	San Rafael	34
Mill Creek Canyon WSA	9,780	Moab/Grand	32
Moquith Mountain WSA	14,830	Kanab	16
Mount Ellen–Blue Hills WSA	81,726	Henry Mountain	24
Mount Hillers WSA	20,000	Henry Mountain	24
Mount Pennell WSA	74,300	Henry Mountain	24
Mud Spring Canyon WSA	38,075	Escalante	20
Muddy Creek WSA	31,400	San Rafael	33
Mule Canyon WSA	5,990	San Juan	30
Negro Bill Canyon WSA	7,620	Moab/Grand	32
North Escalante Canyons/ The Gulch ISA	120,204	Escalante	21
North Fork Virgin River WSA	1,040	Cedar City	41
North Stansbury Mountains WSA	10,480	Pony Express	9

Appendix A

BLM Wilderness Study Areas (continued)

Name	Acreage	Administration	Chapter
Notch Peak WSA	51,130	House Range	11
Orderville Canyon WSA	1,750	Cedar City	41
Paria-Hackberry WSA	136,222	Kanab	19
Parunuweap Canyon WSA	30,800	Kanab	15
Phipps–Death Hollow ISA	42,731	Escalante	18
Red Butte WSA	804	Cedar City	41
Red Mountain WSA	18,290	Dixie	14
Road Canyon WSA	52,240	San Juan	30
Rockwell WSA	9,150	Pony Express	10
San Rafael Reef WSA	59,170	San Rafael	33
Scorpion WSA	35,884	Escalante	22
Sids Mountain/Sids Cabin WSA	80,970	San Rafael	34
South Needles WSA	160	San Juan	39
Spring Creek Canyon WSA	4,433	Cedar City	41
Spruce Canyon WSA	20,350	Price River	35
Steep Creek WSA	21,896	Escalante	21
Swasey Mountain WSA	49,500	House Range	11
Taylor Creek Canyon WSA	35	Cedar City	41
The Blues WSA	19,030	Escalante	20
The Cockscomb WSA	10,827	Kanab	19
The Watchman WSA	600	Cedar City	41
Turtle Canyon WSA	33,690	Price River	35
Wah Wah Mountains WSA	42,140	Warm Springs	11
Wahweap WSA	134,400	Kanab	23
Westwater Canyon WSA	31,160	Grand	36
Winter Ridge WSA	42,462	Price River	35

*Part of this wilderness study area is in Nevada. Only the acreage in Utah is shown here.

Other Recommended Wilderness Areas

The following areas are administered by the National Park Service.

Name	Acreage	Proposed	Chapter
Arches National Park	62,947	1976	37
Bryce Canyon National Park	20,810	1976	38
Canyonlands National Park	287,133	1974	39
Capitol Reef National Park	181,230	1974	40
Cedar Breaks National Monument	4,840	1976	42
Dinosaur National Monument	165,341*	1974	42
Glen Canyon National Recreation Area	668,670	1980	43
Natural Bridges National Monument	5,340	1976	42
Zion National Park	120,620	1974	41

*Most of the proposed wilderness is in Colorado.

Appendix B | Land Administrators, Outfitters, and Guides

Bureau of Land Management (BLM)

UTAH STATE OFFICE
324 S. State, Ste. 400
Salt Lake City, UT 84111-2303
(801) 539-4001

CEDAR CITY DISTRICT (includes Beaver River Resource Area)

176 E. D.L. Sargent Dr.
Cedar City, UT 84720
(435) 586-2401
To report fires: (435) 865-4600

Dixie Resource Area (Paria Wilderness Permits)
345 Riverside Dr.
St. George, UT 84770
(435) 673-4654 • Fax: (435) 688-3258
http://paria.az.blm.gov

Grand Staircase–Escalante Nat'l. Monument
Escalante Interagency Office
Bureau of Land Management
755 W. Main
P.O. Box 225
Escalante, UT 84726
(435) 826-5400
escalant@ut.blm.gov
www.ut.blm.gov/monument

Grand Staircase–Escalante Nat'l. Monument
Big Water Visitor Center
100 Upper Revolution Way
Big Water, UT 84741
(435) 675-3200 • Fax: (435) 675-3215

Grand Staircase–Escalante Nat'l. Monument
Cannonville Visitor Center
10 Center St.
Cannonville, UT 84718
(435) 679-8981

Kanab Grand Staircase–Escalante
National Monument Headquarters
190 E. Center
Kanab, UT 84741
(435) 644-4300

Kanab Field Office
318 North 100 East
Kanab, UT 84741
(435) 644-4600 • Fax: (435) 644-4620

GRAND JUNCTION DISTRICT
2815 H Rd.
Grand Junction, CO 81506
(970) 244-3000
www.co.blm.gov

Appendix B

Bureau of Land Management (continued)

MOAB DISTRICT

Main Office and Grand Resource Area
82 E. Dogwood
Moab, UT 84532
(435) 259-2100

Price River Resource Area
San Rafael Resource Area
Desolation Canyon River Information
125 South 600 West
Price, UT 84501
(435) 636-3622
www.blm.gov/utah/price
www.blm.gov/utah/price/riverinf.htm

San Juan Resource Area
435 N. Main
P.O. Box 7
Monticello, UT 84535
(435) 587-2141
Grand Gulch Reservations: (435) 587-1510

RICHFIELD DISTRICT (includes Sevier River Resource Area)

150 East 900 North
Richfield, UT 84701
(435) 896-1500

Henry Mountains Resource Area
406 South 100 West
P.O. Box 99
Hanksville, UT 84734
(435) 542-3461

House Range and Warm Springs Resource Areas
35 East 500 North
Fillmore, UT 84631
(435) 743-3100

SALT LAKE CITY DISTRICT

(includes Bear River and Pony Express Resource Areas)
2370 South 2300 West
Salt Lake City, UT 84119
(801) 977-4300

VERNAL DISTRICT

Diamond Mountain and Book Cliffs Resource Areas
170 South 500 East
Vernal, UT 84078
(435) 781-4400

National Park Service

National Park Service, Southeast Utah Group
2282 SW Resource Blvd.
Moab, UT 84532-3298
(435) 259-3911
Reservations: (435) 259-4351
Reservations (fax): (435) 259-4285
www.nps.gov/cany

Arches National Park
P.O. Box 907
Moab, UT 84532
(435) 259-8161

Bryce Canyon National Park
P.O. Box 170001
Bryce Canyon, UT 84717-0001
(435) 834-5322
www.nps.gov/brca
www.brycecanyonutah.com

Canyonlands National Park
2282 SW Resource Blvd.
Moab, UT 84532-3298
(435) 719-2313
Hans Flat Ranger Station: (435) 259-2652
Reservations: (435) 259-4351
Reservations (fax): (435) 719-2300

Capitol Reef National Park
HC 70 Box 15
Torrey, UT 84775-9602
(435) 425-3791
www.nps.gov/care

Cedar Breaks National Monument
2390 W. Hwy. 56, Ste. 11
Cedar City, UT 84720-4151
(435) 586-9451

Dinosaur National Monument
4545 E. Hwy. 40
Dinosaur, CO 81610-9724
(970) 374-3000
www.nps.gov/dino

Glen Canyon National Recreation Area
P.O. Box 1507
Page, AZ 86040-1507
Headquarters: (928) 608-6200
Visitor Center: (928) 608-6404

Natural Bridges National Monument
HC 60 Box 1
Lake Powell, UT 84533-0101
(435) 692-1234

Zion National Park
SR 9
Springdale, UT 84767-1099
(435) 772-3256 or (435) 772-0157

State of Utah

Utah Division of Parks and Recreation
1594 W. North Temple, Ste. 116
Salt Lake City, UT 84114-6001
(801) 538-7220
www.nr.state.utah.gov

Utah Division of Wildlife Resources
1594 W. North Temple
P.O. Box 146301
Salt Lake City, UT 84114-6301
(801) 538-4700
Fishing and Hunting: (801) 596-8660
www.wildlife.utah.gov

Appendix B

State of Utah (continued)

Castle County Travel Region
90 North 100 East, #2
Price, UT 84501
(435) 679-8981

Coral Pink Sand Dunes State Park
P.O. Box 95
Kanab, UT 84741
(435) 648-2800
www.stateparks.utah.gov/parks/www1/cora.htm

Garfield County Travel Council
P.O. Box 200
Panguitch, UT 84759
(800) 444-6689

Grand County Travel Council
P.O. Box 550
Moab, UT 84532
(800) 635-6622
www.moab-utah.com/travel/council.html

Green River Visitor Center
John Wesley Powell Museum
(closed in January)
885 E. Main
Green River, UT 84525
(435) 564-3526

Kane County Office of Tourism
78 South 100 East (Hwy. 89)
Kanab, UT 84741
(800) 733-5263
www.kaneutah.com

Moab Travel Council
Center and Main St.
Moab, UT 84532
(800) 635-6622
Multi-Agency Information Center:
(435) 259-8825
info@discovermoab.com
www.discovermoab.com

U.S. Fish & Wildlife

Ecological Services Field Office
2369 W. Orton Cir., Ste. 50
West Valley City, UT 84119-7679
(801) 975-3330
Fax: (801) 975-3331

USDA Forest Service

District Office
507 25th St.
Ogden, UT 84401
(801) 625-5112

Intermountain Region
324 25th St.
Ogden, UT 84401
(801) 625-5306
Avalanche Information:
(801) 364-1581
Travel Info and Road Conditions:
(800) 492-2400
River Flow Information:
(800) 277-7571

Information Office
2501 Wall Ave.
Ogden, UT 84403
(801) 625-5306

USDA Forest Service (continued)

ASHLEY NATIONAL FOREST (includes Vernal Ranger District)

355 N. Vernal Ave.
Vernal, UT 84078
(435) 789-1181 • Fax: (435) 781-5142
www.fs.fed.us/r4/ashley

Duchesne/Roosevelt Ranger District
Duchesne Office
85 W. Main
P.O. Box 981
Duchesne, UT 84021
(435) 738-2482 • Fax: (435) 781-5215

Duchesne/Roosevelt Ranger District
Roosevelt Office
244 W. Hwy. 40
Box 333-6
Roosevelt, UT 84066
(435) 722-5018 • Fax: (435) 781-5237

DIXIE NATIONAL FOREST

Supervisor's Office
1789 Wedgewood Ln.
Cedar City, UT 84720
(435) 865-3700
To report fires: (435) 586-4215
www.fs.fed.us/dxnf

Cedar City Ranger District
1789 Wedgewood Ln.
Cedar City, UT 84720
(435) 865-3206

Pine Valley Ranger District
196 E. Tabernacle St., Room 40
St. George, UT 84770
(435) 652-3100
Camping and Hiking Info:
(435) 688-3246

Powell Ranger District
225 E. Center
P.O. Box 80
Panguitch, UT 84759
(435) 676-9300

Teasdale Ranger District
138 E. Main
P.O. Box 90
Teasdale, UT 84773-0090
(435) 425-3702

FISHLAKE NATIONAL FOREST (includes Richfield Ranger District)

115 East 900 North
Richfield, UT 84701
(435) 896-9233

Fillmore Ranger District
390 S. Main
P.O. Box 265
Fillmore, UT 84631
(435) 743-5721

Loa Ranger District
138 S. Main St.
P.O. Box 129
Loa, UT 84747
(435) 438-2811

Appendix B

USDA Forest Service (continued)

MANTI–LA SAL NATIONAL FOREST
(includes Ferron/Price Ranger District, Price Office)

Supervisor's Office
599 W. Price River Dr.
Price, UT 84501
(435) 637-2817 • Fax: (435) 637-4940

Ferron/Price Ranger District
Ferron Office
115 W. Canyon Rd.
P.O. Box 310
Ferron, UT 84523
(435) 384-2372

Moab/Monticello Ranger District
Monticello Office
496 E. Central
P.O. Box 820
Monticello, UT 84535
(435) 587-2041 • Fax: (435) 587-2637

UINTA NATIONAL FOREST

Supervisor's Office
88 West 100 North
P.O. Box 1428
Provo, UT 84601
(801) 342-5100 • Fax: (801) 342-5144

Heber Ranger District
2460 S. Hwy. 40
P.O. Box 190
Heber City, UT 84032
(801) 342-5200 • Fax: (801) 654-5772

Pleasant Grove Ranger District
390 North 100 East
Pleasant Grove, UT 84062
(801) 342-5240 • Fax: (801) 342-5244

Spanish Fork Ranger District
44 West 400 North
Spanish Fork, UT 84660
(801) 342-5260 • Fax: (801) 342-5272

WASATCH–CACHE NATIONAL FOREST

Supervisor's Office
8236 Federal Building
125 S. State St.
Salt Lake City, UT 84138
(801) 524-3900
Public Lands Info Center: (801) 466-6411

Evanston Ranger District
1565 Hwy. 150 South, Ste. A
P.O. Box 1880
Evanston, WY 82931-1880
(307) 789-3194

Kamas Ranger District
50 E. Center St.
P.O. Box 68
Kamas, UT 84036
(435) 783-4338

Logan Ranger District
1500 E. Hwy. 89
Logan, UT 84321-4373
(435) 755-3620

USDA Forest Service (continued)

WASATCH–CACHE NATIONAL FOREST (continued)

Mountain View Ranger District
321 Hwy. 414
P.O. Box 129
Mountain View, WY 82939
(307) 782-6555

Ogden Ranger District
507 25th St., Ste. 103
Ogden, UT 84401
(801) 625-5112

Salt Lake Ranger District
6944 South 3000 East
Salt Lake City, UT 84121
(801) 733-2660

Other (including Indian Reservations)

Bryce Canyon Natural History Association
Box 170002
Bryce Canyon, UT 84717
(435) 834-4600

Canyonlands Natural History Association
3031 S. Hwy. 191
Moab, UT 84532
(435) 259-6003 • (800) 840-8978
www.cnha.org

Capitol Reef Natural History Association
HC 70 Box 15
Torrey, UT 84775
(435) 425-3791, ext. 106

National Weather Service Forecast Center
Salt Lake City
(801) 539-1311
www.wrh.noaa.gov/

Navajo Nation
Navajo Parks and Recreation
Bldg. 36A, E. Hwy. 264 at Route 12
P.O. Box 2520
Window Rock, AZ 86515
(928) 871-6647 • Fax: (928) 871-6637
info@navajonationparks.org
www.navajonationparks.org

Uintah and Ouray Agency
Ute Indian Tribe
P.O. Box 190
Ft. Duchesne, UT 84026
(435) 636-3600

Outfitters and Guides

Adventure Bound
2392 H Rd.
Grand Junction, CO 81505
(970) 245-5428 • (800) 423-4668
www.raft-colorado.com

Boulder Mountain Ranch
Box 1373
Boulder, UT 84716
(435) 335-7480 • Fax: (435) 335-7352
bmr@boulderutah.com
www.boulderutah.com/bmr

Appendix B

Outfitters and Guides (continued)

Canyonland Tours
543 N. Main
Moab, UT 84532
(435) 259-5865 • (800) 342-5938

Dvorak Kayak & Rafting Expeditions
17921 U.S. Hwy. 285
Nathrop, CO 81236
(719) 539-6851 • (800) 824-3795
www.dvorakexpeditions.com

Escalante Canyon Outfitters
P.O. Box 1330
Boulder, UT 84716
(435) 335-7311 • (888) 326-4453
Fax: (435) 335-7499
www.ecohike.com

Escalante Outback Adventures
P.O. Box 163
Escalante, UT 84726
(435) 826-4967 • (877) 777-7988
tours@utahcanyons.com
www.escalante-utah.com

Far Out Expeditions
7th and Mulberry Streets
P.O. Box 307
Bluff, UT 84512
(435) 672-2294
tours@faroutexpeditions.com
www.faroutexpeditions.com

Holiday Expeditions, Inc.
544 East 3900 South
Salt Lake City, UT 84107
(801) 266-2087 • (800) 624-6323
Fax: (801) 266-1448
holiday@bikeraft.com
www.holidayexpeditions.com

Hondoo Rivers and Trails
Box 98
Torrey, UT 84775
(435) 425-3519 • (800) 332-2696
hondoo@color-country.net
www.hondoo.com

Pine Valley Lodge & Stable
960 E. Main St.
Pine Valley, UT 84781
(435) 574-2544

Sherri Griffith Expeditions
P.O. Box 1324
Moab, UT 84532
(435) 259-8229 • (800) 332-2439
info@griffithexp.com
www.griffithexp.com

Spirit Lake Lodge (open Memorial Day
to mid-October)
Uinta Wilderness
1360 Hallam Rd.
Francis, UT 84036
Lodge: (435) 880-3089
Owner in Vernal: (435) 781-8884

Tag-A-Long Expeditions
452 N. Main
Moab, UT 84532
(435) 259-8946 • (800) 453-3292

Wild Rivers Expeditions
101 Main St.
P.O. Box 118
Bluff, UT 84512-0118
(435) 672-2244 or (435) 672-2200
(800) 422-7654
Fax: (435) 672-2365
wildriv@starband.net
www.riversandruins.com

Appendix C | Conservation Groups

Great Old Broads for Wilderness
P.O. Box 2924
Durango, CO 81302
(970) 385-9577 • Fax: (970) 259-8303
mb@greatoldbroads.org

HawkWatch International
1800 S. West Temple, #226
Salt Lake City, UT 84115
(801) 484-6808
www.hawkwatch.org

High Uintas Preservation Council
P.O. Box 72
Hyrum, UT 84319
(435) 245-6747
www.hupc.org

Sierra Club, Utah Chapter
2120 South 1300 East, Ste. 204
Salt Lake City, UT 84106
(801) 467-9297

Southern Utah Wilderness Alliance
1471 South 1100 East
Salt Lake City, UT 84105
(801) 486-3161
suwa@suwa.org

Southern Utah Wilderness Alliance
122 C Street NW, Ste. 240
Washington, DC 20001
(202) 546-2215
www.suwa.org

Utah Wilderness Coalition
P.O. Box 520974
Salt Lake City, UT 84152-0974
(801) 486-2872
wildutah@xmission.com
www.uwcoalition.org

Wasatch Mountain Club
1390 South 1100 East, Ste. 103
Salt Lake City, UT 84105-2443
(801) 463-9842
www.xmission.com/~wmc

Calf Creek Falls is a watery haven in the arid Grand Staircase–Escalante National Monument.

Appendix D | Map Sources

Trails Illustrated
National Geographic Maps
P.O. Box 4357
Evergreen, CO 80437-4357
(800) 962-1643
www.trailsillustrated.com

Trails Illustrated map numbers, names, and areas depicted:

#210 Canyonlands National Park: Needles & Island in the Sky
Butler Wash WSA
Indian Creek WSA
Bridger Jack Mesa WSA
Horseshoe Canyon North WSA

#211 Arches National Park

#213 Glen Canyon NRA/Capitol Reef NP/Rainbow Bridge NM
Mancos Mesa WSA
Little Rockies WSA
Henry Mountains
Dirty Devil WSA
Dark Canyon ISA Complex
Scorpion WSA
Fiftymile Mountain WSA (eastern edge)

#214 Zion National Park
Red Butte WSA
Spring Creek Canyon WSA
The Watchman WSA
Taylor Creek Canyon WSA
Goose Creek Canyon WSA
Beartrap Canyon WSA
Deep Creek WSA
North Fork Virgin River WSA
Orderville Canyon WSA
Parunuweap Canyon WSA

#219 Bryce Canyon National Park

#246 Canyonlands National Park Maze District/NE Glen Canyon NRA
Dark Canyon ISA Complex
Horseshoe Canyon South WSA
French Spring–Happy Canyon WSA

#701 Uinta National Forest
Lone Peak Wilderness
Mount Timpanogos Wilderness
Mount Nebo Wilderness

Map Sources (continued)

#702 Cedar Mountain/Pine Valley Mountain
Ashdown Gorge Wilderness
Pine Valley Mountain Wilderness
Cottonwood Canyon WSA
Cedar Breaks NM

#703 Manti–LaSal NF/Dark Canyon Wilderness/Natural Bridges NM
Dark Canyon ISA Complex
Cheesebox Canyon WSA
Butler Wash WSA

#704 Flaming Gorge NRA/Eastern Uintas
High Uintas Wilderness

#705 Paunsaugunt Plateau/Mount Dutton/Bryce Canyon NP/Red Canyon

#706 Grand Gulch Plateau
Grand Gulch ISA Complex
Fish Creek Canyon WSA
Road Canyon WSA
Comb Ridge WSA
Valley of the Gods
Goosenecks State Park

#707 Fish Lake North/Central Capitol Reef

#709 Wasatch Front/Strawberry Valley
Mount Olympus Wilderness
Twin Peaks Wilderness
Lone Peak Wilderness
Mount Timpanogos Wilderness

#710 Canyons of the Escalante: Grand Staircase–Escalante NM/Glen Canyon NRA
Phipps–Death Hollow ISA
Box–Death Hollow Wilderness
Fiftymile Mountain WSA
Scorpion WSA
North Escalante Canyons/The Gulch ISA
Steep Creek WSA

#711 High Uintas Wilderness

#712 San Rafael Swell
Sids Mountain/Sids Cabin WSA
Mexican Mountain WSA
San Rafael Reef WSA
Crack Canyon WSA
Muddy Creek WSA
Devils Canyon WSA
Goblin Valley State Park
Cleveland-Lloyd Dinosaur Quarry

Appendix D

Map Sources (continued)

U.S. Geological Survey

U.S. Geological Survey
Denver Federal Center
Box 25286
Denver, CO 80225
(303) 202-4700
infoservices@usgs.gov

U.S. Geological Survey
1594 W. North Temple
Salt Lake City, UT 84116
Send mail to: P.O. Box 146100
Salt Lake City, UT 84114-6100
(801) 537-3300

U.S. Geological Survey
Western Region
345 Middlefield Rd.
Menlo Park, CA 94025
(650) 853-8300
(888) ASK-USGS
http://ask.usgs.gov
www.usgs.gov

Utah Division of Parks and Recreation
Natural Resources Map and Bookstore
1594 W. North Temple
Salt Lake City, UT 84116
Send mail to: P.O. Box 146100
Salt Lake City, UT 84114-6100
(801) 537-3320 or (585) UTAH-MAP
Fax: (801) 537-3395
www.mapstore.utah.gov

USDA Forest Service
Intermountain Region
324 25th St.
Ogden, UT 84401
(801) 625-5306

DeLorme Mapping
P.O. Box 298
Freeport, ME 04096
Customer Service: (800) 511-2459
Sales: (800) 575-5105
Professional Product Sales: (207) 846-7025
data@delorme.com
www.delorme.com

Utah Division of Wildlife Resources
1594 W. North Temple
Salt Lake City, UT 84114
(801) 538-4700
www.wildlife.utah.org
Map series: Lakes of the High Uintas

Forest Service and Bureau of Land Management
These maps are available at the various local offices and in visitor centers. There is a particularly good waterproof topographical map for the High Uintas Wilderness issued by the Forest Service; the BLM does the same for the Arizona Strip District on a map that includes all of the wilderness and proposed wilderness areas near the Utah/Arizona border. See Appendix B for Forest Service and BLM contact information.

Appendix E | Bibliography

Adkison, Ron. *Utah's National Parks*. Berkeley, Calif.: Wilderness Press, 1997.

Allen, Steve. *Canyoneering: The San Rafael Swell*. Salt Lake City: The University of Utah Press, 1992.

————. *Canyoneering 3: Loop Hikes in Utah's Escalante*. Salt Lake City: University of Utah Press, 1997.

Beckstrom, Elizabeth, and Bessie Snow. *Oh Ye Mountains High: History of Pine Valley, Utah*. St. George, Utah: St. George Heritage Press Publishers, 1980.

BLM Utah (Utah State Office, Bureau of Land Management of the U.S. Department of the Interior). *Utah BLM Statewide Wilderness Final Environmental Impact Statement*. Salt Lake City: BLM Utah, 1990.

Chesterman, Charles. *National Audubon Society Field Guide to North American Rocks and Minerals*. New York: Alfred A. Knopf, 1995.

Chronic, Halka. *Roadside Geology of Utah*. Missoula, Mont.: Mountain Press Publishing, 1990.

Craighead, John, Frank Craighead, and Ray Davis. *A Field Guide to Rocky Mountain Wildflowers*. New York: Houghton Mifflin Company, 1963.

Davis, Mel, and John Veranth. *High Uinta Trails*. Salt Lake City: Wasatch Publishers, 1998.

Day, David. *Utah's Favorite Hiking Trails*. Provo, Utah: Rincon Publishing Company, 2002.

Dollar, Tom. *Guide to Arizona's Wilderness Areas*. Englewood, Colo.: Westcliffe Publishers, 1998.

Goodman, Doug, and Daniel McCool. *Contested Landscape*. Salt Lake City: University of Utah Press, 1999.

Kelsey, Michael R. *Boater's Guide to Lake Powell*. Provo, Utah: Kelsey Publishing, 1991.

————. *Climbing and Exploring Utah's Mt. Timpanogos*. Provo, Utah: Kelsey Publishing, 1989.

————. *Hiking and Exploring the Paria River. 3rd edition*. Provo, Utah: Kelsey Publishing, 1998.

Kosik, Fran. *Native Roads*. Tucson: Rio Nuevo Publishers, 1996.

Kuhns, Michael. *A Guide to the Trees of Utah and the Intermountain West*. Logan, Utah: Utah State University Press, 1998.

MacMahon, James. *National Audubon Society Nature Guides: Deserts*. New York: Alfred A. Knopf, Chanticleer Press, 1998.

Massey, Peter, and Jeanne Wilson. *Backcountry Adventures: Utah*. Castle Rock, Colo.: Swagman Publishing, 2002.

Appendix E

Bibliography (continued)

Moore, Michael. *Medicinal Plants of the Desert and Canyon West.* Santa Fe: Museum of New Mexico Press, 1989.

Murie, Olaus. *Animal Tracks.* New York: Houghton Mifflin Company, 1974.

Pearson, Mark. *The Complete Guide to Colorado's Wilderness Areas.* Englewood, Colo.: Westcliffe Publishers, 1994.

Probst, Jeffrey, and Brad Probst. *High Uintas Backcountry.* Bountiful, Utah: Outland Publishing, 1996.

Roberts, David. *In Search of the Old Ones.* New York: Simon & Schuster, 1996.

Roylance, Ward. *Utah: A Guide to the State, Part 2.* Salt Lake City: Utah: A Guide to the State Foundation, 1982.

Scarry, Elaine. *On Beauty and Being Just.* Princeton, N.J.: Princeton University Press, 1999.

Taylor, Ronald. *Sagebrush Country.* Missoula, Mont.: Mountain Press Publishing, 1992.

Thomas, David, Jay Miller, Richard White, Peter Nabokov, and Philip Deloria. *The Native Americans: An Illustrated History.* Atlanta: Turner Publishing, Inc., 1993.

Trimble, Stephen, and Terry Tempest Williams. *Testimony.* Minneapolis: Milkweed Editions, 1996.

USDA Forest Service. *Forest Service Roadless Area Conservation: Draft Environmental Impact Statement, Volumes 1 and 2.* Washington D.C.: USDA Forest Service, May 2000.

———. *What's It All About: Roadless Area Conservation.* Washington D.C.: USDA Forest Service, May 2000.

Veranth, John. *Hiking the Wasatch: A Hiking and Natural History Guide to the Central Wasatch.* Salt Lake City: Wasatch Mountain Club, 1998.

Ward, Geoffrey. *The West: An Illustrated History.* Boston: Little, Brown, 1996.

Weibel, Michael, and Dan Miller. *High in Utah.* Salt Lake City: University of Utah Press, 1999.

Wharton, Tom, and Gayen Wharton. *Utah.* Oakland, Calif.: Compass American Guides, 1998.

Whitney, Stephen. *The Audubon Society Nature Guides: Western Forests.* New York: Alfred A. Knopf, 1990.

Appendix F | Emergency Numbers

NORTHERN UTAH

Wasatch Range	Avalanche Information	(801) 364-1581
Wasatch Range	Road Conditions/Travel Info	(800) 492-2400
All areas, call 911		

SOUTHERN UTAH

Capitol Reef NP	Road Conditions	(435) 425-3791, ext. 1
Cedar City	Highway Patrol	(435) 586-9445
Coconino County	Sheriff	(800) 338-7888
Emery County	Road Conditions	(435) 381-2550
Garfield County	Sheriff	911 or (435) 676-2678
Glen Canyon NRA	Emergency	(800) 582-4351
Grand County	Sheriff	(435) 259-8115
Kanab	Police Department	(435) 644-5854
Kane County	Sheriff	911 or (435) 644-2349
Moab	All Emergencies	911
Montrose County	Sheriff	(303) 249-9611
Montrose County	Highway Patrol	(970) 249-4392
San Juan County	Sheriff	(435) 587-2237
St. George	Police Dispatch	(435) 634-5000

Storm clouds roll over Panorama Point in Capitol Reef National Park.

In Eardley Canyon, Lynna Howard views the largest perennial pool in the San Rafael Reef WSA.

Index

*OPPOSITE: Cascade Mountain in Wasatch Range
of central Utah in fall*

About the Author

FREQUENTLY TEAMED WITH HER BROTHER, photographer Leland Howard, Lynna Howard writes guidebooks, adventure articles, and memoirs. The pair's collaborations include two previous books from Westcliffe Publishers: *Montana and Idaho's Continental Divide Trail: The Official Guide* (winner of the 2001 National Outdoor Book Award) and *Along Montana & Idaho's Continental Divide Trail.*

During the winter months, Lynna focuses on technical writing and publicity for products related to scientific research. In the summer, she leaves the high-tech world behind to spend most of her time on the trails and rivers of Utah, Idaho, Montana, Nevada, and Wyoming. Using her trail name, "PrueHeart the Wanderer," Lynna keeps a travel diary of her adventures. Her current project is a collection of poetry that reflects her wide-ranging interests, from the lives of her two grown children to the mountains of the West and the urban canyons of New York City.

A member of Women Writing the West, Idaho Trails Council, Idaho Alpine Club, and a founding member of Great Rift Writers, Lynna lives in Shelley, Idaho.

About the Photographer

DURING HIS MORE THAN 20 YEARS as an image artist, Leland Howard has cultivated a detailed knowledge of the rough-and-tumble territory of America's Wild West. Exploring areas only accessible by hiking, backpacking, or cross-country skiing is part of the challenge and part of the reward. The patience to wait out a storm, the diligence it takes to travel access routes that aren't on a map, and the mastery of equipment and that ineffable "eye"—these traits are just some of the tools of Leland's trade.

His diverse publishing credits include the National Geographic Society, Hallmark, AT&T, Sierra Press, BrownTrout Publishers, Audubon, Healthy Planet, *PhotoGraphic* magazine, Beautiful America Publications, Angel Graphics, Portal Publications, *Outside* magazine, Blue Sky Publishing, Reiman Publications, Smith Western, Sierra Club, Great Mountain West, Western Image, Westcliffe Publishers, Northwest Publications, and hundreds more. Leland makes his home in Shelley, Idaho.

The work of an extraordinary image artist enchants us even more when it is given room to breathe. Larger, fine-art-quality prints of Leland Howard's images are available in limited editions. For details, please visit www.lelandhoward.com or call (208) 357-3166.